The Secret World of Shugendō

Where Religion Lives

Kristy Nabhan-Warren, *editor*

Where Religion Lives publishes ethnographies of religious life. The series features the methods of religious studies along with anthropological approaches to lived religion. The religious studies perspective encompasses attention to historical contingency, theory, religious doctrine and texts, and religious practitioners' intimate, personal narratives. The series also highlights the critical realities of migration and transnationalism.

A complete list of books published in Where Religion Lives is available at https://uncpress.org/series/where-religion-lives.

The Secret World of Shugendō

Sacred Mountains and the Search for Meaning in Post-Disaster Japan

....

SHAYNE A. P. DAHL

The University of North Carolina Press Chapel Hill

© 2025 Shayne A. P. Dahl
All rights reserved
Manufactured in the United States of America
Set in Charis and Lato Sans by Jamie McKee, MacKey Composition

Cover art: *Yamabushi Enter a Torii Gate*. Courtesy of Adrian Cox.

Library of Congress Cataloging-in-Publication Data
Names: Dahl, Shayne A. P., author.
Title: The secret world of Shugendō : sacred mountains and the search for meaning in post-disaster Japan / Shayne A. P. Dahl.
Other titles: Where religion lives.
Description: Chapel Hill : The University of North Carolina Press, [2025] | Series: Where religion lives | Includes bibliographical references and index.
Identifiers: LCCN 2025015442 | ISBN 9781469690599 (cloth) | ISBN 9781469690605 (paperback) | ISBN 9781469684192 (epub) | ISBN 9781469690612 (pdf)
Subjects: LCSH: Shugen (Sect)—Japan—Yamagata-shi. | Yamagata-shi (Japan)—Religious life and customs. | Yamagata-shi (Japan)—Social conditions. | BISAC: RELIGION / Eastern | SOCIAL SCIENCE / Ethnic Studies / Asian Studies | lcgft: Ethnographies.
Classification: LCC BQ8822 .D33 2025 | DDC 204/.40952/116—dc23/eng/20250423
LC record available at https://lccn.loc.gov/2025015442

For product safety concerns under the European Union's General Product Safety Regulation (EU GPSR), please contact gpsr@mare-nostrum.co.uk or write to the University of North Carolina Press and Mare Nostrum Group B.V., Mauritskade 21D, 1091 GC Amsterdam, The Netherlands.

To Asako, Yoshi, Tora, and my extended family and friends in Japan.
Thank you for your love, support, and hospitality.

Contents

List of Illustrations, ix

Acknowledgments, xi

Prologue, 1
An Oath of Secrecy

Introduction, 5

1 Mountains of Time, 30
  A Tour of Mount Haguro

2 Summits and Waterfalls, 59
  The Shugyō Experience

3 Rebirth in the Mountain's Womb, 87
  Shugyō Interpreted

4 The Buddha and the Kami, 108
  Mountain Politics and Historical Consciousness

5 Autumn's Peak, 129
  Buddhist Temporality and Ascetic Ethics

6 Summits Where Souls Gather, 161
  Ancestral Space-Time and Disaster Pilgrimage on Gassan

7 The Buddha Mummies of Mount Yudono, 180
  Cosmic Bodies of the Future Past

Epilogue, 199
The Mountain Vista

Notes, 205

Works Cited, 227

Index, 241

Illustrations

Map

Dewa Sanzan, 6

Figures

Vehicles pass beneath Mount Haguro's torii gate, 31

A boulder engraved with Matsuo Bashō's haiku, Mount Haguro, 36

The Zuishinmon (Gate of Dual Deities), Mount Haguro, 41

Itō-san ascending the "Stairway of Rebirth," Mount Haguro, 44

Inaho Express Train (Niigata City–Tsuruoka City), 48

Grandfather Cedar with the five-storied pagoda, Mount Haguro, 51

Shintō yamabushi attire, 67

A womb (*tainai*) of boulders near the summit of Gassan with a Buddhist statue inside, 80

A yamabushi performing takigyō (waterfall practice), 82

Group photo after ocean submersion, Awaji-shima, May 2015, 92

Chōnan-san reminding laypeople about the Buddhist, pre-Meiji layout of Mount Haguro, 118

A yamabushi leaps over fire to complete Autumn's Peak, 130

Buddhist yamabushi attire, 139

A Shintō priest summons ancestral souls on the summit of Gassan, 162

A vertically laid stack of funerary tablets, Eighth Station, Gassan, 170

Disaster memorial on the summit of Gassan, 172

Monks remove a sokushinbutsu from a preservation case, Dainichibō Temple, Mount Yudono, 181

A pilgrim prays to the sokushinbutsu, Dainichibō Temple, Mount Yudono, 191

Kōmyōkai, sokushinbutsu of Zōkōin Temple, Shirataka, Yamagata Prefecture, 196

Acknowledgments

If I were to trace the journey of this ethnography back to its inception, I find myself in a small dojo in Swift Current, Saskatchewan, where I started judo at the age of nine. So, I begin by thanking *sensei* Ron DePauw, who introduced me to Japan through judo. I also thank all the judoka at the following dojos for their moral support throughout the writing of this manuscript: Trent University Judo Club (Peterborough, Ontario), Bosei Judo Academy (Toronto, Ontario), Matsusaka Judo Club (Mie Prefecture, Japan), Tagawa Chiku Adult Judo Club (Tsuruoka City, Yamagata Prefecture, Japan), Tsuyoi Judo Club (Charlottetown, Prince Edward Island), and Raymond Judo Club (Raymond, Alberta).

Childhood exposure to Japanese culture through judo is what later prompted me to take anthropology, religious studies, and Japanese studies during undergraduate studies at Lethbridge Community College (now Lethbridge Polytechnic) and the University of Lethbridge (2002–7). I thank Marko Hilgersom of Lethbridge Polytechnic for introducing me to the study of anthropology and religion. In his class, I realized I wanted to be an anthropologist. Also at Lethbridge Polytechnic, I thank students Dustin Gamble and Christian Moir for thoughtful feedback on this manuscript.

I thank Professor John Harding of the Department of History and Religion at the University of Lethbridge for introducing me to the academic study of Japanese religions. His support for me has endured for more than twenty years as I eventually applied for and won a Banting Postdoctoral Fellowship to complete this manuscript at my alma mater under his excellent supervision (2022–24). Professors James Linville, Tom Robinson, and Hillary Rodrigues were also influential in these years. Hillary ignited my desire for world travel, leading me to Japan and on many other journeys. I thank Hillary for lifting the curtain to the world and inspiring me to explore "the garden." Professor Gideon Fujiwara, a historian of northeastern Japan at the U of L, offered very helpful feedback during the final revisions on this manuscript. Thank you, Gideon!

Professor Roger Lohmann, an anthropologist at Trent University in Peterborough, Ontario, supervised my MA thesis (2010–12) and has remained a supportive mentor throughout my career. He introduced me to the anthropology of religion and has invited me to give talks and join conference panels related to research included in these pages. Thank you, Roger, for your long-term investment in my continued success.

Throughout my PhD studies (2012–19), my supervisors, Professors Janice Boddy and Todd Sanders of the Department of Anthropology at the University of Toronto, gave me their full support as I pushed to completion. It is owing to their constant encouragement for me to position my research in an anthropological framework that the argument presented in this book, about the spatiotemporality of sacred mountains in Japan, became visible in my field notes. Professor Michael Lambek, a core committee member, was the first to comment on my work and one of the last to sign off on it. His influence is apparent throughout. I also thank Professor Donna Young, my internal examiner, and Professor Ellen Schattschneider of Brandeis University, my external examiner, for their perceptive comments and challenging questions.

Shortly after I returned from fieldwork in January 2016, Professor Simon Coleman of the Department for the Study of Religion at the University of Toronto invited me to join the Pilgrimage Forum. This led to many lively discussions with leading scholars of pilgrimage studies such as Professors John Eade and Ian Reader. With an encouraging nudge from Simon, who arranged a workshop with Ian Reader, I achieved my first single-authored journal article publication. His scholarship and suggestions in the Pilgrimage Forum have greatly influenced how I conceptualize the landscape and its relation to ritual, pilgrimage, and time. Special thanks to Ian Reader as well for feedback on my writing and support with applications.

I extend my gratitude to the anonymous committee reviewers who saw promise in my scholarship and postdoctoral research funding applications for the Social Sciences and Humanities Research Council (SSHRC) of Canada, the Banting Postdoctoral Fellowship, Ontario Graduate Scholarship, Michael Smith Foreign Study Supplement, David Chu Scholarship in Asia Pacific Studies, and the Department of Anthropology and the Archaeology Centre at the University of Toronto, as well as a generous offer from the Japan Foundation.

In Japan, I thank Professor Oiwa Keinosuke at Meiji Gakuin University and Professor Hayashi Isao at the National Museum of Ethnology for hosting me as a visiting researcher during my primary fieldwork. The resources made available to me while in Japan for fieldwork and the networking connections they helped me form were crucial to my success throughout my stay. In Yamagata Prefecture, I thank the staff at the Ideha Cultural Museum for their assistance in translation and for connecting me with the mountain ascetic community in Dewa Sanzan. I also thank Shozen-in Temple, Dewa Sanzan Shrine, Gassan Shrine, Mount Yudono Shrine, Dainichibō Temple, Chūren-ji Temple, Honmyō-ji Temple, Nangaku-ji Temple, Zōkōin Temple, and the Dewa Shōnai International Exchange Forum for support. I remain indebted to Shimazu Kokai, Hoshino Fumihiro, Kato Takeharu, Miura Takehiro, Naruse Masanori, and Tim Bunting. Special thanks to Watanabe Satoshi, the director of our documentary film project, *The Buddha Mummies of North Japan*. I also thank Suzuki Takashi for translation assistance. The hospitality I received in Yamagata Prefecture is world class, and I look forward to future collaborations with friends there.

I thank Professor Mark Rowe of the Department of Religious Studies at McMaster University for supervising me as a SSHRC Postdoctoral Fellow (2019–21). His mentorship was vital as I navigated my early career during the pandemic, seeking a path forward despite scarce opportunities and extreme uncertainty. Through Mark's guidance at this most difficult time in recent history, I found a narrow passage through a global crisis and was able to continue my research and career. Thank you, Mark!

In 2021–22, I joined the Edwin O. Reischauer Institute of Japanese Studies at Harvard University as a postdoctoral fellow. The appointment included an author's workshop in which leading scholars in my field were invited to read and provide substantive feedback on this manuscript. My research was also featured in a *Japan Forum* talk. I thank everyone at RIJS who mentored and supported me, especially Gavin H. Whitelaw, Stacie Matsumoto, Helen Hardacre, Mary C. Brighton, Abe Ryuichi, Catherine Glover, Hannah Perry, and Jenni Ting. I also thank Scott Schnell, Suma Ikeuchi, and Satsuki Kawano for joining the workshop and giving me excellent feedback on earlier versions of this manuscript.

In the final phase of revisions, I shared sections of this manuscript with members of my creative writing community based out of Analog Books in Lethbridge, Alberta. Special thanks to Scott Paul and Jean McCarthy for their thoughtful feedback and to Scott and Penny Warris, the lovely owners of Analog Books, who have done so much for the community of readers and writers in southwestern Alberta.

This book was made possible by the amazing editorial team at the University of North Carolina Press. I thank Mark Simpson-Vos, Kristy Nabhan-Warren, Thomas Bedenbaugh, Mary Carley Caviness, Valerie Burton, and Laura Jones Dooley for their outstanding support and patience during my revisions. Thank you also to Caleb Swift Carter and Mark Rowe for their thoughtful feedback and editorial suggestions.

I owe a lifetime of gratitude to my family in Canada and in Japan. Asako, my partner in life, has shown more patience than I have with the process of producing this book, twelve years in the making. Her support has been unwavering since day one, and to my last, I will remain grateful. To our sons, Yoshi and Tora, both born during my long spell of graduate school: I hope that someday, when you are old enough to read this book, you can forgive me for the time it took to write. I dedicate it to you both. Whatever mountain you choose to climb in life, do what you must to reach the summit, but always come back home.

The Secret World of Shugendō

Prologue
An Oath of Secrecy

I was standing with a large group of ascetics before the Dewa Sanzan Shrine on the forested summit of Mount Haguro. It was the climax of Autumn's Peak, an eight-day ascetic ritual symbolizing rebirth. The shrine's bright red exterior and moss-covered thatched roof stood in striking contrast to the green, outstretched limbs of centuries-old cryptomeria trees behind. The pulsating buzz of cicadas and the distant cackle of crows shook the late summer air. Then, an ascetic leader spoke:

"Ascetics!" he said in a baritone voice.

"*Uketamau* [received]!" we responded in unison.

"This place is the sacred peak where the strictest secrecy is maintained. You may under no circumstances speak of it to outsiders after you return to the ordinary world. It is strictly forbidden to speak of it to parents, children, brothers, wives, or friends."

"Uketamau!"

"Should you do so, immediately you will fall under the curse of the founder!

"Therefore, make your pledge of silence by striking this gong."

"Uketamau!" we answered in a booming chorus.[1]

After this threatening proclamation, I joined the other ascetics in a long line that led to a small gong. One by one, we stepped forward, received the wooden mallet, and struck it. A sharp metallic clang rang out with each strike. Then we each bowed, pledging to share nothing we had experienced during Autumn's Peak lest the "curse of the founder" befall us. Such oaths of secrecy are why Shugendō, the religion featured in this book, is often referred to as "the secret world" (*himitsu no sekai*).

Before this moment of fieldwork, I had planned to write about Autumn's Peak in detail. Like any good anthropologist, I had filled my pocketbook with descriptive field notes in the brief periods of free time we had during the grueling schedule of ritual activity deep in the mountains. Yet there I was, striking the gong with a mallet before ascetic leaders, committing to honor the secrecy of the rite. And now here I am, publishing a book about it called *The Secret World of Shugendō*. Am I wrong to write this book?

This question, about the ethics of conducting research on a religion involving sworn secrecy, would be the most important one I would ask in my first sit-down interview with the *daisendatsu* (great leader) of Buddhist-oriented Shugendō in Mount Haguro. As you can imagine, I was terribly nervous leading up my interview with him. This meeting was one of those moments of fieldwork where everything was poised to come together—or fall apart. I had received approval from the research ethics board at the University of Toronto. I had been awarded a full scholarship and research funding. What if, after two years of preparation, I was unable to pursue this project? What if, in the end, it was unethical to proceed?

The stakes were high, so I hired a translator named Abe-san to assist me. I wanted to ensure there would be no misunderstanding in the interview. Abe-san worked at the Dewa Shōnai International Forum, a culture center in nearby Tsuruoka City. She was, as was I at the time, in her late twenties. The interview was scheduled at Shozen-in Temple. Located near the base of Mount Haguro in the community of Tōge, Shozen-in is the headquarters for Buddhist Shugendō there. As we entered the temple grounds, I felt a knot tighten in my stomach. I was anxious but also confused: Why did the ascetic leaders allow me to join Autumn's Peak when they knew I was an anthropologist intending to write about it?

Abe-san and I were greeted at the front of the temple by Kei-san, daughter of the daisendatsu. She appeared to be in her mid- to late thirties. Very kind and cheery, she put us at ease as she invited us in. We first kneeled before the Buddhist statues in the *hondō* (main hall) of the temple. Their realistic facial expressions and golden-hued exteriors made a strong impression. It was as if the statues were meditating. In the same moment as I recognized the soothing aroma of sandalwood, Abe-san took some short incense sticks from a small box and handed me a few. She lit hers with a match and then offered the flame to light mine. We poked the incense sticks in the small ash-filled incense burner. As the smoke plume spiraled upward, we steepled our palms together and bowed our heads to the Buddhas.

We then made our way to a tatami (rush straw) mat room to the right side of the *hondō* and kneeled on cushions around a low, wooden table. Kei-san served us green tea from a kettle of freshly boiled water. The wall adjacent to us was covered by a bookshelf. I smiled when I saw titles I had read to prepare for this interview, including Carmen Blacker's book, *The Catalpa Bow: A Study of Shamanistic Practices in Japan*, published in 1975. Blacker was one of the first non-Japanese scholars to experience Autumn's Peak. Her book is a classic in the study of Japanese religions.

The daisendatsu entered the room with quick strides and sat down across from us. My first impression was that he had a concentrated energy about him. Intense and strict. His eyes were noticeably serious: "like if he stared at a stone long enough," I wrote in my field notes, "it would crack." I had taken exhaustive notes during the Autumn's Peak rite. Since I understood little of the meaning of what I had observed at this early phase of fieldwork, this first conversation spanned many subjects. When the timing felt right, I asked the big question: "Why did you permit me to study Shugendō, knowing that I intended to write about it, if all participants of Autumn's Peak are bound to an oath of secrecy at the risk of the curse of the founder?"

Seeing my nervousness about the curse, the daisendatsu burst out laughing. This put me at ease. Then he said:

> There is no problem with respect to you writing about Autumn's Peak. The problem is misrepresentation. This could happen if you take the words and perspectives of individual ascetics to be official interpretations of Autumn's Peak. It could also happen if you project your personal experience and views as official interpretations of temple authorities. Misrepresentation has been a problem for us in the past. Participants have misrepresented Autumn's Peak by mistaking the meaning of its aspects and by presenting individual interpretations or untrue things they've heard as authoritative and official when they are not. If you commit to being truthful in your scholarship of Autumn's Peak and Shugendō more generally, then we have no problem with you writing about it.

"Misrepresentation," I said, "is a problem in anthropology, too. When possible, the best way to prevent it is to share the results of our study with our community of research before finalizing it. That way we can confirm the accuracy of our ethnographic representation. But I must be clear," I emphasized, "that as an anthropologist, I am also obliged to offer unique interpretations of my fieldwork to bring my research into larger disciplinary conversations."

The agreement we reached in this vital interview was that I would commit to clearly distinguishing the sources of information in this ethnography: to not confuse, for example, what a participant ascetic says with what the daisendatsu or senior leaders say. To not confuse what a Shintō ascetic says for what a Buddhist ascetic says. And to always clarify when I am speaking from my own perspective. Really, the daisendatsu was asking of me what I would expect of any good anthropologist: to represent the people we work with and the colleagues we cite truthfully. To clearly contextualize all sources of information.

One way anthropologists ensure accurate representation is by sharing a draft of a manuscript with our interlocutors before our work is published. Given the high degree of uncertainty with research funding and the life circumstances I faced as an early career anthropologist, I didn't know at the time of this interview whether I would be able to honor that approach by returning to Mount Haguro with a full draft of my manuscript to share with the daisendatsu and others before proceeding with publication. Luckily for me, I did find myself in a position to do just that.

In August 2019, after completing twenty-four months of fieldwork conducted in the vicinity of Mount Haguro spanning 2012–16 and three years of writing, I returned to Tōge with a printed manuscript in hand. As I was being driven to Shozen-in Temple, literally a hundred yards or less from the temple, a small truck came barreling out of a side alley at full speed. It passed within inches of the vehicle I was in. A second earlier and our vehicle would have been T-boned on the passenger side, where I was leaning my head against the window. It was a very close call. Close enough to make me wonder. Minutes later and still rattled, with my heart pounding from what could have been a life-threatening accident, I arrived at Shozen-in.

My Japanese-language proficiency was much stronger at this time, but I still brought a translator to ensure accurate communication. Together with the daisendatsu, we reviewed the core text of this manuscript, chapter by chapter. By the end of the meeting, it was clear that although my understanding was inescapably partial—there is simply way more going on in these mountains than any single study can contain—my work had been deemed an accurate and acceptable representation. In the years since, this manuscript has become more nuanced as it met new audiences and received critical feedback. The result is the book you hold in your hands. I am grateful that I have, at least up to now, evaded the curse of the founder.

Introduction

Fieldwork for this ethnography was conducted in the shadows of mountains, on enshrined summits and snowy trails, in cryptomeria forests, and beneath cold waterfalls. It has involved ritual death and rebirth in the symbolic wombs of sacred mountains during ascetic rites, wrestling half-naked men in a forest goblin sumō tournament, observing the worship of mummified ascetics said to be living Buddhas, and late-night drinking with pilgrims who, before a mountaintop bonfire, summoned the souls of their ancestors down from the cosmos for the Festival of the Dead.

These are just some of the images that emerge in my mind's eye when I think back to the field. It's like a dream of a past life. As if a world—all the people I met and the places I visited—is alive and stirring within. Writing it out feels like an expulsion of this inner world. A necessary exorcism in the craft of ethnography. A dream interpreted.

This book is about mountain religion in Dewa Sanzan.[1] Located off the coast of the Sea of Japan in the Shōnai area of Yamagata Prefecture, Dewa Sanzan is one of the most prominent mountain ranges for asceticism, pilgrimage, and recreational mountaineering in Tōhoku, the northeastern region of mainland Japan.[2] The three mountains of Dewa Sanzan are Mount Haguro (Black Wing), Gassan (Moon Mountain), and Mount Yudono (Hot Spring). At 1,358 feet, Mount Haguro is the lowest in height, but it is the central hub of Dewa Sanzan. In the community of Tōge, which lies at the base of Mount Haguro, there are approximately thirty pilgrim lodges (*shukubō*). As the highest mountain of Dewa Sanzan, Gassan (6,509 feet) offers the most dramatic vistas of the surrounding mountains and the plains below, which are mostly used for rice agriculture. Near the summit shrine on Gassan is a well-equipped lodge where pilgrims and climbers typically stay the night before descending to Mount Yudono. As a spur of Gassan, Mount Yudono (4,934 feet) is often described as the most sacred and mysterious mountain of Dewa Sanzan. Owing to heavy snowfall in winter, Gassan and Mount Yudono are open seasonally, from June to October, but Mount Haguro is open year-round.

Most of my interlocutors in and around Dewa Sanzan are mountain ascetics, known as *gyōja*, *shugenja*, or *yamabushi* in Japanese. Some were born

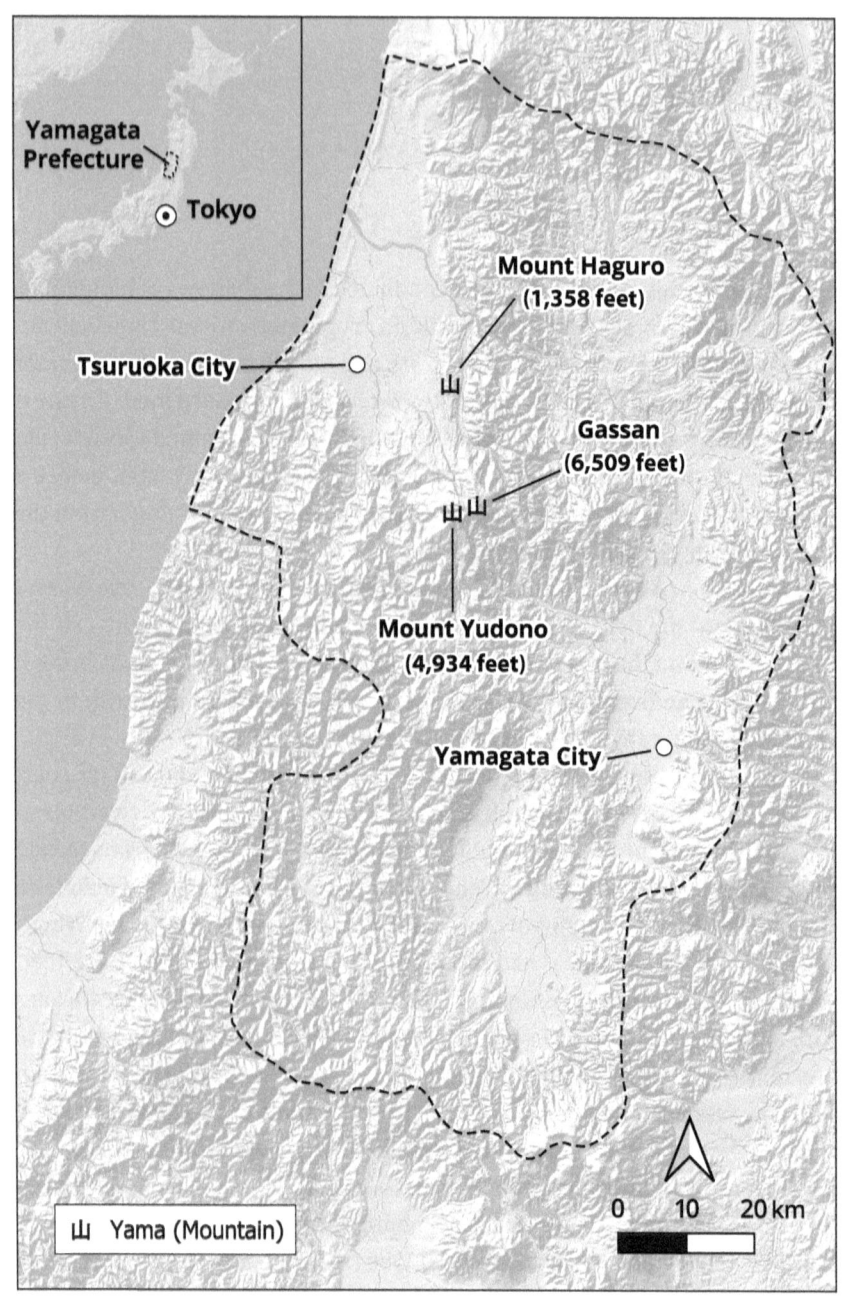

Dewa Sanzan. Map by Kenneth Holyoke.

and raised in urban centers but have abandoned city life to live frugally and closer to a beloved mountain. They have sought to bring themselves, they say, closer to nature and an ancestral way of life. Holding the palm of his hand over his heart, one ascetic described in an interview how he felt that "something is missing" (*nankamono tarinai*) in contemporary society and then indicated that the mountains of Dewa Sanzan and the communities in their orbit have, for him, begun to fill that void. This "missing something" where a heart should be signals a sense of incompleteness. It reflects an identity crisis in contemporary Japan that has been compounded by the earthquake, tsunami, and nuclear disaster of March 11, 2011, often referred to as 3/11.[3] On that day, a way of life was upended and drawn into critical reflection for people across the country, but especially in Tōhoku. The identity crisis that my interlocutors described is as subjective as it is temporal (related to time) and spatial (related to space). It connects the past with the future, society and sacred landscapes, identity, faith, and destiny. It's about where in the wake of disaster, when everything has been stripped away, one can find new purpose and truly belong.

What does the sense of a lost past and an uncertain future leave for those in the post-disaster present? How does one respond to such a crisis of becoming? This ethnography demonstrates that sacred mountains in Japan are symbolically powerful, affective, and socially active placeworlds. By invoking modes of historical consciousness, they counteract a modern sense of rupture from the past and alleviate anxieties about an uncertain future.

Dewa Sanzan is a beautiful and lush natural landscape, but it has deep social and temporal dimensions as well.[4] It conjures history and, in so doing, affects the consciousness of people in the present by augmenting their interpretations of the past.[5] It evokes modes of "historical consciousness" because it exhibits a range of historicities, versions of history, that people in the present draw on to form relations with past times as imagined.[6] How history is recalled and how the future is imagined also imply ethical dispositions toward the past and the future.[7] Dewa Sanzan, like other sacred mountains, is fertile ground for people to generate meaning in life because it is also thoroughly constituted by birth and death symbolism—meaning that seeks balance between the ancestral past and a modern self and that empowers people to envision hopeful futures. Standing apart from urban centers, mountains offer people critical distance from society and a place to reimagine and rejuvenate themselves.

Dewa Sanzan shows us that sacred mountains are places of the past that offer an anachronistic sense of belonging within (but symbolically set apart from) the structural confines of capitalist modernity in contemporary Japan.[8] For my ascetic interlocutors, a deepened bond with the imagined past in the physical place of mountains with fellow ascetics has helped to create critical, affective, and therapeutic distance from the "relationless society" (*muenshakai*) of urban life. In Japan, capitalist modernity is visible in the vastness, verticality, and underground depth of urban architecture, the concrete jungle in which it is common to feel alienated from society.[9] With the critical distance that mountains provide, ascetics can create new forms of hope for a different future, one without faith in or need for material wealth. Hope is temporal because it posits a future in which people can visualize desired improvements to their lives.[10] The hopeful future that ascetics in Dewa Sanzan pursue is, in a sense, an old future, one of cyclical recurrence through annual returns to a premodern past spatialized as mountainous terrain and steeped in death and rebirth symbolism.

Anthropologist Edmund Leach (1961, 125) writes that "time" refers to both a "repetitive time" of intervals or cycles and a "non-repetitive" time of gradual decay. True enough. In the Gregorian calendar, we celebrate the New Year every January 1 (repetitive time), but the calendar year keeps ascending in a nonrepetitive linear progression. Even though we celebrate our birthdays once a year every year, "we are," as Leach writes, "aware that all living things are born, grow old and die, and that this is an irreversible process" (125). Since the "irreversibility of [nonrepetitive] time is psychologically very unpleasant" (125), socially constructed notions of time as a cyclical repetition of intervals works in all cultures to psychologically deny the sense of deterioration. This is most apparent in ritual practice. Maurice Bloch and Jonathan Parry (1982, 9) add that "almost everywhere religious thought consistently denies the irreversible and terminal nature of death by proclaiming it a new beginning." Clifford Geertz (1973, 399) likewise argues that regulated ceremonies and calendrical systems have the capacity to "[blunt] the sense of dissolving days and evaporating years" by attempting "to block the more creatural aspects of the human condition—individuality, spontaneity, perishability, emotionality, vulnerability—from human sight."

Although modern time in Japan is experienced as relatively repetitive with annual festivals and rites (*matsuri*), the Gregorian calendar still emphasizes a linear, ever-progressing march into a future unknown.[11] This is a future that is both financially and existentially uncertain. The nature of precarious work, which has outpaced stable employment in Japan in the past forty years, exacerbates this nonrepetitive sense of time for many Japanese entering the job market. Time is experienced in this sense as scrambling for a handhold in a market of limited-term contracts and of facing the imminent ends of such contracts. Early career scholars, too, know this feeling. Precarious work makes for a precarious temporality and, overall, a precarious experience of life. Yet in post-disaster Japan, the financial uncertainty generated by a precarious labor market is overshadowed by the more existential threat of sudden natural disaster.

Contemporary mountain ascetics refuse to accept such a dire temporality. They are refashioning this nonrepetitive time, experienced as a blind march into decay, with a reimagined "premodern" time of seasonal rebirth. Time is made pliable in the cyclical symbolism of ascetic rituals. Mountain asceticism in Dewa Sanzan offers practitioners a way of ritually denying not only the irreversibility of nonrepetitive time and the inevitable decay it entails but also a way to deny the psychological hold that an increasing sense of uncertainty has over one's life and future. As Nancy Munn (1992, 115) writes, "Ways of attending to the past also create modes of apprehending certain futures or of reconstructing a particular sense of the past in the present that informs the treatment of the future in the present."[12]

Mountain ascetics look forward to returning to Dewa Sanzan annually and, where possible, seasonally. Regular returns to the mountains are cyclical returns to a spatialized past that enable the symbolic death and rebirth of the self. In this context, mountains act as spatiotemporal vortices that tether a rock-solid and geographically fixed foundation to temporally fluid streams of historical and "forward looking" consciousness (Munn 1992, 116). Rituals performed within Dewa Sanzan may not be able to physically blunt or block the flow of time, but they do symbolically evoke modes of historical consciousness. They can bend the uncertainty of nonrepetitive time into a symbolic loop. They can blunt the alienating force of capitalist modernity while (re)connecting contemporary people with an imagined ancestral past, a time when human beings could become Buddhas and when the *kami* (gods), not the economy, were the givers and takers of life.

But why mountains? What makes mountains a useful vantage point to better understand the flexibility of time through space in and beyond contemporary Japan?

Toward an Anthropology of Mountains

Mountains appear unmoving, as if they are eternal fixtures of the landscape, but this is an illusion. They were formed millions of years ago, either by pressurized convergence between continental plates that forced the Earth's crust to crop upward, birthing rocky peaks inch by inch over the course of geological time, or by plates diverging, which enabled magma to gush up from the Earth's mantle and erupt onto the surface, forming volcanoes that went dormant and became mountains. Gassan of Dewa Sanzan is in fact a dormant shield volcano.

The geological process by which mountains form is called "orogenesis." The branch of geography concerning mountains is "orography."[13] In *The Mountain: A Political History from the Enlightenment to the Present*, Bernard Debarbieux and Gilles Rudaz (2015, 2–3) consider cultural interpretations of mountains, how mountains have figured in the human imagination across cultures and throughout history. They expand the meaning of "orogenesis" to refer to social "processes by which societies construct their mountains." As such, mountains constitute "a category of knowledge and of collective action" that emerges from culturally encoded and complex histories with significant variance. As objects of knowledge, mountains are "suspended in webs of significance" that are spun by their human beholders.[14]

An ethnographer committed to understanding the human-mountain interface in any cultural milieu is tasked with cultural orography, studying the social imaginaries that render mountains meaningful in each context, in popular discourse and, more immediately, in the ethnographic encounter. Alpine ethnography (ethnographic research in and around mountains) necessitates cultural orography, an interpretation of why mountains matter, what they mean, and what they have meant in specific cultural and historical contexts. Anthropologists of the past and present have explored the cultural dimensions of mountains in a range of settings, yet an "anthropology of mountains" has mostly eluded the discipline as a distinct field of study with unique theoretical opportunities and methodological challenges.

I draw Debarbieux and Rudaz (2015) into conversation here because their work cuts such a path. They begin by tracing the genealogy of "mountain" as a concept in a prescientific Europe. Before the Enlightenment, the colloquial use of the word "mountain" was a reference to sites of "topological contrast" as well as sites that bore "a contrast in use" from most other places, such as a woodland resource (15).[15] This definition was then used in frontiers throughout the world to naturalize political borders. Mountains became territorial ramparts (45–71) and the source of "new political identities" (134–38), especially through identification with or contradistinction from the alterity of the "mountaineer" (72–81).[16]

Mountain politics, or "oropolitics" (Debarbieux and Rudaz 2015, 164), have played a role in colonial cartographies, where mapping mountains served to claim territory, and more recently in global climate concerns, highlighting the vulnerability of "mountain people" to glacial loss and climatic flux (193–215).[17] The scope of *The Mountain* spans centuries and provides examples from around the globe; however, Debarbieux and Rudaz's otherwise groundbreaking work is limited by its elision of anthropology. The authors write: "Although . . . anthropologists have taken an interest in mountain societies as such since the mid-nineteenth century, they have generally not wished to formulate any analysis of the world's mountains, nor do they seek to define or circumscribe the mountain as such. For them as well, the mountain is primarily a context" (40).

There is some truth in Debarbieux and Rudaz's claim that anthropologists have traditionally treated mountains as an environmental context of human happenings and have not often sought to make universal assertions about them. However, Debarbieux and Rudaz do not share the same disciplinary value of "context" as anthropologists. Situating phenomena in cultural context is the strength, arguably the raison d'être, of the discipline. Making context comprehensible is how anthropologists turn the strange into the familiar. When Debarbieux and Rudaz use the term "context," they are referring to an unacknowledged background that is not an object of analysis itself. In the past decade, a growing number of anthropologists have shifted from anthropocentric approaches toward the world beyond the human. While past anthropological studies of mountains have overlooked how mountains figure into human lives beyond practical need, the anthropology of mountains has steadily shifted throughout the decades toward more post-humanistic approaches. Contrary to Debarbieux and Rudaz's dismissal, the context of mountains in anthropology today goes well beyond resourceful ground beneath human feet or a natural theater of cultural dynamics. Mountains are texts to be read and interpreted in ways that reflect existential needs, historical consciousness, and aspirations for the future of self and society.

James Veteto (2009, 3) traced the rise and presumed decline of the "anthropology of mountains" from the 1970s to the 1990s. He observed that the earliest studies "proceeded from the framework of Julian Steward's cultural ecology." Such works fixed mountain peoples in territorial models of culture and mountains as natural sites of ecological significance.[18] According to Veteto, the cultural ecology approach constitutes the "first wave" of the anthropology of mountains. The "second wave" emerged in the 1980s. It reflected "the need to incorporate the study of history and political economy into mountain anthropology" (4–5). Benjamin Orlove and David Guillet (1985, 16), for instance, connected the ecological adaptation of mountain peoples to "wider economic and political systems," drawing ecological, economic, and historical anthropology together in the context of mountains (Veteto 2009, 4–5).[19]

The 1990s was a "watershed decade" for mountain studies (Veteto 2009, 5). In the United Nations Earth Summit in Rio de Janeiro in 1992, mountains and "mountain peoples" were formally recognized in chapter 13 of Agenda 21, "Managing Fragile Ecosystems—Sustainable Mountain Development." This eventually led the United Nations to declare the year 2002 the "International Year of Mountains." It also led, in 2007, to the formation of the Mountain Forum, an organization drawing together scholars, activists, nongovernmental organizations, and the private sector. The Mountain Forum has unified its diverse membership under the field of "montology." Veteto (13) contends that the emergence of montology has absorbed the anthropology of mountains, which "peaked in the late 1980's and is unlikely to be revived." The ecological dimension of the anthropology of mountains may have been subsumed by a more interdisciplinary "montology," but this did not spell the end for the anthropology of mountains. Examples from nearly every continent demonstrate that the anthropology of mountains was not a fleeting trend but an expanding field of inquiry, one that this book contributes to in addition to considering the anthropology of religion and Japanese religions.[20]

What emerges from an overview of the anthropology of mountains is a model of what I call *orographic perspectivism*: the bricolage of cultural orographies by which people interpret, relate, and react to mountains. Orographic perspectivism lies at the human-mountain interface. It is multidimensional and in constant flux. Whereas the "orogenesis" that Debarbieux and Rudaz describe is a unidirectional social construction of the "mountain" (as a concept), the orographic perspectivism I propose accounts for the creative, interpretive, perspectival space between mountains and human beings. It refers to how one side figures the other or is perceived to figure the other in a cascade of possible meanings, actions, and temporalities.[21]

Mountains are apparently objective but elusively subjective. They are perceived with the eyes and interpreted through culture and personal disposition simultaneously. In a deeper theoretical reading, orographic perspectivism is a mountain-specific application of Friedrich Nietzsche's ([1901] 1968, 339) original formation of perspectivism. Critiquing "physicists [who] believe in a 'true world' in their own fashion: a firm systemization of atoms . . . [that is] the same for all beings," Nietzsche argues that "the atom they posit is inferred according to the logic of the perspectivism of consciousness—and is therefore a subjective fiction." For Nietzsche, the scientific presumption of pure objectivity overlooks "this necessary perspectivism by virtue of which every center of force—and not only man—construes all the rest of the world from its own viewpoint." Here, Nietzsche is emphasizing, as would many anthropologists in the decades to come, the supple and subjective quality of perspective.

Mountains are prisms that refract collective and individual perspectives. Orographic perspectivism refers to the full range of perspectives, engagements, temporalities, and narratives human beings project onto mountains and, in cultures with a relational ontology, the spectrum of perspectives and behaviors mountains are thought to cast onto humans. Mountains are unique features of the landscape. Their verticality and otherness impress from a distance. Seen by all, they are interpreted differently by many. Orographic perspectivism is concerned with situating a given "mountain view" within larger worldviews. Friction between perspectives and interpretations of mountains is what holds the very notion of "mountain" together.[22]

Cultural Orography in Japan

As anyone who has glanced out of the window of a bullet train (*shinkansen*) while traveling in Japan will know, rocky ridges, volcanic peaks, and forested foothills loom over cities as elevated islands in a sea of urban sprawl. In the less populated countryside, mountains overshadow rice fields and farming villages. They are often treated as watchful and morally ambivalent gods (kami). As Kyūya Fukada ([1964] 2015, 215), Shōwa-era author and mountaineer, writes in *One Hundred Mountains of Japan*: "A mountain watches over the home village of most Japanese people. Tall or short, near or far, some mountain watches over our native village like a tutelary deity. We spend our childhood in the shadow of our mountain and we carry it with us in memory when we grow up and leave the village. And however much our lives will change, the mountain will always be there . . . as it has always been, to welcome us back."

I lived in Tsuruoka City, Yamagata Prefecture, during fieldwork, surrounded by mountains on all sides. Mount Haguro, Gassan, and Mount Yudono of Dewa Sanzan fill the horizon to the southeast. Mount Chōkai stands tall to the northeast. To the west, just off the coast of the Sea of Japan, is Mount Kinbō, which has an active shrine with annual festivals but is also the site of a nature education facility for children. I often gazed at Mount Kinbō from my apartment window while typing up field notes. Mountains overlooking villages inspire nostalgia for many people who were born and raised in rural communities but later moved to the city for more opportunities such as postsecondary education and work. Mountains like these are closely connected with people's nostalgic sense of their hometown, or *furusato*.[23]

For contemporary mountaineers (*tozansha*), mountains represent a "challenge" (*charenji*) to overcome. They desire not a nostalgic return to an imagined home village but rather full immersion in and a direct experience of "magnificent nature" (*daishizen*) in the mountains. They ascend the slopes of notable mountains whenever windows of time open in their overworked lives, traveling domestically or abroad to "attack" their summits. Whereas foreign mountains motivate Japanese mountaineers to explore the world beyond Japan, mountains in Japan are still traditionally imagined as an "otherworld" (*ano yo*), sacred places where ancestral souls linger and where the present collapses into the past.

The natural beauty of Japanese mountains and their haunting ambience cannot be easily separated from their ecological significance. Their role in the hydrological cycle illuminates this point. Mountains are immense storehouses of freshwater and are as crucial to Japanese ecology now as they were in premodern times. Where summits are high enough to drop below freezing, massive amounts of precipitation accumulate as snow during winter months. A strong wind from the Sea of Japan brings especially heavy snowfall to the mountains along the Hokuriku (Northland) and Tōhoku (Northeast) regions on the Japanese mainland as well as in Hokkaidō, the northernmost island of Japan. There is so much snow in the mountainous white north that Nobel Prize laureate Yasunari Kawabata ([1948] 1996) famously christened it "Snow Country" (*yukiguni*).

When in spring these colossal snow deposits melt, the water filters through innumerable streams to valley reservoirs and rivers below, where farmers channel what they require to irrigate rice paddies and other crops throughout the spring and summer months. Surging through the veins of the mountain as its lifeblood, spring runoff and rainwater absorb minerals and nutrients particular to the ecology of each mountain. This affects the quality, texture, flavor, and fame of regional rice, sake (rice wine), vegetables, fruit, and water. Some the ascetics I know keep jugs of spring water in their homes that they have gathered from surrounding mountains because they enjoy a variety of flavors and insist that it is far healthier than treated household tap water from the dam. During fieldwork, I was frequently offered a selection of mountain water from different springs in Mount Chōkai, Mount Kinbō, Gassan, and Mount Haguro as a valued beverage.

Gassan receives so much snowfall that new winter festivals have been innovated in townships around it. Engineering students from nearby Yamagata University join locals in crafting villages entirely out of snow. They have stores, shrines, temples, and licensed, neon-lit bars. Symbols of regional, religious, and calendrical significance are carved artistically into the outer walls and inside hollowed-out, candlelit rooms of snow-made structures. The sheep, which was the zodiac animal of 2015 (the year I attended), the rabbit, which is the zodiac animal of Gassan, cherries (a regional delicacy), and dedications to the kami were also represented, crafting a symbolic snow-built village of regional self-representation and rural revitalization. Residents near Mount Kinbō have even created a new annual festival for which heavy machinery is used to sculpt an enormous snow effigy of Daikoku, one of the seven kami of good fortune.[24]

As water towers, mountains serve as "the ultimate source of the rice crop's vitality" in spring (Schnell 2007, 865). Yanagita Kunio (1875–1962), the founder of Japanese folklore studies, argued that in preindustrial Japan, the ecological relationship between mountains and rice cultivation was pivotal in the structure of folk religion and its focus on seasonal agrarian rites. In Yanagita's paradigm, spring rituals for summoning the rice kami down from the mountain and autumn rituals that sent them back up served as a "symbolic complement to the hydrologic cycle" (Schnell 2007, 865). The veneration of mountains in preindustrial times, in many respects, the vicarious reverence of water, rice, and life itself.

Nowadays, with digital media, mountains mean more and less than they ever have in Japan. More in the sense that there is an overabundance of narratives about what mountains mean in general and in specific contexts. Social media, the Internet, and television are clicks away, and books and magazines at the nearest library or bookstore contain an endless trove of information, curated narratives, and diverse perspectives of mountains.

Mountains mean less today than ever before in the sense that traditional metanarratives of mountains, the sort that Yanagita once impressed on national consciousness through his folkloric studies, are fading with time. There is no longer a dominant narrative of what mountains mean, nor a central authority to reproduce a normative paradigm. Although this ethnography presents an argument of sacred mountains in contemporary Japan, it amounts to one ethnographer's interpretation in a greater bricolage of orographic perspectives. The tide of globalization renders the apparently fixed locale into a node of interconnected global flows with shifting currents.

Anthropologist, Scott Schnell (2007) has argued that despite the time-honored claims of Japanese folklorists such as Yanagita who attempt cultural orography, there has never been a universally shared view of what mountains mean to Japanese people living in and beyond their shadows. Orographic perspectivism has long been at work even at the local level in Japan. Schnell contends that in preindustrial times, mountain kami varied greatly in form, function, and character. How mountain kami were imagined depended on one's vocation, geographic distance from and proximity to the mountain, as well as cultural disposition. The way a lowland rice cultivator relates to a mountain and imagines its kami was fundamentally different than that of a hunter or woodcutter, and their views were distinct from those of a foreign mountaineer. As Schnell (867) notes, "Since Yanagita's ideas have been so thoroughly disseminated through books, television, and other forms of mass media, there can now be no guarantee that local informants themselves have not been tainted by his influence." Yanagita's rural essentialism was animated by a nostalgic longing to return to a preindustrial lifestyle. The legacy of his work is still apparent today through tourist advertising that frames the countryside and its people, customs, and landscapes as the true abode of tradition.[25] With the widespread translation of Western mountaineering literature into Japanese, Yanagita's influence appears to be waning. Yet it continues to find new incarnations in popular culture.

Another influential writer contributing to Japanese cultural orography is Kyūya Fukada. *One Hundred Mountains of Japan* is one of the most influential travelogues of modern mountaineering in Japan. The influence of this text has been meteoric. It has inspired plenty of made-for-TV mountaineering documentaries, which contribute to the exponential "mountaineering boom" in Japan. In *One Hundred Mountains of Japan,* Fukada dialogues with his literary ancestors to blend modern views of mountains with traditional narratives. Since this text reflects a historical shift in how Japanese interpret mountains, I want to spend a bit of time contextualizing this work and its author to flesh out the cultural orography at play in contemporary Japan.

Fukada ([1964] 2015, 215) was born in 1903 in Ishikawa Prefecture, as he recounts it, "in the shadow" of Mount Haku, which watched over his village "like a tutelary deity." Fukada's formative years coincided with the "golden age of modern mountaineering," described by Satsuka (2015, 28) as a time when "people's perceptions of mountains were still in transition" between the preindustrial and modern periods. During this time, European notions of the material landscape and individual subjectivity were translated into Japanese for a national reading audience who until then held traditional views about mountains—that they were sanctuaries of the kami and ancestors to be visited for religious purposes.²⁶

According to Satsuka (2015, 29), "The 'discovery' of the alpine landscape [as a material object] took place along with the introduction of geography and natural history, and contemporaneously with the literary, artistic, and intellectual movements of [European] Romanticism." Satsuka attributes the translation of this new, objectifying perspective of mountains primarily to Shiga Shigetaka's ([1894] 1995) *Theory of Japanese Landscape*, but it was writers such as Fukada who would later express a hybrid perspective of mountains that longed for the authenticity of ancestral and storied sacred peaks while seeking to ascend them with the secular sentiments of a modern mountaineer.²⁷

As the title of *One Hundred Mountains of Japan* implies, the text is composed of one hundred mountain portraits. Fukada's ([1964] 2015) central objective, which is made explicit in the conclusion, was to establish a definitive list of "eminent mountains" (*meizan*) in Japan to which mountaineers could refer. Other authors before his time had also attempted to delineate a core group of meizan, but no one in the modern era has surpassed the influence of Fukada's work in this genre.²⁸ Popular NHK (Japanese public broadcasting) documentaries and travel programs feature mountains listed specifically by Fukada.

After guiding the reader through poetic descriptions of each mountain in his list, Fukada attributes his affection for mountains to Japanese ethnicity. Rousing his audience from the slumber of a lingering postwar identity crisis, Fukada ([1964] 2015, 243) writes: "Nowhere in the world do people hold mountains in so much regard as in Japan. Mountains have played a part in Japanese history since the country's beginnings, and they manifest themselves in every form of art. More recently, the Japanese have taken to mountaineering and, although people talk of a mountaineering boom, this is no passing fad. For mountains have always formed the bedrock of the Japanese soul."

The implication is that mountaineering is a timeless method for Japanese people to access the primordial source of their Japaneseness, which, building on Fukada's soul-bedrock metaphor, seems to flow forth from the mountains like spring runoff. His naturalistic vision of national identity preceded but is now reminiscent of the *nihonjinron* (theories of Japanese identity) literature of the 1980s, which sought to determine the distinctiveness of the essential Japanese character.²⁹ Ivy (1995, 2) writes that the ethnic uniqueness emphasized in *nihonjinron* literature is "constituted as the particularized obverse of the West" and in this way fashioned a self-image through contradistinction.

Fukada and other mountain writers of his time authored more than just books about mountains. Such accounts crafted a new sense of pride, refuge, and identity for the postwar generation through a timely reworking of cultural orography through modern literature.

To justify his list, Fukada ([1964] 2015) discloses the three criteria he used to select and exclude mountains. "First," he writes, "a mountain must have stature.... I reject mountains that lack the severity or the power or the beauty to strike people in their hearts.... Mountains, like people, must have character" (244). They must affect climbers from a distance and up close. Second, meizan must have deep histories that prevail in their magnitude despite the trappings of modernity: "A peak that people admire from morning to night, that they crown with a shrine, necessarily qualifies as an eminent mountain.... Unfortunately, the crowds mobilized by mass tourism have debased some of these mountains, hallowed by tradition though they once were... such mountains are no longer eligible" (244). The third quality is something advocates of *nihonjinron* also sought in crafting their self-image of "extraordinary distinctiveness." "What I value," he writes, "is the essence, be it of form, feature, or heritage, that makes a mountain uniquely itself. I do not concern myself with humdrum, run-of-the-mill mountains" (245). Drawing on these three subjective criteria, Fukada canonized a hybrid pilgrimage for modern mountaineers that authenticates a hundred peaks as a special constellation of mountains to inspire awe and wonder. Despite the secular outlook of modern mountaineering, the most eminent of Fukada's catalog of eminent mountains are "spirit mountains" (*reizan*).[30] Gassan of Dewa Sanzan is a reizan on that list.

Beyond the influence of such figures as Yanagita and Fukada, the constant flux of information produced by modern media in contemporary Japan only deepens the labyrinth of orographic perspectivism in Japan today. If mountains have become such complex assemblages that mirror back the web of nostalgic values and modern meanings that globally informed onlookers project onto them, what can one say of mountains in Japan after all?

Ivy (1995, 144) addresses the elusive and foreboding character of mountains in the Japanese imagination by describing them as "sublime unknowns" that are fused with death symbolism and linked "with attendant practices of framing, bounding, limiting, and troping this sublimity"—ways of fixing orographic perspectivism into firmer patterns of cultural orography. Japanese anthropologist Nakazawa Shin'ichi described mountains to Ivy as "terrible multiplicities" because they inspire fear and awe in a way that is "excessive [and] beyond language" (144). It can be said that whatever mountains represent in their "sublime" or "terrible multiplicity," they engender what Michel Foucault (1984, 3) has described as an *espace autre*, an "other space," a "counter-site" to mainstream society. Japanese mountains are the "otherworld" of the dead (*ano yo*) in comparison with "this world" (*kono yo*) of the living. *Kono yo* is the plane of society, but mountains are the manifest trace of the "otherworld" of the dead, its visible aspect. In Japan, mountains are imagined as what society is not, yet also what it will become after death, when souls trek to the peak for posthumous liberation.

One of the most thorough ethnographic accounts of a Japanese sacred mountain and its ascetic traditions is Ellen Schattschneider's *Immortal Wishes of the Soul* (2003). Situated in Mount Iwaki in Aomori Prefecture, Schattschneider presents a comprehensive view of mountains as places that are saturated with reproductive symbolism but also animated by ancestral powers that can and must be tamed by modern ascetics. She writes: "For the northern Japanese women and men with whom I worked, the volcanic mountain functions as a dynamic integrated model of the human mind and body. On the surface the mountain is manifestly placid and life-giving, yet it contains within it raging destructive forces obscured until the moment of eruption. It is for this reason in part, that the mountain so effectively redresses human illness, death, and anger, all of which similarly reside beyond conventional human apprehension and control" (5).

Standing tall above human settlements and presenting a path to the afterlife, the "vertical worlds" of sacred mountains are an espace autre in the popular imagination in Japan.[31] If the Other is essential to the formation of self-awareness through contradistinction, the espace autre of sacred mountains can be understood as mirrors for self-recognition, spaces of self-transformation and vantage points for societal critique. Mountains can be further described in Foucauldian (1984, 3–4) terms as "heterotopias," "places . . . outside of all places, even though it may be possible to indicate their location in reality."

Although sacred mountains in Japan are places, they are places of a wholly different kind and character from most others. This is because, as Fukada hints in his first criterion for meizan, notable mountains in Japan, like people, have character. They are personlike places or, from an animistic perspective, "metapersons . . . engaged with as willful agents."[32] In Japan, this is partly intuited in language. The Japanese language prevents speaking about mountains in the same way as other places, such as cities or sites within a city. Directly or indirectly, Japanese speak of mountains similarly as they do of people—not ordinary people with human bodies but extraordinary people

Introduction 19

with mountainous bodies who may exhibit human characteristics. This is because the Japanese language has a high frequency of homophones, words or compound words that sound the same but have very different meanings. "Mountain" as a standalone word is *yama*; however, when a particular mountain is named, the same ideogram for mountain is pronounced *san* as a suffix. For example, "Mount Fuji" is pronounced "Fuji-san." However, "san" is also an honorific suffix attached to a person's surname. A person named "Mr. Fuji" is also called "Fuji-san" even though the ideogram for "Fuji" has a different meaning from that of the mountain and "san" is an honorary suffix, not an ideogram for mountain. When written, it's immediately clear whether "Fuji-san" is a person or a mountain, but when spoken it is only by reading the social context that one would know whether "Fuji-san" refers to a person or Japan's most famous sacred mountain / volcano.

A common pattern in alpine ethnography is the heterotopic (otherness of place) potential of mountainous spaces. In Japan, this otherness is both a mirror through which modern people are actively searching for self-reflection and a cocoon in which they seek self-transformation. Within their "sublime" but "terrible multiplicity," mountains in Japan have the effect of spatiotemporal vortices. They twist time and history, splitting it off into competing streams of historical consciousness while also reconciling differences through hopeful visions of the future. The emplaced otherness of mountains is owing to a "fatal intersection of time with space," a slippage between history, the future, and consciousness that occurs in the sociotemporal vortex of the mountain.[33] As sites of temporal dislocation, mountains in Japan are also what Foucault (1984, 6–7), "for the sake of symmetry" with the concept of heterotopia, has termed "heterochronies," places "in which time never stops building up and topping its own summit." Mount Haguro, Gassan, and Mount Yudono of Dewa Sanzan are such mountains of time.[34]

If mountains can be generally characterized by alterity, it must be a situated alterity. What motivates people of the present to seek the *other* place and *other* time of the mountain? Does that magnetic quality which draws people to behold them and climb them emanate from the weight of the past because of the conditions of a difficult present and uncertain future? What temporality is the "other time" of the mountain in contrast with?

Capitalist Modernity in Japan

Postwar Japan is characterized by rapid economic growth through to the bubble economy of the 1980s and 1990s and then post-bubble stagnation, exacerbated by the Kobe earthquake in 1995 and then the earthquake, tsunami, and nuclear disaster in 2011 and the Covid-19 pandemic of 2020–23. In this context, Japan has been described as a "relationless society" (*muenshakai*) compounded by pessimism about the future of the country because there are no effective measures against a declining birthrate, an aging population, and the broad effect of economic stress that population decline poses.

At the same time, there is a historic push toward the commoditization of religious tradition for the sake of increasing domestic and international tourism and rural revitalization to boost the economy.[35] Ivy (1995) has considered the complex dynamic between modernity and tradition in Japan—"tradition" not in terms of the actual survival of premodern lifeways but in terms of their "phantasmal" or reimagined continuity.[36] In Ivy's model, the historical consciousness of Japanese modernity is characterized by "the logic of the fetish." By this she means "the denial of a feared absence through its replacement with a substitute presence" (10). The "feared absence" of modernity is a loss of tradition, a disconnect with ancestors and ancestral lifeways. The "substitute presence" is a nostalgic reimagining of tradition. Modernity's "losses" can be attributed to two pivotal ruptures in Japanese history.

First is the Meiji period (1868–1912). This era saw the end of 250 years of political and economic isolation from the West, the revisionist restoration of imperial rule, and, through the colonial annexation of islands and surrounding territories, the formation of a quasi-modern state.[37] Religion and the state were a tightly interwoven theocracy.[38] Western influence was permitted but regulated by the Japanese government at this time. The second major rupture was the Asia-Pacific War (1941–45) followed by the United States occupation (1945–52), when American culture flooded Japan through media and products in the postwar market.[39]

Although there have been numerous ruptures throughout Japanese history, these two are at the forefront of modern historical memory. Where the Meiji period and World War II are often figured as times of radical rupture, the Edo period (1603–1868), which preceded the Meiji era, is often the subject of historical dramas on television and is romanticized as a golden age of Japanese cultural life. A time before globalization, imperial expansion, and international war.[40] The Edo period as lived was markedly different from the Edo period now dramatized, but the dramatization of history is telling of the modern longing to recover an idealized past.

In Ivy's paradigm, modern people experience the feared absence of tradition as a collective sense of loss, which leads to a nostalgic longing to recover what was lost but that never actually seeks to recover it, lest modernity self-implodes. "Despite its labors to recover the past and deny the losses of 'tradition,'" she writes, "modernist nostalgia must preserve, in many senses, the sense of absence that motivates its desires" (1995, 10). Nostalgia is both a longing for the premodern past and a highly marketable affect in the modern Japanese economy.⁴¹

The "substitute presence" Ivy writes of is the fetish that satisfies nostalgic longing. It is manifest in performances, experiences, and places perceived as traditional. Places that bear the mark of the authentic.⁴² While modern people fear the absence of tradition, there is a vast market for its substitutes: objects, places, and experiences that are judged by different measures as to which is more and which is less authentic. The countryside in Tōhoku, in which Dewa Sanzan is embedded, has long been framed as an authentic place when compared with the industrial centers of a sprawling metropolis in central Japan.⁴³

Modernity entails losses of tradition, ancestral connection, and locality. A primary affect of modernity's loss is nostalgia. Nostalgia is stimulated and temporarily cured through encounters with the "authentic" because the authentic represents continuity with the ancestral past.⁴⁴ Things, people, activities, and experiences that act like portals to the nostalgic past are valued for their traditional authenticity. Authentic places are zones in which the past is perceived to resume uninterrupted into the present. In capitalist modernity, such portals, links, and zones are highly valued and commoditized. Fakes and forgeries are the antithetical value. Those in the modern market who seek profits of monetary and social capital compete with one another for legitimacy, as the inheritors of ancestral continuity. This has led to historical revisionism at national and local scales. Within this process is a politics of authenticity, a competition in and between places that have retained their ancestral continuity despite modern historical ruptures and the postwar transition to capitalist modernity. Dewa Sanzan is such a place.

Ethnographic Context

As this ethnography unfolds, the many layers of Dewa Sanzan will come to light, revealing a multidimensional placeworld. For now, I would like to introduce Dewa Sanzan by situating it in a regional context. Dewa Sanzan is in the Shōnai area of Yamagata Prefecture, which is situated in the greater Tōhoku region. Shōnai is a small but geographically diverse area along the coast of the Sea of Japan. Beautiful beaches with waves large enough to surf are less than an hour's drive from the summits of mountains, which are surrounded by rice fields. In winter, it is a snowy plain. In spring, the rice paddies are flooded, mirroring the multicolored hues of spectacular sunsets. In summer, rice stalks are plump, green, and leaning heavy beneath blue skies. In autumn, after harvest, Shōnai becomes a land of soil and stubble but is enlivened with vibrant fall colors. Images of the four seasons in Shōnai often grace the cover of tourist brochures and fashion it a traditional place in harmony with nature. Snowboarders, skiers, hikers, surfers, pilgrims, tourists, ascetics, epicures, musicians, filmmakers, historians, scientists, and hippies of all creeds come from all over Japan and the world to Shōnai. It became, in the wake of the earthquake, tsunami, and nuclear disaster of March 2011, a happening alternative for people who would normally go to the Pacific coast for leisure or vacation.

Over the past forty years, advancements in highways, railways, and airport infrastructure have transformed Shōnai from a remote and hard-to-reach region of exotic interest into a much more accessible and renowned destination for tourism and tradition. As John Traphagan and Christopher Thompson (2006, 11) have observed, the Tōhoku region "is conceptualized by Japanese mainstream society as the nation's repository of traditional lifeways." This national reputation lends itself to regional competition within Tōhoku to draw tourists. Developments in infrastructure have deepened the integration of the local economy in Shōnai with greater metropolitan centers such as Niigata City, Sendai, and Tokyo. Although the infrastructure has greatly increased access to Shōnai and enabled its economy to grow, development has also had its drawbacks. For instance, when the national tourism economy dips, as it did after the earthquake, tsunami, and nuclear disaster of March 11, 2011, and during the COVID-19 pandemic, a major component of Shōnai's economy comes to a halt.

Shōnai and its economic integration with larger urban centers such as Tokyo is apparent in its film industry. *Departures* (2008), which won an Oscar for Best Foreign Language Film, was produced in Shōnai and features images of Dewa Sanzan in the backdrop. Films such as *13 Assassins* (2010), *Twilight Samurai* (2002), *The Hidden Blade* (2004), *Love and Honor* (2006), *Sword of Desperation* (2010), and *After the Flowers* (2010) and the most popular program in Japanese television history, *Oshin* (1983–84), are all highly successful productions that feature some of Japan's most famous actors and were filmed, for the most part, in Shōnai.[45] In 2014, during my fieldwork, the open-air film set Studio Sedic, where most of these films were made, became a tourist attraction. Designed in the likeness of the Edo period, which was the feudal era of *daimyō* (feudal lords) and samurai, Studio Sedic (and by

Introduction 23

extension, Shōnai and Dewa Sanzan) has served many films crews as the background of their nostalgic fantasies of premodern Japan. Studio Sedic has been dubbed "Yamagata's Hidden Hollywood" by the lifestyle magazine *Tokyo Weekender*.

While Mount Haguro is the hub for ascetics and pilgrims in Dewa Sanzan, Tsuruoka City is the hub of the Shōnai region. Just nine miles from Mount Haguro and home to approximately 130,000 residents, Tsuruoka City is a self-described "Utopia of Food." In 2014, it won Japan's first UNESCO designation as a Creative City of Gastronomy owing to its fusion cuisine, which draws centuries-old vegetarian ascetic gastronomy together with contemporary culinary arts.

In July 2012, I visited Tsuruoka for a week. I returned for one month in August 2013 for a pilot research project. From July 2014 to December 2015, I lived in an apartment in Tsuruoka City with my wife, who is Japanese, and our then three-year-old son for my primary fieldwork. I conducted additional fieldwork through homestays in the summers of 2016 and 2019. Overall, I conducted twenty-four months of ethnographic fieldwork. I participated in as many community events, ascetic rituals and rites, and pilgrimages as I was able to. Although my focus was on understanding contemporary Shugendō (mountain asceticism) in Dewa Sanzan, I was also involved in my son's preschool community, combed through local library archives for relevant news articles, traveled widely throughout Tōhoku, conducted interviews with ascetics and pilgrims, and produced a documentary film.

If you recall the oath of secrecy described in the Prologue, it makes sense why Shugendō is not well known outside of scholarly circles. Even within the academic study of Japanese religions, the study of Shugendō has for decades been marginal compared to, say, the study of Buddhism, Shintō, or new religious movements. Despite a recent uptick in scholarly interest, much remains unknown about Shugendō despite what is written in this ethnography or any other book on the subject.[46] This is not only because of its traditional secrecy and social inaccessibility but because it is a living religious tradition changing over time. Shugendō is changing as the world changes, turning over to new generations of ascetics with unique motivations who are responding to the societal complexities and anxieties of their era.

Although Shugendō is glossed as "mountain asceticism" in English, it translates as "the Way to Achieve Miraculous Powers through Ascetic Practice."[47] It can generally be described as a syncretic religion that fuses elements of Tendai and Shingon Buddhism with Shintō animism, mountain worship, and shamanism (in the sense of acquiring supernatural power and applying it for the benefit of others). Depending on the context, practitioners of Shugendō may be referred to as *yamabushi* (those who lay prostrate before mountains), *gyōja* (ascetic practitioners), or *shugenja* (those who achieve supernatural results through ascetic practice).

As a symbolic system of ritual forms that vary across each mountain tradition, Shugendō features mountain entry rites (*nyūbu*) and a range of ascetic acts (*gyō*) immersed in death and rebirth symbolism.[48] A mountain is imagined as a womb from which ascetics, as fetuses, can attain rebirth. As Andrea Castiglioni, Carina Roth, and Fabio Rambelli (2020, 2) write about historical Shugendō: "In general, during mountain-entry rituals, the geophysical body of the mountain was conceived as a mandalic landscape, while the act of ascending or descending it corresponded to equal progressions or regressions within the ten realms . . . of the Buddhist cosmology. The foot of the mountain hosted hells, whereas the top was visualized as the entrance to the realm of the buddhas. The soteriological target of Shugendō . . . was to allow *shugenja* to realize perfect Buddhahood and non-duality with the body of the cosmic Buddha, Dainichi Nyorai . . . while penetrating the inner space of the mountain."

While the Shugendō of today may appear pale in comparison with a more authentic Buddhahood-seeking Shugendō of the past, I see contemporary Shugendō as an adaptable religion undergoing rapid transformation in a now globally interconnected, capitalistic world.[49] Its present transformation is no simple, linear process. It bears all the complexities of capitalist modernity and globalization in the twenty-first century. Shugendō is no longer a subject of study that is restricted to textual research in libraries and archives because it is not merely a matter of the past.[50] It is a matter of the present and the future.[51] As Caleb Carter (2022, 4) writes, "Drawing attention to temporal and regional variations reinvigorates our awareness of the fluid interpretations practitioners have applied to Shugendō throughout its history." To gain a full perspective on contemporary Shugendō requires skills in archival, textual study as well as long-term, full immersion in ethnographic fieldwork involving participant-observation, mountaineering, a budget for international travel, digital ethnography, and the will to endure all the physically demanding ordeals of *shugyō* (ascetic training). Thinking back to the more gnarly aspects of fieldwork, I can recall moments where I felt there was a real risk of severe injury, even death. Courage is required. So is trust in one's *sendatsu* (ascetic guide).

To this day, Shugendō is protected and sustained by religious orthodoxies in key sacred mountains, but its practice is not confined to any one mountain. An aspiring ascetic may undergo shugyō in a particular Shugendō tradition such as in Mount Haguro of Dewa Sanzan but then practice Shugendō in mountains around Japan on their own or with other groups. They may even create their own groups or travel overseas to overlay foreign landscapes with Shugendō ritual. Contemporary Shugendō is experimental, dynamic, and global.

That said, every mountain has its lore. Unlike many Shugendō traditions in Japan that trace their origins to En the Ascetic (634–700?) as their founding figure, the oral tradition of Dewa Sanzan begins with Prince Hachiko (542–641), eldest son of Emperor Sushun (530–92). A shrine atop Mount Haguro honors him to this day. According to legend, after the Soga clan assassinated his father in 592, Prince Hachiko renounced his position in Nara and became a wandering ascetic. His journey led him to Dewa (modern-day Yamagata Prefecture), where he followed a mysterious purple cloud into the forest and became lost. A three-legged crow appeared and guided him to the summit of what is now Mount Haguro. Descending into a secluded valley, he spent years in ascetic training, cultivating spiritual power. One day, a hunter sought his help for an ailing patriarch. Prince Hachiko advised reciting the Heart Sutra, which healed the man. As word spread, disciples gathered, and Haguro Shugendō took shape.[52]

Dewa Sanzan may be a geographically bounded locale and may have a reputation for its remote, secretive, archaic Shugendō traditions, but it is now thoroughly animated by global flows of people and friction between competing orographies and their associated temporalities. Anna Tsing (2005, 4) describes friction as "the awkward, unequal, unstable, and creative qualities of interconnection across difference" that constitute global connections. She adds that "friction" also "inflects historical trajectories, enabling, excluding, and particularizing" streams of time (6). The friction of Dewa Sanzan's global connections parallels the friction its space generates between multiple temporalities within Japanese religious history—pasts, presents, and futures entwined in a multistranded braid of time. This ethnography is not a definitive account of Dewa Sanzan. It is an invitation to other curious souls (perhaps you?) to engage with the fascinating, interdisciplinary subject of Shugendō and sacred mountains in Japan. There is still so much more to learn.

Book Synopsis

Each chapter of this book is episodic. It presents an ethnographic take of the living placeworld of Dewa Sanzan and a unique angle from which I argue that sacred mountains represent spatiotemporal alterity in contemporary Japan.

Chapter 1 introduces Dewa Sanzan through Mount Haguro. The ethnographic narrative is an account of my first visit to Mount Haguro in July 2012, when I was guided up the mountain by a yamabushi. I use key sites that my guide explained to me along the path of Mount Haguro as entry points into a larger discussion of the multiple temporalities of Dewa Sanzan, the ways in which it figures into historical and societal dynamics in Japan, especially in terms of its relationship with regional narratives of Tōhoku. This chapter sets the spatial and temporal stage for subsequent chapters.

In chapter 2 I take a step deeper into the contemporary scene of Dewa Sanzan with an account of "yamabushi experience" retreats. A senior yamabushi in Dewa Sanzan has shortened what is normally a ten-day ascetic rite (Autumn's Peak) into a three-day weekend training program. Participants may be religious or not, and there is no long-term commitment or membership required. This chapter demonstrates the proximity between religion and tourism in Dewa Sanzan but emphasizes the central draw of the yamabushi experience retreat: its temporary symbolic break from capitalist modernity in the spatiotemporal alterity of the mountains through "alpine affects"—a term I use to describe bodily porosity with the sacred mountainscape.

In chapter 3 I explore some themes that ascetics discuss in their reflections on the yamabushi experience retreat. I attend especially to the gendered aspect of the mountains, which are closely related with the theme of rebirth, and how it impacts individual ascetics' interpretations of themselves in relation to modern society. This chapter reveals a counterculture element to contemporary Shugendō, which reflects my point that mountains are an "other space" in contemporary Japan in which people think critically about the agency of their lives in the structure of capitalist modernity. I suggest that ascetics seek a cyclical temporality of annual rebirth in the symbolic womb of the mountains, a rebirth experience they struggle to find in the linear time of capitalist modernity.

Chapter 4 explores competing streams of historical consciousness in Dewa Sanzan through rival institutions of Buddhist and Shintō Shugendō. Applying the notion of ressentiment (historical alienation) to Japanese religious history, I argue that religious tensions in contemporary Dewa Sanzan are rooted in a historical dispute between Shintō nativism and Buddhism, a religion originating from the Asian continent. I show how a power dynamic has emerged between Shintō and Buddhist forms of Shugendō in Dewa Sanzan through strategic uses of history and engagements with the media and scholarship.

Chapter 5 presents an account of the Buddhist-oriented form of Shugendō in Mount Haguro and its annual mountain entry rite, Autumn's Peak. I suggest that while the rite is said to present participants with symbolic death and rebirth in the mountain's womb, it is now generally experienced as a suspension of and return to capitalist modernity and a chance for self-improvement. A shift in membership has also led to a new ethics of participation where the temple authorities seek to prevent members from exploiting their status as yamabushi for personal and professional gain. I suggest that this negotiation of ethics presents a model of ascetic *phronesis*, an exercise in "practical judgment" in which ascetics attend to their religious devotion without succumbing to modern temptation. This tension, between loyalty to the temple and the temptation to capitalize esoteric knowledge gained in the rite, illuminates the challenge that the temple faces to maintain the traditional integrity of Shugendō in a globally interconnected contemporary Japan.

Chapter 6 considers mountain pilgrimage on Gassan, one of the best-known reizan (spirit mountains) in northeastern Japan. I begin by describing the death symbolism of the mountain and how it can manifest in visions for pilgrims while ascending. I focus on a bonfire ritual that occurs on the summit every August 13, the first day of the annual Festival of the Dead. I describe how the bonfire serves as a beacon to the sky-dwelling ancestors, who are imagined descending onto the peak and then down the slope to visit their families for the duration of the holiday. The earthquake, tsunami, and nuclear disaster of March 11, 2011, added deeper significance to the mountain when a local mountain ascetic organized an effort to erect a memorial on the summit for the victims of the disaster, reorienting the temporality of the peak from the ancestral past to the future reconstruction of the inundated coast and igniting a sense of hope for the future in the wake of disaster.

In chapter 7 I examine the case of self-mummified ascetics whose robed remains are on display and worshipped in a few temples in Mount Yudono.[53] They are revered as "living Buddhas" (*sokushinbutsu*) by temple patrons who petition them in prayer and who, in some cases, claim to receive telepathic messages from them while awake or dreaming. Within the Mount Yudono community, there is a politics of authenticity between the temples with the mummies. Monks at different temples have competing claims about which mummies are forgeries and which are real. Such claims are grounded in historicities of the automummification process and if it was undertaken properly but are also, as I demonstrate, connected to competition in the domestic and international tourism industry.

In the final chapter I conclude with general reflections on sacred mountains in Japan. I suggest that in Japan mountains act as "key symbols" that are filled with "root metaphors" (Ortner 1973) through which modern ascetics cultivate critical distance from society and seek self-knowledge and spiritual rejuvenation. I also urge ethnographers and scholars of religion to attend to the mountains that lie in the periphery of their field sites. Mountains are not just background features of the landscape but are bountiful sources of knowledge deserving of sustained inquiry. Mountains are open season for interdisciplinary research.

1 Mountains of Time
A Tour of Mount Haguro

Northeastern Japan was thrust into the global spotlight March 11, 2011, when a magnitude 9.0 earthquake struck, followed by a tsunami and an unfolding nuclear disaster.[1] I remember it clearly. I was in Japan a day before, visiting Mie Prefecture. From 2008 to 2009, I had taught English at a school in Matsusaka. The director of the school invited me to fly over for a special anniversary event that March. I stayed with my in-laws for a week, arriving on March 3 and returning home to Canada on March 10. I woke up in the middle of the night after my return. Typical jetlag, but my phone was also buzzing. Friends were messaging me, asking if I was OK. I didn't know what had happened until I turned on the news and saw for myself the unbelievable scale of the disaster that had unfolded less than twenty-four hours since my departure. So many lives lost so suddenly. The global media focused on images of tsunami destruction and the unfolding nuclear crisis for weeks to come, but the unique culture of Tōhoku was mostly omitted from the coverage.

The next summer, my wife, our one-year-old son, and I returned to Mie Prefecture to visit her family. I then went on a tour of Tōhoku to explore the region for myself. Dewa Sanzan stood out in my guidebook. It was described as a place where "you can see white-clad pilgrims (equipped with wooden staff, sandals, and straw hat) and the occasional yamabushi (equipped with conch shell, checkered jacket, and voluminous white pantaloons) stomping along mountain trails or sitting under icy waterfalls as part of severe ascetic exercises intended to train both body and spirit" (Rowthorn et al. 2007, 549). A yamabushi "training camp" was listed. It was based in Tōge, the township surrounding Mount Haguro, and operated through the Ideha Cultural Museum (Ideha Bunka Kinenkan). The fee to attend the training camp was 30,000 yen (US$300 at the time). It included two nights, three days of "fasting, mountain sprints, and 4:30 am wake up calls." "These boot camps," the guidebook warned, "are not for the faint of heart" (549).

I had called the museum from my in-laws' mountainside village in Mie to see if the three-day yamabushi training camps were still in operation. I

Vehicles pass beneath Mount Haguro's torii gate. Photograph by Shayne Dahl.

learned from the receptionist over the phone that they were no longer available. My guidebook was outdated. The edition I had was the last to advertise the so-called training camps.[2] When I mentioned that I was considering ethnographic research in Dewa Sanzan, the receptionist changed her tone and made a special arrangement. I was then scheduled to meet a yamabushi named Itō-san (pseudonym) at the museum on July 18 for a guided tour of the mountains.

It took nearly twelve hours via express and bullet trains (*shinkansen*) to get to Tsuruoka City from Mie Prefecture. The most efficient route is to go from Tokyo to Niigata City and, from there, to take an express train called the Inaho (ear of rice) directly to Tsuruoka City, which is an hour and a half north along the rugged coast of the Sea of Japan. The final leg of the journey to Mount Haguro, which is the same for most without a vehicle, is a nine-mile bus ride from Tsuruoka Station to Tōge.

Halfway through the ride, the bus exits the cityscape of Tsuruoka and enters a green plain of rice paddies leading to the elevated forest of Mount Haguro. Towering over the road at the base of the mountain is a large, bright red Shintō gate, called a torii. All vehicles driving up Mount Haguro must pass through it. Torii are made in many styles and are commonplace at the entrances of shrines or paths leading to religious sites throughout Japan. Thomas Kasulis (2004, 18), a scholar of Japanese religions, writes that torii are "holographic entry points" that "specify a particular place or object as having . . . concentrated power" and link people "with the *kami*-filled

Mountains of Time   31

world."³ Passing through Mount Haguro's torii, one quickly realizes that civilization does not end at the gate. Mount Haguro and its township, Tōge, are fully developed with modern infrastructure and, as the international ATMs, restaurants, ice cream shops, souvenir stores, camera-toting hikers, and large parking lots filled with cars, vans, and buses indicate, a lively tourist center. These days, a torii is as much a marker of sacred space as it is a tourist beacon.⁴

Whether viewed as sacred space or as a tourist site, the space of Dewa Sanzan still possesses some quality that renders it in travel advertisements, magazines, and blogs as a formidable "power spot" (*pawāsupotto*). Even the Shōnai Visitors Association website advertises Dewa Sanzan as a place of "power spots." Caleb Carter (2018, 145) defines power spots as "certain places [that are thought to] emanate special energies from the earth."⁵ Since the New Age movement came to prominence in Japan in the 1980s, there has been increased interest in key religious sites as a source of "power." Through "word of mouth, family relations, media attention, celebrity personalities, and independent spiritual counselors," power spots are not only places that emanate power but places from which that power can be absorbed, through proximity and touch (168). The so-called power spot boom (*pawāsupotto būmu*) that has taken place over the past three decades in Japan has become a driving force in modern tourism.

What constitutes the power of Dewa Sanzan as a power spot for modern visitors? From what source might this power of place derive? I suggest that beyond the intensity of the natural landscape, with its rivers, waterfalls, high slopes, and thick, green vegetation, it is the nostalgic and ancestral temporality of Dewa Sanzan's mountainous space that factors strongly in its designation as a place of power. The power of its place is the way it spatializes the ancestral past (as imagined) for contemporary people through religious architecture fashioned centuries ago that is seamlessly embedded in an impressive natural landscape. Where some visitors consciously pursue this imagined past, others engage it passively. Intentions aside, visitors to Dewa Sanzan are bound to encounter other times in the other space of the mountains.

For Allan Grapard (1994, 373–74), to understand what counts as "sacred" space, we must attend to the social relations of power that outline the boundaries of the sacred. He writes that "scholars of religious history have studied the forms of space they term 'sacred' as though they were devoid of historical conflict in their origins as well as in their maintenance. . . . They treat the power of sacred spaces as though it were intrinsic to those places and always already there, with little regard for sociological or political factors, and as if power were a numinous entity that has never changed."[6]

Delineating what he calls an "ideology of space" in Japan, John Nelson (2000, 57) writes that "any location, whether deemed sacred or not, can be thought of as a deeply layered text to be decoded at each level or . . . as composed of underlying layers (structures, strata, and encrusted meanings) some of which are immediately accessible to the eye while others require excavation." When "excavating" the strata of meaning in any place, "the historical record becomes important less for the exact dates it provides than for its serviceability in forging explicit connections between particular places and a sense of regional or national consciousness and community."

Through a virtual tour of Mount Haguro, a "thick description" of the places behind its torii gate, I argue that what makes Dewa Sanzan attractive is not some sense of intrinsic sacred quality but the natural beauty of the environment compounded by multiple modes of historical consciousness the place evokes in visitors, moments in which they encounter for themselves the past as spatialized in the medieval architecture and curated landscape.[7] For urban Japanese feeling disconnected with the past, an experience of being immersed in the spatialized past of the mountains make the space powerful relative to the alienation common to life in a metropolis. As Tim Ingold (2010, 153) writes, "To perceive the landscape is . . . to carry out an act of remembrance and remembering is not so much a matter of calling up an internal image stored in the mind, as of engaging perceptually with an environment that is itself pregnant with the past."

Whether framed in religious or secular terms, this remembering and re-imagining of the past through the mountain is a driving force in the modern tourist economy of Dewa Sanzan. Its biggest asset for modern Japanese visitors is its link to the premodern Japanese past. Contrary to historical studies and the tourist promotional materials of Dewa Sanzan, in which there is a presumed rupture between the past and the present, I demonstrate some of the ways in which Dewa Sanzan refracts the present with echoes of the past in Mount Haguro. Through cultural orography (the anthropological study of cultural representations of mountains) and alpine ethnography (ethnographic fieldwork conducted in mountainous landscapes), this chapter shows how perspectives of Dewa Sanzan are crafted from specific places that are connected to specific moments, periods, and perceptions of the past. Also, how some of these places connect with larger regional narratives. The placeworld of Dewa Sanzan retains its magnetic draw in the twenty-first century because its mountainous landscape is crowded with places of religious and literary heritage that stimulate national cultural nostalgia and the satisfaction of ancestral communion.[8]

The Ideha Cultural Museum

The Ideha Cultural Museum is a large, gray concrete building with tinted windows, tourist banners lining its perimeter, and a large parking lot. It lies at the top of the narrow road that winds through Tōge, a block or so from the entrance to the mountain path. I arrived in the late morning of July 18, 2012. I decided to go earlier than my appointment because I wanted to inquire about what sort of customary gift I might be able to give Itō-san, my yamabushi guide. After all, he agreed to this special arrangement despite the museum's five-year hiatus on yamabushi experience (*yamabushi taiken*) tours.

Entering through the sliding glass doors, I came upon a small shop of trinkets, souvenirs, and a large collection of books about Dewa Sanzan. There was a mannequin *tengu* (forest goblin) dressed in yamabushi garments beside the receptionist's desk and a yamabushi's conch trumpet (*hora gai*) on display behind with a price tag for 120,000 yen. There was a small table with different sizes of hora gai for visitors to try. I introduced myself to the receptionist, but she promptly sent for one of her co-workers. A slender, handsome, and professionally dressed man with a sharp goatee soon appeared. He shook my hand and introduced himself as Masatoshi. Masatoshi was in his mid-thirties. He spoke good English. Once he learned that I was from Canada, he told me that he had studied English and animation in Montreal for a few months in his early twenties. We established rapport quickly.

I had presumed that the receptionist called Masatoshi over because of his English skills, so I reiterated to him that I was supposed to meet a yamabushi named Itō-san at 1:30 p.m. Also, that I wanted to buy Itō-san a gift, but I did not know what would be appropriate for a yamabushi, or even if they were able to receive gifts owing to their ascetic discipline. Masatoshi said that I did not need to bring a gift: "You coming here all the way from Canada to learn about Shugendō is, itself, a gift that he greatly appreciates." Wanting, stubbornly, to make a good impression, I insisted that there must be something I could provide Itō-san, but Masatoshi strongly insisted that Itō-san did not require a gift. I conceded.

He then asked: "Would you prefer to be guided by Itō-san wearing normal clothing or to be dressed up as a yamabushi?" Naively, I did not expect that a yamabushi would need to dress up as a yamabushi. My eyebrows furrowed, signaling confusion. Masatoshi then qualified his question: "Dressing in yamabushi attire will cost extra." Despite a sense of disappointment in the piecemeal pricing and embarrassment for having to disclose my desire with cash in hand to see an authentic yamabushi, I opted to pay extra, hoping the photos would be useful someday.

Masatoshi soon went back to his office. I wandered around the museum for the next hour and a half, exploring the exhibit, which features mannequin yamabushi in checkered robes with conch trumpets and wooden axes marching in a procession. There were also alphorns on display, suggesting past cultural exchanges between the yamabushi who sound their hora gai into the mountainous amphitheater of Dewa Sanzan and the Swiss alphornists who play their melodies throughout the Alps.[9] The museum also has a library with every academic, journalistic, audiovisual, and popular publication or broadcast related to Dewa Sanzan. I then went for lunch.

I expected to meet Itō-san at 1:30 p.m., and returned at that time, but the receptionist told me that he was running late. While perusing books, I kept an anxious eye on the front entrance waiting for a yamabushi. Suddenly, a man startled me from behind. It took a second to recognize him in the all-white yamabushi uniform, but it was Masatoshi who had emerged from his office. His full name, he then told me, was Itō Masatoshi.

He had introduced himself by first name to accommodate the English custom of referring to people by their given name. I hadn't thought to ask what Itō-san's first name was because the Japanese custom is to refer to others in formal settings by surname. As it turned out, our efforts to accommodate each other's naming culture set a friendly tone to our meeting. He later told me that once he realized I had thought "Itō-san" was a separate person from "Masatoshi," he decided to play along. He decided to conceal his identity to teach me a lesson about the multiple identities that yamabushi possess. Many yamabushi have special names that are used exclusively in the mountains. After years of participation in Shugendō rituals, they gradually develop a yamabushi identity that is distinguishable and secreted from their ordinary life.

The Poem in the Stone

On our way to the entrance of Mount Haguro, we came upon a large boulder in front of a pilgrim's lodge. It had a small statue of Matsuo Bashō, the famous haiku poet, before it. A haiku was engraved onto its surface. Itō-san explained its meaning as we walked by. The significance of it became clear as we ascended Mount Haguro since other statues of Bashō and his haiku are

A boulder engraved with Matsuo Bashō's haiku, Mount Haguro.
Photograph by Shayne Dahl.

found along the trail and on the summit. The first thing to know about Dewa Sanzan, which this boulder signifies, is that it is embedded in larger regional narratives of Tōhoku that Bashō himself played a strong role in shaping.

The story of this haiku-engraved boulder and others like it in Dewa Sanzan and throughout Tōhoku begins in spring 1689, when Bashō tied on his straw sandals, gripped his staff, and embarked on a two-and-a-half-year journey from modern-day Tokyo into "the Interior," the northeastern region of the Japanese mainland now referred to as Tōhoku.[10] Contemporary Tōhoku includes Akita, Aomori, Fukushima, Iwate, Miyagi, and Yamagata Prefectures, but the first use of Tōhoku as a regional designation was in the 1890s following the Meiji Restoration. Before that, the northeast was referred to as Ōshū, Ōu, or Michinoku (Hopson 2017, 68).

In 1694, a few years after his return to Tokyo but just months before his death, Bashō published *The Narrow Road to the Interior*, a travel sketch based on this journey that blended prose with haiku.[11] Included in this travel sketch and etched into monuments throughout Dewa Sanzan are three haiku dedicated to Mount Haguro, Gassan, and Mount Yudono:

how cool it is here
a crescent moon faintly hovers
over Mount Haguro

the peaks of clouds
have crumbled into fragments
Mount of the Moon

I cannot speak of Yudono,
but see how wet my sleeves are
with reticent tears[12]

Bashō's lean but vivid travelogue has become one of the most domestically and internationally celebrated works of Japanese literature.[13] It is important to consider not only for its appearance in select sites throughout Dewa Sanzan but because it has, over the centuries, influenced popular perceptions of the space and time of Tōhoku, a region long fashioned as a primitive place of the past. As Traphagan and Thompson (2006, 11) write, "Culturally, the Tōhoku region [is] conceptualized by Japanese mainstream society as the nation's repository of traditional lifeways." For more than a millennium, since the colonization of the northeast in the eighth century, Tōhoku's reputation among power centers of Central Japan has been subject to racism against the Indigenous peoples of the northeast, the Emishi and the Ainu. Following the devastation of World War II, Japanese scholars repurposed Tōhoku to reimagine Japanese ethnicity and identity through a "noble savage" narrative (Hopson 2017).

The Narrow Road to the Interior, which links Dewa Sanzan to Tōhoku in the Japanese imaginary, has been described as "a monument . . . set up against the flow of time" through which Bashō sought "a vision of eternity in the things that are, by their own very nature, destined to perish."[14] The method through which this "study in eternity" rendered the ephemeral everlasting was Bashō's poetic depiction of fleeting events and experiences in nature, like the nocturnal chirping of a cricket or the cool scent of snow on the spring breeze. One affect, or shared feeling, that haiku inspires is called *sabi* in Japanese, a kind of existential loneliness. *Sabi* is like realizing that "all living things are evanescent is sad, but when one sees a tiny creature enduring that sadness and fulfilling its destiny one is struck with a sublime feeling."[15]

Bashō's concise haiku enable transient moments in nature to be perpetually reimagined. His haiku are written in the present tense. With each reading, the motion in nature captured in a haiku recurs as if eternally present in the imagination of the reader. Haiku, as a literary art that enables fleeting moments to be endlessly reimagined and eternalized throughout the ages, has interesting consequences when considering the impact that *The Narrow Road to the Interior* has had on Tōhoku and Dewa Sanzan in the popular imagination. Although Bashō was influenced by a Buddhist aesthetics of impermanence and Daoist ideals of immortality, nearly every scene in *The Narrow Road to the Interior* is tethered to place.[16] By animating places within Tōhoku through haiku, Bashō succeeded in "remapping the cultural landscape of the Interior" as well as its temporality for future generations.[17]

The Narrow Road to the Interior can be situated in anthropological theory as literary "place making" (Basso 1996, 5–7). In Keith Basso's ethnographic context, among the Western Apache of America, placemaking occurs in several ways. In one instance, it is "retrospective world-building" where his Apache interlocutors would read into a place through its name, associated stories, and environmental features. By imagining what it signified for the ancestors, his interlocutors would fashion a place for the present that is in spatial and temporal continuity with an ancestral and storied past. Basso writes that for his interlocutors, "instances of place making consist in the fleshing out of historical material that culminates in a posited state of affairs, a particular universe of objects and events—a placeworld—wherein portions of the past are brought into being" (6).

Matsuo Bashō's poetic place-making also conveys spatiotemporal continuity with an ancestral and storied past. By venturing to the same "poetic places" that poets of the past once did, Bashō sought to "dialogue" or "commune with the ancients" through a shared rumination of place across the span of centuries.[18] His style was to invoke the established poetic essences of known places, objects, and subjects (their associations and established meanings) while asserting a "newness" to them in succinct but expressive haiku.[19]

By visiting poetic places and expanding the horizon of their meaning and perceived essence, Bashō reformed poetry while reimagining Tōhoku for urban Japanese of his time and for centuries after. Place-making was the practice and result of Bashō's craft, though it was undertaken in a way unique to his artistic, historical, and cultural context. Bashō chose "the Interior" for his final journey because "the north was largely an unexplored territory" at the time, representing "all the mystery there was in the universe" for him and his contemporaries.[20] Even the linguistic equation between the northeast and the "interior" is telling of the mystique of the region for Bashō—that it is hidden or enclosed in a barrier of wilderness. Scholars suggest that "the Interior" inferred in the title has a double meaning.[21] In a superficial sense, it is a geographic reference to the region now called Tōhoku, but in a metaphoric sense, it is introspective. The narrow road represents "the difficulty of the spiritual journey within" since *oku* can be translated as "interior," "deep," or "within," depending on the context.

The Narrow Road to the Interior is "a kind of fiction, loosely based on the actual journey, leaving out most of what happened."[22] Its structure conforms to an aesthetic symmetry of place. The nocturnal, cloudy, and emotional haiku about Mount Haguro, Gassan, and Mount Yudono of Dewa Sanzan, which are on the northwest coast of the Sea of Japan, were written in symmetrical contrast to the brightness of Mount Nikkō on the Pacific coast, whose "benevolent power," Bashō ([1694] 1966, 100) wrote, "prevails throughout the land, embracing the entire people, like the bright beams of the sun."

The Narrow Road to the Interior has stood the test of time and remains one of the most popular introductions to the people, customs, and places of Tōhoku for urban Japanese and non-Japanese alike. The lasting and now global influence of this early modern travel sketch, which is a part of the national school curriculum, cannot be overstated. Bashō's posthumous fame reached such heights that within two centuries after his death, nearly a thousand stone monuments dedicated to his legacy and works were erected around the country and he was deified, for a time, by the imperial court.[23]

A strong tourist infrastructure in key sites that Bashō visited, including Dewa Sanzan, has physically altered the landscape of Tōhoku with statues, museums, paved mountain trails, stylized souvenirs, and busloads of "literary pilgrims" tracing Bashō's path.[24] I have seen his statue on other mountains in Yamagata Prefecture as well, places he made famous with the three simple lines of a haiku. Yamadera is most notable.[25]

Given the temporal structure of Bashō's haiku and the long-standing fame of *The Narrow Road to the Interior*, it has, like a haiku to a fleeting motion in nature, fashioned a particular moment in Tōhoku's history and particular images of Dewa Sanzan as eternal in popular culture. In seeking eternity in the ephemeral yet tethering his poetry to place, Bashō wedded the geographic interior with "the Interior" of his literary project, instilling the regional cartography with the storied affects embedded in his prose and haiku that are engraved in stones, monuments, and statues throughout the region. Tōhoku is inscribed by Bashō's sketch into a mysterious, harsh, timeless, exotic, traditional, and remote territory, the domestic and rural "Orient" and Other to the urban, and a place to seek inner truth.

The Narrow Road to the Interior reveals that even as far back as the Edo period (1603–1868), Tōhoku has been subject to regional exoticism by people from the more densely populated areas of the mainland. This tendency to emplace Tōhoku as a special spatiotemporal region of ancestral continuity and timeless natural beauty has been replicated in numerous scholarly works and popular media in the centuries following Bashō's legendary journey.[26]

This haiku-engraved boulder I saw near the entrance to Mount Haguro, to which alcohol offerings are made by shukubō (pilgrim's inn) owners, is just one manifestation of Bashō's enduring influence on the multiple temporalities of Dewa Sanzan, but it reveals a clear link between Dewa Sanzan and Tōhoku. The two are bound together by geography, history, literature, and the popular imagination in Japan. Dewa Sanzan is enfolded into Tōhoku, and Tōhoku represents national cultural tropes of ancestral continuity and heritage.

Descent into Hell

After passing by the haiku-inscribed boulder, Itō-san and I soon approached the gate leading to the stairway up Mount Haguro. It's called the Zuishinmon, or Gate of Dual [Shintō] Deities. Statues of Shintō kami are enshrined in columns on either side. I saw a pilgrim exit the gate, turn around, bow to the mountain one last time, and then walk past us.

Itō-san told me that before the 1870s, Buddhism was the dominant religious order of Dewa Sanzan. At that time, the entrance was called the Niōmon, the Gate of Dual [Buddhist] Deva. The term *niō* refers to muscular guardian statues.[27] While making deeper than usual eye contact with me, Itō-san explained: "The niō were able to look into people's souls to see if they were pure to enter. They deterred the unworthy by cursing them if they cross." The two niō also have asymmetrical facial expressions. One has its mouth open, representing あ(Ah), the first syllable of the Japanese syllabary. In Buddhism, this is associated with the sound of birth. The other niō has its mouth closed, representing ん (Un), the last syllable of the Japanese syllabary, which has symbolic associations with death. Enshrined together in a gate, the niō materialize the alpha-omega (阿吽 [A-Un]) of Esoteric Buddhism and Shugendō, which unites birth and death symbolism in sacred

The Zuishinmon (Gate of Dual Deities), Mount Haguro. Photograph by Shayne Dahl.

mountains. Since Shintō became the dominant religious order of Dewa Sanzan in the late nineteenth century, "just 150 years ago," Itō-san would say with emphasis, "the niō statues at the entrance of Mount Haguro were replaced with Shintō kami."

Itō-san and I bowed before the Zuishinmon, passed through it, and then descended a flight of stone steps into a deep green forest animated by the sound of rushing water and the rhythmic buzz of cicadas. It became immediately obvious why Mount Haguro's stone stairway is referred to as "the green tunnel" (*gurin toneru*) in tourist brochures. The forest floor is lush with vegetation, and 585 cryptomeria cedars tower over the stairway. This is the result of afforestation accomplished over several decades from the Keichō to Kan'ei period (ca. 1596–1624). The impressive feat of landscaping was offered as an aesthetic act of devotion to Buddhist deities and their Shintō avatars in the mountains. Tullio Lobetti (2014, 101), an Italian anthropologist, writes of his experience entering Mount Haguro: "Centuries old trees (cryptomeria) are everywhere, while enormous fern leaves cover the ground. Broken rays of the sun filtering through the leaves illuminate this dream-like landscape, where all signs of human civilization suddenly disappear. The sensation of entering a different dimension is indeed powerful and one's senses are lost in this contrasting reality."

Mountains of Time   41

Once Itō-san and I reached the bottom of the stone stairway, he asked: "Don't you think it is odd that to climb Mount Haguro, we must first descend? Why do you think that is?" I was too absorbed in the scenery and floral scents of the forest to think analytically. I said, matter-of-factly, that it was just the unique geography of the mountain. He shook his head, then explained: "Since the mountain is actually a mandala [an orographic microcosm of Buddhist cosmology], we just descended into hell (*jigoku*)."[28] The mountains of Dewa Sanzan, like other sacred mountains throughout Japan, were "mandalized" in the centuries following the introduction of Esoteric Buddhism (Tendai and Shingon) in the early Heian period (ca. 800 CE).[29] From the ninth century, mountains were modeled into mandalic landscapes signifying different realms of Buddhist cosmology and were invested with the symbolic power to turn humans into Buddhas.[30]

In Esoteric Buddhist cosmology there is a doctrine of Ten Worlds (*jukkai*), generally modeled in a vertical hierarchy. From bottom to top: hell (*jigoku*), hungry ghosts (*gakidō*), beasts (*chikushōdō*), warring spirits (*tengudō*), humanity (*ningendō*), heavenly beings (*tenjōdō*), and four stages of Buddhahood: discipleship (*shōmon*), self-enlightened Buddhas (*engaku*), Buddhas dedicated to the liberation of others (*bosatsu*), and Buddhahood (*butsu*).[31] In the mandala of the mountain, hell is found on the outer edges and lower altitudes, Buddhahood on the summit, and the rest, gradated between. In this symbolic framework, climbing a mandalized mountain symbolizes ascending progressive stages of Buddhist awakening.[32]

I replied to Itō-san: "If this is hell, then it's far more beautiful than we're led to believe!" I intended it as a compliment about the beauty of the place while trying to share a laugh and develop rapport, but Itō-san seemed to take it as insensitive to the seriousness of his place-making claim about the mandala of the mountain. Although he was serving as my tour guide, Itō-san is an active yamabushi who partakes in annual rites that make serious ritual use of the mandalic framing of space in Mount Haguro. It's not an abstract matter for yamabushi like him.

The name of the initial segment of the stairway when descended is Falling-Descent-into-Hell Hill (*jigoku he ochiru kudari saka*), and one of the shrines at the base of the hill is dedicated to the King of Hell (*enma*). Since the mandalization of mountains is a continental phenomenon, the fusion of hell (*jigoku*) imagery with the alpine landscape is not unique to Mount Haguro. Mount Tateyama in Toyama Prefecture is well known for its "alpine hells," as is Mount Osore (Dread or Fear) in Aomori Prefecture, with its strong geothermal activity and volcanic lake.[33] As the outer edge of the mountain's mandala, Falling-Descent-into-Hell Hill indexes an Esoteric Buddhist temporality reaching back into the Heian period (794–1185) but, more generally, a premodern past of Buddhist dominance in Dewa Sanzan.

Grapard (1982, 221) writes that mountains throughout Japan were configured as complementary mandalas: the Womb Mandala (*taizōkai*), the feminine component, and the Diamond Mandala (*kongōkai*), its masculine pairing. For pilgrims and yamabushi, entering mountains became a symbolic means of self-transformation by "penetrating the Realm[s] of the Buddha." As a transformative space, the symbolic bond between mountains and wombs is especially pronounced in Mount Haguro, where yamabushi assume an embryological status during annual rites (Sekimori 2016). Although visitors to Mount Haguro may not know the historical symbolism of the mountains before arriving, signs posted in front of key sites explain the history and the symbolism in both Japanese and English.

The Womb of the Mountain

Itō-san then turned to me and asked, "Do you know why my clothes are white?" I shook my head. He explained, "When I wear these clothes, I am a dead man. Even my name is different. The *dō* of Shugendō means 'way.' Shugendō is the way of dying and being reborn in the womb of the mountain. The path we are walking on is called the 'stairway of rebirth.' Until one is reborn as a Buddha, all practice is like a dream."

Just over a mile long, the stone-step stairway leading to the plateaued summit of Mount Haguro is the second longest in Japan. It includes 2,446 steps, each carved from river stone. It is frequently advertised as the "stairway of rebirth" (*umare kawari no ishidan*) since the interior of the mountain is, on one level of symbolic interpretation, an alpine womb. Mount Iwaki, about 215 miles north of Dewa Sanzan, has similar associations. Ellen Schattschneider (2003) conducted fieldwork on Mount Iwaki in the early 1990s. She writes that the main shrine's "ritual practices are organized with reference to the disturbing symbolism of human childbirth and the regenerative cosmological womb of the life-giving mountain" (213). This framing of mountains is prevalent in Japan, though not many make it a travel advertisement as in Dewa Sanzan. Many ads that I have seen since my initial tour feature yamabushi dressed in white and ascending the stone steps of Mount Haguro beneath a descriptive caption referring to the uterine symbolism of the mountain.

As I ascended the stairway with Itō-san, I began to understand why the museum charges extra for him to wear the yamabushi uniform. Its contrast

Itō-san ascending the "Stairway of Rebirth." Photograph by Shayne Dahl.

against the green sylvan backdrop—or, if on Gassan, the bright blue sky—is picturesque and, for Japanese, nostalgic of a bygone era. At certain moments during my tour Itō-san struck a pose and stood in silence, looking stoically into the distance. It took me a few seconds to realize he was waiting for me to snap a photo. It was, after all, the package I paid for.

One artistic brochure I located in library archives a year after this guided tour and that was distributed by a township sightseeing agency stated that there are thirty-three images of small sake cups carved into select steps along the trail. It said that the wishes of those who can spot eighteen or more are likely to come true while the wishes of those who can locate thirty-three are certain to be granted. For the more practically inclined, the brochure features a contest where a person who could locate all thirty-three carvings could win a free night's stay with meals at the shrine on the summit or, if they could find only eighteen, they would receive a consolation prize of "pesticide-free, locally brewed blueberry juice." The numbers eighteen and thirty-three, I later learned in a public lecture at the Ideha Cultural Museum, are specific in Buddhist numerology to Kannon, the Bodhisattva of Compassion and overseer of Mount Haguro.[34] Eighteen was said to represent Kannon's number of arms and auspicious festival day (*ennichi*), while thirty-three refers to how many times Kannon will reincarnate to save humanity.

Only a hundred yards or so down the path and the fusion of the tourist industry with Buddhist cosmology and Shintō innovations becomes obvious in the "power spot" of Mount Haguro. A key element of this captivating scene is the presence of the yamabushi moving through the religious architecture in the mountain. Itō-san, with his anachronistic attire and ritual actions, adds a striking dimension to the cultural orography as he performed Shugendō rituals at sacred sites all along the stairway.

The Conch Trumpet

After crossing an arced red bridge, Itō-san forced a deep breath into his hora gai, piercing the relative quiet of the forest. He said that it is necessary for yamabushi to sound their conches when entering a new threshold of the mountain's mandala. We had just passed through "hell," though into what I was unsure at the time. "The sound of the hora gai," he said, "is the sound of *Aum*"—the cosmically diffuse drone of Buddhist awakening. He cradled the conch trumpet in his right arm like a baby the entire climb, its red cord hanging around his neck.

The hora gai is the signature possession of a yamabushi. In Japan, there are many different sizes and shapes of hora gai with mountain-specific styles of playing, mouthpiece designs, and meanings. The origins of the hora gai, as with the origins of Buddhism, reach back to India. In the Indian context, it is referred to as the *śaṅkha* and is used by the blue-skinned preserver god, Viṣṇu, who sounded it to "spread terror in his enemies" (Saunders 1985, 150).[35] This parallels its practical use for premodern military leaders to announce commands through melodies in war, but its sonic power is much greater than this. In the Hindu context, the śaṅkha bestows fame, prosperity, and degrees of influence on those who play it and those who receive a blessing from it. It also has healing power, both through its melodies and, if ingested, after having been broken apart and crushed into powder.

The idiosyncrasy of shell formations, whether they whorl clockwise or counterclockwise as well as their size and coloration, takes on all sorts of mythological, philosophical, and sexual associations for yamabushi. The high-pitched drone is, as Itō-san mentioned, generally equated with *Aum*, the vibrational hum of the universe. This is a Buddhist interpretation. For Shintō yamabushi, the hora gai, like the sound of a baby crying or the stamp of a sumō wrestler's foot, is a purification of space through sound. Shugendō adapted this magical conch trumpet early on as an audible symbol of spreading the dharma, the universal law and truth realized by Buddha. In the Dainichikyō Sutra, it states that the Buddha "transmits the law through the shell . . . by means of a single sound, he diffuses the law in all the worlds and in all directions and puts all beings into a state of awakening" (Saunders 1985, 150). In Shugendō, which is strongly influenced by Esoteric Buddhism, the blaring resonance of the hora gai is the voice of the cosmic Buddha, the source and substance of the universe—in Japanese, Dainichi Nyorai, the Great Sun Buddha.[36]

The hora gai may be described as the sound of Aum, it may be used to mark transitional points in pilgrimages up the mandalic mountain, and it may purify the senses to awaken Buddhahood within, but it is also a powerful resonance that inserts a sonic pitch and melody of the nostalgic past into the present for contemporary yamabushi, pilgrims, and tourist-hikers on the path. In Dewa Sanzan, the frequent cry of the hora gai draws both visitors and modern yamabushi into a sonic-nostalgic affinity with the past. At any point on the trail when Itō-san blew into his conch and there were tourists nearby, they would hastily reach for their cameras to snap a photo of his archaic figure. From their sighs of awe, it was clear that they were impressed. Itō-san would later tell me that seeing an old picture of yamabushi playing a hora gai in an anthropology textbook inspired him to become a yamabushi and that learning to play the hora gai has solidified his bond with the yamabushi of centuries past.

The hora gai is just one element in a much larger constellation of practices and material culture in contemporary Shugendō. For Itō-san and other yamabushi I would meet over the years, the antiquated temporality the hora gai signals is its most superficial aspect. During ascetic training (shugyō) in the mountains, it is used more practically to keep bears away. It is also used for long-distance communication between yamabushi in mountains since it can make a range of coded calls. Yamabushi can distinguish the identity of the player through their style. Certain melodies are affiliated with specific aspects of Buddhist doctrine and Shintō liturgy in Shugendō rituals. Yamabushi take pleasure in blaring the hora gai at high viewpoints and listening to the melody they have generated from their diaphragm echo far into the mountainous expanse as if their spirit has drifted over the landscape like a fast-moving morning mist. The longest hora gai echo I would hear reverberated in the mountains for over ten seconds.[37]

I have also observed regional discrimination between yamabushi who associate different hora gai playing styles with stereotypes of ascetics from other regions of Japan. I once attended a group hora gai practice session led by a senior yamabushi from Mount Hakkai in Niigata Prefecture. He criticized the playing technique of yamabushi from the Kansai region, especially Osaka. He said that people in Kansai are "loud and annoying" (*urusai*). Because they release their energy through constant chatter, they cannot hit the high notes of the hora gai. They cannot reach as deeply into their abdomen for breath because they perpetually diminish their diaphragm power through chatter. To the contrary, he said, yamabushi from Tōhoku are quiet and reserved. They retain their vital energies because they are modest and can draw on them to play more powerful, Dewa Sanzan–specific hora gai melodies.[38]

In the context of modern tourism in Dewa Sanzan, the hora gai is an exotic object of urban tourist fascination. For tourists with only a superficial sense of the history of Dewa Sanzan, the hora gai is an audible emblem of the authentic, nostalgic mountain ascetic traditions in the far north. As Laura Bear writes (2016, 496): "Soundscapes are generated . . . to alter perceptions of temporality by enlisting the flux of time. . . . Music is a condensed temporal artifact that can help us understand how various aspects of social time appear simultaneously in action. . . . Within capitalist modernity, therefore, music is . . . a profound sensory counterpoint to . . . abstract market time."

Representing an enduring continuity with the ancestral past, the hora gai is now embedded in touristic regionalism of Dewa Sanzan as the signature possession of a yamabushi. Even the express train I took from Niigata City to Tsuruoka bears this symbolism—the Inaho (ear of rice). Like many trains in Japan, the Inaho has become linked to the geography, character, and history of the regions it passes through as well as the tourist sites along the way. The association between routes and the trains that pass through them is so strong that the trains themselves have become a tourist attraction, occasionally animated with characters that represent regional values.

When the Inaho pulled up to my platform in Niigata City the day before my tour with Itō-san, I noticed a cartoon yamabushi blowing into a conch shell on the exterior. The text below the cartoon figure read: "The yamabushi Shō-chan." Shō is short for Shōnai, the region of Yamagata Prefecture that contains Mount Haguro and other tourist attractions along the coast of the Sea of Japan. The honorific "*-chan*" gives this dwarfed mascot a childlike persona and an aura of familiarity. One would only use "-chan" to refer to a close friend, family member, or child. Among adults, "-san" is the standard honorific.

Featuring Shō-chan on the Inaho is a clever tourist promotion because it associates relational closeness and social ease with the Shōnai region through

Inaho Express Train (Niigata City–Tsuruoka City). Photograph by Shayne Dahl.

this animated train car mascot. The Inaho is the only place I have seen Shō-chan, but his animated yamabushi brethren populate the tourist economy of Dewa Sanzan. The hora gai conch trumpet is his central prop.

Ivy (1995, 29) has argued that the "Discover Japan" and "Exotic Japan" railway tourism advertising campaigns of the 1970s and 1980s pushed a "nativist project of national (re-) discovery" that led to the "trans-figuring" of traditional sites (such as temples, shrines, and castles) and rural regions. Such campaigns urged "Japanese to discover what remained of the pre-modern past in the midst of its loss" by traveling to the regions that retained the connection (10). She writes: "The interlinked industries of tourism, transportation, advertising, mass media, and publishing have created institutionalized circuits that channel local eccentricities into a standardly pluralized nation-culture" (31). Shugendō, as represented by Shō-chan, qualifies here as one such "local eccentricity."

This attempt to unify cultural diversity under the banner of a "Japanese" national ethnic identity has led to the irony of Japanese people "discovering" Japan, of traveling away from home but remaining at home. In the industrial period, "rapid industrial growth had led to high levels of pollution and urban sprawl as well as rural devastation and depopulation" (Ivy 1995, 34). The "vanishing" rural landscape against the backdrop of industrialization "came to symbolize a generation's desire to escape to its origins," which were to be found in the hinterlands, especially the northeast (34).

The apparent irony in Japanese domestic tourism is spatiotemporal in form: a kind of nostalgic exoticism that seeks an encounter with "the vanishing" traditions of Japan. Domestic tourism is also fixated on the "exotic" because touristic experiences of tradition in the rural areas are temporally Other to the urban lifeworlds of many modern tourists (Schnell 2005). The domestic tourist economy and its nostalgic exoticism have only grown since the "Discover Japan" and "Exotic Japan" advertising campaigns discussed by Ivy. The Inaho train is one example of how the placeworld of Dewa Sanzan has been integrated into the national cultural imagination through the mascot of the boyish yamabushi, Shō-chan, playing his hora gai.

Tourist shops near the Zuishinmon gate also sell snacks and trinkets featuring the hora gai and the yamabushi. As Millie Creighton (1997, 252) writes: "Images of yesterday's rural lifeways (whether real or invented) are eagerly consumed because they help today's Japanese cope with the fear of culture loss in the present and allow them to move into the future." In a shop near the Zuishinmon, I found the image of a yamabushi with a hora gai imprinted on a box of crackers waiting to be literally consumed. Such examples represent the consumption of place, the *power* of a heterotopic place, in the context of Dewa Sanzan.[39]

Exorcism River

Itō-san pointed downward to the river. He said that during certain Shugendō rites, "yamabushi walk almost naked into the flowing water" below the red bridge next to where we stood. There they recite Buddhist sutra and Shintō incantations. The river is called Haraigawa, which can be translated either as Purification River or as Exorcism River. The antonyms of *oharai* (to purify or exorcise) are *tsumi*, a "pollution" of the soul, and *kegare*, "impurity." Carmen Blacker ([1975] 1999, 41–42) writes that *tsumi* is "directly antipathetic to sacred power . . . the principal source of magical weakness" and that "the ascetic, if he wishes to approach the world of numina [kami] must . . . rid himself of the unclean hindrances which make his presence unwelcome."

Adding layers to the symbolic strata of Exorcism River is the common motif of river crossing in Buddhist literature and myths. River crossing is symbolic of crossing into the otherworld (*ano yo*), the realm of the dead, and traversing illusion toward enlightenment.[40] River crossing draws death, enlightenment, and purification symbolism together. The river is a "root metaphor" working within the "key symbol" of the mountain in Japanese Buddhism because it "provides a set of categories conceptualizing other aspects of experience" (Ortner 1973, 1340).

The seriousness of river symbolism (or mountain symbolism) is intact among contemporary yamabushi such as Itō-san but has waned in popular consciousness with modernity. The entangled web of semiotic association that rivers traditionally possess has become an object of touristic interest that yamabushi guides (called sendatsu) feature in their packaged tours. As such, tourism has become a means for sendatsu to reassert the meaning of key symbols and root metaphors, which keeps traditional symbols (such as the river as a world crossing) alive.[41] Although tourists in Dewa Sanzan may know little about the symbolic associations of what they encounter in the mountains, the sendatsu have varying degrees of knowledge about the symbolic meaning that they communicate as they guide people up the stairway of rebirth in Mount Haguro and along the slopes of Gassan and Mount Yudono.[42]

The Grandfather Tree

Itō-san once again blared his hora gai as we crossed the bridge over Exorcism River. We then approached a massive cedar tree wrapped in a large, knotted rope, a *shimenawa*. This tree, Itō-san explained, is called the Grandfather Cedar (*jiji sugi*). At 34 feet in circumference at its base, he told me, it is over a thousand years old and was designated a natural monument by the government in 1951. There was once a Grandmother Cedar (*baba sugi*), next to it, "but a windstorm knocked her down in 1902."

Itō-san bowed twice before the tree, clapped twice, and bowed again in proper Shintō form. I awkwardly tried to mimic the gesture but, on the first day of research, was confused with the sequence of claps and bows. I was not alone. I saw other Japanese visitors laughing among themselves as they tried but failed to get the order right. It seemed just as foreign a practice to them as it was to me. In the years since, the Dewa Sanzan Shrine has put up signposts with bilingual instructions explaining how and where to bow and clap in proper Shintō form.

This ritual is common practice while hiking the trails of Dewa Sanzan. The paths are filled with many venerable sites, including trees, ponds, and boulders marked with *shimenawa* knotted rope, Buddhist statues and effigies tucked in caves, and shrines with associations to kami and events in Shintō mythology. All these sites receive reverent bows and claps and sutra recitations, along with snapshots and selfies.

Grandfather Cedar with the five-storied pagoda, Mount Haguro.
Photograph by Shayne Dahl.

In terms of trees and forests as places of the kami, Fabio Rambelli (2007, 144) has argued that their status was determined before the Meiji Restoration in 1868 by the doctrine of *honji suijaku*, which translates as "original foundation, manifest traces." This is the doctrinal position that kami are local manifestations of universal Buddhist deities. For example, special trees were thought of as Buddhist deities manifest as local kami. Pushed by esoteric logic in which everything is a manifestation of Dainichi Nyorai, the Cosmic Buddha, trees "were not merely simulacra, receptacles of the sacred, but presences—animated icons, living Buddhas" (144). Buddha nature was manifest as a Buddhist deity, manifest as a local kami, manifest as a tree.

Before the Meiji Restoration, when Tendai and Shingon Buddhism represented the dominant religious orders in Dewa Sanzan, honji suijaku was a dominant mode for interpreting and engaging the environment. After the persecution of Buddhism following the edict proclaiming the separation of Shintō from Buddhism (*shinbutsu bunri*) from 1868 through the early 1870s, sacred trees such as Grandfather Cedar and other sacred sites of Dewa Sanzan would be viewed through a Shintō lens as kami or abodes of kami. With the passage of time, this, too, has changed. Now a major component of contemporary religion in Japan is characterized by what Ian Reader (1991, 15–20) calls the "primacy of action." This is an emphasis on the outward, socially visible form of worship. The subjectivity that the outwardly expressed form of worship signifies may be there, but it's secondary at best. In the primacy of action, ritual observance becomes social etiquette expressed through bodily comportment.[43] Think of it as having the appearance of prayer without the intent or even the underlying faith. In Dewa Sanzan, the primacy of action is apparent in visitors who perform the prescribed bows and claps not necessarily because they believe in and wish to express reverence for the Buddhist deity or kami that may animate the Grandfather Cedar or other sites but rather because it is the socially prescribed way to demonstrate respect.

Reader's notion of the "primacy of action" in Japanese ritual parallels Roy Rappaport's (1992, 5) definition of ritual: "the performance of more or less invariant sequences of formal acts and utterances not encoded by the performer." While people ascending Mount Haguro's stairway of rebirth do not "encode" the symbolism of the ritual themselves, "they are *participating in*—that is to say becoming *parts of*—the orders to which their bodies and breaths give life" (6). So, whether Shintō-style expressions of worship by tourists in Mount Haguro align with their religious beliefs or not, they are, by conforming to Shintō protocol, accepting the Shintō order.

As Rappaport (1992, 7) writes: "In performing a ritual, the participants accept, and indicate to themselves and others that they accept, the order encoded in that ritual. Acceptance of an order may be a consequence of belief in it, but acceptance does not require such belief." In Dewa Sanzan, the acceptance of the liturgical order inferred by ritual performance is also an acceptance of its temporality. This acceptance will take on new meaning as this ethnography unfolds, but for now, being as broad as possible, the temporality that such ritual observances signify is clearly of the past. Imbued with the past and being of nature, mountainous space possesses a kind of power that is not only worthy of reverence but can be absorbed through proximal contact, as many ascetics, pilgrims, and tourists do by undertaking place-based observance rituals, called *omairi*. It is in this ritual behavior, the absorption of power within power spots through omairi rites, that contemporary animism in Japan remains active through both religion and tourism.[44]

The Five-Storied Pagoda

Less than a hundred yards from the Grandfather Cedar is a five-storied pagoda (*gojū no tō*). A few tourists were gathered around its entrance. Some were snapping selfies. Others with cameras on tripods were trying to capture the quintessential photo of Mount Haguro: a family portrait with the pagoda in the background. Itō-san quickly led me past the photographers to the front of the pagoda. I could not tell if he was flattered or hiding his annoyance, but he smiled as tourists angled to snap a photo of him.

Standing before the pagoda, Itō-san began reciting the Heart Sutra. This is a popular sutra for pilgrims and ascetics around Japan and in Dewa Sanzan especially.[45] The Heart Sutra repents delusion through the acknowledgment of bodily impermanence and cosmic interdependence.[46] As Itō-san chanted, he was rhythmically clanging his *shakujō*, a Buddhist sistrum designed with a wooden handle topped with metal rings. The sound of the clanging rings, like the hora gai, was used by medieval yamabushi and monks in performing exorcisms.[47] I have seen it used for the same purpose today.

After his intense recitation of the Heart Sutra, Itō-san performed *mudras*: esoteric hand gestures that, he told me, serve to protect him and his patrons in the mountains. As I would later learn during Shugendō rituals, mudras also symbolize different aspects of Buddhist awakening within Shugendō and Esoteric Buddhist rituals. E. Dale Saunders (1985, 30) writes that in the formative stages of Esoteric Buddhism, "the hand became a sort of universe in miniature, representing a complete cosmogonic system with its own vocabulary." Mudras are ritual gestures of this Esoteric Buddhist doctrine that harness its magical power but also conjure the historical presence of Buddhism in Dewa Sanzan before the Meiji Restoration. The five-storied pagoda represents the significance of the five elements in Buddhist cosmology: earth, water, fire, wind, and emptiness envisioned as the sky.

Travelers in a Tea Shop

After a series of sharp inclines, just when my legs began burning from the strain, we arrived at a tea shop on the left side of the stairway. It had an open area with benches offering breathtaking views of the Shōnai plains below. The shop had a rustic thatched roof. A few people were seated inside, drinking steaming cups of tea. Itō-san was greeted warmly by the owner, an elderly woman with a slight hunchback. He ordered us some tea and conversed with the shop owner. They seemed to have known each other for years.

Curious about the motivations of some of the travelers there, I introduced myself to several of them and asked if they would like to be interviewed. The first people I spoke with were a young couple from Shikoku, a large island about 600 miles to the southwest. They introduced themselves as dental technicians. When I asked if they were visiting for religious purposes, they said, "Nope. Just sightseeing." I pressed further and asked if when they visit a shrine, they perform the proper sequences of bows and claps, the omairi, which I had noticed people having trouble with below. They said they do, but it is just a formality (*katachi dake desu ne*). They perform the ritual without firm belief in the kami, though they do not necessarily doubt their existence either, they said, expressing agnosticism with nonchalance. They mentioned that they intend to make a prayer for a child at the shrine, but they did not come specifically for that purpose. They were more interested to see the sites of historical significance in Mount Haguro, such as the five-storied pagoda, a famed power spot. They were also interested to see the similarities and differences between the Dewa Sanzan pilgrimage trail and the Shikoku pilgrimage trail of their home island (Reader 2005).

I also spoke with a mother-daughter pair from Tokyo at the tea shop. The mother said that twenty-five years earlier she had been told by a psychic (*reinōsha*) to visit Dewa Sanzan. She climbed it shortly after. Although she would not disclose why or what happened on that trip, she had decided to return this year. Her daughter, worried for her mother's safety (but also wanting to go sightseeing in Tōhoku), decided to come along and make it a bonding experience. The daughter came to support her mother, but her mother clearly indicated that she had a fated relationship with Dewa Sanzan, one that the psychic was able to discern for her years ago and that she was still exploring.

As Itō-san and I made our way out of the tea shop, a middle-aged man with sweat streaming down his bald head arrived alone. He had jogged all the way up. He mentioned that he was a farmer and that he lived nearby. He announced to everyone in the tea shop that it was his birthday. He said that for the past ten years or so, he had climbed Mount Haguro on his birthday to celebrate his yearly "rebirth."

While the temporality of the mountainous spaces may not be the stated motivation of these travelers, each of whom has a unique story and perspective of the mountains, the history of the place, the medieval architecture, the stone stairway, and the impressive natural surroundings is the context in which they each pursue their idiosyncratic purpose. Performing acts of place-based reverence, omairi, where necessary as they gradually ascend to the peak of Mount Haguro, they "accept, and indicate to themselves and others that they accept, the order encoded in that ritual" as well as its temporal dimensions (Rappaport 1992, 7).

The Chinese Zodiac

After the final stone step of the 2,446 leading to the plateaued summit of Mount Haguro, there is another large torii gate. Before entering, visitors are expected to wash their hands and rinse out their mouths at a basin of water (*temizuya*), which is standard practice in Shintō shrines and qualifies as a *harai* (exorcism) through self-purification. Passing through the final gate to the sacred yet touristic summit (there is a large parking lot on it with many buses from around the country), one finds a two-tiered courtyard with several Shintō shrines that were combinatory Shintō-Buddhist temples until the 1870s.

Dewa Sanzan Shrine, the main Shintō shrine for all three mountains, is at the center of the summit of Mount Haguro, across from a large pond of lotus flowers called the Mirror Pond (*kagamiike*). Itō-san invited me to look at the stairs leading up to the shrine. There were ten, he noted, because each step represented a realm of the Ten Worlds cosmology: "Ascending the stairs represents the ascent of the mandala of the mountain and symbolizes the attainment of enlightenment."

Inside the shrine was a stone statue of a horse. Some people were rubbing it. There were many offerings at its feet. Itō-san explained that each mountain of Dewa Sanzan is associated with a particular animal and its corresponding year in the twelve-year cycle of the zodiac calendar.[48] Mount Haguro's zodiac year animal is the horse, Gassan's is the rabbit, and Mount Yudono's is the ox. Statues of these zodiac animals can be found near and within shrines on each mountain. The zodiac of each mountain was determined by the zodiac year that the mountain was established as a place of religious significance in Shugendō. Special ceremonies and celebrations take place on each mountain's zodiac year. Mount Haguro had elaborate zodiac celebrations in 2014 (year of the horse) that included architectural floodlighting called "light ups" (*raito appu*) and musical performances.[49] Gassan celebrated the year of the rabbit in 2011 and 2023. Mount Yudono celebrated the year of the ox in 2009 and 2021.[50]

The twelve-year, twelve-animal zodiac calendar signifies eight directions and eight Buddhist deities.[51] Each mountain in Dewa Sanzan is associated with a particular Buddhist deity and a particular kami. Confusingly, the Buddhist deity of each mountain is not the deity that aligns with its zodiac year. While Mount Haguro's zodiac animal is the horse, which aligns with Seishi Bosatsu (Bodhisattva of Wisdom, associated with the south), the principal Buddhist deity of Mount Haguro is Kannon (Bodhisattva of Compassion, associated with north).[52] Gassan's principal Buddha is Amida (Buddha of the Afterlife) and Mount Yudono's is Dainichi Nyorai (the Great Sun Buddha). The Shintō gods of each mountain are both singular and a multiplicity. Each mountain has its chief kami, and yet each mountain is animated by numerous kami that are enshrined along the trails. In Dewa Sanzan Shrine, as well as in Buddhist temples, the zodiac is crucial for the ritual calendar. The modern calendar may make for an "empty, homogenous time," but the Chinese zodiac operates in tandem with it.[53] Most rituals in the liturgical order of Dewa Sanzan move in annual cycles. The zodiac presents a premodern cyclical time of repetition within a secular Gregorian calendar that corresponds with global society.

The Birth Canal

Just before we descended, Itō-san said, "The very last thing yamabushi do in Autumn's Peak is dash from the summit of Mount Haguro, down the stairway of rebirth, as fast as they can, all the way through the Zuishinmon gate." In local Shugendō tradition, the dangerous sprint down the stairway represents "a baby exiting the birth canal." Once the yamabushi exits the gate—which, Itō-san finally revealed to me, "is a vagina"—they will scream "*Nya! Nya!*" like a newborn baby. The place-name of the descending stairway immediately after entering the Zuishinmon is Falling-Descent-into-Hell Hill, as mentioned above. This changes when exiting Mount Haguro. Then, it is a sharp ascent and is called Taste-of-the-Suffering-of-Birth Hill (*mamago saka*).[54] The death and rebirth symbolism in Mount Haguro shifts with the direction of movement in and out of the mountain's gate, reaffirming the mountain-as-womb motif in the cultural orography of Dewa Sanzan.

Conclusion

In this chapter, I have explored some of the ways Mount Haguro has been represented, how such representations condition contemporary perspectives of the place as a power spot, and how Mount Haguro becomes infused with multiple temporalities through the historical retrospection that sites within the mountain evoke through architecture, signage, ritual, and the curated landscape. Teeming with storied places, Mount Haguro, as experienced on a guided tour, arouses in visitors distinct modes of historical consciousness while immersing them in a vibrant and audible mountainscape, where the rush of water backgrounds a chorus of birdsong and the buzz of cicadas. Itō-san's tour presented me with a meaningful encounter of Mount Haguro, introducing me to some of the ways in which modern tourism, religion, and natural beauty intersect with history and literature on the trails of Dewa Sanzan. It is a fully animated placeworld, a place of places invested with the power of past times.

A preliminary look at Mount Haguro reveals a "vibrant interface between tourism and religion" in which visitors experience multiple temporalities interacting and overlapping at every step along the "stairway of rebirth."[55] And yet, as the travelers in the tea shop indicated, each visitor has individual motivations as well. A mother-daughter reunion, a honeymoon sojourn, a request to the kami for a baby, a solitary birthday celebration. Time in the space of Mount Haguro, in tandem with its verticality and alterity, is what makes it a desirable getaway. Dewa Sanzan is, like the entire region of Tōhoku, envisioned as a holdout of premodern times for many urban tourists. The religious and the touristic have become interconnected in ways that can make it difficult for an outsider to discern. In later chapters I dig deeper into the religious dimensions of Shugendō and pilgrimage in Dewa Sanzan, where tourism is explicitly resisted, but here I have sought to demonstrate that Dewa Sanzan has been advertised and packaged figuratively and literally for touristic consumption through the temporal multiplicity and natural beauty of its multilayered placeworld.

Whereas the haiku-time of Bashō enlivens past moments to be relived in the present and future through boulders and statues, tourist-time in modern Dewa Sanzan is retrospective and nostalgic, reaching after "the vanishing" traditions of premodern Japan—even if the past presented to tourists is a "phantasm" of the actual (Ivy 1995). This chapter has explored points of contact between the past echoing into the present and retrospection in the present peering into the past. It has also shown how the simulacra of Dewa Sanzan's interfused temporality overlay an orographic landscape that has itself been subject to afforestation, Buddhist and Shintō architecture, and mandalization. By connecting the two aspects of this chapter, modern framings of the past and religious tourism in the present, I interpret Dewa Sanzan as sacred tourist space framed as and within a land before industrial time even while as it remains deeply enmeshed in and dependent on the modern tourist economy.[56]

2 Summits and Waterfalls
The Shugyō Experience

....

When I returned to Dewa Sanzan in August 2013, Itō-san had a large tatami mat room in the corner of his rustic countryside house prepared for me. I was surprised by the sight of his home, inside and outside. It was a *bukeyashiki*, an old samurai residence. It had a traditional hearth (*irori*) in the center with a kettle hanging down from the ceiling. From the road, the house was difficult to see since it was half hidden in thick, green vegetation. The unkempt, tangled ecosystem of plants, insects, snakes (which I saw in the trees!), and other mountain critters in Itō-san's yard, I soon learned, was by preference. Most of his neighbors had well-managed properties with orderly gardens. Nature was domesticated within their yards. Itō-san did not have, need, or want a domesticated yard, or even a garden. He preferred to have his house hidden in overgrown brush and to forage in the mountains for vegetables instead. A part of his income came from selling his surplus mountain vegetables (*sansai*) to restaurants in metropolitan areas.

Weather permitting, Itō-san opens all the sliding doors around his house in the morning and works in the interior veranda next to the tall stalks of green grass and bushes that waft around in the breeze.[1] Large bees and gadflies (*abu*) often buzz through, but Itō-san does not flinch. Once while I was interviewing him, a giant hornet (*ōsuzumebachi*), which is venomous, got stuck in a curtain. With bare hands, Itō-san casually caught the hornet in a teacup and released it outside. His house, like his yamabushi self, is in a state of free-flowing porosity between the inner (*uchi*) and the outer (*soto*) divide.[2]

Within days of my arrival, Itō-san insisted that I meet a sendatsu (ascetic guide) named Hoshino Fumihiro. I had seen pictures of him on social media before but had not known who he was. At this time, Hoshino-san was in his mid-sixties. He was bald with flowing white locks on the sides of his head. He also had a thick, white beard and strong eyes. He had all the markings of what I imagined an authentic yamabushi to look like when I initially arranged my tour of Mount Haguro in July 2012. In photos I had seen of him, he was either leading a group of yamabushi in the mountains or seated in the middle of large groups of young adults. He claims thirteen generations of yamabushi heritage and is now, at my time of writing, in his late seventies. Despite his age, he is still very active.

One warm August morning, around 9:30 a.m., Itō-san and I got into his small *kei*-car and drove down a gravel road squeezed between fields of plump rice stalks. We turned onto the highway that led beneath the large torii gate entrance into Mount Haguro. A few miles up the road, in the village of Tōge, we entered Cherry Blossom Street (Sakurakōji), which is lined with shukubō (pilgrim lodges). The street was once famous for its beautiful cherry blossom trees, but most of them were cut down to make way for paved roads, car garages, and parking lots in the postwar tourism boom around the 1960s. We soon pulled up to Hoshino-san's residence, a mid-sized shukubō called Daishōbō, Dwelling of the Great Sage.

We passed under the torii at the entrance of the property. Itō-san opened the front door and announced our presence with a morning greeting, "*Ohayo gozaimasu!*" (Good morning!) A grumbling voice called us in. We took our shoes off in the entrance and walked in. Hoshino-san was seated at the head of the table in a spacious tatami mat room. His intricately decorated family altar was behind him. The altar looked as if it was enshrining his figure. He sat in the half-lotus position, wearing a white muscle shirt and loose-fitting monk's pants. Itō-san and I kneeled next to him while his wife served us green tea. His white beard made a strong impression. Throughout my travels in Japan, I had never met anyone with a full beard.

Kneeling across the table from Hoshino-san, I was too nervous to speak beyond a basic greeting. Realizing my insecurity, Itō-san took the lead and introduced me in detail, listing my academic affiliation, accomplishments, and interest in studying Shugendō. Hoshino-san just sat there with his arms crossed and his eyes closed. I could not tell if he was listening or if he had dozed off.[3]

When Itō-san finished introducing me, Hoshino-san flashed open his eyes, made eye contact with me, and asked a question, but it was in a dialect I did not understand. He then started to laugh and spoke quickly in between hearty chuckles. I understood Japanese well enough to know I was being mocked and to notice when his tone shifted from mockery to annoyance, but the meaning of his words escaped me. Itō-san indicated that it was time to go, so I quickly presented Hoshino-san a gift, which he placed in his family altar without opening.[4]

On our way out of Tōge, I asked Itō-san what Hoshino-san had said to me. Apparently, he had mocked and then scolded me for assuming that I could conduct research in Japan before having completely mastered the language. "Why is it," he had asked me, "that when Japanese go abroad to study, they always study English first, but you foreigners hardly ever seem to undergo the same preparation before coming to Japan? It's arrogant! Good luck trying to study Shugendō! Look, you don't even understand a thing I am saying!" That's when he burst out laughing. I had failed to mention to him that my visit at that time was only for a pilot study and that I intended to return with more language training the following year. I thought I had lost a golden opportunity with Hoshino-san.

A few days later, when I was climbing Gassan in the late afternoon to attend a ceremony on the summit, I approached a man resting on a boulder halfway up the mountain. He was alone, admiring the vista of Mount Chōkai in the distance. We were the only two in sight. To my surprise, it was Hoshino-san. He was dressed in his white yamabushi attire. He was cradling his conch trumpet (hora gai) in his right arm and had a white cloth wrapped around his head that dangled down the sides of his face like bunny ears. Seizing the moment, I reintroduced myself in the best Japanese I could muster, emphasizing how grateful I was for his time during our previous meeting. He replied, "Oh? I don't recall meeting you . . . ?" I then described the meeting and summarized his comments about my weak Japanese, trying to laugh with him at how naive I must have appeared. He replied, "Oh yes, I remember now. You were with Itō-san. Well, you foreigners all have the same face to me!" He then picked up his walking stick, turned around, and climbed onward to the summit. A bell dangling at his hip rang into the breeze as he disappeared into the rolling clouds of mist ahead. I was stunned. Through Itō-san, I had already registered and paid for Hoshino-san's three-day ascetic training the following week.

My first impression of Hoshino-san, whom Itō-san claimed was one of the most influential yamabushi in Dewa Sanzan, was that he might simply not like foreigners (*gaijin*). This was not the case, though. As I would learn in the years to come, Hoshino-san is not at all hostile to foreigners. To the contrary, he enjoys traveling and making international friendships more than most people his age that I have met in Japan or anywhere.

The next day, while descending Gassan toward Mount Yudono, I met an older pilgrim on the path. We walked down together. She knew Hoshino-san well and put everything into perspective for me. She speculated that his actions were not motivated by prejudice. He had accepted me as a "foreign apprentice" even before Itō-san introduced us. I was accepted, she said, when I committed to undertake his three-day shugyō (ascetic training). She told me that the about-face he gave me on the mountain was already his "second lesson." The first was "strong encouragement" to strengthen my Japanese. His feigned amnesia on the slopes of Gassan, she interpreted, was to show me that "I am not special" or memorable just because I am a foreigner and I should not presume to be: "It is now up to you whether you want to accept his teachings or not," she said before we parted ways.

Hoshino-san, I would come to understand over time, is a kind and charismatic man in private with a rollicking sense of humor and grandfatherly warmth. Despite his age, he glides up and down the trail with a lightness I have rarely seen. On the mountain, especially during shugyō, he becomes a severely strict but highly respected sendatsu. I have met no one who was not, at one point, scolded by him for some moral infraction. Perhaps his strictness is how he performs his role as sendatsu. He prefers affective pedagogy over lecturing and often uses the "potent sanction" of shame to assert his authority to teach and discipline in his capacity as sendatsu.[5] By the measure of many aspiring yamabushi who come to Dewa Sanzan, Hoshino-san is the master. As one of his most senior assistants explained, "When we jokingly talk about Master Hoshino, we say he is like a manga character or like Yoda from *Star Wars*. Rather than being 'sacred' and acting like a holy being, he is very earthly."[6] Years later, as I deepened my knowledge of ascetic politics, I learned that he also has his critics.

This chapter is about the anachronistic figure of Hoshino-san and his three-day shugyō retreats. Hoshino-san's shugyō is experimental in comparison with the institutional Shugendō that Dewa Sanzan is typically known for. Structurally, Hoshino-san's practice is a hybrid of Shugendō and tourism. During the time of my fieldwork, he was offering shugyō up to five times or more a year. It was, I later learned, Hoshino-san himself who had founded the "yamabushi experience" program through the Ideha Cultural Museum (the one I had seen advertised in my guidebook).

Hoshino-san, who worked for the Tsuruoka City office before retirement, also played a central role in securing municipal funds to construct the museum. His three-day shugyō is a fusion of Shugendō and tourism for a few reasons. First, participants are paying customers who travel from cities throughout Japan and from abroad for an all-inclusive weekend of shugyō. For many, it is their first time to Yamagata Prefecture, perhaps even Tōhoku or Japan. Shugyō with Hoshino-san may even be the climactic "cultural" experience of a longer sightseeing trip. A senior yamabushi, one of Hoshino-san's local apprentices, volunteered as a photographer during shugyō so that participants could focus on their training but still get photos of their time on the mountain, which are often shared with comment on social media afterward. T-shirts with yamabushi mottos are also sold at the end of shugyō. Promotional videos about Hoshino-san and his practice have been featured in advertisements by the local and prefectural tourism industry.

By framing his retreats as both shugyō and a touristic yamabushi experience, Hoshino-san has managed to give Shugendō rituals a secular appearance without desacralizing them. In this way, he has made Shugendō accessible to an agnostic public while retaining the religious form of ascetic ritual. His shugyō can be described as both an immersive touristic experience of Shugendō and a ritualized tour of Dewa Sanzan.[7]

Through his hybrid approach, Hoshino-san has made shugyō meaningful to people who may or may not believe in the magical or doctrinal aspects of Shugendō but who seek a spatial and temporally exotic, existential, self-empowering experience in the faraway mountains of Tōhoku. Those who do wish to engage faithfully in the rituals are able to do so and are softly encouraged but not required. Yamabushi who commit and return at least once a year for shugyō can and do gain status within Hoshino-san's community of yamabushi. A quantifiable measure of "ascetic capital" accrues every time one undertakes shugyō.[8] Hoshino-san's shugyō, which is now available and advertised for international tourists, is unique in Dewa Sanzan because it occupies a gray zone between secular and religious ritual. Participants are free to choose their place on the spectrum of belief and commitment while engaging in ritual practice.

I have already provided a brief translation of shugyō, describing it as "ascetic training," but there are nuances to the term and past treatments of it in anthropology that require a deeper reading. A linguistic analysis reveals how common *shugyō* is in the Japanese language and culture. Also, how it can, as Hoshino-san's practice does, shift freely between secular and religious meanings. Once *shugyō* is clarified linguistically and in terms of its ritual structure, I will continue to describe the practice of shugyō in Dewa Sanzan under the guidance of Hoshino-san, exploring some of the ways he has configured it anew, making it compatible with the tourist experience and contemporary sentiments.

Shugyō in Translation

Shugendō is often glossed as "mountain asceticism," but as Tullio Lobetti (2014, 9–10) has observed, "there is no word in Japanese indicating asceticism in the abstract sense; instead, there is a generalized use of the suffix *gyō* to mark all of the specific practices' names." The ideogram for *gyō* (行) depicts a crossroads and implies movement and action. When paired with other ideograms, the action becomes specified. For example, *suigyō* means "water practice" (splashing cold water over one's body), *kangyō* means "cold practice" (winter trekking with minimal protection from the cold), and *takigyō* means "waterfall practice" (standing beneath a waterfall). The most general term for "ascetic practice" is *shugyō*, and those who undertake shugyō are called *gyōja*. *Shugyō* cannot be easily translated as "asceticism" because it can and is often applied outside of a religious context. In English, ascetic acts, ascetics, and asceticism typically bear religious association.

The broad meaning of *shugyō* is apparent in Shiho Satsuka's (2015, 46) ethnography, *Nature in Translation*, which focuses on Japanese tourism in Banff, Canada. One of Satsuka's interlocutors described his job working for a Japanese corporation as "shugyō" because of the repressive aspect of his labor: "I devoted myself to the work as if it was the whole stake of my entire life," he said. "I had never used a paid vacation because it would be admitting defeat in my struggle to improve myself." *Shugyō* can also mean committing oneself to mastering a particular skill or deepening one's knowledge on a particular subject or art. *Shugyō* is also used to frame difficult aspects of life as existential challenges to be overcome to improve oneself. As Satsuka (49) puts it: "to 'polish' the self . . . and, by doing so, to find *ikigai*, a reason that makes one's life worth living." *Shugyō* entails a sense of self-overcoming through sustained effort, a striving to surmount challenges and be strengthened through this laborious trial.

The *dō* (道) of Shugendō is the same *dō* of Judō and Aikidō. It means "way" and refers to a particular way of doing things, a way that is prescribed and governed by rules and guidelines issued by the founders and successive authorities of a sect, art, or school. When shugyō is undertaken but there is no way guiding the practice, the meaning of *shugyō* becomes general use. Satsuka's interlocutor exemplifies this. When shugyō is undertaken in a specific way, then it entails specific practices with corresponding guidelines and protocol. While *shugyō* has a broadly nonreligious meaning in common usage, it finds unique religious expression in Shugendō. *Gyō* (ascetic acts) are ordeals that expand the horizons of spiritual and personal agency to new limits, granting one increased power. This is why Shugendō is often defined as the way to cultivate "supernatural powers through ascetic practices in the mountains" (Miyake 2001, 13).[9]

Shugyō and the Ritual Process

On the slopes of Dewa Sanzan, hikers may do shugyō on their own terms, to "polish" the self in a personalized sense, but Dewa Sanzan is known as a place to undertake shugyō in specific ways that empower oneself by molting it and then rebirthing it in the womb of the mandalic mountain. It is also the means through which one can purge the spiritual pollution (*tsumi*) and impurity (*kegare*) that cling to the self through symbolic death, then recover the purity of being in utero and reenter the present world born anew. The alpine affects of shugyō in Dewa Sanzan are unique because they offer intense sensory stimulation with physical features of the mountain and its unique climactic conditions.

The ritual process of shugyō can be interpreted in the language of Arnold van Gennep (1960) as a classic rite of passage that follows three stages: "pre-liminal–liminal–post-liminal." The liminal phase is betwixt and between, a time of acute personal and social transformation. Shugyō can also be brought into Victor Turner's ([1969] 2008) framework in which ritual is a process of "structure–anti-structure–synthesis." I find Jean Comaroff's (1985, 231) critique and modification of Turner's model instructive here. She argues that Turner's notion of "anti-structure" implies "a universal state of formless communion which would in all societies be the antithesis of structure." Alternatively, she proposes "counter-structure" as a more precise description of what the ritual process creates for a person. "This [counter-structure] liminality is not formless," she writes. "Its deconstruction of established sociocultural arrangements entails a reconstruction which both subverts and seeks a permanent transformation of a historically specific system" (231). Yamabushi make no explicit attempt to transform society through shugyō, but they do gain a critical "counter-structure" perspective from which many have transformed their own lives and even their communities. Shugyō is an emplaced practice that symbolically reverses the impact of capitalist modernity, easing the sense of estrangement it generates, while giving yamabushi a renewed sense of purpose and control over their lives in uncertain times and an unstable world.

The "counter-structure" phase of the shugyō process allows yamabushi to inhabit the "counter-modern" space and time of Dewa Sanzan and to be changed by it.[10] In Hoshino-san's program, the three-part structure of shugyō takes place over three days. Day one is a transition from structure to counter-structure; day two is fully counter-structure; day three is a transition from counter-structure to synthesis. Every day of shugyō involves "territorial passages," a "magico-religious ... crossing of frontiers" through the heterotopia of the mountains.[11] Observations in the field reveal that yamabushi constantly shift back and forth between their "modern" mode of being (even if that means time out for a cigarette or a bus ride) and the orthodoxy of Shugendō ritualism, but the general structure of the three-day rite follows van Gennep's classical three-part model.

In this context, shugyō is a composite ritual that not only encapsulates elements of initiation, birth, pilgrimage, and funerary rites but, through Hoshino-san's contemporary remodeling, has become fused with the tourist infrastructure of the Shōnai region and Yamagata Prefecture. While it follows the three-part structure of rites of passage, Hoshino-san's shugyō marks no elevation of social status beyond Daishōbō, his own shukubo. In what follows, I describe the ritual form of Daishōbō's three-day shugyō, the "techniques of the body" through which yamabushi interface with the culturally encoded orography of Dewa Sanzan.[12]

The Shugyō Experience

Symbolic separation from the "structure" of capitalist modernity begins immediately on arrival at Daishōbō. Moments after participants enter, they undress from their daily clothing and put on yamabushi attire. There is a specific sequence to putting on the uniform. It consists of a *fundoshi* (loincloth), a robe, a *hakama* (loose pantaloons that tie around the knees), cloth shin guards (*kyahan*), a head wrap (*hōkan*) (the bunny ears I saw on Hoshino-san when I met him on Gassan), and a knotted paper stole (*shime*) that hangs around the neck like a necklace. When outdoors, yamabushi also wear white, split-toe boots (*jikka tabi*), preferred for the thin sole because it deepens the tactility between one's feet and the rocky terrain. The uniform must be worn with appropriate tautness. Too loose and it will fall off. Too tight and the ties can create painful tourniquets. I can't count how many times I couldn't stand after hours of sutra recitation during shugyō owing to the tightness of the pantaloon ties around my knees.

The changing of garments is a significant starting point of shugyō and is an aspect of *shōjin kessai*, purification through religious abstinence. As Itō-san told me during my tour of Mount Haguro, the significance of white in the context of Dewa Sanzan and other sacred topographies in Japan is that it symbolizes being "dead to the world."[13] The deathly status of yamabushi at the onset of shugyō positions them to gestate in the womb of

Shintō yamabushi attire. Photograph by Miura Takehiro.

the mountain and, through the completion of their training, be "reborn" (*umare kawari*).

Within a half an hour of their arrival, people who had traveled to Daishōbō as young, stylish individuals with multicolored brand-name mountain gear transform into a uniform crew of white-clad yamabushi. By midafternoon, everyone is kneeling on the tatami floor before Daishōbō's main altar, which features a handscroll painting of Seoritsuhime, a kami associated with water purification.[14] Hoshino-san enters the room with fast strides, his feet swishing across the mats. He kneels before a large drum, picks up two drumsticks, and starts pounding a rhythm with gradually increasing intensity that peaks and then gradually decreases, a sonic ascent to a summit that then descends and ends with a final heavy thump. He picks up his hora gai and generates a melody frequently heard in the mountainous amphitheater of Dewa Sanzan.

Hoshino-san takes attendance through an altered voice, a deep baritone speech with a fast and accented rhythm. It is the same voice he uses to summon the kami. During roll call, each person's hometown is announced. Then, their surname and first name. Yamabushi respond to their names being called with a strong, existence-declaring, "Uketamau!" This roughly translates as "Received!" or "I accept!" but has, for Hoshino-san, come to define the quintessential disposition of a yamabushi: receive and accept anything, pleasant or unpleasant, that happens to you. Do not resist life's challenges. Do not make excuses. Absorb all events and gain power by expanding the horizon of oneself through acceptance.

Following roll call is *gongyō*, the devotional gyō (practice) of Shintō incantations (*norito*) and the recitation of the Heart Sutra (*hannya shingyō*) of Buddhism. Each yamabushi is given a sheet of paper with the Shintō norito written on one side and the Heart Sutra written on the other. Yamabushi will carry this paper with them throughout the three-day ordeal or until they manage to memorize the entire set, which many do. The Heart Sutra emphasizes the nonduality between form and emptiness, birth and death, the illusion of the senses, and the interdependent nature of reality. It is one of the shortest but most popular sutras in Japan.[15]

There are two forms of norito practiced by yamabushi during Hoshino-san's shugyō, and they are very melodic and entrancing when performed. One is called Three Word Prayer (*sango haiji*). It is dedicated to purification and prosperity:

1. "Cleanse all impurities. Purify all sins. Exorcise and rejuvenate" (*Moromoro no tsumikegare haraimisogite sugasugashi*).[16]
2. "May the distant kami smile upon and bless honorable spirits with good fortune" (*Tōtsukami emitamae izunomitama wo sakihaetamae*).[17]
3. "May the descendants of heaven prosper and be as everlasting as heaven and earth" (*Amatsuhitsugi no sakaemasamukoto ametsuchinomuta tokoshienarubeshi*).[18]

The Three Mountain Prayer (*sanyama haiji*) uses the same formulaic expression of reverence for Mount Haguro, Gassan, and Mount Yudono. The name of the mountain is changed with each utterance. With Gassan in focus, it would be: "With utmost reverence, I worship the divinity of the kami of Gassan" (*Ayani ayani kuzushiku tōto tsuki no miyama no kami no mimae wo orogami matsuru*).[19]

Through exhaustive repetition, yamabushi undertake gongyō with increasing intensity during shugyō, often falling asleep as they chant for hours in the middle of the night. Shortly after the first gongyō session, yamabushi are called to prepare their backpacks and line up outside, two by two, with

Hoshino-san in the front. A senior yamabushi, who carries a conch, stands directly behind him. Then the women, and then the men. One senior yamabushi stays in the back to make sure everyone is accounted for. Over the course of my fieldwork, the ratio between women and men altered greatly. During my first shugyō in 2013, the gender ratio was about 85 percent men and 15 percent women (with typically thirty participants). By the end of fieldwork, it was at times 70 percent women, 30 percent men. This reflects Hoshino-san's evolving feminist discourse, which encourages women, through social media, to reconnect with an inherent "wildness" (*yasei*) that was lost to a hypermasculinized and patriarchal modernity.

Following a rule of silence, the procession of yamabushi hiking up the verdant mandala of Mount Haguro appeared to me as a white centipede. Hoshino-san is the head and yamabushi are the body and legs. Yamabushi walk in unison and in silence, with beginners having no sense of direction. All that can be heard are the pattering of steps, the tapping of walking sticks on the 2,446-stone-step "stairway to rebirth," heavy breathing, and the powerful melody of Hoshino-san's conch trumpet as it pierces the natural ambience. Walking in silence and in unison is a meditation in which individuality, the freedom to move and act by one's individual volition, is subsumed into group coordination. One false step or stumble and collective attention centers on the individual. Any disruption of uniformity and group flow is an intuitive breach of an unspoken rule to move as one. Silence is crucial to Hoshino-san's practice. "When people are undergoing my shugyō program," he would often teach, "they are not allowed to speak. Not even a word! If they say anything, shugyō would be in vain because they are required to understand what they can gain not with their head but with their body."[20]

In the conclusive feast that follows shugyō (called a *naorai*)—a jolly event involving great food and sake in Daishōbō—yamabushi offer reflective testimonies about their experiences before the group. The most common comment I have heard is about inner and outer silence. According to a young woman from Tokyo: "In the beginning of shugyō, my mind was busy. Thoughts of work and unresolved responsibilities circulated loudly in my head as we climbed the steps. Gradually, as I began to tire into the second day, the sound of our steps became a metronome without the background noise of my thoughts about miscellaneous things. My focus attended to my footing, pace, the view, and the scents and sounds of the mountain. I feel very rejuvenated now! Reborn, I suppose."

Lorna Parkes (2023), a journalist for *National Geographic*, went on a shugyō experience with Hoshino-san and his fellow sendatsu. She also described the quieting of the mind after hours of hiking: "At first, I find it impossible to concentrate. I fiddle with the plant leaves that are tickling my legs, and slap away what I'm convinced is a mosquito. But eventually I find myself uncoiling. It's like turning up a TV's colour saturation. Sounds are richer. The fluttering of leaves becomes a roar. The rustle of insects is more defined—almost as if I could hear the air being sliced by the flap of a butterfly wing."

Eventually, through the monotony and exhaustion of trekking in silence during shugyō, the mind becomes quiet, entertaining fewer miscellaneous thoughts and arriving at fewer realizations but becoming more sensorially receptive. Yamabushi testimonies speak of attending less to one's internal dialogue and more to the morning birdsong, the wind on their faces, the patter of the rain, the grinding of rocks beneath their feet, and the sweat dripping off their brow.[21] The inner silence that is achieved through a strict rule of outer silence and physical exhaustion is one example of alpine affects. Shugyō leads yamabushi not just to perceive their interrelationship with nature but to feel it viscerally. Yamabushi drink water from mountain springs as sweat drips from their pores, mixing with rain falling from the sky. Hoshino-san's philosophy of shugyō attends to water (*mizu*) as a key metaphor for the existential unity between humanity (*ningen*) and nature (*shizen*).

Over the course of fieldwork, I heard many iterations of this impression, all of which emphasize the gradual silencing of an overstimulated mind, musing as it does over the challenges of life in capitalist modernity: thoughts of work, work-related relationships, anxiety about the future. Many yamabushi I have met say that the mind muses about in internal dialogue, laboring to solve many of the problems not only of daily life but of childhood trauma. By walking in silence, solutions to the problems circulating in a yamabushi's mind spontaneously occur as epiphanies. This is one reason why Hoshino-san also refers to shugyō as an experience of "realization" (*kizuku*). Most of his ideas, which are expressed as aphorisms and axioms, unexpectedly appeared to him during shugyō.

I recall Hoshino-san, in one of his more laid-back moods, telling a group of yamabushi after shugyō: "To connect with nature through shugyō is to connect with your inner nature as a human being. The nature you see outside of you is also inside of you." In the same way Fukada Kyūya (2015) described carrying an image of his hometown mountain in his memory even as he moved away, yamabushi describe closing their eyes in the days and weeks after shugyō and seeing flashing images of their shugyō experience in Dewa Sanzan as they go about their ordinary lives. As critical as Hoshino-san is about the term "nature" (*shizen*), he makes use of it to explain key concepts of his philosophy to people. Using *shizen*, he gradually works toward the notion of *jinen*, a premodern Buddhist concept that fuses human and nature but that was abandoned when modernists translated "nature" into Japanese.[22]

For many yamabushi in Hoshino-san's three-day shugyō, the idea of religion emerges only as an afterthought. Shugyō is, as Lobetti (2014) observes, a "bodily hermeneutic": a "technique of the body" in which alpine affects are read as a text through the cultural orography of Dewa Sanzan, which is, itself, overlaid with reproductive symbolism.[23] Under the rule of silence, none of this is spoken aloud during shugyō. It emerges afterward during the post-shugyō feast, on social media, and with further discussion.

Halfway up Mount Haguro's stairway of rebirth is the tea shop that overlooks the Shōnai rice plains below, where I had met some travelers the year before. There, yamabushi, who are on an otherwise strict diet, are permitted and encouraged by Hoshino-san to enjoy crushed ice with syrup. Women working at the teashop crush thirty bowls of ice with a hand-wheel apparatus. Even as yamabushi enjoy the cool treat, silence is expected. Emulating Hoshino-san, many peer into the forest as they savor the sweetness. "How can yamabushi accept such a sweet treat during shugyō?" I would later ask Hoshino-san during a sit-down interview. "Uketamau" was his answer: "As a yamabushi, you are encouraged to receive what is offered to you and accept whatever happens to you in shugyō. Uketamau is the practice of acceptance."

Along the way to the summit of Mount Haguro, yamabushi clap and bow in Shintō form and recite gongyō at every auspicious site, including Grandfather Cedar and the five-storied pagoda. It's standard omairi practice with the addition of gongyō. Only a couple of breaks are permitted during our ascent up the stairway of rebirth. Breaks are short and used for self-care: readjusting one's outfit (tightening or loosening ties), gulping down water, putting on or putting away rain gear, using the washroom, and so on. Washroom breaks must be timed to ensure access to public facilities.

Following a circuit of gongyō at shrines on the summit is a rapid descent down Mount Haguro. Yamabushi go all the way back to Daishōbō without stopping. There, for the first time since changing into yamabushi garments, participants are permitted personal time. I always took notes when such moments arose during shugyō, but most people would sit in silence, staring at the floor, meditating, napping, or going outside for a cigarette.

Hoshino-san soon returns to the main hall and instructs yamabushi to form a circle. He tells everyone to bow to the center of the circle, then turn around and sit down in the half-lotus position to perform *zazen*, seated meditation.[24] No explanation is provided by Hoshino-san about what to focus on, but the sonic environment of Dewa Sanzan is audible. The soft sounds of the breeze, if there is one, sweeping through the forest. Rain pattering softly or aggressively on the thatched roof of Daishōbō. Subtle sensations like these were described by yamabushi from metropolitan areas as a delight of shugyō. For a mind full of city noise, the effects of such sounds and songs resonates beyond everyday experience like a relaxing massage for an overstimulated mind. Less delightful are the gadflies (*abu*) that buzz around meditating yamabushi before settling on exposed skin for a bite to eat.

Gakigyō, hungry ghost practice, follows meditation. Four wooden planks are placed on the tatami mats in the altar room as tables. Everyone receives two pickles, a bowl of rice, and a bowl of miso soup. Kneeling before their meager meal, yamabushi wait for Hoshino-san. He then glides in with big strides and kneels at the head of one of the tables. He calls out "*Sanjo, sanjo, go sanjo!*" and yamabushi quickly devour their food. I was surprised the first time I experienced this. Some yamabushi downed the entire meal in under a minute, shoveling food in their cheek-stuffed mouths faster than they could chew or swallow it. Gakigyō is reflective of Buddhist Shugendō doctrine in Dewa Sanzan. It emulates and identifies with the "hungry ghosts" of Buddhist cosmology. *Gaki* are the souls of people who died with unfulfilled desires and who now haunt the living. They exist in a state of perpetual hunger.

Sakamoto Daizaburo (2012), an illustrator and author from Chiba Prefecture, has experienced Hoshino-san's shugyō many times. He writes in his book, *Yamabushi and I*, that shugyō, including the rationed meal of gakigyō, taught him to appreciate the subtle things in life: "When I first thought of shugyō, I imagined it as a continuous series of hardships. It wasn't like that. The unadorned beauty of nature I saw in the mountains during the day, the deliciousness of just two slices of pickled radish. . . . These are things I hadn't really noticed in everyday life."[25]

After gakigyō, Hoshino-san instructs everyone to go outside. The nocturnal journey that follows leads to unexpected directions in the dark. Yamabushi are often disoriented, tripping over roots and stones. Hoshino-san guides everyone by candlelight in a nonlinear circuit between dimly lit village streets and forest trails thick with vegetation to perform gongyō at shrines hidden in the forests of Mount Haguro. Hoshino-san also leads yamabushi to a clearing, directing gongyō to the plateaued peak of Gassan under the stars. Nightwalking in Dewa Sanzan is a cosmic experience that also inspires fear. Sakamoto (2012, 44) writes: "It was a night sky that you cannot see in the brightly lit city. Some yamabushi were searching for constellations. The number of stars was almost frightening. The Milky Way was also visible. The stars seemed like eyes, all looking at me at once. I remembered hearing that until around the Edo period, there were people who found looking at the stars terrifying. I understand that feeling."[26]

Sakamoto's description of the atmosphere of Mount Haguro goes further to envision it as a place deeply connected with the ancestral past. He writes:

> Walking through Mount Haguro's forest . . . I feel the presence of the world of death. In the forest of Mount Haguro, there's a kind of beastly, sticky smell. It feels like the air gets slightly heavier and clings to my body with each step I take. . . . It feels like something that has always been close to me. It was like the darkness that appears when you close your eyes to go to sleep. . . . I felt that the ancient people's perception—that the spirits of the dead stay in the lower mountains and eventually ascend to the higher mountains to become gods—flows similarly within me, a modern person.[27]

Nightwalking also gives yamabushi a unique view of society. Tsuruoka City's lights are a distant glow below. As Sakamoto writes, this perspective inspires a bird's-eye view perspective of urban life and insightful reflections on the human condition:

> Beyond the forest was a hill with a good view. All around were fields. Below, the night view of Tsuruoka City spread out. I gazed at the city lights. I wondered if families were enjoying time together there, if friends were hanging out, if lovers were being affectionate. . . . Even though it's only been two days of shugyō, I had distanced myself from such everyday life. In the chaotic world of nature, I seem to find a simpler version of myself. When I'm in the mountains, the things I usually worry about seem insignificant. I feel like I lose myself and can see what it means to be a universal human being.[28]

Returning to Daishōbō later in the night, yamabushi are led to a separate building near the edge of the yard for *nanban ibushi* (pepper smoke). My first experience of nanban ibushi was unforgettable. First, the women, then, after fifteen minutes or so, the men. When the men were called, I went with others and saw the women coughing and gagging, keeled over on the ground. Some were laughing out of disbelief. Inside the two-story shack, in a tatami room on the second floor, a candle was lit. A single flame illuminated the small room. At the front was a handscroll featuring images of the kami of Mount Haguro, Gassan, and Mount Yudono. A pungent scent filled the room. Hoshino-san was hidden in the shadows at the back, sitting half-lotus over a brazier of smoldering embers. His eyes and beard were glowing amber in reflection of the red-hot cinders.

"Hurry! Get in here now!" he bellowed to the men. "When I say come, I mean immediately! Never leave me waiting!"

With the other men, I knelt before the flickering candlelit images of the kami of Dewa Sanzan on the handscroll and began performing gongyō. I could hear Hoshino-san scraping something onto the embers behind us. Then I heard a fiery crackle. The room filled with thick, agitating smoke. The senior yamabushi were unaffected. Soon, most ascetics, including myself, erupted into uncontrollable fits of coughing that got worse the more we coughed until the coughing felt like suffocating because of the tears, phlegm, and mucus that the smoke stimulated. When the mucus became too much to swallow, people started gagging. Vomiting is not unheard of in the context of nanban ibushi. Oddly, there is also some laughter in between all of this because some people's reactions are unexpected and comedic in a slapstick kind of way.

Still, everyone tried to get through the gongyō: the Three Word Prayer, the Three Mountain Prayer, and the Heart Sutra. When no one could tolerate it any longer, Hoshino-san, who had been fanning the brazier to produce smoke in the back without a single cough, permitted everyone to leave. There was a rush to the door that prevented some of us from leaving immediately. He then called for me to open the window because I was closest. I opened it and stuck my head out with four or five others, gasping. From the outside it must have looked as if we were victims in a burning house as the smoke plumes poured out the window above us and we struggled to breathe. Inhaling the humid evening air of Mount Haguro at that moment produced a kind of synesthesia yamabushi would later comment on. The air was heavy with a thousand forest flavors. It was later described as "delicious" (*oishii*). Other, more masochistic yamabushi would say the opposite: that the smoke was "delicious." Nanban ibushi is "hell practice" (*jigokugyō*) and is undertaken by Buddhist and Shintō yamabushi alike in Dewa Sanzan. It is meant to simulate hell (*jigoku*) and is a genuine experience of suffering.

Sakamoto's description of nanban ibushi is notable:

> To avoid inhaling as much smoke as possible, I took slow, deep breaths through my nose and reduced the frequency. Suddenly, I felt a sensation in the back of my nostrils that I had never experienced before. "This is bad!" I thought. "If I inhale this directly, it will be a disaster!" Instinctively, I lowered my posture to avoid the smoke. With each crackle of the burning spices, the smoke thickened, and I could no

longer see ahead. Tears streamed down my face, and my nose was running profusely. As for breathing: so far so good. Then, I heard the chanting from behind, *"Moromoro no tsumikegare haraimisogite sugasugashi"* [Cleanse all impurities. Purify all sins. Exorcise and rejuvenate]. It felt as if all my sins and impurities were turning into liquid and flowing out of my eyes and nose. Feeling that I might somehow manage to maintain composure within the smoke, I opened my mouth to join everyone in the Three Word Prayer. That was a mistake. I opened my mouth, and this is what came out: *"Moromoro no tsumi . . . kega . . . re . . .* cough, cough, cough!!!" Once I started coughing in the smoke, I couldn't breathe anymore. "If this continues," I thought, "I'm going to pass out." The sound of my labored breathing echoed. It didn't feel as if nanban ibushi was invigorating my life force. Rather, it seemed as if my soul was about to fly away from my body. I didn't want to leave the room in the middle of the practice, though, since I had come all the way to Mount Haguro to train as a yamabushi. A whirlwind of emotions surged through me. I was in such distress that I couldn't make sense of anything.[29]

When the time comes to sleep, men and women are separated by floors. Women upstairs, men downstairs in the altar room. Everyone receives a basic futon, blanket, and pillow. With militaristic efficiency, bedding is arranged. After lights out, yamabushi are fast asleep. No one is permitted to wash themselves in any way or brush their teeth before going to sleep or at any other point during shugyō. This is an aspect of "beast practice" (*chikushōgyō*), which corresponds with the second realm of the Ten Worlds cosmology. Within five minutes, the entire lower floor of Daishōbō is covered with sleeping yamabushi. On the men's side, this means a shukubō-shaking chorus of snoring within minutes and other strange sounds of people sleeping, such as grinding teeth, involuntary itching, sleep talking, and farting. If it's hard to fall asleep the first night, the second night is usually no problem since the exhaustion catches up to you quickly. Within just a few hours, everyone is awakened by a senior yamabushi blaring a conch trumpet. In a flash, everyone packs up their futon and gets dressed.

Day two begins with a predawn zazen seated meditation session and a speedy, hungry ghost breakfast. Just before sunrise, yamabushi board a bus bound for Gassan. Most yamabushi are unaware of the time since they do not bring watches. They are not generally permitted electronics, and there are no visible clocks in Daishōbō. The hike to the summit begins from the eighth station parking lot. Most days on Gassan are cold and windy. Clouds roll in from the Sea of Japan and crash into the mountainside, unfolding into gossamers of mist. On the slopes of Gassan, yamabushi begin breaking the code of silence, laughing at each other's stumbles, and commenting on the mystical (*shinpiteki*) landscape views.

After a steady ascent up the rocky slope, Hoshino-san guides yamabushi into Gassan shrine, which rests on the summit like a crown. An attendant priest, who lives in the shrine during the summer months, gives each yamabushi a paper effigy inscribed in red ink. Like other visitors, yamabushi bow before the priest. He then performs a loud and melodic norito incantation, forcefully waving a wand (*ōnusa*) covered with sacralized folded paper (*shide*) over yamabushi heads. Yamabushi then wipe the paper effigy, which is shaped like a human figure, over their bodies and place the paper in a pool of rainwater. Architectural and ritual boundaries lead to the innermost sanctuary of Gassan shrine. This is a purification rite, preparing visitors for entry. Once inside, yamabushi perform gongyō on the summit before the mountaintop shrine. Photographs are strictly prohibited. After gongyō on the peak, yamabushi eat a quick lunch of rice balls in the nearby mountain lodge (*yamagoya*).

Descending a spur of Gassan, called the "neck of the ox" after Mount Yudono's zodiac animal, yamabushi traverse windy ridges and down a series of steep rusty ladders to Mount Yudono. As the yamabushi hike down a mist-swept, boulder-spotted slope to a natural spring in between Gassan and Mount Yudono, Hoshino-san serves water to each yamabushi straight from the open vein of the mountain. Further down, we enter a canyon. Its walls, as with the soil, gradually increase in shades of ocher, reflecting a shift in the mineral composition between Gassan and Mount Yudono. Below the narrow trail is a small river that spills into waterfalls, each marked with barriers of sanctifying *shimenawa* rope and zigzagged *shide* paper. Coins are scattered across the path, the offerings of past pilgrims.[30] Reflecting on the spatiotemporality of the path between Gassan and Mount Yudono, Sakamoto writes:

> The path to Mount Yudono is very steep and almost deserted. There are places where you must rely on rusty iron ladders to descend dangerous cliffs. I once heard from a member of the confraternity of pilgrims from Chiba, who have been venerating Dewa Sanzan for generations, that they consider such paths as those walked by their ancestors. They traverse the same routes, feeling a sense of unity with their ancestors. At Gassan, the home of ancestral souls, pilgrims meet the spirits of their

ancestors, walk the paths their ancestors trod, and weave the cycle of life into the next generation. How many people have walked this path over the long years? Every step I take might be part of a journey I unknowingly inherited from someone else as if it were passed down through generations.[31]

Approaching the main shrine of Mount Yudono after a long hike that began at 4:00 a.m., yamabushi are instructed to remove their jikka tabi boots and socks. Undergoing the same purification ritual that everyone did before entering Gassan Shrine with the waving *ōnusa* and incantations, yamabushi then enter a torii to the inner sanctum of Mount Yudono barefoot. The first time I entered, I was thrown into a shared sense of awe along with other beginner yamabushi, most of whom broke the code of silence with audible sighs of wonder: "*Wa–!*" (Wow!) or "*Eh–?!*" (For real?!). We approached slowly as we gazed upward at the enormous two-headed ocher mound towering about fifteen feet above us. White-clad pilgrims were already bowed before it, chanting the Three Word Prayer and the Three Mountain Prayer with hands raised steepled together, incense smoke swirling around with candles burning. Milky yellow hot spring water was pulsating from openings in the mound's rounded heads, cascading down its textured ocher surface of hardened mineral in soft, rhythmic waves. The hot spring gushed straight up from the depths of the Earth out from the apex of the mound, all the way down to our bare, aching feet. The water was as hot as a perfectly heated bath. If I had to guess, it was about 108 degrees Fahrenheit. After hours of climbing up and down Gassan in thin-soled split-toe jikka tabi boots over rocky terrain, the hot water was deeply soothing, especially when combined with the tactile massage of the uneven stone surface on bare feet. The physical and psychological exhaustion of shugyō had made us vulnerable on a personal and emotional level to even the slightest atmospheric change. Our first encounter with this hot spring mound, especially when we had no previous knowledge of its existence or that we would see it, was deeply affecting. The soothing sensation of hot spring water on aching bare feet while standing in awe of this natural phenomenon wasn't just physical. It was emotional. I can only describe it as the humbling feeling of being loved, the kind of love a baby feels in a mother's embrace. In Japanese, *amae*.[32] It filled the space between my shoulder blades like a warm breath inhaled from the soles of my feet. Waves of goosebumps cascaded around my body like the waves of hot water cascading down the surface of the hot spring mound.

This pulsating mound, known as Great Boulder (ōiwa) among Shintō yamabushi, is what endows Mount Yudono (Hot Spring) with its name.[33] As we beheld its truly anomalous nature while standing in a surging puddle of its yellow water, Hoshino-san led us into gongyō. For him, and other priests and pilgrims of Shintō faith, the Great Boulder is a kami, the actual "god body" (goshintai) of Mount Yudono.[34]

There is a traditional rule that those who witness this sight must never speak of it. To this day, travelers are forbidden from photographing it. Bashō's haiku of Mount Yudono refers to its secrecy while capturing the sense of awe it inspires: "I am forbidden to speak of Mount Yudono but see how wet my sleeves are with reticent tears."[35] Now, as I saw pilgrims and yamabushi break down in tears before the Great Boulder with my own eyes, Bashō's poetic allusion to something forbidden and affecting became clear. It may seem taboo for me to write about it, but things have changed since the time of Bashō, when all aspects of Shugendō, not to mention certain forms of Buddhism and Shintō, were cloaked in strict secrecy.[36] Respected yamabushi have written about their experiences with the Great Boulder in books, and there is no central authority to consult as to whether one is able to speak of or write about it. In the time of Bashō, Buddhist ascetics oversaw Mount Yudono. Now it is operated by Shintō priests of the Dewa Sanzan Shrine.

After performing gongyō before the Great Boulder, we climbed on all fours up the backside of it and reached near the top. From there, you have not only a spectacular view of the lower valley on the other side but also a view of the top of the two-headed mound. It was amazing to see the water surge out with the same frequency of a human heartbeat. Sakamoto writes about this anomalous hot spring mound in a gendered and sexual paradigm: "The moment I placed my hand on the mound to climb it a shock ran through my body. I felt a raw elasticity. 'The rock is alive,' I thought. It felt like a human body. I recognized the sensation. It was the same as the feeling of touching a vagina. The hot spring water, like warm lubricant, slid smoothly between my fingers. The rock is the same as a human. A human is the same as a rock. Thinking this, I felt like I was being truly absorbed into nature."[37]

Through the uterine symbolism of Mount Haguro and here, in the sexual descriptions of the Great Boulder of Mount Yudono (which I have heard from other yamabushi and Buddhist monks), I learned that Dewa Sanzan is a deeply gendered landscape. Places where there are boulders that have fallen on top of other boulders, leaving a small passage between for a person to squeeze through, are called wombs (tainai). They are used by hikers, pilgrims, and yamabushi alike who, on entering, may also make a prayer before a small Buddhist or Shintō statue inside.[38] On the slopes of Gassan, a place called Higashi Fudaraku (Eastern Paradise) has an oval-shaped lake named Ohama. For Buddhists, it is imagined as a vagina associated with the Womb Realm and is located adjacent to a large rocky pillar, which is imagined as a phallus, the Diamond Realm. During annual rites, ascetics perform gongyō on the shores of the lake and, after a swift ascent, atop the phallic pillar. At the base of the boulder-phallus is another womb-crevice in which ascetics pray before a small golden Buddhist statue. Although the efficacy of rituals is enhanced by the sexual union of their gendered sites, a fair number of contemporary yamabushi, especially the men, are also amused by the symbolism.

After our omairi visit to the inner sanctuary of Mount Yudono, our crew of yamabushi found some yellow-orange water footbaths (*ashiyu*) with different intensities of heat near the exit and settled in. We placed our feet in the water. Just when we began to enjoy ourselves a bit, breaching the code of silence, Hoshino-san appeared and motioned with a stern voice for us to put our jikka tabi back on immediately.

The shugyō process is one of constant flux. Yamabushi are always moving. Transitions are swift. Food is not eaten, it is devoured. Jikka tabi are put on and removed. Futons are prepared and stowed away with militaristic efficiency. Yamabushi arrive to depart and depart to arrive. Thus come, thus gone. They glide through forests under moonlight and ascend and descend mountains as the Sun does horizons. All these movements work to silence the intellect. Our movements are constant, monotonous, exhausted, and decisionless, guided by Hoshino-san, the head of our yamabushi centipede creeping through the mountains.

Immediately after departing Mount Yudono Shrine, yamabushi are separated between men and women. A senior yamabushi leads the men and Hoshino-san leads the women. During my first shugyō, the men followed Itō-san out of the shrine, quickly down a winding paved road. Bright yellow tour buses frequented this narrow switchback road. Several times we had to dodge them by leaning into the bushes. I had assumed we were done for the day and were just heading down to catch a bus when suddenly Itō-san turned sharply to the left and dashed into the thick bushes. The rest of us followed. Quick-footed and half-crouching down a barely visible muddy trail, we bushwacked headlong through big green leaves and tangled branches.

Down the thickly forested trail, there was another rusty ladder. We all climbed down. Once we reached the river, which flowed down the ocher

A womb (*tainai*) of boulders near the summit of Gassan with a Buddhist statue inside. Tombstones from centuries past are stacked on top and near the entrance, adding death symbolism. Photograph by Shayne Dahl.

canyon we had just seen from above, Itō-san announced that we were to strip down to our *fundoshi* (loincloths). We all stripped down, placing our sweaty yamabushi clothing onto wet boulders along the riverbank. I wanted to make a good first impression with senior yamabushi, so I rushed to the front with Itō-san and Oki-san, a yamabushi from Tokyo. They led everyone upstream through a canyon, over sharp rocks, and through deep pools of cold rushing water. The red rock canyon looked and sounded so different from below. One had to be extremely cautious in choosing steps to avoid lacerations yet fast enough to keep up with our group of half-naked men. The women were told to change in a separate location. They remained in their undergarment robes, removing only their outer layer.

Itō-san and Oki-san seemed to be racing each other. I sensed a spirit of competition between them. They moved lightly over the rocks, while I trudged and crawled and winced when the sharp rocks dug into my feet. I constantly anticipated some big pool of water ahead that we would submerge ourselves into, but suddenly we came to the canyon's end, where two immaculate waterfalls billowed down. Then it hit me. We were not racing to do gongyō in a cool pool of rushing water. We were racing to the Great Waterfalls (Ōtaki) of Mount Yudono.

Shortly after we arrived, Hoshino-san and the women joined us. Hoshino-san took his clothes off and stood on a large boulder with the two sparkling waterfalls roaring behind him. His white *fundoshi* (loincloth) matched his white beard. He called for our attention and then taught us how to draw up energy (*ki*) before performing takigyō, "waterfall practice." Hoshino-san instructed us to turn left, extend our arms with palms open, make fists, and pull our arms back to our chests as we said with guttural force: "*Eh–sa! Eh–sa!*" This was done with quick repetition. Then we shifted to the right and did the same: "*Eh–sa! Eh–sa!*" This aggressive warm-up gets the blood flowing quickly. It is followed with a yogic breathing exercise in which one squats, like a sumō wrestler, and extends their arms out to the sides. While rising to stand, we were instructed to draw our arms all the way up, inhaling deep, until our palms met above our heads. Our steepled palms were then lowered as we exhaled until they were directly over the center of our chests. The prayerful position when the palms are together is called *gasshō* in Japanese. From gasshō, the left palm is pivoted so the fingers point to the inside of the right elbow and the right palm is pivoted so the fingers point to the inside of the left elbow. Then the fingers are curled together. From this position, yamabushi raise an interlocked grip over the belly button while inhaling through the nostrils and force the grip downward, exhaling from the mouth, all with deep abdomen breaths. This is one cycle of the breathing exercise. Revitalized, Hoshino-san then summoned various kami with a booming voice and directed us to enter the waterfall with a wave of his arm.

I have experimented with psychedelics before. In my experience, nothing compares to the intensity of takigyō. The cold hits one's involuntary nervous system immediately. It takes your breath away and leaves you gasping for air, especially if you are a beginner. With each gasp, water fills the mouth and may go down the wrong tube, making you cough. The water of this waterfall is a mixture of rain, snowmelt, and the mineral water surging out of the Great Boulder a couple hundred yards upstream. It tastes like iron. Beneath the waterfall, I could barely stand. The weight of the tumbling columns of water repeatedly knocked me down. I remember screaming a *kiai* (a martial arts power scream) to gather strength and offset my frustration, but I could not find my balance on the sharp, shifting rocks while receiving the relentless beat-down of the waterfall. The water felt like a torrent of pebbles pouring on my head. Itō-san and Oki-san, who were blurry figures to my right and left, had no trouble. I could vaguely hear them performing the Three Word

A yamabushi performing takigyō (waterfall practice). Photograph by Shayne Dahl.

and Three Mountain gongyō through the deafening sound of rushing water and the smack it makes when it slams against one's head and shoulders.

It is difficult to put into words what takigyō feels like. Experienced yamabushi draw on different metaphors to express their impressions, but always in the hours, days, and months after the actual experience. Some have described it as a "mother's embrace," paralleling "the divine mother of the mountain" trope (see Ichiro 1968, 141–80). Interestingly, some gamers have described takigyō as a "power-up, like catching a flashing star in Super Mario Brothers." In several books and magazines for sale in the Ideha Cultural Museum, takigyō is called an "exorcism" (*oharai*), "a purification of the heart" (*kokoro ga arawareru*), "entrance to the afterlife" (*ano yo no iriguchi*), "the gateway to a sanctuary" (*seiiki he no mon*), "an out-of-body experience" (*taigairidatsu*), a way of "realizing the destiny of one's spirit" (*tamashii no shimei wo shiru*), and a technique to "meet your new self" (*atarashii jibun to deau*).[39] One yamabushi I met described the experience as initially painful but said that if one performs gongyō effectively, "the kami and the Buddhas make the waterfall lighter and warmer."

Beyond metaphors, takigyō is, in the most general sense, a complete sensory overload. Because of the uneven distribution of the streams within the torrent, it brings the body into a chaotic vibration. Near the end of my first takigyō, perhaps a minute after I entered the waterfall, I stopped resisting. I found my balance with knees bent. My posture straightened. My eyes were closed. All I could see were flashes of red from the sunlight penetrating my eyelids and black from the rapid and ephemeral shadows that the falling water cast. This moment of cold, vibrating, strobe-lighting corporeal intensity in the waterfall eventually shifted from pain to ecstasy. Other yamabushi would unceremoniously describe this to me as "the moment adrenaline kicks in." Sakamoto (2012, 62) likewise describes the onset of internal warmth in his body after reaching a certain threshold of pain that makes the experience more enjoyable. So enjoyable, in fact, that he exerted himself to a dangerous extent and was bedridden the next few days with a high fever. Hoshino-san warns against this sensation, though, calling it "dangerous" because it signals thermoregulatory warming from cold shock. I remember when I came out of the waterfall, Oki-san teased me for trying too hard with my kiai scream. Laughing, he said, "Nice fight!" Hoshino-san later taught me that resisting the waterfall is the wrong strategy. Acceptance, *uketamau*, is the key.

Asumi-san is a petite woman from Fukushima Prefecture who moved to Shōnai and started doing shugyō after the tsunami of 3/11 devastated her hometown, Minami Soma. She shared an interesting interpretation of takigyō.

In an interview, she said, "Water is nature. I am human. During takigyō, nature overwhelms my human body, but I must stand. Nature's power is coming down on my head and shoulders, on my entire being, but my inner power is heating up and my body fights to stand straight. My will to live is greatly empowered as I struggle, and I feel my humanity ascending upward into the hard-falling water." She was depressed both in the months following the disaster and still occasionally in the present, she said, but shugyō is a way to renew her *ikigai*, purpose in life and path to a new future.[40]

After takigyō, we got dressed and hiked all the way down to the large torii marking the entrance for visitors who come directly to Mount Yudono, which is the torii featured on the cover of this book. The yamabushi passed through the torii and piled into the bus that was waiting for us in the parking lot below. I remember writing field notes through all the bumps and turns. Nearly everyone else had fallen asleep, their heads nodding in all directions. Some with faces leaned up against the window, exhausted and euphoric. It was silent but for the bus engine hum all the way back to Daishōbō.

On the morning of day three, yamabushi wake up early to ascend the stairway of rebirth of Mount Haguro once more for a visit to the Dewa Sanzan Shrine. Once there, we ascended the ten steps, took our jikka tabi boots off, and entered. Inside, Hoshino-san leads a special ritual in its main hall (*honden*). Kneeling there together before closed doors that hide the central object of worship (the god body, or *gōshintai*, of Mount Haguro), yamabushi are told to prostrate themselves by placing their foreheads on the tatami floor. A Shintō priest then thumps a thunderous rhythm on a large drum while another performs a melodic norito incantation, uttering the names of various kami. The back of each yamabushi is struck with a metallic staff with folded streamers (*gohei*), blessing each yamabushi with the power of Dewa Sanzan's innermost sanctuary.

The final descent from the summit following this climactic ceremony is fast and uninterrupted. When the yamabushi return to Daishōbō, Hoshino-san makes a small fire out of cedar sticks. Yamabushi are instructed to jump over the fire while releasing a scream like that of a newborn baby: "*Nya!*" It is called *basaitō* and represents rebirth after the completion of shugyō, the first step toward post-shugyō synthesis.[41] After one final gongyō session in Daishōbō, each yamabushi is awarded a thin wooden talisman (*ofuda*) with the yamabushi's personal name inscribed beside the names of Mount Haguro, Gassan, and Mount Yudono, formally establishing each participant's relationship with the mountains as the talisman will be set up in their home altar (*kamidana*). Group pictures are taken while participants are still in yamabushi clothing. Then everyone dresses, once again, in their colorful modern clothes. Together with Hoshino-san, everyone goes to a nearby hot spring called Yamabushi Onsen for a soak. After three days of sweating from nonstop movement through mud, rain, cold, wind, cold shock in a waterfall, and sleep deprivation, many yamabushi often joke that the *onsen* is "heaven" (*tengoku*), one of the upper stages of the Ten Worlds in Buddhist cosmology. I always found it hard to disagree. As Sakamoto writes: "Having safely completed our training, we headed to a hot spring near Tōge to wash away the dirt and fatigue of the past three days of shugyō. At this long-awaited moment, everyone, though they are all adults, had their eyes wide open and shining, with faces like elementary school students on summer vacation. After all, we had just been reborn."[42] As we soaked in the onsen, naked and quietly reflecting on our passage through the orographic and spiritual thresholds of shugyō in Dewa Sanzan, the bond between yamabushi had come full circle as a unique form of communitas—a spontaneous, egalitarian communion described by Turner ([1969] 2008), where ritual practice washes away all social distinctions and, in this case, is replaced by a shared experience of rebirth in the mountain's womb.

Conclusion

In this chapter, I have introduced a very influential contemporary yamabushi named Hoshino Fumihiro. I have described his three-day shugyō through my own experience as well as through some descriptions of other yamabushi who have trained under his guidance. This is a basic sketch of shugyō, focused on one specific form under the guidance of one specific sendatsu in one specific mountain range. There are other forms of shugyō practiced in Dewa Sanzan, and there are many more practiced in other Shugendō mountains throughout Japan.[43]

My intent in this chapter has been to introduce the notion of *shugyō* (ascetic training) in general terms and differentiate it from the English term "asceticism." The terms are superficially similar but fundamentally distinct. "Asceticism" is exclusively religious. The term *shugyō* is broader, more flexible. It slips in and out of religion, depending on the context. This is part of the reason why Hoshino-san has been able to market his three-day shugyō as being whatever a patron wants it to be. It can be a touristic experience of the Shugendō traditions of Dewa Sanzan or a genuine religious experience through Shugendō rituals. What usually happens is that a person's experience falls on a spectrum between these poles. Shugyō is in this respect inherently liminal, betwixt and between, a "countermodern" experience of a "counter-structure" ritual—time outside of capitalist modernity in the time-warped mountains of Dewa Sanzan.

I find it useful to draw on Simon Coleman's term "laterality" to describe Hoshino-san's shugyō in that it is constituted by discrete movements between the secular and the sacred as well as between Shintō and Buddhist ritual. "The very point of laterality," Coleman (2023, 741) explains, "is that it is constituted by moving across the semiotic and social territories of any given ritual field." In a ritual context such as Hoshino-san's three-day shugyō, laterality means "reaching ambiguously across spaces, times, and behaviours . . . separating 'set-apart' and 'everyday' action. It prompts negotiations, intersections, and articulations between behavioural frames." Coleman (730) adds, "While Turnerian liminality emphasizes intensity of immersion, laterality encompasses much more varied affective responses from those unsure how or even whether to participate. As an attitude, it implies being located at one remove from formal ritual action while also being oriented, however partially, toward such action." In contemporary Japan, figures such as Hoshino-san are successful in promoting their religious practices because they find creative ways to capitalize on the laterality between the secular and the religious, shugyō and tourism, Shintō and Buddhism.

In the years since the completion of my fieldwork, Hoshino-san has collaborated with some of his more business-minded yamabushi to create a tourism outfit specifically for foreigners seeking an authentic yamabushi experience. The company is called Yamabushidō, the Way of the Yamabushi.[44] A range of shugyō options for tourists include both secular framing and more spiritual orientations. For example, the company operates a three-day "Reset Training," framed in secular language, as well as "Basic Yamabushi Training" and "Master Yamabushi Training," a seven-day experience under the guidance of Hoshino-san in coordination with Zen monks in Shōnai. In this form of "lateral Shugendō," there is something for everyone.

3   Rebirth in the Mountain's Womb
Shugyō Interpreted

After three days of exhaustive *shugyō* topped off with a nice hot soak in the nearby Yamabushi Onsen, we returned to Daishōbō for the final feast, called a *naorai*. Everyone is served *shōjin ryōri*, an originally Buddhist vegetarian cuisine that is now served by Shintō-oriented sendatsu to their guests. In 2014, shōjin ryōri contributed to Tsuruoka City, which encompasses Mount Haguro, becoming recognized as Japan's first UNESCO Creative City of Gastronomy. Cherries, mushrooms, bamboo shoots, lotus roots, fiddlehead greens, beans, and other mountain vegetables foraged from the Dewa Sanzan range taste extraordinary after the minimal rations of rice, miso soup, and pickles during gakigyō (hungry ghost practice). The naorai feast begins with a big *kanpai* (cheers!) of sake. An oversized cup makes its rounds with many yamabushi taking the challenge to chug as much as they can. Things loosen up quickly, introducing a ludic element to the conclusive feast.[1] Even Hoshino-san will drop his strict sendatsu persona and joke around a bit. As Sakamoto Daizaburo recounts: "While the drinking progressed, a large red cup that could hold two big bottles of sake appeared. We all took turns drinking the generously poured sake from it. I drank quite a bit as well. Then, Hoshino-san called out: 'Hey, do the *Yokachin*!' Yokachin [nice dick] is a type of entertainment performance with regional variations. . . . It's basically a humorous erotic dance where a man will wiggle his hips and dance in sync with the chants, imagining the 1.8-liter bottle of sake as his penis."[2]

The Yokachin may appear from the outside, from an ethnocentric point of view, to be rude behavior, something totally inappropriate in a religious context. In this cultural milieu, it prompted only laughter from men and women. After all, the landscape of Dewa Sanzan has many rock formations and natural features that are interpreted as male and female genitalia. We had just spent three days performing *gongyō* before many such sites together. Shugendō rituals often express sexual, embryonic, and reproductive symbolism.[3] It quickly becomes normal. I've seen ludic jokes in Shintō and Buddhist contexts. That said, societal norms are always changing. By the time you read this, ludic sexual humor may no longer be tolerated during shugyō.

When the mood of the naorai party quiets down, yamabushi each take turns speaking before their peers, reflecting on their shugyō experience through personal testimony. The prolonged silence over three days and the quiet epiphanies that shugyō incubates must have a rebound effect because each person speaks at length, offering insightful interpretations of shugyō. In this chapter, I share a broad range of interpretations that yamabushi have shared at the naorai and with me in sit-down interviews. An overview of their testimonies shows the diverse interpretations yamabushi have of shugyō. Yet clear patterns related to gender, agriculture, sexuality, and counterculture do emerge. Ultimately, shugyō creates a space for reflection on self and society, a chance for both renewal and transformation, through the reproductive and religious symbolism of Shugendō ritual.

Shugyō Interpreted

A typical account emphasizes heightened sensory perception to the environment after a period of internal dialogue (about one's own personal issues, work-related problems, and so on). As one yamabushi explained: "I dragged matters from my daily life with me as I walked in the mountains at first. I couldn't focus at all on my surroundings. After the second night of forest walking . . . I don't know how to describe this sensation, but I noticed the Earth moving outside of my mind. The world appeared differently to me. Then, I was moved. I felt *alive* on the moving Earth. Usually, I don't attend to such sensations, but in shugyō, I could vividly sense the wind and other natural movements." As Hoshino-san (2017, 31) himself writes: "Entering the mountain makes problems vanish."[4]

Some describe this process of working toward inner silence and enhanced sensory perception using the metaphor of an onion: "I thought my mind was like an onion being peeled away to the core, layer by layer. I went deep within my mind during shugyō." I have heard a few yamabushi report childhood memories, including trauma, spontaneously emerging while hiking up the mountainous slopes: "Shugyō drew my childhood memories out. I was not actively thinking, but they came to mind nonstop, bubbling up like a wellspring. I feel like my spirit was dry and shugyō put some water on it or like my spirit was in a dark forest and shugyō brought sunshine. I realized that I had become lost inside of myself."

I have seen many yamabushi moved to tears during shugyō. As I described in the case of Mount Yudono, the combination of immersion in a beautiful and sacred mountainscape, exotic rituals reminiscent of ancestral times, and physical exhaustion produces strong emotional reactions. Sometimes these emotions are expressed as a nostalgic longing to connect with a national cultural essence or identity. Here is a testimony of a middle-aged man that reflects the nostalgic perspective: "I think that we Japanese need to know more about our Japaneseness. Before shugyō, I realized I don't know anything about Japan. After these three days of shugyō, I realized that shugyō or something like it is necessary to gain this knowledge. Last night, when we were doing gongyō at the summit of Mount Haguro, I wept uncontrollably. I'm not sure why, but something inside of me was released. I want in the future to put myself in this situation again."

In his second book, *Yamabushi Notebook*, Sakamoto Daizaburo shared a similar sentiment:

> When I first stepped into the world of yamabushi, the most surprising thing was my own body. Having spent my days working at a computer, barely moving, my body had become dull from urban living. However, by walking in the mountains and fasting, I noticed even the slightest changes. This isn't some grand tale. It's more about realizing the simple joy of eating a rice ball or pickled radish when I was really hungry. For me, it was a truly significant discovery. People often ask me, "What changed when you became a yamabushi?" I feel that it wasn't about changing something but rather rediscovering what was already within my body. Some might suggest that outdoor activities or mountaineering would suffice. I disagree. While modern outdoor recreation is rooted in contemporary Western culture, the world of yamabushi is based on a culture that has been nurtured since people first began living on the Japanese archipelago. This aspect drew me in more deeply. Human beings must navigate through life alone, but by focusing on our own bodies, we can discover a vibrant, raw nature that resonates with the rhythms of nature and the universe through its aspects such as food and sexuality. It might be something obvious, but when I realized this, I was quite moved.[5]

As these testimonies indicate, there are a range of metaphors and frameworks through which yamabushi interpret the shugyō experience before their peers. Hoshino-san himself often concludes the series of testimonies with an impromptu lecture in which he shares not only his philosophy of shugyō but thoughts on his role as sendatsu. As he sees it, "The role of sendatsu is simply to make a space for modern yamabushi to feel [*kanjiru*] their spirits [*tamashii*]." In his teaching, *tamashii* (spirit) is the unconditioned essence of a person, their true self in a natural or untrammeled state of being. Shugyō is framed in his philosophy as a technique to revive one's tamashii.[6] It suffers not only under the pressures of capitalist modernity but also through the pull of societal obligation, which can be intense in Japan, and the general suffering of life. For Hoshino-san, our tamashii is who we as human beings are born as and destined to be if we can liberate ourselves from all the limits and conditions placed on us by the circumstances of society. The way to revive one's tamashii is to be sensitive to and abide by one's intuitive feelings (*kanjiru*). Shugyō enhances this sensitivity.

Although he has his own unique views, Hoshino-san accepts all interpretations of the shugyō experience. This is why he focuses mostly on making an opportunity for modern people to connect with nature, creating a space for them in the sacred landscapes of Dewa Sanzan to have a transformational experience. At the end of my last naorai with Hoshino-san in May 2015, he said: "My form of Shugendō is not a return to the original Shugendō of the past. What I want to do is a 'soft' (*yuruyakana*) Shugendō that is flexible and adapted to modern life. We don't need doctrinal texts in this day and age! I want to encourage everyone to find such a soft union between modern life and tradition. Shugyō is about feeling [*kanjiru*], not doctrine."

Another interesting aspect of this post-shugyō synthesis, the return to modern life, is how new networks and communities form through social media. After every shugyō I undertook, my social media accounts would light up with dozens of friend requests from yamabushi I had just met, most of them linked to Hoshino-san's accounts. Over social media, yamabushi would openly share information and photos about various sacred sites they had visited, food they had eaten, and where they hoped to organize and coordinate future events, some featuring Hoshino-san. This has extended his practice far and wide, well beyond Yamagata Prefecture and well beyond Japan (in Brazil and New Zealand, for instance), connecting his followers with nature around the globe through the rituals of Shugendō as he knows and practices it.

Gender, Landscape, and Time

As Sakamoto's description of the pulsating hot spring of Mount Yudono reveals, gender and sexual references often figure into yamabushi testimonies of shugyō. A male yamabushi I did shugyō with in spring 2015 reported: "It's my first time speaking after three days so I don't know if I will speak well. This is my second time doing shugyō under Hoshino-san. Compared to my first time last year, my mind was very quiet. I especially enjoyed walking through the forest. The forest scents were the best! The song of the birds and other forest sounds is truly the best music! Another thing . . . I apologize for my language, but every step I took felt like I was having sex with the earth. It felt so good! Thank you for this precious experience."

Hoshino-san himself approaches the mountain and the ocean as maternal entities. He sometimes describes the waterfalls he does takigyō in as a flow of "amniotic fluid." When possible, he undertakes *misogi* (water submersion) in the ocean. During a three-day shugyō he hosted in Awaji Island, just off the coast of Shikoku Island, he led male and female yamabushi into the ocean to perform gongyō before a diamond-shaped boulder that is featured in Japanese mythology as the first drop from the "spear" of Izanagi that generated the Japanese archipelago.[7] Describing the ocean as a womb of amniotic fluid, Hoshino-san later explained: "I realized in my body that the mountain and the ocean are maternal existence. When I finish shugyō, I really like to go into the ocean. I find a place where no one else is around. Then, I take off all my clothes and jump into the ocean naked. Floating there, I think, 'Ah, I am truly inside of my mother's womb now.' Being reborn into a new life, I feel embraced in happiness."[8]

Many male yamabushi experience a form of gender complementarity between their bodies and the mountainous landscape they perceive as feminine (for Hoshino-san, the ocean as well).[9] It is in this gender complementarity between the male human body and the feminized landscape (or body of water) in which shugyō inspires not only the symbolic sense of rebirth from a maternal power but sexual interpretations of the shugyō experience—whether it is to the texture of hot spring water in Mount Yudono, the shape of the conch trumpet, or stepping on the soft forest floor.[10] Women connect with the feminized landscape of the mountains in a way that does not reflect complementarity but rather harmonized corporeal empowerment. One female yamabushi reported feeling her womb heat up during shugyō: "Before coming to Dewa Sanzan, I stopped by my parent's house and had a really good meal. They were like "Please, eat this . . . and this and this!" preparing me for shugyō. Once I started to climb the mountain, I felt energy [*enerugi*] emanating from the ground beneath me as if all the plants were glowing. As a woman, I felt a deep connection. My womb felt increasingly hot as I climbed. So much energy was coming up from the ground into my body."

Group photo after ocean submersion, Awaji-shima, May 2015. The diamond-shaped boulder, the mythic first drop of the Japanese archipelago, is featured in the back. Photograph courtesy of Miura Takehiro.

The gendered landscape may take different forms in yamabushi testimony depending on one's gendered relation with it, but it also figures into Hoshino-san's sense of time and history in interesting ways. Hoshino-san sees the patriarchy and chauvinism of Japanese society as only a modern development. In his view, women are, by nature and in deep history, more powerful than men. To prove this point, Hoshino-san cites the case of Queen Himiko. According to early Chinese historical records, she ruled peacefully over twenty-two chieftains near the end of the Yayoi period (400 BCE–300 CE). She is said to have had a thousand female attendants and only one male attendant.[11] For Hoshino-san, she is the prime example of ancient matriarchy. Queen Himiko was chosen to lead because under male rule there had been decades of warfare. Modernity and its patriarchy are, in Hoshino-san's paradigm, a fall from an ancient matriarchal utopia. Shugyō in the heterotopic, heterochronic, and gendered space of the mountain is a way to revive that ancient spirit (tamashii) and its inherent wildness (yasei) in the modern age.

Another historical example Hoshino-san draws on to emphasize the prevalence of ancient matriarchy in Japan is the change in the national calendar from lunisolar to Gregorian:[12]

Before the Gregorian calendar was introduced in Japan, we used the lunisolar calendar [*taiin taiyōreki*]. Dates were counted using the lunar calendar based on the moon's cycles, while the solar calendar based on the sun's cycles added the seasonal changes. In those days, the annual cycle and the sense of seasons were perfectly aligned. Moreover, up until the early modern period, women's natural instincts were preserved. This is because women's bodies are connected to the moon. The strong *yasei* [wildness] of women is absolutely related to their monthly menstruation cycles. However, in the fifth year of the Meiji era [1872], the calendar changed to the Gregorian solar calendar, severing society's temporal connection with the moon. Over 150 years have passed since then. Nowadays, when I say to women, 'Your tamashii is strong,' they respond with 'No way!' The sense of having strong yasei has nearly disappeared. Until the early modern period, it was well preserved. With modernization from the Meiji era, lifestyles and customs have changed. In the Edo period, women wore *koshi-maki* [traditional wrap skirts]. In those times, without modern sanitary products, it is said that women could control their menstrual flow. Such abilities have disappeared now. The yasei and tamashii that women originally possessed back then are now lost. What a waste! In the past, when they wore koshi-maki, everything went well with the lunisolar calendar, the sense of seasons, and customs. Their yasei was preserved. All of that has been destroyed. Even if it's just for three days, if women do shugyō in the mountains and become immersed in nature, their faded yasei will be awakened, and their body will naturally become revitalized. That feeling of liveliness is tamashii. That is the true beauty of women. When women are lively without makeup, their beauty shines from within. I realized this during shugyō.[13]

Reacting to this teaching, some female yamabushi have reported that they have undertaken shugyō while menstruating and have even practiced controlling menstrual flow to revive their female wildness (yasei), which, they come to feel under Hoshino-san's influence, has been lost to modernity. That women now seek to do shugyō entails for him that women in society have forgotten or fallen out of synch with the power of their inherent wildness (yasei). This wildness, he says, is evident in female reproductive power and in the menstrual cycle. Once, when he stated this point before an audience at a public speaking event in Kobe, he then openly criticized men for saying disrespectful things about women and the menstrual cycle, declaring: "It is essential for life itself!" I remember a woman bursting into tears, then hugging and thanking Hoshino-san for his comment. In a different idiom, especially for audiences of women, he describes shugyō as "menstruation for men." Women have natural renewal cycles in their bodies, but men do not, so they need to go into the womb of the mountain for rebirth.

"A Mountainlike Man"

Hoshino-san's three-day shugyō has become one of the most convenient and portable models of institutionally affiliated Shugendō for contemporary laypeople in Japan today, and it has only expanded to attract international clients since the conclusion of my primary fieldwork. It is a bold, reformative move within the Shugendō world, which has, until the past decade, been too arcane to garner popular interest. Hoshino-san's success has made any attempt at ethnographic anonymity futile. He does not wish to be anonymous, anyway. He aspires to draw more visitors to Dewa Sanzan and truly believes that Shugendō has value for the modern world.

Hoshino-san's fame skyrocketed as the go-to yamabushi master of Tōhoku over the course of my fieldwork. He was invited to speak across Japan and to partake in symposiums at universities, and he was invited as a guest of honor in New Zealand at an interfaith gathering with New Age and Indigenous spiritualists from around the world. Hoshino-san has published two books articulating his yamabushi outlook on life. The first is titled *Live by Feeling: A Yamabushi Method*.[14] In one of the book reviews featured on the cover, a Japanese professor writes: "Hoshino-san is a mountainlike man. A mountain does not speak, but if it had a mouth, it would speak like Hoshino-san."[15]

Sensing the importance of this man in the unfolding history of Dewa Sanzan, I tried to accompany him wherever he went. At a certain point, I just could not keep up. Even while trekking through the mountains, I had trouble keeping up. I recently saw a video on his social media of him at the age of seventy-eight, ascending the snow-covered slopes of Gassan. One slip, and a person would slide all the way down the slope! He is soft-hearted and fun-loving outside of shugyō, a jolly, charismatic grandpa figure in many respects. That is certainly the countenance portrayed in the *Uketamau* film, in which he speaks of the mountain as a motherly figure and can be seen performing takigyō in Mount Yudono's waterfalls (Ruffell 2012).

Hoshino-san's model of the yamabushi as someone who realizes their untrammeled state or wildness (yasei) within is quite Daoist, but it also strikes interesting parallels with Jean-Jacques Rousseau's ([1755] 2009) *l'homme de naturel* (natural man), a prerational hominid the philosopher imagined and used to critique inequality in Western civilization.¹⁶ Both l'homme de naturel and Hoshino-san's ideal type of the yamabushi, a kind of *l'homme de monte* (mountain man), are creatures of affect. Where l'homme de naturel lacks metacognition and is bound to affectivity not by choice but by disposition, the contemporary yamabushi undertakes shugyō with the purposeful intent of increasing affectivity because it is a vital quality that modern people have forgotten. It may seem surprising why Hoshino-san, a mountain ascetic, is espousing a philosophy of living by the whims of feeling and wildness—the embrace of natural instinct or yasei—but this apparent contradiction disappears when considering the failure of "asceticism" and its self-denying, instinct-disciplining connotations via Christianity to serve as a fair translation of yamabushi. For Hoshino-san, to "live by feeling" is an extension of the yamabushi motto "uketamau!" (I receive!) and of the affectivity of shugyō, of feeling the mountain, its waterfalls, hot springs, and rugged slopes. He wants his disciples to awaken to their true self, which has been repressed by societal conditioning. Hoshino-san's understanding of what it means to be a yamabushi aligns more closely with the Daoist ideal of a sage—one who renounces society to be in nature and seek mystical union with the cosmic flux (see Zhuāngzǐ 2024)—than with the Christian model of a self-denying ascetic (see Laidlaw 2002).

There are also notable parallels between Hoshino-san's philosophy on the necessity of shugyō in modern times and Sigmund Freud's discussion of the cause of neurosis in *Civilization and Its Discontents*. Freud ([1930] 1961, 39) wrote that "a person becomes neurotic because he cannot tolerate the amount of frustration which society imposes on him in the service of its cultural ideals, and it was inferred from this that the abolition or reduction of those demands would result in a return to possibilities of happiness." For Hoshino-san, shugyō offers individuals a temporary abolition of societal demands, a psychologically necessary break from the state of *gaman* (emotional repression) required to function in capitalist modernity and pursue its materialistic ideals.

Hoshino-san views "the ancients" (*mukashi no hito*) as being in tune with the yasei (wildness, natural instinct) of human nature. His rule of silence during shugyō is intended, he often tells yamabushi, to teach modern people how to once again "think with the body" (*karada de kangaeru*) as the ancient people once did. Hoshino-san claims that this kind of "body thinking" is actual "wisdom" (*honto no chie*) because it emerges from a dialogue between one's embodied being and the physical world. Finding one's balance beneath the cold crush of a waterfall, cultivating the will to remain there after crossing the threshold of pain, learning to read the mountainous terrain by choosing the best footholds, and learning to silence the urge to qualify affects—of awe, pain, fear, happiness, exhaustion—through words; all these practices engender "thinking with the body" for Hoshino-san.

By contrast, "knowledge" (*chishiki*) is "thinking with the head" (*atama de kangaeru*). For Hoshino-san, it is representational thinking that lacks substance. During the post-shugyō naorai feasts I attended, Hoshino-san often said that those who think solely with the head find singular answers that merely echo what others have said, but those who think with the body discover a multiplicity of truths within. He often leveled his critique of knowledge, or chishiki, on the figure of the scholar and was especially bold in the presence of scholars (myself included), denouncing the superfluities of intellectual abstraction. However, Hoshino-san did express hope in the potential for an anthropology of Shugendō since the primary method of ethnography is participant observation and prolonged fieldwork.[17]

Hoshino-san often cites "uketamau" as the ideal philosophy to live by: to accept or receive, not resist, the flux of life in the same way yamabushi learn to accept, not resist, the torrent of the waterfall in the throes of takigyō. In an interview, he clarified:

> "Uketamau" is a phrase unique to Shugendō practitioners of the Mount Haguro sect. No matter what is said, no matter when one's name is called, and no matter what one is called upon to do, the practitioner replies, "Uketamau!" If you think about it, Shugendō is a highly syncretic religion. It was influenced by Shintō, Buddhism, Onmyōdō, Daoism, and animism. It is not a monotheistic religion but a polytheistic one, and therefore it needs to be capable of accepting a wide range of ideas and other religions. Uketamau is indeed an expression that well represents this aspect of Shugendō. Sometimes within our daily lives, we might feel that something isn't right. This generates conflict within us. Conflict will not lead to good things, so the attitude represented by uketamau should be fundamental to how human beings live in human society. Whatever happens, we must start with acceptance. This expression of the Haguro yamabushi is truly outstanding.

Hoshino-san's use of uketamau makes Shugendō accessible and represents one way for him to incorporate ancient wisdom in the modern world. However, it is not without critics. Some of Hoshino-san's most senior yamabushi have emphasized to me the "necessary limits of uketamau." Once, while at the

Tsuruoka library with my family, a senior yamabushi whom I had not noticed in his regular clothes greeted me and we began speaking about Hoshino-san's teaching of uketamau outside of shugyō. He said it was great that laypeople were finding uketamau a useful approach to life's many challenges, but one must also set limits to such acceptance. He then cited the example of radiation exposure in nearby Fukushima Prefecture, which, following 3/11, was an ongoing problem: "Should we, when faced with such a situation as in Fukushima, simply accept our lot?" This comment reveals that although influential in yamabushi circles, the self-subjugating aspect and fatalism inherent in Hoshino-san's philosophy of uketamau is not accepted by all. Even with those who do accept it, there are some reservations.

Hoshino-san's philosophy is explicitly antirationalist. His critique of modernity is framed as a critique of "knowledge." He claims that the bodily "wisdom" of the ancients must be revived and that shugyō is a contemporary means of restoring it. Acknowledging his place in history yet striving for the revival of the ancient wisdom of Shugendō (at least his vision of it), Hoshino-san has said on numerous occasions: "I realize that we cannot return to the past world of our ancestors who lived closely with nature. What I am aiming for instead is a new return." This "new return" is premised on bringing people "face-to-face with nature" in the mountains through shugyō, leading them to realization (*kizuku*). As places of the past and repositories of ancient wisdom, bodily engagements through alpine affects draw yamabushi into a kind of ancestral communion with the history and the wisdom of Dewa Sanzan. As my summary of yamabushi experience testimonies demonstrates, each person has their own realizations and Hoshino-san is open to all. Even still, he does have his own paradigm that he expressed with increasing conviction throughout my fieldwork.

Hoshino-san's views of the human-nature relationship, for instance, have evolved over time. He explained: "I realized that humans are nature through shugyō. Yamabushi stand beneath waterfalls and when they do, mind and body are activated. As I understood, the use of this activation was to receive energy from the waterfall as a kind of power-up. However, a few years ago, while I was doing takigyō [waterfall practice], the word 'mixing' [*mazaru*] came through my body. My energy and the waterfall's energy were mixing. I feel as though my spirit realized the truth and translated it into this word." For Hoshino-san, when one speaks of truths realized in the mountains "from the belly" (*hara kara hanasu*), then it qualifies as wisdom (*chie*), not knowledge (*chishiki*), which is in the head, even though it is expressed through the representational form of language. To become wise like the ancients, according to Hoshino-san, one must enter bodily dialogue with the landscape.[18] This means fully immersing themselves in alpine affects during shugyō.

While yamabushi dialogue with the mountains through their bodies, they are also generally aware of the temporal alterity animating the trails. Hoshino-san's lectures on the historical significance of key places before and after shugyō, televised documentaries about different aspects of the mountains, and written works about Dewa Sanzan such as Sakamoto's books, as well as signposts along the trails, signal its connections with the past. Shugyō makes the body multitemporal through alpine affects, but the past may be specific representations of history, or it may be a vague sense of primitivism. The "ancient people," Hoshino-san explained in one of his post-shugyō lectures, had a heightened sense to "feel the sacredness of place": "They had a very active spirit. The ancient people lived through spirit [tamashii], but modern people live through thinking. They think too much! That is why they cannot create such epic mythology. Modern people work so hard to create, but they cannot make something nearly as epic. Ancient people create from spirit, so it becomes universal. That is why we can feel its power even today."

Hoshino-san teaches that "shugyō is a way to forge an ancient spirit in the modern body."[19] It is a bodily practice that enables modern people to reconnect with tamashii (spirit). In Hoshino-san's usage, tamashii implies a perspective driven by intuitive feeling and bodily affect, not a thinking intellect. By empowering modern people to connect with the ancient sensitivity of tamashii, Hoshino-san and his followers contend that Shugendō has the potential to awaken a grassroots transformation in modern society.

The Counterculture of Shugyō

Itō-san's take on shugyō and Shugendō places different emphasis than Hoshino-san's more nostalgic, spiritual framework. The very day I first arrived at Itō-san's house in August 2013, he had not yet returned from running errands. His wife invited me in for tea. Within minutes, while my tea was still steaming, a vehicle rumbled into the yard. I could hear Itō-san's voice. When he walked into the house, a man with a large black video camera hoisted on his shoulder, another man with headphones and an audio boom, and a woman with a notepad followed him in. Itō-san introduced me, but I didn't understand what was happening. The three-person film crew was from NHK, the national broadcaster in Japan.

I then learned that Itō-san had resigned from his position at the Ideha Cultural Museum shortly after he guided me through the mountains in 2012.

At the museum, he was charged with promoting Dewa Sanzan through various tourism projects, but he had decided to pursue his own entrepreneurial ambitions. In the year since I had last seen him, he had conducted research on the waning textile tradition of handcrafted straw sandals (*oezori*) in Shōnai. He not only interviewed senior craftspeople in the region about the *oezori* (which straw was required, when and how to harvest and treat it, and how to assemble it into durable footwear) but also created a business network among regional craftspeople to help them more effectively distribute and profit from their work. The success of his regional revitalization projects is what attracted the attention of NHK. Naturally, they were also interested in his life as a yamabushi.

I was behind the camera and beside the film crew when they began interviewing Itō-san in his living room. With permission, I flipped on my recorder and captured an interesting exchange between the young woman interviewer and Itō-san that was not aired. She was curious about his life as a yamabushi and his experiences of shugyō:

NHK: When did you first do shugyō?

ITŌ-SAN: When I was a university student. It was a part of an academic seminar. Within those three days [of shugyō] . . . hmm . . . how can I explain . . . ? It is difficult to express. Shugyō is unproductive time. What do I mean by that? For example, if I do some work in society and produce something, I will receive remuneration for it. This is how we generally make a living. Shugyō is outside of this. You are not selling your labor. The labor of shugyō is not for economic livelihood. It is for your own spiritual development.

Itō-san described shugyō as a form of non-capitalistic labor.[20] For Itō-san, working a job "is not a natural way to live." Most people I met during shugyō came from larger urban areas. They were accustomed to working long hours for mediocre wages on temporary contracts. Yamabushi "labor" during shugyō is not appraised and exchanged for yen. Itō-san's notions of the labor of shugyō are comparable to Karl Marx's ([1844] 1978, 70–81) notion of "species being" as unalienated labor. This means labor invested in activities and products that are valued and exchanged not for currency but for one's own benefit and the benefit of one's community. This was the first but not the last time Itō-san would critique capitalist labor or, as he calls it, "routine work." He would later tell me that although he made the most of his job at the Ideha Cultural Museum, he could not achieve the degree of freedom he truly desired while working under the authority of others.

Sato-san was another senior yamabushi who assisted Hoshino-san at the time of my fieldwork. Although he was from Tsuruoka, he traveled for years in France, Okinawa, and Hokkaidō as an artist before returning to settle in Tsuruoka. One sticking point for his decision to return was the realization of his spirituality, which he discovered during Hoshino-san's three-day shugyō. In an interview, he expressed aversion to capitalism, describing it as "the religion of atheism":

> The scariest thing is atheism, when the company or corporation a person belongs to, and the economy itself become gods [kami]. If a person works for a company, the commands they receive must be obeyed. In this system, you cannot oppose anyone above you in the hierarchy. Bosses are gods and workers don't even realize it. I think that is terrifying. It's not only major cities like Tokyo. Even in rural areas this is happening. The government and politicians, mayors, governors, . . . for the average worker, they are the gods to appease. This is what I mean when I speak of a brainwashed society. Their bosses are their gods, and the economy is their religion. If you can escape this society, you realize something is strange about it, but if you live inside of it, you cannot understand.

Shugyō, for Sato-san, is a dwelling outside of capitalist modernity, its atheistic religion, and its temporality. He also talks a lot about the Jōmon, who lived 14,000–300 BCE, and expresses a desire to return to their primitive and more natural lifestyle. This includes foraging for mountain vegetables, gardening, and living closer to sacred mountains. In the backyard of his house at the time of fieldwork was an ancient Shugendō trail leading up Mount Kinbō.

I once traveled with Sato-san to a countryside region in Japan about 600 miles to the west where a community of artists, friends of his, were living in a depopulated farming village. Owing to rapid economic growth in metropolitan centers, the countryside areas of Japan have suffered intense depopulation. However, counterculturalists who are critical of capitalist modernity have gone the other direction to seek out a higher quality of life at lower cost despite lower income.[21] Sato-san's friends, a family of three, lived in an abandoned elementary school for which they paid 10,000 yen for monthly rent (US$62 at the time of writing). They traded art for food and yoga lessons with their neighbors and had a handcrafted stone bath outside that was fire-heated. During this trip, Sato-san, a fully trained yamabushi, brought his hora gai and played it all around the area and spoke about the possibility of reviving an old Shugendō trail nearby, which excited our hosts and their countercultural community of artists.

Thinking about why Shugendō and a return to the countryside has resonated with young people lately, Sato-san mused: "Perhaps those people who awakened after the disaster sought a guiding principle for a new way of life and found it in Shugendō? It possessed what they were looking for. In shugyō, they entered nature, became one with the rhythm of nature, and thought: 'This is good. This is it. This is what I was seeking. Until now, I have been brainwashed, but the things that brainwashed me have suddenly washed away.' I think the people who have felt this way are many. I know I have."

Asumi-san, whom I mentioned earlier (from Fukushima), fits this profile. She worked a desk job leading up to the disasters but could not go back to work afterward:

> My job before the tsunami was basically deskwork. I was a receptionist. However, after 3/11, everything changed. I doubted my career. I could have died on that day, but luckily, I survived. The distance between life and death is the width of paper. I thought, even if I went back to the same job I had, if the same thing happened, I would live the same life. Since 3/11, my whole existence was shaken. I could not go back. Even though I was working at a hospital, nothing there could even protect my life. I worked to get money, of course. You can buy food at a store, but if no one is selling or if there is no longer a store, you cannot. Even if you have money, you cannot buy what is no longer sold. After 3/11, all the stores were either destroyed or emptied and distribution stopped. Seeing that, I realized that money is meaningless. If I can make food or my own stuff, I don't need money to buy it.

Asumi-san was initially evacuated to Tokyo owing to radiation concerns but had difficulty relating to people there: "I couldn't find the words to describe my experience or my feelings about the disaster to anyone in Tokyo. I just couldn't relate to anyone." She had a brother-in-law living in Tsuruoka City, so she moved north. Having lived in the snowy north for a few years, Asumi-san has come to interpret shugyō through the metaphor of winter:

> People think of spring as the season of blossoming. Living here, I have come to realize that it begins in winter. Winter is when the plants are preparing to bloom. Without winter, there is no spring blossom and no harvesting in autumn. The origin of the word *fuyu* [winter] is "to store the spirit," or "to shake the spirit." This not only applies to plants,

but I suppose it applies also to humans. . . . I think the culture of Dewa Sanzan was born of this environment. In winter, everything is white, covered in snow. People are stuck inside. They are confined. This is clearly connected with the confinement practice [komorigyō] of Mount Haguro. I feel as though even a baby in the mother's womb is a komorigyō compared to the spring of birth. In Autumn's Peak, people say, "Komorigyō is everything." . . . To emerge, to be reborn, confinement is necessary. All things originate from an unseen place. This is difficult to express in language. That's why it is better enacted, for example, though shugyō. . . . I enjoy the lively interactions between [human and nonhuman] living beings in Shōnai. Some people say, "We are a part of nature." . . . Living here, I feel it deeply in my body, especially during shugyō.[22]

Asumi-san went from feeling powerless before nature in the wake of the tsunami to finding a way to align herself with nature's power through living in Shōnai and regularly undertaking shugyō. Her reference to the seasonal power of winter is echoed by other yamabushi. Itō-san also referred to the generative power of winter in his unpublished interview with the NHK journalist who visited his home:

NHK: Do you remember your first impression of shugyō?
ITŌ-SAN: Before I could have an impression or was able to reflect on my experience, I was just trying to keep up with the fast pace of shugyō. It took me a long time to be able to think objectively about my experience and express these thoughts in language. I'm not sure what it was, but something about it resonated with me. "What was that? What was that resonance?" I thought. A question was born. To find the answer, I returned the next year and the year after that. Through participating, I gradually came to understand. It became ripe within me. This became my core.
NHK: So . . . what was that thing that resonated with you?
ITŌ-SAN: It can be explained through many different perspectives. . . . When I was in graduate school, I studied no-till agriculture. . . . In the middle of the winter, farmers would put water in the rice fields. It is cold at that time, isn't it? There are two purposes to putting water in at that time. First, by irrigating the fields, you stimulate an ecosystem. Also, by planting rice seedlings there, the rice becomes wild. Usually, rice seedlings are cultivated in a greenhouse in the winter and planted in the spring when ready. If you plant rice

seedlings in a wild place in midwinter, they become strong. Since the rice becomes stronger when wild, we do not need to use fertilizer or pesticides. They grow strong without it. I thought that was so interesting! What would happen if we put a human being in the same situation as these rice seedlings planted in midwinter? Well, it seems like shugyō, doesn't it? When you throw a human being into nature and scramble them up thoroughly [*gucha gucha*] there, when they return, their faces are lit up. Their hearts and minds have been cleansed. Shugyō invokes the inner wildness [yasei] of human beings. Although we must live in a society of economic transactions, it is also important if we can live in a different kind of place, one where you can come face-to-face with yourself and face-to-face with nature. I think it is good if we can have such a place.[23]

Itō-san speaks of shugyō through the agricultural metaphor of winter rice. It is stronger and more potent owing to its harsher conditions of gestation, which strip the comforts of greenhouse warmth and shelter away. Itō-san uses the onomatopoeia "*gucha gucha*," which means to cast into disarray, "to scramble," to describe the experience of shugyō. He then suggests that shugyō transforms people by "activating an inner wildness [yasei]," which is contrasted against an outer domestication by "a society of economic transactions."[24] Within the heterotopia of Dewa Sanzan, shugyō presents yamabushi an opportunity for personal transformation. In Hoshino-san's view, this transformation is also historical practice, a way of forging an "ancient spirit in the modern body," but for yamabushi such as Itō-san and Sato-san, it is more generally a noncapitalistic way of life.

Itō-san, who studied philosophy at the graduate level, is confident when he contributes his own voice to the spectrum of orographic perspectives giving meaning to Dewa Sanzan. To the NHK interviewer, Itō-san added:

When you look at nature, many different forms are visible. For example, the grass, the trees, and so on. Within nature, there is a birthing power [*umidasu chikara*] behind this. In spring, this power is revealed when the plants grow thick and quickly flourish. When this creative power becomes fixed, when it crystallizes, it becomes this tree, this wind, this soil, then it takes shape. This creative power itself is nature, not only its visible manifestations. . . . I think this birthing power of nature is also within a human being. It becomes expressed in art and other forms of creativity. There is a connection here. I wanted to keep thinking about something like this invisible nature. Where can one find a place or find a community to think about such a thing? Well, shugyō is a very suitable space for this. Around the same time that I was studying no-till agriculture, I was participating in a heritage preservation project focusing on *satoyama* [sustainable mountain villages]. I was thinking: there are so many ways to protect visible nature, but for invisible nature, for the spirit of nature itself, I do not think there are any preservation efforts. As a word, it sounds strange, but I'm talking about the preservation of a "spiritual ecology" [*seishin seitai*]. I decided to cultivate this kind of effort as my career, as my path in life. It could be a think tank that contributes to regional revitalization. I eventually decided to make a business. That is when I made my first appointment to meet Hoshino-san. That is when I became a yamabushi.

Sakamoto's perspective of shugyō differs from others. He is explicitly nonreligious. It is more existential, philosophical, and anthropological. He writes:

I don't believe at all that earnest prayer can lead to enlightenment, financial prosperity, or the fulfillment of wishes. Some aspects of being a yamabushi involve acquiring a type of supernatural power called "*genriki*" through intense shugyō. I have no interest in that either. However, when I enter the mountains, I feel invigorated. My body becomes lighter. When I witness the richness and harshness of nature, powerful emotions arise from deep within me, emotions that I don't even want to describe as mere "inspiration." Nature is mysterious. In my interactions with nature, I try to uncover the reason for my existence: "Why am I here?" I believe that the culture of yamabushi, descendants of primitive nature worship, still retains the essence of this relationship between humans and nature. By practicing as a yamabushi, I seek to understand what nature truly is and find clues about the meaning of life. This quest to understand the meaning of life is the reason I remain a yamabushi, despite my weak sense of religious faith.[25]

It's worth noting that even though Sakamoto states that he has no desire to acquire supernatural powers through shugyō and denies having a sense of religious faith, he does express belief in ancestral agency in guiding his actions. He writes, "It seems it wasn't by chance that I entered the world of the yamabushi. It was as if the ancient people were beckoning me."[26]

As Itō-san, Sato-san, Asumi-san, and Sakamoto indicate, shugyō has a strong countercultural element. Framed by Hoshino-san as "a way to cultivate an ancient spirit in the modern body," the significance of shugyō for

Hoshino-san's pupils is inclusive but broader than the "new return" to ancestral ways that he espouses. For them, it is countermodern and noncapitalist, a moral response to materialism and the industrial degradation of the environment. Sakamoto (2013, 15) states specifically, "For me, becoming a yamabushi means reinterpreting society through the culture of the yamabushi"—in other words, gaining a critical perspective of society through repeated experiences of shugyō. For Itō-san, shugyō is a means of "spiritual ecology," a way to honor and celebrate the reproductive power of nature, the power that, though unseen in winter months, as Asumi-san said, is pregnant in the Earth beneath the snow, preparing to give birth to nature's diverse forms every spring. Shugyō, through alpine affects, draws yamabushi into direct contact with this birthing power, this umidasu chikara, effecting a sense of rebirth in the body and an awakening of the spirit (tamashii).

Conclusion

Dewa Sanzan's relative proximity to larger metropolitan centers and its accessibility via transportation infrastructure puts it in the Goldilocks zone for urban retreats. Local yamabushi, such as Hoshino-san, the curators at the Ideha Cultural Museum, and other tourist businesses have been able to market the econostalgia of Dewa Sanzan through weekend shugyō that offer anachronistic experiences in the symbolic wombs of sacred mountains. The popularity of shugyō has prompted Hoshino-san to clarify his views of it and have led dedicated yamabushi to develop new perspectives of themselves and critical outlooks on society. One apparent contradiction in Hoshino-san's practice and discourse is his position on language. In an interview, Hoshino-san explained his philosophy of experiential truth: "People often ask me: 'What sort of shugyō do yamabushi do? What are the contents of shugyō? What activities do yamabushi do during shugyō? For me . . . an understanding of Shugendō can only be realized through the situation of shugyō. The meaning of shugyō cannot be truly understood in language!"

Even so, he has written two books on the subject, gives talks around the country to this day, and has been featured in domestic and foreign films. All his efforts seek to make sense of shugyō for modern people. The thread of his argument that I have emphasized here is how he frames shugyō as a method by which the bodies of modern people can connect with ancestral wisdom through the womb of the mountain, which helps contemporary yamabushi navigate the challenges of modern life by reviving their wildness and strengthening their spirits (tamashii).

Hoshino-san's philosophy of "living by feeling" (*kanjiru mama ni ikinasai*) is to accept one's own natural inclinations as opposed to constantly repressing them for the sake of social obligations. Being true to oneself enables contemporary yamabushi to pursue life with more joy. He emphasizes this point in many ways: "When you feel moved in a good way, it is because your tamashii feels something. So, keep doing the things that move you to live in alignment with your tamashii."[27] In this way, Hoshino-san's shugyō is a counter-structure release from the truly ascetic, self-denying strictures of capitalist modernity. For Hoshino-san, shugyō is the inversion of the "asceticism" of society. It is aimed at releasing one's inner wildness (yasei), not repressing it, out of social obligation. It is about freeing and strengthening one's tamashii (spirit), not oppressing it. For Hoshino-san, shugyō, its alpine affects, and religious heritage as expressed in ritual, renders the body multitemporal by awakening an ancient spiritual essence within.

Certainly, in medieval Shugendō, there were no such weekend yamabushi as there are today. Contemporary yamabushi who live in a metropolis such as Tokyo fit shugyō in their busy schedules when they get the chance. Even still, the mountains remain heterotopic spaces that yamabushi perceive as being outside society even though their trails are frequented by tourists. It's as close as one can get and that is good enough for them. Mountains are spaces in which yamabushi can experience spiritual renewal through an affective and bodily engagement with the spatialized past rendered as a womb. As Itō-san, Sato-san, Asumi-san, and Sakamoto illustrate, shugyō also helps young people to gain critical distance from society so that they can rethink their life course and reconsider their values. It's not merely nostalgic idealism or primitivism, though that may be a motivating factor at first.

Whereas the terrain of Dewa Sanzan is a temporal landscape, it also constitutes, as yamabushi testimonies clearly indicate, a gendered landscape. For many male yamabushi, shugyō is an encounter with a feminine nature. "She" appears for some as a maternal figure. The mountain and assembled structures of boulders within it are manifestations of her womb and her waterfalls are amniotic fluid. For other men, "she" is a sexual partner. Stepping on the soft forest floor is having sex with her, sacred hot springs are her vaginal fluid, and stairway gates and oval lakes are architectural and geological manifestations of her vagina. Alternatively, for an increasing number of female yamabushi, shugyō is experienced as bodily empowerment, an affirmation of their gendered communion with feminine nature. As the vital energies of the ground emanate, heat is felt in the womb. A woman's womb is a microcosm of the mountain's womb. Both are imbued with birthing power (umidasu chikara).[28]

Hoshino-san may be a "mountainlike man," yet he is only one (though very influential) voice of many who contribute to the orographic perspectivism of Dewa Sanzan. Yamabushi have their own perspectives in which the mountains are placeworlds beyond the self-estrangement and atheist religion of capitalist modernity. As Sato-san suggests and Asumi-san's story reflects, many people have reoriented their priorities in the wake of 3/11, unsubscribing from the postwar sentiment (as they see it) that material wealth is the key to happiness. They realize instead that there must be other paths that lead to a greater form of immaterial wealth. For the yamabushi I've met, Shugendō is such a way and Dewa Sanzan is an ideal place to practice it.[29]

4 The Buddha and the Kami
Mountain Politics and Historical Consciousness

・・

As Oki-san deposited some coins into a vending machine in the sunny hot spring lounge, he turned to me and asked, "What did you say the topic of your research was again?" He pushed a button, and an ice cream sandwich fell out of the dispenser. I did not know what to make of my research in this early phase of fieldwork, so my response to Oki-san's question was vague: "Um... contemporary Shugendō." He looked puzzled by my simple response and inquired further: "Temple-form (*tera-gata*) or Shrine-form (*jinja-gata*)?" He was asking whether I would focus on Buddhist-oriented or Shintō-oriented Shugendō. The way he phrased his question implied that the answer could only be one or the other, not both, though "both" is how I answered because both forms are practiced in Dewa Sanzan. "I see," he said with a subtle nod, as if I was missing something.

I have since come to understand his query as stemming from a fault in the bedrock of the yamabushi social world. Oki-san's either/or framing of the question hints at the religious politics of Dewa Sanzan. Practically, Oki-san's question indicates a scheduling conflict between Buddhist and Shintō institutions of Shugendō in Mount Haguro. Both groups simultaneously perform Autumn's Peak, the main, annual ascetic rite. The Buddhist version is held from August 24 to August 31, while the Shintō version is held from August 25 to September 1. Buddhist ascetics enter the mountain a day before and exit a day before Shintō yamabushi. During Autumn's Peak, ascetics from each group reside in either a temple or a shrine complex that are just a few hundred yards apart near the summit of Mount Haguro. Since the rite is synchronous for both groups, participants can participate in only one version per year. Loyalty is expected from new and existing members.

At a deeper level, Oki-san's question refers to a historic rift between these two institutions of Shugendō. Tracing the rift back approximately 150 years reveals the fault line from which it emerged. The Meiji Restoration of 1868 precipitated a cascade of societal reforms, including a crucial event in Japanese religious history when Shintō and Buddhism split from a former syncretic union, consequently dividing the Shugendō traditions of Mount Haguro into two rival organizations: Haguro Shugen Honshū (The Real Chapter of Haguro Shugendō), which is Buddhist-oriented, and Haguroha Koshugendō (The Ancient School of Haguro Shugendō), which is Shintō-oriented.[1]

In this chapter, I clarify the political dynamic between Buddhist and Shintō Shugendō in Mount Haguro as it stands today. Although the current divide between Buddhist and Shintō Shugendō in Mount Haguro can be traced back to an imperial edict issued at the beginning of the Meiji period when syncretic religions such as Shugendō were ordered to purge all Buddhist elements, this is only the most obvious source of the current schism. Underlying centuries of interaction between Buddhism, a religion imported from the Asian continent, and Shintō, the putative indigenous religion of the Japanese archipelago, is a historical disposition that shifts between nativist resistance to foreign culture and cosmopolitanism, the embrace and integration of foreign culture. The Meiji-era Shintōization of Shugendō in Mount Haguro signifies a breaking point of nativist ressentiment against prolonged Buddhist dominance in Japanese religious history more generally. The reversal of power in the Meiji period when Shintō was elevated in statecraft and Buddhism was persecuted has led to the current state of Buddhist ressentiment against Shintō dominance in Dewa Sanzan.

Ascetic Ressentiment

The notion of ressentiment that I draw on here derives from Nietzsche ([1887] 1989). Ressentiment is a potent affect that swells in the collective ethos of a people living in a prolonged state of political subjugation. The intergenerational animosity of the ruled, who feel themselves powerless against their rulers, is the common affect from which the subjugated class creates new moral values for themselves over time. These values oppose the ruling class, who epitomize immorality for the subjugated.[2]

Although ressentiment is reactive affect, not reactive action, it strengthens over time and across generations to motivate future action. Nietzsche described this as a kind of spiritual-political revolution and a societal shift in moral values, a "slave revolt." Didier Fassin (2013, 260) has reformulated the term *ressentiment* for anthropology, defining it as "a reaction to historical facts, which generate an anthropological condition. . . . It implies not primarily revenge but recognition. It signifies the impossibility to forget and the senselessness to forgive. The man of ressentiment may have been directly exposed to oppression and domination, or indirectly, through the narratives of his parents or grandparents."³ In other words, ressentiment is a state of historical alienation shaped by a power dynamic that is hierarchical, oppressive, and intergenerational, even over millennia.

I find it instructive to draw on Fassin's reformulation of ressentiment to understand the dynamic in present-day Mount Haguro between Buddhist-oriented and Shintō-oriented Shugendō, which reflects fundamental tensions in Japanese religious history. For example, since the introduction of Buddhism into the Japanese archipelago in the sixth century, it has been framed by nativists as foreign and contrasted against a shifting assemblage of indigenous religiosity.⁴ Nativist hostility toward Buddhism after its introduction to the people of the Japanese archipelago was quelled when the powerful Soga clan influenced emperors to adopt Buddhism and violently suppressed their nativist opponents through "a campaign of war and assassination" in the Asuka period (538–710 CE) (Hardacre 2017, 28).⁵ In the following centuries, syncretic movements such as Shugendō emerged. They combined Buddhism with forms of indigenous animism, shamanism, ancestral veneration, Daoism, and mountain worship.⁶ Despite the eventual prominence of Buddhism in Japan, nativist ressentiment against Buddhism as a foreign religion remained present for more than a millennium after its introduction.⁷ Contact with American traders in the 1850s prompted a societal crisis in Japan that led to a nativist cultural revolution, the Meiji Restoration of 1868, during which nativist ressentiment toward Buddhism peaked and a period of active Buddhist persecution ensued.⁸ Like a swirling eddy in the great river of time, the dynamic between Shintō and Buddhism in the Shugendō traditions of Mount Haguro is a localization of this history that persists in the present.

The ressentiment in Japanese religious history between Buddhism and Shintō is crucial to understanding contemporary Shugendō in Mount Haguro because both Buddhist-oriented and Shintō-oriented institutions of Shugendō claim to be the legitimate successors of this millennium-old mountain religion. Where Buddhist-oriented Shugendō was once the dominant power in Mount Haguro, Buddhist ascetics are institutionally disempowered under the hegemony of a Shintō religious order today owing to the events of the Meiji period. Their disempowerment has led contemporary Buddhist ascetics to express ressentiment toward the post-Meiji Shintō establishment of Dewa Sanzan. There are now competing narratives in the ascetic social world that seek to assert historical legitimacy.

To understand the political dynamics in Dewa Sanzan today, we must attend closely to ascetic historicities—socially constructed perspectives of the past that shape present-day relations.⁹ In this chapter, I draw on historical narratives told by both scholars and ascetics, as each offers distinct insights into the contemporary political dynamics of Dewa Sanzan. I show that the ongoing tension between "temple-form" and "shrine-form" Shugendō in Dewa Sanzan today is driven by ressentiment. This conflict reflects deeper patterns in Japanese religious history between nativist and cosmopolitan tendencies.

Historicities of Shugyō

There are many ways one can practice Shugendō, but the primary method is shugyō, as discussed in previous chapters. The most traditional form of shugyō in Dewa Sanzan is the Autumn's Peak rite at the end of August. Hoshino-san's three-day shugyō is less traditional but more publicly accessible. There are also private arrangements a person or a group seeking to do shugyō can make. Tourists and company vacation groups can arrange to do shugyō through the Ideha Cultural Museum or through local pilgrim's inns (shukubō). There are over thirty such shukubō around the base of Mount Haguro, all of which are now affiliated with the Dewa Sanzan Shrine. In past eras, shukubō operated in tandem with Buddhist temples, but since the separation orders of the Meiji period in 1872, they are all now linked with the Dewa Sanzan Shrine, which is Shintō. Shukubō are operated by resident yamabushi who have deep ancestral history in the Shugendō traditions of Mount Haguro. Hoshino-san's Daishōbō is one such shukubō.

During fieldwork, I was able to attend the Buddhist version of Autumn's Peak three times but did not partake in the Shintō version. This decision enabled me to gain rapport with Buddhist ascetics but presented a clear limitation in my understanding of the Shintō version of Autumn's Peak. I would encourage curious readers looking for a research project to consider studying the Shintō version of Autumn's Peak.

I tried to supplement this methodological limitation by participating in Hoshino-san's three-day shugyō program because he is a Shintō-oriented yamabushi affiliated with the shrine. As such, the shugyō he offers is a truncated form of the Shintō version of Autumn's Peak. It was my primary access to Shintō Shugendō in Dewa Sanzan. Hoshino-san has condensed what is normally an eight-day procession into a three-day formula. This has allowed him to host his three-day shugyō over a weekend, which has made it accessible to urban people with inflexible work commitments and has enabled him to transpose his ritual formula onto other sacred mountains in Japan and abroad (in Brazil, for instance) where he runs his shugyō program with the support of local teams.

I first interviewed Hoshino-san a few days following my first participant-observation experience of his three-day shugyō. I asked if it was a recent development. Unexpectedly, he responded with a long historical narrative. I quote it in full to reveal how he situates his practice within the complicated history of Dewa Sanzan:

> Until the Meiji period, what we would call the modern period, Shintō and Buddhism were united in *shinbutsu shūgō* [Buddhist-Shintō syncretism]. In the Meiji period, the government had many initiatives and policies to modernize society. To do that, the government made State Shintō and designated the emperor as a *kami* [a descendent of Amaterasu, the Sun goddess]. So then, in the first year of the Meiji period, the government initiated the separation of Shintō and Buddhism. It was not a simple transition. Since Shugendō was an ideal form of shinbutsu shūgō, the government decided they must destroy it to proceed.
>
> In Meiji 5 [1872], the "Shugendō prohibition" law was legislated.... The new government recognized that without quashing Shugendō, the separation of Buddhism and Shintō would not proceed. In Dewa Sanzan, this entailed that Shugendō had to take a purely Shintō form. Until this point, Buddhist influence was strong in Mount Haguro, especially through Tendai Buddhism. During the Meiji period, all civil servants were Shintō nationalists and scholars. Since it was a time of State Shintō, everyone was influenced by Shintō.
>
> In Meiji 6, the first Shintō priest was sent here. His name was Nishikawa Sugao.... He made Dewa Sanzan a place of totally Shintō gods. He received the notice in March to become Dewa Sanzan's main priest and he came in October. He went to Tokyo in between. There, he decided which places would be associated with which gods and then made it a place of Shintō gods.
>
> Nishikawa removed all the Buddhist statues around the mountains, but his *great aspect* is that he made concessions for the local mountain religious practices. Typically, in a mountain of Shintō gods, there is no shugyō, but he permitted it. He also kept Autumn's Peak and Winter's Peak *firmly intact*. In this way, he preserved Shugendō and shugyō. After the separation of Buddhism and Shintō, there was a movement to abolish Buddhism [*haibutsu kishaku*], but despite that, the Buddhist form of Shugendō remained at Shozen-in Temple and survived.

They also kept Autumn's Peak, which they still practice. So, on Mount Haguro today, on the same mountain, we have two Autumn's Peak rites. On the shrine side, the Shintō side, we practice it from August 25 to September 1. The Buddhist, temple side is from August 24 to August 31.

Regarding the question: "Why did I start my three-day shugyō?" The people who come to the mountains often ask about shugyō. "What is shugyō? What kind of shugyō do you do? What sort of things do you practice? What's it like?" Well, shugyō is fundamental to Shugendō, but you cannot know shugyō without experiencing it. Since I was asked so many times, I started to offer the yamabushi experience program. From a verbal explanation of shugyō, one cannot fully understand. So, when I was forty-five years old [in 1991], I started a program for the three-day shugyō. Because modern people do not have one week to spare for Autumn's Peak, I condensed it and made it compact.

There are a couple of interrelated points in Hoshino-san's historical narrative worth emphasizing. First is his representation of Buddhist persecution in Dewa Sanzan through the figure of Nishikawa Sugao. Although Hoshino-san acknowledges the removal of all Buddhist statues from Dewa Sanzan, his speech was quick and without emphasis, presented as a straight overview of historical facts. This was then followed by a verbally emphatic qualification: Nishikawa's "great aspect" of compromising with locals to keep Shugendō rituals such as Autumn's Peak and Winter's Peak "firmly intact." Hoshino-san, a yamabushi affiliated with the Dewa Sanzan Shrine, here asserts a fundamental continuity from pre-Meiji to modern Shugendō in Dewa Sanzan. His narrative represents a historical transition, not a historical rupture.

The second point is how he situates his three-day shugyō in this narrative of historical continuity by explaining how it is merely a condensed form of Autumn's Peak. Although Hoshino-san strings together historical facts in his narrative, he emphasizes continuity over rupture and situates his three-day shugyō in a millennium of history to demonstrate his own authenticity and that of his program. My question was, after all, about how "new" his shugyō was. His roundabout answer was that it is essentially as old as Autumn's Peak itself, though with modification.

Tullio Lobetti (2014, 113) attended the Shintō version of Autumn's Peak. He has observed Shintō historicity up close. He recounts one senior ascetic explaining to novices why Shintō-oriented Shugendō retains aspects of Buddhism in the Autumn's Peak rite. They instructed that it was to serve as a "reminder of the previous contamination of the practice by Buddhist influence."

Such politics, as I have observed among Buddhist ascetics, are ever present but subtle. As Lobetti notes: "It is not simple to obtain information about this, as the leaders seemed to be somewhat uncomfortable with the issue. They tried to explain the persistence of Buddhist terms in what was otherwise officially defined as a 'pure Shintō' practice as a way of preserving a certain degree of . . . continuity with the historical past and not create too deep a fissure within the history of Haguro Shugendō" (113).

As controversial as it may appear, this position suggests that the Meiji-era shrine officials were put in a quandary by their contradictory need by imperial edict to reform Shugendō in Shintō fashion while, at the same time, respect the allegiance that the local populace felt, and still feel, toward traditional Buddhist symbolism, language, and ritual. Gaynor Sekimori (2005b, 126–27), who has studied this schism more closely than anyone, writes:

> Haguro-san is still divided into Shintō and Buddhist factions, and the gap that emerged between them during the Meiji era remains deep. The priests of the Dewa Sanzan Shrine are educated at Shintō universities and trained at organizations like Meiji Jingu [in Tokyo], and they have no interest in bridging the gap between Shintō and Buddhism. The Buddhist *yamabushi* consider themselves the true inheritors of the Shugendō tradition and are not very concerned with the shrine's autumnal peak rituals. The former Shugendō practitioners, who have *shukubō* in Tōge, find themselves in a delicate position between the two. Although they belong to the shrine, they are aware that they bear the burden of the Haguro Shugendō tradition. However, fundamentally, it is unlikely that the severed threads of Haguro Shugendo will ever be woven back together into one.[10]

Curious to know more about Hoshino-san's relationship with Buddhist ascetics today, I asked him specifically about his connection with Shimazu-san, the daisendatsu, or leader, of Haguro Shugen Honshū. Hoshino-san replied:

> Shimazu-san was my classmate as a child. His parents [who led Haguro Shugen Honshū a generation ago] and their community of Buddhist ascetics were hostile toward the shrine, but Shimazu-san's generation is less so. As a yamabushi of the shrine, I want to have more of a relationship with Shozen-in Temple, but we do not really get together. Our current relationship is determined by history. It is not the shrine's fault, nor is it the temple's fault. That is why we do not discuss it. From my perspective, we are doing two Autumn's Peak rites simultaneously

on the same mountain and so this is still, in a way, a shinbutsu shūgō [Shintō-Buddhist syncretic] mountain, which is unique in Japan.

Hoshino-san's narrative is optimistic about the current relationship between the temple and the shrine as it compares to past generations. Yet it is ultimately fatalistic. For him, history is at fault for the current divide. The actions of contemporaries that reinforce the divide are inconsequential. History becomes a temporal scapegoat for unreconciled grievances in the community that have lingered across generations. It is easier to defer to the past, which is imagined as fixed and unchangeable, than to actively negotiate tensions in the community today that would challenge a polarized interpretation of the past. Although Hoshino-san expresses a clear understanding of the history of Shugendō with selective emphasis, he absolves the shrine of today from responsibility for the persecution of Buddhism through deference to history.

Historical Consciousness and Tourist Infrastructure

The selective emphasis of Hoshino-san's Shintō-oriented historical narrative is also pronounced in the Dewa Sanzan tourism industry. We can see this at the nearby Ideha Cultural Museum. A detailed display there outlines yamabushi practices and Shintō historicity. The centerpiece of the museum is a procession of mannequin yamabushi dressed in Shintō garments, modeling mountain entry during the Shintō version of Autumn's Peak. The display does not qualify that it is a specifically Shintō procession, as opposed to Buddhist, just that it is a procession of yamabushi for Autumn's Peak. Likewise, all other mascots and logos featuring yamabushi, such as the cookie packages, brochures, and train designs, are all Shintō yamabushi.[11] There is minimal reference to the existence of Buddhist Shugendō in Mount Haguro in any of these popular representations. Where mentioned, Buddhist Shugendō has been designated to the past tense. Even I was drawn into promoting Shintō historicity without realizing it.

In winter 2015, I requested translation assistance from the Ideha Cultural Museum. I had compiled a large collection of relevant newspaper articles and offered my services in exchange for their help. In return, they requested that I assist them in revising a rough English translation of all the Shintō place-names and explanations along the "stairway of rebirth" in Mount Haguro, which I did. When I returned in summer 2016 to conduct follow-up research, I found that all the translations I provided the museum were inscribed on wooden signs and posted before every significant site along the

2,446-stone-step stairway of Mount Haguro. Without knowing what the translation was to be used for, I had unintentionally assisted in translating and promoting Shintō historicity. Where cited on the signposts, the pre-Meiji Buddhist place-names and meanings are framed in the past tense, as if they were no longer relevant and Buddhist ascetics are no longer an active presence, which is untrue.

The place-making claims on the signposts strike me as a palimpsestic recalibration of Buddhist heritage in Mount Haguro. A man-made waterfall pouring into Exorcism River near the Falling-Descent-into-Hell Hill captures this sense of historical rupture. The wooden sign in front of the waterfall reads that from the 1650s to the 1870s, it "was" named Fudōdaki, the Waterfall of Fudō, a fierce avatar of Dainichi Nyorai, the Cosmic Buddha. In the 1870s, Nishikawa altered the name of this waterfall to Suga no Taki, in reference to a Shintō myth in which two gods felt refreshed on arriving in Suga. While doing fieldwork with Buddhist ascetics, I saw that they still refer to the site as Fudōdaki. Sites all the way up to the summit are framed as formerly Buddhist sites and have been placed into a constellation of Shintō mythology for visitors, Japanese and foreign.

How Shintō-oriented Shugendō has managed to exert so much influence in and around Dewa Sanzan despite the continued existence of Buddhist Shugendō was further revealed to me when I visited the Tsuruoka City office in August 2016. I sought only to acquire some statistical information about the tourist industry. When I inquired at the front desk, I was directed to the elevator and told to go to the fifth floor. When the elevator door opened, I was in the middle of a room of Tsuruoka City employees. All eyes glanced up and I was immediately escorted to a table by a window with a view. Green tea was served. Five employees sat around me, introducing themselves one after another with business cards. They were leaders of the tourism department.

Although they were willing to share information with me about the statistics of tourist visitation and their strategy to draw tourists, they were equally interested in my research. When I revealed that I was studying Shugendō and had participated in Hoshino-san's three-day shugyō as well as the Buddhist version of Autumn's Peak, four out of five of the people at the table revealed that they were senior yamabushi in Haguroha Koshugendō (Shintō-oriented Shugendō). In fact, on the back of their business cards was their yamabushi name and title with a picture of the shrine and a hora gai (conch trumpet). I even recognized one city official from a brochure where he was dressed in Shintō yamabushi attire before the five-storied pagoda. The relationship between the shrine, museum, and the municipal government, I then learned, extends much further than Hoshino-san. Shrine yamabushi are managing city funds for Dewa Sanzan tourism and have been doing so for decades.[12] Through such efforts, Shintō-oriented Shugendō has become a driving motif in the regionalism of the Shōnai area of Yamagata Prefecture.

In a subsequent interview with the curator of the Ideha Cultural Museum, I learned that the museum (established in 1991) was formed and is sustained through a joint funding arrangement between Dewa Sanzan Shrine and the city of Tsuruoka. It is no wonder, then, that the museum, the signposts, tourist brochures, and souvenirs are all Shintō-oriented. The separation orders of the 1870s transformed not just the religious organization of the mountain but also the entire community, its identity, and politics across generations.

Buddhist Ressentiment in Mount Haguro

Owing to the political dynamics in the community of Tōge, it was difficult to get Buddhist ascetics to speak candidly about their views of the shrine, Hoshino-san's three-day shugyō, or the activities of the museum. However, there were subtle expressions that emerged throughout fieldwork. Apart from the modern practice of Autumn's Peak and the conversations I have had with participating ascetics, yamabushi of Shozen-in Temple (headquarters of the Buddhist-oriented Haguro Shugen Honshū) facilitated a lecture series in cooperation with the Ideha Cultural Museum during my fieldwork.[13] Chōnan-san, the son-in-law of Shimazu-san (the daisendatsu and leader of Haguro Shugen Honshū) was the instructor. There is a clear personality and generational difference in style between him and his father in-law. Although very knowledgeable, Chōnan-san does not approach Shugendō in the same academic style as Shimazu-san. He includes humor and is a very dynamic, animated speaker. Chōnan-san's eight-part lecture series was called "Easy to Understand Haguro Shugendō." It was structured for broad public appeal.

Each lecture focused on a particular theme that demonstrated various aspects of Buddhist Shugendō in Mount Haguro, indirectly asserting the authenticity of Haguro Shugen Honshū. Chōnan-san spoke of the origins and pre-Meiji use of talismans (*ofuda*) in Dewa Sanzan. He described the structure of pilgrimage and mountain entry rites when the mountain was mostly constituted by Buddhist temples and lectured on Buddhist sutras and their significance in relation to the Buddhas of Dewa Sanzan. Chōnan-san's demonstrations encouraged participation from the audience, which led to the recitation of Buddhist sutras in spaces typically governed by Shintō

The Buddha and the Kami 117

Chōnan-san reminding laypeople about the Buddhist, pre-Meiji layout of Mount Haguro. Photograph by Shayne Dahl.

yamabushi while encouraging participation from the audience, many of whom were affiliated with the Dewa Sanzan Shrine.

Chōnan-san lectured in the museum and at different temples around Tōge. He also gave a tour of Tōge with a series of pre- and post-Meiji maps, encouraging his audience to imagine how it once was. I would characterize his efforts as a form of nostalgic place-making, "retrospective world-building" that involves "an adventitious fleshing out of historical materials" (Basso 1996, 5–6). The pre-Meiji Buddhist placeworld that Chōnan-san conjured for his audience presents a historical counterbalance to the signposting project of the museum in which the toponyms and histories of sacred sites in Mount Haguro were rendered in specifically Shintō terms. For his tour of Tōge, Chōnan-san guided attendees through the village, explaining how the layout of the mountain gradually changed from the 1600s until the Meiji period, when the separation orders permanently transformed Shugendō in Dewa Sanzan.

In one comment, which shocked his audience of people mostly affiliated with Dewa Sanzan Shrine, Chōnan-san asked, "Do you see the spot on the map where it says Niōmon (Gate of Buddhist Guardians)? After the Meiji period, it was moved to where it now stands and was renamed Zuishinmon (Gate of Shintō Deities). The original location of the Niōmon gate now serves as the site of the public toilets." The audience was visibly aghast, their expressions a mix of disbelief and dismay. Sensing their discomfort, he added with a confident tone: "I am sorry, but that is the truth!"[14]

The narrative Chōnan-san generally presents in his talks is one of decline, but it is also a clear declaration of the historical legitimacy of Haguro Shugen Honshū. As presented by Chōnan-san, Buddhist historicity is a narrative of persecution, of imagining what was once a great mountain of shinbutsu shūgō, Buddhist-Shintō syncretism, with temples all around and then comparing that nostalgic image with the present in which the absence of temples that were razed to the ground is felt as unjust. Public toilets where Niōmon once stood is symbolic of the entire situation, as many Buddhist ascetics see it. Chōnan-san's vision of the Meiji period is one of tumultuous change. His narrative is marked by a period of persecution against Buddhist-oriented Shugendō by Shintō nationalists, Buddhist decline, then postwar revival. Ultimately, it is a narrative of Buddhist continuity in Mount Haguro because the severity of persecution was unable to break Buddhist Shugendō, the original and legitimate Shugendō of Dewa Sanzan. It is a narrative of historical resilience and unreconciled injustice. This is more demonstrated through place-making and ritual performance than it is outwardly declared. The schism is so deep in the ascetic social world that it is difficult to speak about directly.

More than once, after the audience of Chōnan-san's "Easy to Understand Haguro Shugendō" lecture series left the museum, I have seen other Buddhist ascetics who reside in other areas throughout Japan chide Chōnan-san for his diplomacy. Instead, they urged him to be more forthright against the past persecution and continued suppression of Buddhist Shugendō in Dewa Sanzan. However, as the son-in-law of Shimazu-san and permanent resident of Tōge, he is obliged to maintain his diplomatic tact in addressing the schism. In one case, a visiting Buddhist ascetic condemned Shintō ascetics for walking past Koganedō, one of the main Buddhist temples in Mount Haguro, without paying their respects (that is, performing an *omairi*). Since Buddhist ascetics perform omairi at significant Shintō sites, it is disrespectful, he argued, that the gesture of goodwill is not reciprocated. In a subsequent lecture held in Koganedō, Chōnan-san raised the subject with the following comment:

> Many different ascetics come to Dewa Sanzan for pilgrimage. In modern times, they come by car or other means of transportation. However,

before modern vehicles, people came by foot. People used to do *omairi* [ritual observance] at Koganedō Temple here in Mount Haguro to begin their pilgrimage. Many still do, as they should. There might be people who think, "Oh, you are just saying this because you represent the temple," but Dewa Sanzan is a *seiiki* [sanctuary] and there are limited ways to enter the area.... I want you to know not only the history but also the continued spiritual significance of this temple called Koganedō.

Considering the context in which this comment was made, the tone in which he made it, and the comment of his Buddhist companion just weeks before, I interpret this statement as a veiled critique of Shintō ascetics and the Dewa Sanzan Shrine as an organization for refusing to perform omairi at Koganedō before or after Autumn's Peak or for pilgrimage. Refusing, in other words, to acknowledge the historical authority of the temple and its Buddhist heritage as a crucial entry point for pilgrimage in Dewa Sanzan.

The most direct expression of Buddhist ressentiment toward the Dewa Sanzan Shrine that I observed during fieldwork is on August 31, the final day of Autumn's Peak. After seven days of shugyō, Buddhist yamabushi depart Kōtakuji Temple near the summit of Mount Haguro and walk directly through the forest and across a road to the Dewa Sanzan Shrine. The ascetics ascend the ten steps, symbolizing the Ten Worlds of Buddhist cosmology, and squeeze together on the veranda before the main hall. There is usually a Shintō service underway with pilgrims dressed in white kneeling before the inner sanctum. Seeing the Buddhist ascetics gathered on the veranda, Shintō priests abruptly halt their service. Every year that I attended, I saw Hoshino-san kneeling just inside the entrance. He appeared to be waiting for the Buddhist procession. Buddhist ascetics would then take out their *shakujō*, a metal-ringed sistrum that clangs in rhythm with the recitation of sutras, and Buddhist ascetics would lead everyone into a series of chants with the Heart Sutra at its core. There was an intensity to the chanting on the veranda of Dewa Sanzan Shrine that was noticeably different from any previous *gongyō* session in Kōtakuji Temple. It was more aggressive. It sounded angry. This climactic moment, above all others in the annual ritual cycle in Dewa Sanzan, is where Buddhist ressentiment toward the Dewa Sanzan Shrine is put on clear public display. I recall seeing senior ascetics cupping their hands over their mouths to amplify their already loud chanting voices. There was fierceness in their eyes as they peered into the inner sanctum. This was the one moment in the year when Buddhist ascetics ascended the stairs of the Dewa Sanzan Shrine in a procession, announcing their continued existence on the mountain. Hoshino-san chanted along with Buddhist ascetics during the recitation of the Heart Sutra every year I attended. I interpret this as a modest reconciliatory gesture.

Anti-Western Resentment

So far, I have described Buddhist ressentiment toward Shintō-oriented Shugendō in Dewa Sanzan. Although there is a deep local history here, many Buddhist ascetics come from elsewhere in Japan. Those who are from elsewhere and have minimal commitments to Haguro Shugen Honshū outside of Autumn's Peak do not feel the same degree of ressentiment against the Shintō establishment as those who are more situated in the internal divisions and subjected to the contemporary politics of Dewa Sanzan. These less situated ascetics find value in both Buddhism and Shintō, like most religious people in Japan. Even still, they develop their own views of the local divide between Buddhism and Shintō in Dewa Sanzan, seeking to reconcile their commitments to Buddhist practice with their belief in Shintō.

Inserted in my Buddhist-oriented Autumn's Peak application package in 2015 was an anonymous letter written by someone from Iwate Prefecture who had joined the year before. It is interesting because it expresses nativist resentment not at Shintō but against the rising influence of Western civilization in Japan. A section reads:

> In recent years, Western values have spread throughout Japan. This presents a crisis in society because we are losing Japanese spirituality [*seishin sei*]. Where can we find the origin of this spirituality? In Shugendō, of course. Shugendō was crucial to the formation of our spirituality. In ancient times, Japanese people were living from the gifts of mountains, rivers, the ocean, and all forms of nature. We didn't divide between Buddha or kami. We lived in awe and fear of them but received sustenance with gratitude. Our respect for Buddha and the kami was embedded in daily life. Regional culture bloomed at this time through local performing arts, traditions, and so on, all of which embody Japanese spirituality. . . . It may not be written in our textbooks, but Shugendō has been a monumental influence in Japanese traditional culture for the arts. Before the Meiji period, Western countries such as Britain or America, among other countries with such fortitude, started to conquer Africa, Southeast Asia, and so on. Japan was left with no choice but to enter a confrontation with the

West. After the Meiji period, the Japanese government confronted these strong countries with Shintō as the national religion. To make State Shintō, they separated the Buddha and the kami and prohibited Shugendō by law. As a result, Shugendō was severely damaged. Yamabushi were forced to belong in either a shrine or a temple.

All over Japan, there was also a movement to persecute Buddhism [*haibutsu kishaku*]. Valuable treasures such as statues and temples and significant religious instruments were destroyed. Owing to State Shintō, Japan grew as an empire, but we ultimately lost World War II. State Shintō was then dismantled and here we are. Seventy years passed after the war and Japan grew and became the fastest-growing economy in the world. We have more than enough food, amenities, cars, nice homes, and so on, but I feel that at an inverse proportion, Japanese spirituality weakened. After postwar liberalism came egoism, individualism, indifference, and loneliness, leading to isolated deaths. Children and parents lose their patience and snap with violent aggression. Rationalism has made our relationships tasteless, bland, and automatic. For example, stepping into a convenience store, we see that the cashiers are programmed robots with a script. The sense of self-entitlement that people have now leads to monster parents who brazenly harass teachers for their and their children's shortcomings. There are people seeking small claims over petty incidents, most of which are their own fault. We have lost trust among ourselves and must depend on written and signed documents to take each other seriously. Business has become a matter of profit supremacy and the worship of money. There are also young thieves who scam the elderly by phone, and so on. These Western values have spread to Japan, and as a result we are losing the high spirituality we once had. Shugendō embodies the origin of our high spirituality. It represents the opposite of Western values. I will continue to participate in Autumn's Peak to go back to the origin of Japanese spirituality.

This letter expresses, not ressentiment (historical alienation) against Shintō, but resentment (ideological alienation) against Western values. Didier Fassin contrasts *ressentiment*, a French term, with its English correlate, "resentment," derived from Adam Smith's ([1759] 1976, 34–40) moral philosophy.[15] Fassin reworks Smith's framework of resentment to mean "ideological alienation." It is "a reaction to a relational situation which results from a sociological position" that "involves diffuse animosity and tends towards vindictiveness. It shifts its object of discontent from specific actors toward society at large . . . via imaginary projections" (Fassin 2013, 260).

The historicity presented in this letter begins like Hoshino-san's account. There is a vaguely described golden age in the pre-Meiji era where the Buddha and the kami, humans and nature, coexist in harmony and Shugendō's influence was evident in various traditional arts. This golden age overlooks the millennium of tension between the foreign Buddha and the indigenous kami that has existed since the introduction of Buddhism to the Japanese archipelago. In his narrative, Western imperialism encroaches on the world and Japan is positioned as a vanguard of Asian sovereignty, which in a mirror image to the West, sought increased influence through colonial expansion.

In my reading of this letter, "State Shintō" is not rendered as the determining agent in the abolition of Shugendō. Rather, it was the global encroachment of the West, which forced the reactionary and defensive emergence of State Shintō and its damaging policies (such as the kami-Buddha separation edict). In this letter, Japan's loss in World War II represents a succumbing to Western values, which has led to the corrosion of Japanese society. Where Hoshino-san treated history as a scapegoat for unfulfilled social obligations from the shrine to the temple in the Mount Haguro community, the author of this letter directs blame to the influx of Western values into Japan after World War II. Shugendō, as practiced in Dewa Sanzan, is imagined to be resistant to "Western values" and is therefore essential to the preservation of the "high spirituality" of ancient Japan, which is continuous in both Shintō and Buddhist forms. The author speaks of a common "we" from the imagined golden age to the present, which is characteristic of *nihonjinron* discourse (nationalistic theories of Japanese ethnicity and identity).[16] The internal ressentiment (historical alienation) between Buddhist and Shintō ascetics in Dewa Sanzan today, therefore, is omitted in the narrative and replaced with ressentiment (ideological alienation) against a common nemesis—namely, the West.

A senior Buddhist ascetic I met in Autumn's Peak also expressed ressentiment against the West as opposed to ressentiment against Shintō. He introduced himself to me as a guide of the Shikoku pilgrimage. He did not historicize his anti-Western resentment but clearly expressed it. Many times, he would tell me how Western tourists have completely overrun the Shikoku pilgrimage trail in recent years. He attributed the problem to the distribution of Shikoku pilgrimage brochures to pilgrims and tourists on the Camino de Santiago pilgrimage in Spain.[17] Without understanding how to arrange their accommodations, he alleged, Westerners attempting the Shikoku pilgrimage would sleep on toddler changing tables in bathroom stalls, use the side of the road instead of washroom facilities, and disregard necessary customs and etiquette along the way. All in all, he said, the sacred journey was becoming a sightseeing adventure, and it was polluting the path.

Buddhist ascetics in Dewa Sanzan express ressentiment as historical alienation against the Dewa Sanzan Shrine to varying degrees, but some clearly express resentment as ideological alienation against the West as they interpret it and the capitalist modernity it introduced to Japan. In emphasizing the clash of Japanese traditional values with Western values, such narratives redirect internal tensions of Mount Haguro outward to a less proximal target.

Critical views of Shintō Shugendō in Dewa Sanzan and capitalist modernity converge for some Buddhist ascetics who disapprove of Hoshino-san's three-day shugyō. They see it as a tourist outfit. Over a cup of green tea during the Buddhist version of Autumn's Peak, I observed a group of Buddhist ascetics speaking about the modern scene in Dewa Sanzan. Hoshino-san's three-day shugyō came up. One senior ascetic expressed his view in the form of a circuitous critique. He said, "Shugyō is only Shugendō if it has a 'way' (dō). Without that, it becomes something else. Those who practice shugyō without a 'way' are not practicing Shugendō." In a twist of irony, Hoshino-san would go on to form a company called Yamabushidō (Way of the Mountain Ascetic) designed for higher-end clients from other countries.

The Politics of Shugendō Scholarship

In an ethnographic account of the political dynamic of Mount Haguro, Andreas Riessland (2000, 194) describes Dewa Sanzan Shrine as a "thriving religious enterprise" with a "well-functioning publicity machine" that strives to make Mount Haguro a more attractive destination for tourists and pilgrims. One method to achieve this goal has been to grant filmmakers, documentarians, and scholars access to their religious ceremonies and events. Riessland argues that this active public relations campaign has been designed, in part, to legitimize the authenticity of Haguroha Koshugendō as the destined successors of Shugendō in Dewa Sanzan. At the time of Riessland's research, Buddhist leaders of Haguro Shugen Honshū described this public relations campaign as "profanity." They were also strongly opposed to a road construction project endorsed by Haguroha Koshugendō that would cut right across the path leading from Kōtakuji Temple to the summit of Mount Haguro. Ascetics now cross this road during Autumn's Peak with sendatsu as crossing guards to prevent accidents with tour buses.

Although professional and diplomatic, Haguro Shugen Honshū's response to the shrine's public relations has involved strategic engagement with academia, using it (especially history of religions) as a medium to educate the public about its historical authority in Mount Haguro. Carmen Blacker ([1975] 1999, 2000a), H. Byron Earhart (1965, 1970), and Miyake Hitoshi (2000, 2001, 2005) were among the first scholars of a select group permitted to partake in and partially document Autumn's Peak. Although it remains locally eclipsed by Haguroha Koshugendō, a growing amount of scholarship has been dedicated not only to understanding Haguro Shugen Honshū's legacy in Dewa Sanzan but to establishing this history internationally. In 2005, Shimazu Kokai, the daisendatsu and leader of Haguro Shugen Honshū, collaborated with Kitamura Minao in editing an influential Japanese-language volume on the history and philosophy of Haguro Shugen Honshū entitled *A Thousand Years of the Haguro Shugen Yamabushi* (Shimazu and Kitamura 2005). Kitamura (2009) also filmed the Buddhist Autumn's Peak for the first time in history and released an ethnographic film entitled *The Autumn Peak of Haguro Shugendō*. In addition to the film, he produced an album containing audio recordings of all the sutra and mantra recitations practiced in the rite, which is accompanied by a booklet, *Haguro Shugen: A Liturgical and Sound Cosmos*, that details the philosophical meanings of Haguro Shugen liturgy (*gongyō*).

The rapid increase in Buddhist-oriented Haguro Shugen Honshū–approved academic publications and multimedia documentations since the 1960s seems to reflect an effort to reestablish the historical, religious, and political legitimacy of Buddhist-oriented Haguro Shugen Honshū. This makes sense considering the more visible and economically prominent domestic public relations campaign of Shintō-oriented Haguroha Koshugendō. In an essay included in *A Thousand Years of the Haguro Shugen Yamabushi*, edited by the daisendatsu himself, Japanese religions scholar Gaynor Sekimori writes:

> At first glance, there does not seem to be a significant difference between the Buddhist-style Autumn's Peak and the Shintō-style Autumn's Peak. However, the Shintō rituals are merely adaptations of the former Sanzan liturgy and the opening mountain hymns into Shintō form. The rituals performed by Kōtakuji Temple and the worship ceremonies conducted by the shrine are entirely different. By eliminating Buddhist elements, the shrine's Autumn Peak has lost much of its original symbolic expressions and dramatic structure. . . . There are criticisms [within the Buddhist community of Mount Haguro] that the Dewa Sanzan Shrine is only using Shugendō to attract tourists. When comparing the *saitōgoma*

[fire ceremony] performed by the shrine and Kōtakuji Temple, for instance, the shrine's saitōgoma has changed to focus on visual appeal and general popularity, while the rituals at Kōtakuji Temple retain their original mysticism and secrecy.[18]

The battle for legitimacy and the politics of authenticity between these rival sects through academia and multimedia puts domestic and international researchers in a delicate position because simple research decisions—for instance, on which side of the dynamic to study, to refer back to Oki-san's question at the beginning of this chapter—have deeply political and ethical consequences in the yamabushi community. As Riessland (2000, 200) observed: "With my participation in the Autumn's Peak, I have become located in the local competitive environment."

Aspiring yamabushi must choose between Buddhist and Shintō versions of Autumn's Peak because they occur at the same time and because it is the most essential rite for yamabushi in Dewa Sanzan. Autumn's Peak confers membership, bestows yamabushi names, and elevates status in the hierarchy of ascetic sociopolitical organization.[19] Outsiders who first encounter the "secret world" (*himitsu no sekai*) of Shugendō these days are often unaware that Buddhist-oriented Shugendō even exists in Dewa Sanzan. This is because Haguro Shugen Honshū keeps a low profile despite academic collaborations.

Most first-time yamabushi whom I have met presume that the Autumn's Peak offered through the shrine is the only venue in Dewa Sanzan. Buddhist-oriented Haguro Shugen Honshū has no website, no advertisements, and until very recently, a near-total absence in popular media. Reputable scholarly books have been written about Haguro Shugen Honshū, as mentioned, but unless one is a skilled researcher or has visited Dewa Sanzan before and spoken to other yamabushi, Haguro Shugen Honshū is difficult to track down. Initiates are accepted by invite-only. One must know and be trusted by a member to become one. Even then, resumes are vetted. I was extremely lucky to gain access.

The initiates that I have met over the course of fieldwork tend to enter the political dynamic between Buddhist and Shintō Shugendō with minimal bias, but those who are committed gradually find that political neutrality on the mountain is tenable only in naivete. Loyalty is expected. The unspoken but pervasive tension between the two groups, whose headquarters are a few hundred yards apart in a small community, is so contentious that one could risk damaging their relationship with both if they did not remain loyal to one.

My answer to Oki-san, that I would study both "temple-form" and "shrine-form," was, in retrospect, very naive. I had presumed I could study both because the shugyō that we attended under Hoshino-san's guidance operates in affiliation with Dewa Sanzan Shrine and I was already registered for Autumn's Peak with Haguro Shugen Honshū at Shozen-in Temple. At this early stage of research, the politics were unknown to me. When I returned to conduct the main period of fieldwork from August 2014 to December 2015, I had thought that living in the nearby city of Tsuruoka rather than in the community of Tōge would help me retain neutrality between the temple and the shrine; however, weaving between each group to broaden the scope of my research subjected me to competing suspicions from members of both sides about what my true intentions were and with whom I sided. As an anthropologist, I understand myself as a relativist seeking a good balance of information from every angle.

Near the final weeks of fieldwork, my relativism began to make me feel as though I was a double agent in a century-and-a-half-long cold war. Yamabushi from each side inquired indirectly, through their members, if I was spying for the other. At one point, near the final week of research, I requested a last interview with Chōnan-san. He initially refused because he was suspicious of me owing to my growing association with Hoshino-san. Only by clarifying that I was not a devotee of Hoshino-san, that I was only studying his representations of Shugendō, was I able to retain rapport with the Buddhists.

Conclusion

Allan Grapard (1994, 373–74) writes that "to understand what counts as 'sacred' space in Japan, we must attend to the social relations of power that delineate and contest the boundaries of the sacred." The contemporary sanctity of Dewa Sanzan is a result of centuries of conflict, revolution, and resistance. The historical negotiation of power relations in Mount Haguro specifically between Buddhist and Shintō institutions of Shugendō is, as my account demonstrates, ongoing. "The burden of the past," as Michael Lambek (2002, 9) notes, "is not a dead weight." It is an active force in the yamabushi present.

In this chapter, I have revealed the political dynamics that shape historical consciousness in Mount Haguro, showing how rival Shugendō institutions selectively emphasize certain histories to legitimize their authority in the present. The Dewa Sanzan Shrine and affiliated Shintō yamabushi frame the Meiji period as a time of tumultuous transition but with the fundamental continuity and superiority of Haguroha Koshugendō, whereas Buddhist ascetics see Shintō-oriented Shugendō as an attempted rupture that failed to obstruct the fundamental continuity and superiority of Haguro Shugen Honshū. From either perspective, the political history of Mount Haguro is and has long been fractured by ressentiment (historical alienation).

The diplomatic response of contemporary ascetics on both sides who interpret the coexistence of Buddhist and Shintō Shugendō in Mount Haguro as a modern form of syncretism (shinbutsu shūgō) despite the historical divide is an idealistic view, a story that ascetics tell themselves about themselves to hold their community together. Reconciliatory gestures have been made, and continue to be made, by ascetics on both sides of the divide. Despite the politic dynamics in Dewa Sanzan, these practitioners share a deep appreciation for the mixed heritage of Shugendō—a millennium-old, nature-based, and animistic religion that expresses strong themes of spiritual rebirth and existential awakening.

5 Autumn's Peak
Buddhist Temporality and Ascetic Ethics

On the final day of Autumn's Peak, our group of seventy or so ascetics (*gyōja*), fully adorned in the attire of the Haguro Shugen Honshū, walked in a flag-bearing, conch-sounding procession through a forest of tall cedars to the summit of Mount Haguro. For the past week, we had been staying in Kōtakuji Temple, a mile or so away, undertaking *shugyō* associated with the Ten Worlds cosmology of Buddhism.

Crossing a muddy trail, we soon entered the training grounds of Shintō yamabushi who were nearing the end of their Autumn's Peak. Their space was marked by a *shimenawa* rope with several *shide*, zigzag-folded white paper, dangling from it. More than 150 of these uniformly white-clad Shintō yamabushi were lined up on either side of the path, clapping with congratulatory smiles as we approached. Some Buddhist ascetics of lower rank bowed to friends on the Shintō side with a smile. I remember seeing Sakamoto Daizaburo, author of the books I've been citing, nestled in with others on the Shintō side. Their faces and clothes, like ours, were stained with a week's worth of sweat and dirt, creating a sense of solidarity. The daisendatsu and other high-ranking Buddhist ascetics maintained their focus on the path ahead, offering only subtle acknowledgment as we passed through Shintō space. The divide was clear.

Bellowing out Buddhist declarations of repentance (from desire and the illusions produced by the senses), we marched across a large, paved parking lot lined with souvenir shops and food stalls with affecting aromas. Tourists paused in their tracks to observe and take photos. Some already had their tripods set up, waiting. Before long, we were standing at the foot of Dewa Sanzan Shrine on the summit of Mount Haguro, which was called Jakkōji (Light of Wisdom Temple) before the Meiji period. We ascended the ten stairs of the staircase, which correspond with the ten worlds of Buddhist cosmology, and squeezed together on the veranda before the main hall. A Shintō service was underway, with pilgrims dressed in white kneeling before the inner sanctum, but the priests abruptly halted their service when

A yamabushi leaps over fire to complete Autumn's Peak, symbolizing the first bath after rebirth (*basaitō*). Photograph by Shayne Dahl.

we arrived—a Buddhist irruption from the past. Kneeling just inside the entrance was Hoshino-san. He seemed to have anticipated our arrival. He was dressed in a business suit, not his usual Shintō attire.

After running through a sequence of sutra recitations, we descended the stairs and kneeled on the ground before the shrine. Tourists gathered, snapping photos and watching curiously. In medieval speech, the *dōshi*, a heavyset ascetic from Aomori Prefecture who facilitated ceremonies throughout Autumn's Peak in his gritty baritone voice, spoke with our cued response:

"Ascetics!"

"Uketamau!" [We receive!]

"As I have said before, this place is the sacred peak where the strictest secrecy is maintained. You may under no circumstances speak of it to outsiders after you return to the ordinary world. It is strictly forbidden to speak of it to parents, children, brothers, wives, or friends."

"Uketamau!"

"Should you do so, immediately you will fall under the curse of the founder. Therefore, make your pledge of silence by striking this gong."

"Uketamau!"[1]

One by one, each ascetic tapped a small gong with a wooden hammer and bowed. After everyone struck the gong, committing to secrecy, the daisendatsu then declared the completion of Autumn's Peak: "You are now reborn!" At once and with vigor, everyone jumped up, belted out a loud, climactic "birth cry" (*ubugoe*) accompanied by the blasting melody of the conch trumpet. With a sudden burst of energy, everyone then sprinted down the stairway of rebirth. The rapid tap of *jikka tabi* (split-toe boots) descending the stairs sounded like the patter of raindrops I had listened to as I fell asleep the night before and that made the stairway very slippery. I remember one older ascetic slipping on a step and cracking his forehead on the stone surface. I stopped to help, but he insisted on getting up and continuing his descent despite the purpling lump on his forehead. I soon found myself near a small group of ascetics calling out "*Nya! Nya!*" imitating the sound of babies crying and laughing about it all the way down.

Like other ascetics in front of me and behind, I sprinted out of the gate, the Zuishinmon that used to be a Niōmon. When I burst through the gate, I was immediately startled by a barrage of camera flashes. A crowd of photographers and journalists were waiting to capture our annual moment of rebirth. Some ascetics were already being interviewed before large cameras and handheld microphones. I heard them remark over heavy breath how grateful they were for having the opportunity to participate and for being able to complete it owing to "the aid of the Buddha and the *kami*." Others mentioned how they expected their business to improve "by the power of the Buddha." Ironically, some ascetics used their round bamboo hat (*ayaigasa*), which symbolizes a placental shield in the "cosmic womb" of the mountain, to shield their faces from being photographed.[2]

After everyone exited the gate, we gathered once again into a linear procession and made our way to Shozen-in Temple, where Autumn's Peak had begun eight days earlier. A fire was set outside of the temple gate, and we all leapt over it as "the first bath" (*basaitō*) following rebirth. The same ascetic who was laughing at his own birth cries all the way down tripped on a loose pantaloon string after jumping over the fire and scraped his knee bloody on the pavement. Then he stood up and laughed it off just like the guy with the lump on his head. The bliss of completing Autumn's Peak seemed to make ascetics impervious to pain. A carnival of flashing neon lights was set up around the temple with popcorn, french fries, and bean paste snacks for sale, and there were prize games for the children of Tōge. The community was celebrating our return.

We entered the temple. Each of us received a talisman (*ofuda*) certifying completion of Autumn's Peak and our advancement in ascetic rank. After we returned the garments to the temple, an ascetic I met invited me to accompany him to a hot spring resort on the summit of the mountain for a public bath and ice cream. After a week without bathing, despite clambering up and slipping down muddy slopes in the rain, and a vegetarian diet without dessert, this sounded perfect. We hopped into his black BMW with its nice leather interior and drove up to the summit we had just descended by foot for a hot soak.

For Shintō ascetics, Autumn's Peak is one of several significant rites throughout the year.[3] However, for Buddhist ascetics, who restored Haguro Shugen Honshū after a seventy-four-year hiatus (1872–1946) and who do not condone "yamabushi experience" retreats facilitated through the museum, it is the main practice of the year. In both groups, people with diverse backgrounds come from all over Japan and the world to participate. This includes civil servants, academics, tradespeople, retirees, salarymen, farmers, illustrators, artists, environmental and antinuclear activists, voice actors, martial arts competitors, and many others. Few Buddhist ascetics are local. The Autumn's Peak of the Dewa Sanzan Shrine, to the contrary, has mostly local members, including employees of the municipal government. The Autumn's Peak of the shrine is interwoven into the fabric of the regional identity of Shōnai, whereas the Autumn's Peak of the temple is situated in a national network of Buddhists, lay and ordained. I participated three times (2013–15) in the Buddhist version of Autumn's Peak but, regretfully, did not join the shrine version. The rivalry between the two groups would have made it difficult for me as a resident researcher to move freely between them: I would have lost the trust of both had I not committed to one.

The vignette that opens this chapter is a partial description of the concluding rituals of the Buddhist version of Autumn's Peak. It illuminates the transitional period between the counter-structure of the rite and the synthesis following its completion, which is a rebirth less into Buddhist awakening and more into capitalist modernity. This is made evident by the camera flashes, the festival around the temple, and a BMW ride to the summit. The death and rebirth symbolism of Autumn's Peak appears to me as a ritualized suspension of and rebirth into capitalist modernity.

In the Buddhist context, this temporal shift is engendered through medieval Buddhist ritualism and language, which stands in sharp contrast to Shintō ritual and historicity. While the spatiotemporality of Autumn's Peak is revealing of the ways in which Mount Haguro hosts competing modes of historical consciousness stemming from a Buddhist and Shintō divide, moral tension has also emerged within Buddhist Autumn's Peak. This tension reveals the struggle Haguro Shugen Honshū is having to preserve tradition and resist the exploitative tendencies of capitalist modernity.

In this chapter I demonstrate how the Buddhist approach to Shugendō expresses resistance to aspects of capitalist modernity that, by contrast, Hoshino-san and Dewa Sanzan Shrine have embraced. I also attend to the ethics that such resistance produces. To aid my analysis of the moral tensions in contemporary Autumn's Peak, I draw on the notion of *phronesis*, the "continuous exercise of [moral] judgment to find the right balance of virtue between two extremes which would be vices under the circumstances."[4] Michael Lambek (1997, 140) writes that "*phronesis* describes how we make our way, exercising moral judgement, doing or trying to do the right thing." Laura Bear (2016, 494) has extended anthropological approaches of phronesis to consider its temporal implications. In her paradigm, phronesis is "an ethics of right action that contains . . . what time is and what it should be used for. We anticipate the future on the basis of both learned experience and ethical representations of the past and future that found our sense of agency. Our phronesis is experienced as personal discernment, aesthetics, and duties of care. It takes the form of an explicit working on yourself, the world, and social relations."

Autumn's Peak offers ascetic participants a rare opportunity to enter an intense but temporary period of medieval Buddhist space-time. Buddhist shugyō empowers individuals by permitting them "to refill time with symbolism and to regain agency" (Bear 2016, 496). Buddhist shugyō involves "personal discernment" and "duties of care" for the knowledge one gains, especially to resist the temptation to capitalize on that knowledge outside of shugyō. Through an ongoing negotiation that requires a continuous exercise of judgment (that is, phronesis) between temple elites and lay practitioners about the proper intent and responsibility of shugyō, I suggest that Autumn's Peak represents ascetic phronesis in Buddhist space-time. The ritual shows participants how to be responsible ascetics in modern times, how to find moral equilibrium between traditional Shugendō values while living in capitalist modernity.[5]

In what follows, I look beyond the historical politics of Mount Haguro and more closely at the content and ethics of contemporary practice that have emerged in Buddhist-oriented Autumn's Peak—in other words, how ascetic ethics arise as a reaction to capitalist modernity and its temptations. I demonstrate how the Autumn's Peak of today presents material and ritual forms of Buddhist space-time. Like Hoshino-san's practice, the "counter-structure" duration of the rite is rooted in the past, but as we see, it is a Buddhist past that is invigorated in the present, not a Shintō past. Although there are syncretic elements that integrate kami worship in Buddhist-oriented Shugendō, rituals are rooted in Tendai Buddhism. The ethics of participation are also remarkably different, signaling a tension between capitalist modernity, traditional values, and temple loyalty. Ascetic phronesis in Buddhist-oriented Shugendō, a moral balance between tradition and modernity, emerges vis-à-vis the activities of Shintō Shugendō, past incidents of capitalist exploitations, and other public promotions of Shugendō ritual.

Rethinking Rebirth

The ritual structure of Autumn's Peak is based on the Ten Worlds Practice (*jukkai shugyō*) of medieval Buddhism in which the ten realms of Buddhist cosmology are ritualized as mountain austerities. In Haguro Shugen Honshū, the Hell Realm (*jigokudō*) is enacted through inhaling and choking on acrid smoke produced by chili pepper powder (like *nanban ibushi* described in chapter 2, but in a Buddhist ritual context). The Realm of Hungry Ghosts (*gakidō*) is practiced through fasting and speed eating. The Beast Realm (*chikushōdō*) is emulated by abstaining from bathing and oral hygiene. The Warring Spirits Realm (*shuradō*) is realized through a "forest goblin sumō" (*tenguzumō*) tournament. The Realm of Humanity (*ningen*) is expressed through the repentance of illusion and impurities through a *saitōgoma* fire ritual. Last, the Realm of Heavenly Beings (*tenjō*) takes shape as a pilgrimage to a secret area deep in the Gassan range. The four stages of Buddhahood are not included in modern practice. Emphasis is placed on the first six worlds (*rokudō*), which are subject to karmic rebirth.

The daisendatsu was very clear with me in an interview that it is a mistake to think of the realms as entirely self-contained:

> Everything is related. There are realms of hell, hungry ghosts, beasts, warring spirits, humanity, and divine beings. These are the six worlds or stages before Buddhahood. They are not totally self-contained or independent. All realms are intertwined and overlapping. For instance, during nanban ibushi, you are smoked out. It's a hard practice, right? It's associated with the Hell Realm. But everything you find difficult can be a kind of suffering. It could constitute Hell and Hungry Ghost Realms simultaneously. We divide the shugyō into worlds to facilitate

understanding and explanation, but they do not make sense if they are not interpreted as a whole. They overlap. It is not like climbing steps one by one. . . . Everything is presented in a mixed form.

Although the daisendatsu and other senior ascetics worked hard to help me comprehend what the six worlds really represent, it took years and some difficult personal life experiences for me to understand. Yes, the six worlds are featured in the rituals of Autumn's Peak. Yes, they are an aspect of Buddhist cosmology and soteriology. But why? I used to think of them exclusively as realms a person may be reincarnated into depending on their karma in this life. For example, that a person with bad karma would be incarnated in the next life in a lower level and a person with mostly good karma would be incarnated as a human or a heavenly being. This is a true reflection of Buddhist beliefs when it comes to reincarnation, but Autumn's Peak offers a more immediate and existential perspective on the six worlds.

The daisendatsu and other ascetics have impressed upon me over the years that the six worlds are not just destinations in the cycle of rebirth but universal aspects of the human condition reflected in our experience of life. Have you ever suffered? Then you have experienced Hell. Have you ever felt desperate? Then you have experienced the Hungry Ghost Realm. Have you ever been in a conflict? Then you have experienced the Warring Spirits Realm. This is what ascetics mean when they say: "Shugyō is life itself." From this perspective, shugyō is a ritual simulation of the different dimensions of the human condition. Ultimately, as the daisendatsu explained, all the dimensions mix and collapse into one another. In a single day, you may pass through several worlds. Shifting between them is a kind of reincarnation. Until one attains Buddhahood, a deep realization of the nondualistic nature of reality, our lives phase in and out of the six worlds. Participating in Autumn's Peak raises awareness of how ascetics' lives, as with all lives, are stuck in the six worlds and how, with proper practice, they can be liberated from these illusionary realms. By participating in Autumn's Peak, ascetics not only deepen their insight into different dimensions of the human condition but also engage with reality through the lens of Esoteric Buddhist cosmology.

Autumn's Peak begins with a funeral and then the symbolic conception at Koganedō. A *bonten* pole topped with white *shide* is handled by the daisendatsu, who swirls it and then throws it down onto the steps of the temple. On his back is a portable wooden altar (*oi*) representing a womb. He is wearing a conical hat (*ayaigasa*) that symbolizes the placenta. Swirling and throwing the bonten down onto the entrance of Koganedō is said to emulate the erotic movements of Izanagi's "spear" in the creation myth of Japan discussed in chapter 2 (Earhart 1970, 115). Ascetics then enter the mountain to perform the Ten Worlds shugyō with emphasis on the six realms. This represents their embryological gestation (Sekimori 2016). The embryological symbolism is explicit in many of the rituals. In one instance, three fans (*uchiwa*) are fitted together into a circle and placed on the ceiling of the temple in the main hall. Streamers are placed in the center of the fan circle that extend to the floor. This represents a placenta and an umbilical cord in the womb of the temple. Ascetics are embryos gestating through shugyō.[6] Liberation from the six realms is emulated through a conclusive sprint down the Stairway of Rebirth with a birth cry (ubugoe).

The death-gestation-rebirth aspect of Autumn's Peak aligns with the three-part model of ritual discussed in chapter 2, but also with Eliadean ([1964] 2004, 64–66) descriptions of shamanistic initiation through death, resurrection, and obtaining shamanic powers. Historically, ascetics are known to use the power they have gained in the precincts of sacred mountains through shugyō in religious services for their sponsors. Patrons seek to benefit from the spiritual merit of the ascetics. In return, patrons sponsor ascetics' religious activities. The fact that ascetics use the power gained through shugyō to aid supporters with magical rites related to healing or curating good fortune draws Shugendō into the orbit of shamanism, especially when considering more esoteric practices such as spirit possession and exorcism. Miyake Hitoshi (2001, 131–42) considers ascetics as comparable to shamans because both are poised between humanity and spiritual dimensions. Where the otherworld of shamanism is accessed through "techniques of ecstasy," the otherworld of the Shugendō ascetic is the sanctuary of the sacred mountain. Like shamans, ascetics draw power from the otherworld in the service of their communities. They are liminal beings. Half here, half "there."

In the contemporary ritual of Autumn's Peak there is also, as I noted in Hoshino-san's practice, a sense of laterality, of matters from the secular world slipping into the sacred world throughout the rite.[7] Friendships and rivalries form between ascetics, and jokes are told about recent happenings in pop culture. Incriminating rumors about ascetics in other Shugendō mountains are sometimes spread. It is as intensely religious an experience as it is intensely social, but relations are structured through a temple hierarchy based on seniority and rank.

Tullio Lobetti (2014, 103) argues that the religious experience of Autumn's Peak, the sense of symbolic death, gestation, and rebirth it produces on completion, is a consequence of temporary spatial dislocation, a "loss" of self through exhaustion, and "gain" of power from the bodily affects of emplaced practice (106). Lobetti's interlocutors, as with mine, describe a "discarding" (*suteru*) and "forgetting" (*wasureru*) of the modern self during shugyō as one gradually draws attention away from ruminating thoughts and toward the cultivation of willpower and bodily effort: "I was thinking only about walking and nothing else," explained one of the ascetics he interviewed. "It was like I was dead" (106). And yet the spatial dislocation of being in a beautiful mountain with a community of ascetics for a time is revitalizing and produces a sense of gain. Lobetti argues that these interpretations of shugyō reflect the union of "bodily hermeneutics" and "doctrinal hermeneutics" expressed in a sense of death, gestation, and rebirth: "As the relationship between the two . . . hermeneutical dimensions is dialogical by nature, it is thus complex to determine which one is influencing the other the most. Furthermore, the ways in which individual practitioners conceptualize the practices are also very personal and it would be impossible to trace a complete map of these relations as well as define univocal directions of influence" (108).

The space of Dewa Sanzan is inseparable from its time. The mountainscape is also a timescape. If shugyō is a spatial dislocation, it is also temporal dislocation. The death-conception-gestation-rebirth structure of Autumn's Peak has, in all prior studies of Shugendō in Dewa Sanzan, been explored in terms of Buddhist cosmology and doctrine. In this chapter, I consider the spatiotemporal aspects of ritual—the various ways that Autumn's Peak signals a return to a specific past, one that is premodern and Buddhist. I emphasize the temporality of Autumn's Peak, the ways in which it cues a mode of historical consciousness for Buddhist ascetics that contrasts with capitalist modernity and Shintō historicity. I suggest that the temporality of Autumn's Peak can be divided into material and ritual dimensions: the material dimension of and within Buddhist temples (that is, ascetic garments, ritual items, and statues) and the ritualism (that is, ritual structure and liturgy) of the Ten Worlds Practice.

Autumn's Peak reflects a distinctively Buddhist temporality and historical consciousness in Dewa Sanzan. Here, the temporal dimension of the rite is anachronistic. It is nostalgic for modern ascetics, most of whom live otherwise ordinary lives in contemporary Japan. In some respects, Buddhist ascetics end up reproducing the capitalist modernity they wish to escape. Some pilgrimages into the mountains begin with a commute up narrow roads by rumbling, gas-powered buses. Ascetics sneak chocolate bars, instant coffee, and snacks during the Hungry Ghost Realm fast. There are, as Lobetti (2014, 102) observed, many such instances of "cheating." There is also the touristic impulse: posting post-shugyō selfies on social media or the misuse of yamabushi names for profitable ends.

Although Autumn's Peak exercises a particular mode of historical consciousness, it is permeated, like Hoshino-san's three-day shugyō, with lateral moves to capitalist modernity. From this friction between the ritualized suspension of modernity and the permeation of modernity in Autumn's Peak and temple politics there emerges a partially embodied, partially objectified and constantly evolving ethics of participation, an ascetic phronesis. Although my description of the temporal dimension of Autumn's Peak clarifies the Buddhist space-time that the rite produces for participants, my main argument in this chapter concerns the tension between temple elites and lay members about the ethics of participation. This tension is born of friction between Buddhist morality and capitalist modernity in an increasingly globalized world. It is under constant negotiation and requires practical moral judgment (phronesis) to navigate.

The Multitemporal Ascetic

Many aspects of Autumn's Peak signal a temporal shift from the capitalist modernity of the urban present that ascetics normally inhabit to a premodern Buddhist space-time. This shift is enacted at the outset when, shortly after all ascetics arrive at Shozen-in Temple on August 24, they are called by rank to receive their ascetic garments and ritual items for the week from temple authorities. These items must be returned on completion of the rite unless ascetics are willing to pay the high cost to acquire them.[8]

The first garment is a headband (*hachimaki*). When worn, it places over the forehead the name of Haguro Shugen Honshū, an image of a rising sun, and Sanskrit letters for the Buddhist deities representing each of Dewa Sanzan's three mountains: Kannon for Mount Haguro, Amida for Gassan, and Dainichi Nyorai for Mount Yudono. Worn over top of the headband is the *tokin*, a small, circular black cap that ties around the back of the head by a string. The tokin has twelve pleats across its surface, representing the twelvefold chain of causation in Buddhist doctrine. One of the twelve pleats is indented. Ascetics wear the tokin with the indented pleat pointing downward during mountain confinement (*komorigyō*) and, on completion of Autumn's Peak, flip it upward to signify rebirth and the attainment of Buddhahood. The tokin is black to signify ignorance, but its twelve pleats are also associated with an eight-petal lotus flower and the jeweled crown of the five wisdoms. The placement of the tokin over the hachimaki on the forehead, the site of

Buddhist yamabushi attire. Photograph by Shayne Dahl.

consciousness, marks the head as a transformative space. In this case, the metamorphic symbolism of awakening and rebirth is fused with the mountains and Buddhas of Dewa Sanzan. It also has practical utility for some yamabushi who use it for a drinking cup.

The checkered robe with long sleeves that ascetics wear is called a *suzukake*. Most ascetics wear a blue checkered suzukake. The higher-ranking sendatsu (including the dōshi) wear different colors that are in symbolic association with the five directions (the cardinal directions, plus a center) and the five elements (wood, water, earth, fire, and air), collectively representing the constituent spaces and substances of the universe. On each sleeve and on the back of the suzukake is the image of a lion. Symbolically, the ascetic's torso is a nondual union of the Diamond and Womb Realms. As the daisendatsu explained: "The left of the body corresponds to the Diamond Realm [*kongōkai*] and the right to the Womb Realm [*taizōkai*]. The staff held in the left hand is called the Diamond Staff [*kongōzue*]. It represents the Diamond Realm, which is male. The right represents the Womb Realm, which is female. That is why we carry hora gai in the right

Autumn's Peak   139

hand. The conch shell, or any shell, represents a woman. We are created through the unification of man and woman. Without their unification, we would not be born. *Gasshō* [steepled palms together in prayerlike form] represents this unification."

When ascetics wear the suzukake, they are symbolic embodiments of Fudō Myōō, a Buddhist deity that is an avatar of Dainichi Nyorai, the Great Sun Buddha also known as the Cosmic Buddha. Wearing the suzukake during processions, ascetics symbolize a fractal aspect of the Cosmic Buddha in human form, though the figure of the daisendatsu is more explicitly connected with that symbolism during Autumn's Peak.

The Buddhist surplice is called a *yuigesa* or *kesa*. Ascetics receive yuigesa based on their rank. Beginners receive a knotted paper rope, like the *shime* of Shintō practice. Second- and possibly third-year participants wear a green cloth kesa, and fourth years onward wear a kesa crafted of blue silk with six pompoms, which represent the six senses (the standard five, plus consciousness) and bear association with the six realms of suffering that ascetics symbolically enact through Ten Worlds Practice. In the past, an ascetic who completed seven years of Autumn's Peak would be given a yuigesa by the temple. However, the new ethics of participation are changing such norms and the customary yuigesa has become a point of tension between the temple and some senior ascetics.

Ascetics wear pantaloons (*hakama*) and cloth shin guards (*kyahan*) as they do in the Shintō version, but in Buddhist Autumn's Peak there is also a *hashirinawa* or *kainō*: a red rope wound tightly and knotted into a cord that hangs around the waist. It signifies the umbilical cord. Although the body is divided (and united) left and right, in association with the Diamond and Womb Realms of Buddhist cosmology, it is also divided and united by the kainō into upper (cosmic, masculine Diamond Realm) and lower (earthly, feminine Womb Realm). These united divisions of the body symbolize the nondualism of Esoteric Buddhism.

In addition to these garments, participants in Autumn's Peak have a list of items they are required to purchase either before the rite or at the temple, where a small vendor is set up in a corner. Some items are optional that come with added cost. The *nenju* or *juzu* is a Buddhist rosary of 108 beads, one for each of the 108 *bonnō* (polluting desires, obstacles to awakening in Buddhism). As with the hora gai, the nenju is used in the beginning and end of every ritual chant. The beads are rubbed together between the palms, signifying a repentance of the 108 bonnō as well as adding a resonant layer to the sonic texture of sutra recitation. Ascetics also carry a hora gai in the right hand and an elaborately inscribed staff (*kongōzue*) in the left. They may also have a *shakujō* (Buddhist sistrum). Everyone wears jikka tabi boots.

The last item to mention is the *ayaigasa*, the wide-brimmed hat some ascetics wear during pilgrimage in the mountains. There are two forms of ayaigasa in Autumn's Peak. One is strictly for the ritual use of elite ascetics and relates specifically to the ritual structure. The other is a straw hat that anyone who has purchased it privately can wear. However, both forms have a similar association with the placenta. As Gaynor Sekimori (2016, 529) writes: "In the womb, the placenta protects the foetus from heat and cold, and from poisonous vapours, just as in the outside world the ayaigasa protects the wearer from heat and cold, wind and rain. By wearing it constantly, we remember the obligation we owe our mother." Incidentally, as my opening vignette depicts, the ayaigasa was used by one ascetic not as protection from heat, cold, or rain but rather to block his face from the cameras of eager photographers.

Evident in the ascetic's wardrobe is a multilayered symbolism that points to gendered complementarity when discerned apart and sexual union when considered as a whole.[9] Modern ascetics have interesting reactions to the sexual symbolism of ascetic attire and sacred items. One senior ascetic I got to know invited me to his home in Osaka once and showed me a large collection of hora gai he had handcrafted over his many years in the mountains. His favorite, he said was the one with a shell that looked and felt the most like a vagina.[10]

Apart from the sexually charged symbolism of ascetic garments and the hora gai, changing out of one's modern clothing into the attire of a Haguro ascetic bears other differences from changing into the garments of a Shintō ascetic. One such difference is the signification of rank and personal style, but another is the depth of symbolism. In Hoshino-san's three-day shugyō, everyone is uniformly dressed in white and there are few formal markers of status. The white garments signify death and purity. This is common knowledge. Buddhist ascetic attire permits signifiers of status and personalization within a complex array of symbols that bear doctrinal connections. For instance, beginners must tuck their suzukake robe inside the waist of their pantaloons, whereas all upper-year ascetics do not. Instead, they wear a red *hashirinawa* belt. The kesa surplice also signifies rank. Sitting arrangements during rituals are organized hierarchically. Ascetics may add a shakujō sistrum, a hora gai, or a *hisshiki* (sitting mat made of animal skin) to further personalize their style. During Autumn's Peak, there is room for individuation within an encoded hierarchy.

Changing from brand-name designer clothing into Shintō or Buddhist ascetic attire signifies an embodied departure from capitalist modernity, yet they are departures into different streams of historical consciousness with competing claims over contemporary legitimacy in Dewa Sanzan. Wearing Shintō attire is a temporal shift into post-Meiji Shugendō, which claims, contentiously, to be indigenous but is characterized by many Buddhists as being a new religion—one that is, as Itō-san said, "*just* 150 years old." To the contrary, Buddhist attire evokes a pre-Meiji, medieval Shugendō. That said, the Haguro Shugen Honshū of today is the result of a post–World War II revitalization. As to be expected in any religious context in contemporary Japan, the Buddhist version of Autumn's Peak also has novelties and modern additions. Nevertheless, a decidedly premodern Buddhist frame of historical consciousness is configured by wearing ascetic attire that stands in temporal and political contrast to the dominant presence of Shintō ascetics in Dewa Sanzan today. Sakamoto (2012, 29) has participated in Hoshino-san's shugyō, Buddhist Autumn's Peak, and Shintō Autumn's Peak. From the perspective of broad experience in different groups in Dewa Sanzan, he writes: "When I wear the attire, I feel as if I have become a member of the yamabushi from a much older era [*furui jidai*] rather than a modern person, and it makes me feel more focused and disciplined."[11]

Temples, Statues, and Buddhist Spacetime

The temples in which ascetics perform rituals throughout Autumn's Peak are another material aspect of its temporal alterity. For most of the year, participants of Autumn's Peak live, as most Japanese do, in modern homes and apartments in highly populated urban centers, surrounded by the convenience and instant gratification of city life. For the duration of Autumn's Peak, however, they will sleep and perform rituals in Shozen-in Temple on the first (August 24) and the last night (August 31) of the rite and in Kōtakuji Temple, which is deep in the forest, near the summit of Mount Haguro for the duration. Immediately before entering the mountain on August 25, ascetics are symbolically conceived at Kōganedo Temple, which is across the street from Shozen-in Temple in the township of Tōge. Immediately after leaping over the fire (symbolizing their first bath) after descending Mount Haguro on August 31, ascetics conclude Autumn's Peak with prolonged chanting in Kōganedo as well.

Each of these temples is full of Buddhist iconography salvaged from the early Meiji persecution of Buddhism in Dewa Sanzan. Golden-hued statues of Buddhist deities are seated larger than life in the main altar of each of these candlelit temples. Throughout Autumn's Peak, ritual form plays out within the material architecture of the temple. Incantations of Buddhist deities and full-bodied prostrations take place at the feet of Buddhist statues that are spoken of not as statues but as fractal and animate embodiments of Buddhist deities. They are referred to by ascetics not as *butsuzō* (Buddhist statues) but as *butsu* (Buddhas). The statues are not objects that signify. They are subjects, signified.[12]

Autumn's Peak offers ascetics an opportunity to enter a prolonged engagement with the Buddhas of Dewa Sanzan. Shozen-in, Kōganedo, and Kōtakuji are the temple spaces in which these relationships are pursued within the womb of the mountain. In Mount Yudono, there are three temples in which mummified Buddhist ascetics of past centuries are robed and worshipped. Despite their mummified state, they are called "embodied Buddhas" or "living Buddhas" (sokushinbutsu). As described in chapter 7, they are, like statues, worshipped as Buddhas incarnate. During Autumn's Peak, some ascetics travel by bus to these temples to venerate them with sutra recitations.

In addition to the arrangement of golden statues in Shozen-in, Kōganedo, and Kōtakuji are a long series of ritual items imbued with meaning that have been described in depth in former studies of Autumn's Peak, each a constitutive element in a mosaic of materiality representing Buddhist space-time and modes of historical consciousness. Ritual has a relatively fixed structure in Autumn's Peak that is repeated year to year with slight variation. Changes take place, but the fundamental configuration, which draws on the Ten Worlds Practice, is strictly observed, weather permitting.[13]

Ascetics' living arrangements in Kōtakuji Temple during the core duration of Autumn's Peak are organized in accordance with the twelve animals of the Chinese zodiac. In the basement of the temple, which was installed within the past decade, are twelve rooms (*heya*): Mouse, Ox, Tiger, Rabbit, Dragon, Snake, Horse, Sheep, Monkey, Rooster, Dog, and Pig. Each room is occupied by a senior ascetic who reports to temple elites, ascetics of varying degrees of seniority, and a beginner who is responsible for most chores of each room: preparing tea, cleaning toilets, and making food offerings to the hungry ghosts (*gaki*). These are not rooms with dividers but small demarcated areas within a larger open space.

The use of the zodiac to divide up the living quarters within Kōtakuji is significant because it draws on premodern horology and chronometry when hours and years were calculated in reference to the zodiac and were imbued with levels of meaning beyond a serialized numeric quality. Nowadays, most Japanese think in terms of the Gregorian calendar and a Western chronometry of seconds, minutes, hours, weeks, months, and years. Although it is "2025" in Japan as I write, many institutions still use the imperial calendar to mark the year, and so it is also "Reiwa 7" (the seventh year of the Reiwa era). The use of the zodiac during Autumn's Peak (not to mention the abandonment of Western chronometry of minutes and seconds in exchange for zodiac time) marks a temporary suspension of capitalist modernity into premodern zodiac space and time. "Essentially," the daisendatsu explained, "the zodiac represents the universe."

The ritual structure of Autumn's Peak is divided by three "lodgings" (*shuku*) which represent the past, present, and future of embryonic transformation.[14] Rebirth is imagined as ascetic conception in the womb of the mountain, signified by mountain entry. "The first *shuku* is the Buddhist world found within the womb. The second *shuku* is the world of all creatures, the great sea found outside of the womb . . . The third *shuku* is the crossing of the sea of eternal death."[15]

It used to be that each lodging took place in three different temples, but since the early Meiji persecution of Buddhism in Dewa Sanzan led to the razing of most temples in Mount Haguro, the crossing between lodgings is symbolized by crossing through a staggered set of rice stalks in the forest. Ascetics are housed at Kōtakuji for the duration of Autumn's Peak. The five sendatsu also represent Buddhist space-time, symbolizing the five elements (earth, water, wood, fire, and sky), the five directions (four cardinal directions, plus the center, embodied in the daisendatsu), and five Buddhist deities, each associated with a direction. Collectively, the sendatsu symbolize the Esoteric Buddhist cosmos.

The temple is like a fractal expression of the macrocosmic Buddhist universe. Its symbolic role as a womb within the womb of the mountain is made visible when ascetics enter the third lodging of Autumn's Peak. During this phase of the ritual process, the inner sanctum of the temple is decorated as both a womb and the Buddhist cosmos. I mentioned that three handheld uchiwa fans are fitted together in a circle on the ceiling, representing a placenta, and multicolored streamers dangle from their center point as an umbilical cord. Senior ascetics craft paper cut-outs of various "constituents" in the Buddhist cosmos (dragons, forest goblins [*tengu*], temples, shrines, torii gates, and so on) that are arranged in a dazzling display in the main hall. At night, candlelight illuminates the cut-outs, casting shadows of these mythic figures across temple walls and across the golden faces of Buddhist statues. The time of embryonic gestation is fused with Buddhist cosmography within the space of the temple.

Another way Buddhist space-time manifests is through its social coordination. Time is not synchronized by a twenty-four-hour clock. Instead, time is marked by sound, the piercing melodies of the hora gai. The hora gai marks the beginning and end of all rituals within Autumn's Peak. It is sounded in a variety of melodies, each with its own symbolic reference, at different stages in the ritual process. In the middle of the night, ascetics are awakened by the hora gai. This resembles the conch trumpet's power to awaken human beings from the slumber of samsaric existence, which is illusory like a dream. Owing to the contrast of one's surroundings within the temple during Autumn's Peak when compared with one's life in modern Japan, waking up by the conch call of the hora gai and shuffling into the decorated, candlelit hall dressed in robes can feel like a dream. When I asked Itō-san what he thought of Autumn's Peak, he said, "During Autumn's Peak, it becomes my whole life. My regular life feels like a dream. After, the memory of Autumn's Peak is foggy and blurred, like a dream." Sakamoto writes that he felt as though he was living in a folk tale (*mukashi banashi*).[16]

While the materiality and ritualism of Autumn's Peak conjure up a medieval Buddhist space-time, there are also moments of "time out of time" (Rappaport 1992), a disorienting sense of living outside a world of calendars and clocks, even outside the zodiac and conch calls. Such moments often arise during intense gongyō (sutra recitation) while severely sleep deprived, weaving in and out of consciousness while chanting for hours in the middle of the night. This includes the Heart Sutra, Amida Sutra, Lotus Sutra, and many others. Mantras are dedicated to Dainichi Nyorai, Amida Nyorai, Yakushi Nyorai, Kannon, Fudō Myōō, Jizō, and other important figures in Buddhism.[17]

All rituals, sutra and mantra recitations, and official commands throughout Autumn's Peak are spoken using medieval grammar and vocabulary. Some phrases and grammatical conjugations are the same as one would find in contemporary samurai movies, but they have long since fallen out of common parlance. One basic example is the verb "to be." In modern Japanese, *aru* (to exist) or *desu* (is) can be made formal through the conjugations *arimasu* or *de gozaimasu*. At the end of rituals in Autumn's Peak, the dōshi, who facilitates most rites, says, "*De gozaru*," which is an archaic conjugation, one that I've heard some younger ascetics parody as they joke around in spare time. Most sutras are composed of the Japanese rendering of Chinese characters and Japanese pronunciations of Sanskrit terms, but the ascetics chanting them, unless they have undergone intensive language training, generally have only a vague sense of what they are chanting. Even the Heart Sutra, which many ascetics can recite by memory, is mostly nonsensical in modern Japanese. For ascetics, though, what is important is not what these sutras mean; it is the ecstatic experience of chanting them under candlelight in a temple on the summit of a sacred mountain, far from the sirens and artificial lights of the city.[18]

The olfactory sense is also drawn into Buddhist space-time by the burning of various kinds of incense, Japanese cedar, and the scent of sandalwood powder that some ascetics rub all over their hands before rituals. During the Hell Realm, midnight gongyō are concluded by the dumping of powder made from crushed chilis onto braziers throughout the hall, producing plumes of acrid smoke that quickly fill the room. As with the Shintō version described in Hoshino-san's three-day shugyō, this ritual is called *nanban ibushi*. While sendatsu cover their mouths and fan the smoldering heaps of chili powder, ascetics cough and gag on the smoke. For a few days after Hell Practice, the lingering smell of this harsh smoke saturates the temple.

Perhaps one of the most interesting and affecting manifestations of Buddhist space-time in Autumn's Peak is spirit possession during the Hungry Ghost Realm Practice. Every year that I participated in Autumn's Peak I observed female ascetics enter different forms of spirit possession. One form, the most general and widespread, manifests as a great sadness that sweeps through the ascetic community during the ritual placation and memorialization of hungry ghost spirits. There are eruptions of tears and sobbing as everyone recites sutras for the hungry ghosts. For the preceding two days, participants have undertaken exhausting pilgrimages up and down Mount Haguro while fasting from food, simulating the suffering of hungry ghosts. As the daisendatsu explained: "We think that spirits of the deceased tend to fall into the gaki realm. This is why we have *segaki*, a memorialization service for the souls fallen into the gaki realm. We're trying to save them."

In 2013, my first Autumn's Peak and just the third to follow 3/11, I recall feeling concern for Asumi-san. At this early stage of fieldwork, we had not yet met. She seemed distraught as we broke our hungry ghost fast with a bowl of miso soup. I thought to introduce myself to see if she was alright. She seemed to be put at ease by my greeting. Naive of the fact that many ascetics were from the tsunami-inundated coast, I asked, "Where are you from?" attempting to redirect her focus from what was bothering her. She barely managed to speak, but she uttered, "Fukushima" before erupting once more into tears. Days later, she and other women would tell me that every year at Autumn's Peak, during Hungry Ghost Practice, a dark emotion out of their control would temporarily overcome them. "It was as if others were crying their sadness through me," Asumi-san said. The "others" she spoke of were, she felt, not only the souls of victims of the disaster but the souls of other hungry ghosts. I have also observed senior ascetics performing exorcisms through the recitation of Buddhist sutras and mantras and the clanging of a shakujō sistrum over the bodies of female ascetics experiencing a form of spirit possession during Hungry Ghost Practice.[19]

When I asked the daisendatsu about spirit possession during Autumn's Peak, he said:

> Possession-like phenomena can happen at any time. Walking in the mountains, suddenly a person can no longer walk. We might say they have become possessed by a gaki and we perform an exorcism by giving them food and performing some sutra recitations or mantras. There are many such incidents. People whose sensitivity is enhanced through shugyō become more susceptible. Here is a simple analogy: You enter a space full of radio waves and your mind tunes to a specific radio wave. We do not endorse spirit possession as a part of Autumn's Peak, but certainly, such phenomena are long known to happen.

Many examples demonstrate the spatiotemporal aspects of the materiality and ritualism of Autumn's Peak and how it fosters a Buddhist space-time for modern ascetics. Apart from the religious value of the rite for participants, there is also something very nostalgic about it all. It connects modern people with a past lost to modernity, specifically the modernity brought on by the persecution of Buddhism in the Meiji period. Postwar modernity, with its strong American influence, is, ironically, what allowed Haguro Shugen Honshū to revitalize the Buddhist version of Autumn's Peak in Mount Haguro through the expansion of freedom of religion laws.[20] Seeing the market value of nostalgia and religion, some people have undertaken Autumn's Peak to gain accreditation to capitalize on their knowledge. This has caused concern among temple authorities and prompted a nuanced negotiation of ascetic phronesis, a developing moral sense of what it means to be a good ascetic in modern times.

Moral Dilemmas in the Mountain's Womb

The ethical tension with capitalist modernity in Autumn's Peak is made evident weeks before it is even undertaken in the form of a letter sent out to all prospective participants. The first section is a practical guide, explaining the necessary supplies that ascetics will need for the week. Electronics are prohibited. In place of electric lights in Kōtakuji are oil lamps that hang from the ceiling (against which ascetics comically bang their heads when they stand) and candles. Headlamps are permitted for ascetics who have difficulty reading sutra books in candlelight, but electronics that access the Internet are strictly forbidden. There is also a detailed guideline with strict proscriptions. It reads:

> In recent years, some people who have joined Autumn's Peak have not followed the rules. This is very disappointing. Please ensure that the reason you intend to undergo shugyō is sincere. In Autumn's Peak, we share the same place and schedule, but the contents of the experience will vary based on one's status. Beginners and experienced members will have different experiences. This is as it should be. For beginners: Face yourself and look within. Do shugyō for yourself. For experienced members: To further improve, be strict with yourself and guide others. To all members: Please consider deeply why you wish to spend your precious time and hard-earned money for this shugyō. Participate with a clear objective. Even as you undertake the same practices as everyone else, those with clear purpose will gain more from shugyō than those without. There are many worthy objectives for undertaking shugyō. For instance: self-cultivation [*jikotanren*], memorialization [*kuyō*], or repentance [*sange*]. However, if you think: "I hope to meet a spirit medium," "I want to acquire psychic powers," if this is for tourist leisure, as if shugyō were a mountain camp or novel experience, if you want to receive a yamabushi name from Haguro Shugen, or if you want to apply what you learn for the sake of your own religious group—these are all unjustifiable and completely unacceptable objectives for Autumn's Peak. Those who desire to undertake shugyō for such ends will not be permitted. Furthermore, there will be no fighting, screaming, dancing, singing, or inappropriate behavior. This is a group activity. Please do not disrupt the group with selfish acts. If we hear reports of such activities, you will be asked to leave. We used to allow you to carry a cell phone in case of emergency, but past ascetics did not respect this privilege and took photos of our practices and uploaded them to social media, which is strictly prohibited. It is a matter of personal responsibility to follow the guidelines set forth. A person who cannot follow simple rules loses purpose in shugyō. If you are interested in the form and not the content of shugyō, please go elsewhere. We ask that you

face and think deeply about your actions throughout Autumn's Peak, whether they are necessary. It is very annoying for experienced members who pursue their practice sincerely to be disturbed by beginners who do not follow the instructions of their room leaders. Even if you have acquired a high status in other Shugendō mountains or in your career in secular society, it is irrelevant in Autumn's Peak. A beginner is a beginner. You must follow instructions from superiors. Age is also irrelevant. To enhance the experience of Autumn's Peak, we have strict guidelines, but we pray wholeheartedly that you will have an excellent shugyō.

There are important points to glean from this letter. From the first few sentences, we see that the mountain is a place for self-reflection. Everyone will gain unique experiences during shugyō in the mountains, reflecting my notion of orographic perspectivism set forth in the Introduction. We also learn that past participants have pursued shugyō with insincere intentions, that they have broken rules, and that the temple authorities are disappointed about the situation. The letter describes self-reflection and mentoring, self-cultivation, the memorialization of the dead, and repentance as sincere and virtuous objectives. Notably, becoming a Buddha is not among them. Blacker (2000b, 197) wrote of her first Autumn's Peak: "Certainly, none of the party who climbed Mount Haguro in 1963 had any thought in their minds of becoming Buddhas. . . . The Buddhist intention in devising the passage through the ten worlds seems to have fallen short of fulfillment." The use of Autumn's Peak as a networking opportunity to seek out spirit mediums (*reinōsha*), as a means to obtain psychic power, as a novel form of religious tourism, or to receive a yamabushi name, are all strictly condemned. The last section of the letter reveals how vertical relationships between members are not only based on experience but how they are enforced through a hierarchical system organized by seniority.

Lobetti (2014, 99–100) notes that on the Buddhist side, Autumn's Peak is organized through "a system of vertical relationships" with "temple heads" at the top of the hierarchy, followed by "experienced practitioners" and, at the bottom, "occasional practitioners and newcomers." He adds, "There is a remarkably solid and articulated doctrinal structure underlying the whole practice and this, coupled with the presence of a legitimate leadership, enhances the sense of orthodoxy of the ascetic acts performed. The sense is so strong that the influence of lay practitioners during the practice becomes virtually nonexistent. Lay ascetics let themselves be led, passively assist with rituals that they often do not understand entirely and follow a strict hierarchical order in their relationship with other participants and the leaders" (56). It is owing to hierarchical relations determined by ranking that Autumn's Peak is also called Promotion Peak (*shusse no mine*).[21]

As indicated in this letter, there is an expressed concern regarding the intentions and misappropriation of knowledge acquired through participating in Autumn's Peak. It has, as Shimazu-san, the daisendatsu, told me in an interview, become a persistent problem:

> These kinds of people are increasing. Aspiring "exorcists-for-hire" and so on. They don't say anything to us beforehand and just go ahead with their exploitative activities after. When this happens, the real meaning of Shugendō and its core Buddhist aspect is lost. Participating in Autumn's Peak does not mean one is a "yamabushi." If you do one week of shugyō in a year, you cannot call yourself a "yamabushi." Some do. Unfortunately, this is becoming more common. The purpose of shugyō is to improve yourself and achieve a realization, but these people use shugyō to improve their businesses. I wonder how much they understand about Shugendō and what it really means to be a yamabushi. We try to prevent these kinds of people by reviewing their resume when they apply to join.

We can see a sharp difference here in the use of the word *yamabushi*. This is a very important point of departure between Shintō and Buddhist Shugendō. For Hoshino-san, the term applies to anyone who "connects people with people and people with nature." It is one of the ways in which Hoshino-san seeks to draw people into his practice. For the Dewa Sanzan Shrine, someone who participates in its Autumn's Peak is a yamabushi. For Shimazu-san, it is difficult to achieve such a title as yamabushi. He does not use the term *yamabushi* to refer to modern practitioners of Autumn's Peak. Rather, they are called "ascetics" (*gyōja, shugenja*) or simply "participants" (*sankasha*). That is why I have consistently used the term "ascetic" when describing participants of the Buddhist version of Autumn's Peak.

To be recognized as a yamabushi by the daisendatsu, one must participate in all aspects of Haguro Shugen Honshū throughout the year for multiple years. Such opportunities are inaccessible to all but the highest-status, most respected, and most trusted members—the moral exemplars of ascetic phronesis who strike a virtuous balance between ascetic practice and modern life. Some yamabushi are ordained monks in Buddhist temples in other areas of Yamagata Prefecture and other parts of the country, even as far away as Hiroshima Prefecture.

An example of a moral exemplar who is not a monk would be Inoue-san, who works as a gardener in Tokyo. He's a very earnest and hardworking man, creating green spaces in the world's largest metropolis as his purpose in life. Every chance he gets, he comes to Mount Haguro to fulfill official yamabushi responsibilities but also comes for unofficial social visits. His devotion led him to become ordained in Haguro Shugen Honshū, which is affiliated with Tendai Buddhism. I asked him once how he maintains his yamabushi practice while living in Tokyo, especially when training hora gai melodies. I imagined it being very difficult to do so without immediately attracting a lot of attention. He said he often goes to Mount Takao, which is a ninety-minute commute. When I asked, "Isn't it too crowded there?" he answered, "Not on a rainy day." An image flashed in my mind of him dressed in his yamabushi attire with his large conical hat shielding him from rain, playing his hora gai while walking through the foggy forests of Mount Takao, his melodies muted by the patter of heavy rain on the ground. No one would know, apart from any intrepid hikers who went into the mountains on a rainy day. Even then, they would only hear the faint echo of a mysterious melody weaving through the trees.

Shimazu-san is also strict about members of Autumn's Peak writing about their experiences without permission and publishing anything on the Internet, including pictures of themselves dressed in Haguro Shugen attire. Inoue-san shows no trace of his yamabushi spirituality on his social media. Shimazu-san's caution of the Internet in general is very reasonable given the political problems misinformation has caused in recent years: "Information is made freely available on the Internet. It is therefore not difficult for people to become confused about what is true and what is false. For people who seek information on the Internet, there are so many different answers available. One cannot know what to believe. Society becomes confused when saturated with misinformation. It distorts their very reality. This is the core of my doubt regarding the value of the Internet, especially as it pertains to Haguro Shugen."

The daisendatsu's concern regarding the exploitation of Autumn's Peak and the loss of Shugendō's inherent meaning was emphasized further when in 2015 a letter was included with everyone's record of completion document. It begins and ends with encouragement toward Buddhist realization but centers on a serious criticism of the misappropriation of yamabushi status and names. Here I include three points in the letter that outline further ethical guidelines for participation:

1. Look deeply into yourself and be conscious about the Buddha nature within you. Even in your daily life, before and after Autumn's Peak, try to maintain this consciousness by approaching your life with the attitude that life itself is shugyō. We experience the Ten Worlds daily. Experiences of non-ordinary consciousness such as feeling euphoric, as if you are floating, or mystical visions are not the goal of shugyō. You must instead attend to your inherent Buddha nature.
2. After you descend the mountain and complete Autumn's Peak, your yamabushi status is no longer applicable. You cannot use your yamabushi name, or your affiliation with Kōtakuji or Haguro Shugen, outside of Autumn's Peak. If a situation should arise where you were to misuse our affiliation, we will disavow you, and you will be subsequently prohibited from Autumn's Peak.
3. The name you receive (*ingo*) is not a new given name to be called by. The fundamental meaning of the name-suffix "*in*" is "one who follows the way of Buddha." This one may or may not be human. It means having a heart-mind that wishes to protect and advocate the teachings of the Buddha. Although we use the *ingo* during Autumn's Peak, we do not formally certify the names. To the people who are reborn in the womb of Kōtakuji through a connection with the Buddha, I hope you establish *in* in your heart. In modern times, religious spirituality is in decline. People who relate to religion need to be critical of the problems that arise from religion while protecting religious laws. *Do not criticize others to legitimize yourself*! For example, before you criticize cults or new religions, think about yourself and consider whether you carry the same dangerous potential. Look within yourself all the time. I wish you not to step off the path. *Gasshō*!

This letter indirectly refers to cases where participants have used the affiliation of Kōtakuji and their ingo acquired in Autumn's Peak to pursue profitable and other personal ends. It was difficult for me to obtain direct information about individual cases during fieldwork because it is a sensitive matter, but I have heard from senior ascetics that in the past, the daisendatsu was required to travel to Central Japan to disavow Kōtakuji from a case of fraud involving someone who had attended Autumn's Peak and subsequently used the knowledge gained to perform exorcisms for a fee. The customer reportedly contacted the temple to confirm whether their "exorcist-for-hire" was legitimate. Over the years, other related incidents have occurred.

The Internet and social media have also led to a surge in interest from New Age types. I have met a few. I once met a beginner ascetic who is a voice actor for a famous Nintendo game, *Kirby's Adventure*. Speaking with me over a brief lunch, she compared her Autumn's Peak experience with other exotic experiences she has had with Indigenous people around the world, including at ayahuasca retreats in Peru.[22] In between rituals and during breaks, I saw her giving tarot card readings, Reiki healings, and massages to other ascetics, including higher-ranked sendatsu.[23] Another senior ascetic I met who regularly undertakes shugyō in Shikoku and other regions of western Japan offered to heal an injury I had developed on my knee after the forest goblin (*tengu*) sumō wrestling tournament. I had seven bouts. He placed his hand over my knee and proceeded to gesture as though he was pulling something out with a clenched fist. He grunted and coughed. His breathing became labored as he performed an extraction of my pain.

He asked, "Do you feel better now?" Everyone was watching, so I affirmed to avoid the awkwardness of saying "No." After many drinks of sake, I asked where he learned this healing technique. He asked if I had ever seen the movie *The Green Mile*. He then confirmed that he learned the healing technique from the film's protagonist, John Coffey, who draws ailments out of afflicted characters into himself before exorcising the spirit of it from his own body.

The situation of New Age ascetics has got the temple authorities so concerned that they have requested some senior members to investigate. They continue to add rules and modifications to Autumn's Peak throughout the years to prevent this behavior. Ten years ago, ascetics would be taught *mudras* (symbolic hand gestures) in their first year of participation, as a key aspect of their initiation. Because some members misappropriated mudras outside of Autumn's Peak for their own exorcist enterprises, temple instruction was delayed to the third year, to ensure the trustworthiness of members. Yet in Autumn's Peak in 2015, when my cohort was expecting to learn the mudras, it was revealed that the temple would no longer be imparting that knowledge on a general basis. In addition, members who were entering their seventh year were expecting to receive their own *kesa* (Buddhist surplice) as a milestone acknowledgment of their dedication. Some were disappointed to learn that they would not receive it—the *Green Mile* exorcist-ascetic among them. A highly ranked representative of the temple simply told me: "If *everyone* cannot comply with the rules, then *no one* will gain access to esoteric knowledge. It poses a risk."

Despite written warnings and precautionary measures, individuals with motives deemed questionable continue to come. Even experienced members are subject to scrutiny, which makes it a complex issue for the temple. What to do when loyal members, people who have participated for a decade or more and who are generally very dedicated, use the rite for their own economic or personal benefit?

Yamabushi in Mexico

Nomura-san presents an interesting example. When I was entering my third year of Autumn's Peak, Nomura-san was entering his seventh. He is one of the most serious and dedicated members among the younger generation. Outside of Shugendō, he is engaged with many projects, including regional revitalization. Nomura-san, like a few other ascetics in Autumn's Peak, uses an image of himself dressed in the garments of Haguro Shugen for his social media profile and has, in several ways, incorporated "Haguro yamabushi" into his identity outside of shugyō, often introducing himself as such.

Among his many talents, Nomura-san is a dancer. In the one performance I saw of his troupe, just two days before Autumn's Peak in 2015, he played the part of an exorcist. He appeared to exorcise a spirit from a possessed dancer, who is himself a Mexican living in Yamagata Prefecture. During this performance, he read aloud from an ethnography of the Huichol Indigenous people of Mexico, which was translated into Japanese. He went on a cultural exchange program to Mexico earlier that year. This dance performance, which was excellent, was a part of the collaboration.

During Nomura-san's cultural exchange in Mexico, he traveled to the Sierra Madre Occidental and joined Juan, his Mexican dance partner, in a peyote ceremony with a Huichol shaman. Nomura-san was quiet about his activities in Mexico to Buddhist ascetics—I presume he did not want to raise suspicion—but Juan, who also participated in Autumn's Peak, told me that Nomura-san dressed in full Haguro Shugen yamabushi attire and "drank as much peyote as the shaman." He performed mudras and chanted before a ceremonial fire during the peyote rites. According to Juan, "the fire blazed" when Nomura-san performed Shugendō rituals before it, and this impressed the Huichol, for whom Nomura-san was respected as a shaman from Japan. After they had consumed peyote together, said Juan, "they flew to the sky." It followed that Nomura-san spent one week in the mountains with the Huichol shaman, taking peyote and performing rituals with the shaman along the way. Nomura-san has also toured Europe with his yamabushi clothing in the promotion of ascetic culinary traditions of Dewa Sanzan (*shōjin ryori*).

This presented a difficult situation for Shozen-in Temple authorities: Nomura-san remains one of their most respected and highly ranked members, but he, too, had used the yamabushi title and garments to pursue personal ends, a practice the temple sought to deter diplomatically by sending out the general letter to members, reminding them of the rules. I have noticed moments where other ascetics asked Nomura-san about his business affairs in which he uses his yamabushi identity in the presence of senior ascetics (some of whom also incorporate their yamabushi identity into their work lives). Even though such difficulties arise in the fluid ethics of participation in Autumn's Peak, this does not mean it will permanently damage the relationship between members and the temple, who benefit from loyal and continued membership. Every situation is unique and requires a delicate negotiation of ethics.

As my social network expanded beyond Dewa Sanzan, I would meet yamabushi around the same age and who share similar sentiments as Nomura-san but who belong to different Shugendō traditions in other areas of Japan. Nomura-san may appear to be an outlier in Dewa Sanzan for his international engagements, but he is not an outlier in the broader context of contemporary Shugendō. He may, in fact, represent a generational shift in the kinds of people seeking to participate in Shugendō. Many younger ascetics are dynamic, globally minded spiritual seekers not unlike the voice actor who reads Tarot cards and flew to Peru to for an ayahuasca retreat. I've also met an ascetic who, just like Nomura-san, flew to Mexico and went on a pilgrimage with a Huichol community, in his case, to Real de Catorce in the Mexican state of San Luis Potosí.

This ascetic did not dress in his yamabushi clothing during the trip, but he did carry hora gai with him, playing it in the arid mountainous landscape of Real de Catorce. With a Huichol community, this yamabushi harvested peyote buttons from the desert and participated in ceremonies involving peyote consumption. Although his case is not directly connected to Dewa Sanzan, his experience in Mexico illuminates the global networks that link contemporary mountain ascetics in Japan with forms of indigenous spirituality that practitioners feel a deep affinity with overseas despite cultural differences. Of his experience in Mexico, this yamabushi wrote on social media:

> In the dry desert land, while being careful of prickly cacti, I searched for peyote. Rather than searching, peyote calls to me. Focusing my

attention downward while surrounded by cacti and plants, I found myself separated and out of sight from others. I existed alone in the serene silence of the world. I blew my hora gai, making my presence known to the world. There is joy in encountering peyote. When I blew the hora gai for a woman who got lost and separated from everyone, the sound reached her, and she safely returned. It was my first time helping someone with a hora gai. . . . We stayed in the desert for two nights. We lit a fire, ate peyote, and the shaman sang, prayed, and danced. . . . Happiness is sleeping on the ground while looking up at the starry sky. In the morning, I woke up to the sound of singing. The pink-colored sunrise and sunset here are truly beautiful. I greeted the morning sun with the hora gai. Finally, we reached the sacred site of Wirikuta Bernalejo, a mysterious place in the desert where there is a large pile of rocks forming a mountain. A meteorite fell on the land of Wirikuta, enhancing its energy. Peyote grows there. It is a place that connects with the universe. Food that connects with the universe. At this sacred place, the Huichol people offer peyote, goat blood, candles, money, and pray. I also set up my hora gai and prayed. Peyote is very unpalatable but as you keep eating it, you get used to the taste. I ate a lot.

Reflecting on the unique dynamics of contemporary Shugendō, Caleb Carter (2022, 4) writes: "Although some practitioners may prioritize continuity with the past, others have been drawn to Shugendō through rising trends in spirituality (*supirichuariti*), mental wellness, and a desire to connect with the rigors and the beauty of the mountains. The act of preservation can bring meaning to the present but can also legitimate forms of discrimination." The key tension in contemporary Shugendō is between continuity and change, tradition and innovation. This tension is visible in the case of Autumn's Peak temple authorities who seek continuity of tradition in an ever-changing world and ascetics such as Nomura-san and others who are experimenting with their religious practice in a globalized world.

The Case of Koshikidake

Nomura-san's matter, as with others, is internal to the temple and addressed indirectly, managed by everyone involved in a constant and tactful negotiation of ethics. It never struck me as a big deal. Other cases are more politically delicate with higher stakes. The example of Koshikidake Shōkai, a long-time participant in Autumn's Peak, and his Shugendō sect, Koryū

Shugen Honshū, is a bigger deal.[24] Koryū Shugen Honshū was established in 2005 in Mount Koshikidake near Higashine City in Yamagata Prefecture by Koshikidake Shōkai at Kannon-ji Temple. The history of the temple, which Sekimori (2009a) describes in more detail than I will here, is well documented with hundreds of Shugendō ritual manuals from centuries past. The last Buddhist abbot overseeing the temple laicized in 1871. Koshikidake, "the instigator of the revival of Koshikidake Shugendō" (now known as Koryū Shugen Honshū), is the great-great-grandson of the last Buddhist abbot of Kannon-ji Temple.

Koshikidake-san was born in Hokkaidō because his father had relocated there for work. He moved back to Yamagata as a child to live with relatives, eventually pursuing a career in film production. According to Sekimori (2009a, 58), "From around age 30, he felt increasingly committed to continuing his family's religious tradition, partly in memory of his *shugenja* [mountain ascetic] ancestors and all those who were victims of the *shinbutsu bunri* [kami-Buddha separation orders]." He then underwent ordination and postordination rites though Hakusan-ji, a Tendai Buddhist temple near another Shugendō mountain. To familiarize himself with the Ten Worlds Practice, he began participating in Autumn's Peak in 1992 and would continue, he told me in an e-mail exchange, for twenty years.

The controversy with his sect and Autumn's Peak is nuanced among ascetics and the temple monks. There is legitimate respect for the effort Koshikidake-san has taken to revive Kannon-ji. The discomfort with his practice has more to do with presenting rituals he learned from Autumn's Peak in an accessible forum, where aspiring yamabushi from anywhere—Japan or abroad—can seek ordination through his temple, in person, or via live video lessons for a reasonable price. The vetting process has become stricter in recent years, but there were numerous incidents reported on his sect's social media platform where his students were caught misbehaving. He repudiated such behavior in a social media post:

> Some foreign students want to use their Japan visit to generate marketing propaganda back home. One person dressed in robes and visited a temple where the abbot was absent and took photos for his blog to make it look like it was his temple. He also posted a photo at my friend's karate dojo with a comment about passing the test for black belt, which did not really happen. The abbot and the karate teacher both complained to me. With such disrespectful behavior, that student lost credibility and we as Shugendō ascetics lose face and honor.

To attract new members, Koshikidake-san has also filmed rituals that were drawn from the Ten Worlds Practice of Autumn's Peak and advertised his sect by posting the videos on YouTube and sharing them via social media. He also formed the International Shugendo Association (2019), which hosts shugyō around the world, including in Switzerland, Canada, and the United States. The association's website states: "Our mission is to plant Shugendo across the world, in ways matching the needs of different people and cultures."

This transparent approach to Shugendō ritual stands in contrast to the secrecy of Shozen-in and the daisendatsu's critical comments about the Internet. When I raised the issue with the daisendatsu, asking him if he knew about Koryū Shugen Honshū and its online activities, he became visibly uncomfortable and said: "The *ko* of *Koryū* means 'ancient,' but their sect is not ancient." He would then tactfully avoid making any direct accusations against the group by speaking abstractly about the difficulties of maintaining integrity in Autumn's Peak membership. Indeed, if the behavior of members with two decades' seniority in Autumn's Peak are still questionable, trust becomes hard-earned in this community.

Critics of Change

Another point of tension in Autumn's Peak has to do with conservative ascetics who are critical of changes that the temple leaders are alleged to innovate year to year. One longtime member, Okuda-san (pseudonym), once confided that he was "disgusted" with a new ritual. In the evening of August 29, following the forest goblin (tengu) sumō tournament but before the *saitō goma* fire ceremony, the dōshi performed spirit possession in which he speaks and acts as the fierce Fudō Myōō, the avatar of Dainichi Nyorai. The first time I witnessed this ritual, the dōshi danced with flaming stalks of rice straw, smashing them together, making embers fly. Holding one flaming stalk of rice in between his teeth in a lunge position, he leapt high into the air with a guttural *kiai* power scream, switched legs in midair, and landed, tossing salt everywhere, while all ascetics surrounded him and recited sutras and mantras. More than once, he pulled flaming stalks through the sleeves of his suzukake robes.

Following this intense ritual dance, an oversized cauldron was placed over a fire until the water was steaming. The dōshi was lifted by his arms into the cauldron. The flames licking the sides of the cauldron nearly caught his suzukake sleeves on fire. While ascetics chanted sutras, he made guttural cries and eventually exited the cauldron, smashing bundles of straw into the water and then slapping them onto the fire, generating clouds of steam as he spoke in the deep, altered voice of Fudō Myōō. Okuda-san was angry after each performance of this rite, alleging that the temple was succumbing to the "pressure to perform," to compete against the shrine and retain membership by presenting exotic experiences to members—experiences that were, in his view, unnecessary and superfluous. Okuda-san was angriest and most overtly upset about this "new" innovation, often using ad hominem insults to the dōshi (calling him "eggplant man," for instance, because of his purple suzukake). Some sided with him, but most others seemed content with such practices, whether they are new innovations or not. They accept changes since contemporary Autumn's Peak is in revitalized form.[25]

Conclusion

In this chapter, I have attended to the spatiotemporality of the modern Buddhist practice of Autumn's Peak while considering the ethics of participation it generates. Struggling to maintain integrity with doctrinal principles and their religious legacy despite historical transformations, temple leaders and their ascetic membership are constantly negotiating an emerging ethics of participation, cultivating a sense of ascetic phronesis—a fluid application of "wise judgment" for ascetic practice in the modern, globalized world. Phronesis lies at the interface of Buddhist morality and capitalist modernity in Japan, where the incentives to capitalize on esoteric knowledge abound in a precarious economy. In official letters from the temple to its ascetic membership, guidelines to ascetic virtue may appear as a list of prescriptions and proscriptions, but they offer a navigable path for ascetics in modern times, pointing to the original intent of shugyō in Dewa Sanzan: self-transformation in the womb of the mountain.

Phronesis is, as Lambek explains, "a matter of exercising judgement rather than following rules. A truly virtuous person may come to do so spontaneously."[26] The moral exemplars of Autumn's Peak such as Inoue-san, the gardener in Tokyo, are ascetics who have cultivated such an ability and exercise it spontaneously. Ascetic phronesis, a sense of how to be a "good" ascetic in modern times, is cultivated through ongoing dialogue between temple elites and lay members about what constitutes wise practical judgment and what does not. Ascetic phronesis is a moral response to the risks of disseminating traditional knowledge to contemporary practitioners in capitalist society. It is the way ascetics balance respect for the Shugendō traditions in the mountains of Dewa Sanzan and the demands of the modern, rapidly changing world below, seeking moral equilibrium between traditional virtue and modern value.

As the examples in this chapter indicate, there are expectations from the temple of their ascetics and the ascetics of the temple. The space in between is what I have been referring to as the ethics of participation. It is both a creative and critical space between Buddhist space-time and the socioeconomic challenges of capitalist modernity and globalization. In this liminal space, ascetic phronesis remains under constant negotiation.

6   Summits Where Souls Gather
Ancestral Space-Time and Disaster Pilgrimage on Gassan

"Look! Look! Can you see them? They are everywhere!" Naitō-san is a self-described spirit medium (*reinōsha*) who claims to "see the unseen" (*mienai koto ga mieru*). We were hiking the short distance between the parking lot of Gassan (6,509 feet) to the shrine at the eighth station when he had suddenly pointed to a nearby slope and insisted, ecstatically, that I try to "see the unseen," too. To my eyes, the grassy slope was laid bare to the blue sky. For Naitō-san, a crowd of men, women, and children clad in white stood there with walking sticks. Ghostly pilgrims waiting for the ceremony to begin. They were, he said, standing in a long line that stretched all the way to the summit, some three miles in the distance. Every year on this day, August 13, a vertically laid stack of funerary tablets is set ablaze on the summit of Gassan before pilgrims to memorialize and summon ancestral souls for Obon, the Festival of the Dead.

Naitō-san and I were with Tanaka-san, my homestay host. For decades, she has volunteered with the Dewa Shōnai International Forum for international exchanges. Her grandfather was a well-respected spirit medium in the Shōnai region who undertook countless pilgrimages to Gassan throughout his life. His grave is in a temple yard in a village in the Shōnai plains below, but within the past few years, owing to his fame and dedication in Dewa Sanzan, an engraved stone monument was erected in his honor at the eighth-station shrine of Gassan.

Tanaka-san would later tell me that pilgrimage up Gassan and *shugyō* in the Shintō version of Autumn's Peak were the methods by which her grandfather acquired and strengthened his psychic powers. Every August 13, the first day of Obon, she brought flowers and food offerings to place before her grandfather's stone memorial and rinsed it with water to quench his thirst in the afterlife. When I leaned over some *jizō* statues to take a photograph, Naitō-san grabbed my arm firmly and pulled me back.[1] I thought I may have offended him with my photography, but to my surprise, he yelled

A Shintō priest summons ancestral souls on the summit of Gassan.
Photograph by Shayne Dahl.

emphatically and in broken English: "Watch out! There are children! Oh my god! Oh my god! They are climbing up your legs! Get back!"

Naitō-san's ghostly visions are not uncommon in Gassan. It is one of the most formidable reizan, or "spirit mountains," of Tōhoku.[2] *Reizan* is often glossed in English as "sacred mountain," but the ideogram for *rei* has a deeper relation to ghosts and the ghostly (for example, *yūrei*) than it does to an arbitrary sense of sacredness defined in contradistinction to an arbitrary sense of the profane. Such categories are blurred in contemporary Japan. One could translate *reizan* as "haunted mountain," as some Japanese have to me, but I prefer to use the term "spirit mountain" to capture the balance between the sacred and the ghostly.[3]

In this chapter, I explore the haunted temporality of Gassan. Up to now, I have treated Dewa Sanzan as a place that connects modern people with different streams of historical consciousness based on nostalgic and religious perspectives of a contested past. Here, we will see that the mountains are also a portal through which ancestors—and, in special circumstances, souls of the recently deceased—are imagined to reenter the present world of the living. A consideration of mountain pilgrimage in Gassan reveals the ancestral space-time of Dewa Sanzan, which is one of the defining features of its cultural orography. The peak of Gassan, the highest point of the Shōnai plain, is where "this world" (*kono yo*) and the "otherworld" (*ano yo*) make contact.

As a rendezvous point between worlds, the space of Gassan is a two-way street through time. It enables pilgrims to connect with ancestors while serving as a spatiotemporal gateway for ancestors, formless figures of the past, to return, for a time, to their families in the present. The peak of Gassan is a place where ancestors from the past become present and where pilgrims can alleviate ancestral suffering through posthumous memorialization rituals that prevent ancestral souls from becoming "relationless Buddhas" (*muenbotoke*). The climbing season on Gassan spans July 1 to the first week of October. A mixture of mountain climbers, pilgrims, and ascetics frequent the trail. Pilgrimage and ancestor veneration hit their peak moment of the annual ritual cycle on the first day of Obon, August 13. An analysis of annual memorialization rites on the evening of this specific day reveals not only the defining feature of Gassan's cultural orography—that it is a spatiotemporal artery between worlds—but also that it is a site of post-disaster healing.

As a disaster memorial on the summit shows, 3/11 has modified both the meaning and the temporality of the peak, expanding its orientation from traditional ancestor veneration to retrospective reflection on the event of disaster, the memorialization of the souls of disaster victims in the present, and the future reconstruction of the Sanriku Coast. On the summit of Gassan, ancestral space-time and the multiple temporalities of disaster—of its past event, its present victims, and its future recovery—are interwoven into the performance of annual memorialization. By providing a ritual framework to mourn, memorialize, and look to the future with hope on the summit of Gassan, yamabushi have innovated a moral response to disaster that is unique to Dewa Sanzan.[4]

In the wake of disaster, Anne Allison (2013, 202) wrote that "hope" has become "the affect and effect of 3/11," a force of "collective action . . . a working partnership, recovering, relieving, reconstructing the stricken area, moving it—and Japan—forward." She asserted that despite the tragic losses of 3/11, pundits have deemed the post-disaster period as a "return of hope" because it has shocked people out of the "social disaster" of an increasingly "relationless" society—a socioeconomic condition caused by the neoliberal reforms implemented after the recession of the 1990s.[5] Richard Samuels (2013, xii) also writes of the "rebirth" discourse following disaster in which pundits projected that the "3.11 generation would find a fresh motivation and stimulate a new national resolve" just as the postwar generation had done. Allison (2013, 200) describes post-disaster hope as "an ethics of care built from . . . precariousness," where communities are working together to tackle the socioeconomic problems that already existed but were exacerbated by the disaster. On the summit of Gassan this post-disaster ethics of care extends into the afterlife. By caring for the suffering souls of disaster victims, memorialization rites, such as funerals, are therapeutic for pilgrims, too. Memorialization rites on the summit of Gassan present an emplaced ritual catharsis for pilgrims, helping them to move forward from the devastating past event of disaster into the future with hope.[6] Gassan is a symbolically charged space in ways that overlap with Mount Haguro but that are also distinct. Like Mount Haguro, which is imagined as a womb, Gassan is imagined a "divine mother" in one respect.[7] In another, more prominent sense, it is the abode of the dead. To clarify Gassan's status as a spirit mountain, I first describe the narratives that support its associations with death.

The Cosmic Deathscape of Gassan

The late Robert J. Smith (1974, 63) wrote: "There can be no doubt that one of the oldest and most widespread beliefs as to the final destination of the soul is that it resides in the mountains. All over the Japanese islands there are mountains and high plateaus that are believed to be the abode of spirits." To this effect, Gassan, like other spirit mountains, is a "deathscape," a place "associated with the dead and for the dead" where death is spatialized as orography.[8]

As Naitō-san's vision signals, souls are imagined (and "seen") ascending, or attempting to ascend, the slopes of spirit mountains over the course of years, and not by their effort alone. Surviving family members and descendants must periodically memorialize their souls, as Tanaka-san did for her psychic grandfather. This enables the formless figures of ancestral souls to continue upward to the peak, where they transcend their individuality and, ultimately, their humanity, either by becoming a kami or by attaining posthumous Buddhahood. The cultural orography of Gassan is not as ritually active as it was before the Meiji period or even before World War II, but it is often narrativized in nostalgic discourses about its traditional significance. Such narratives, which are reiterated by scholars, tourists, pilgrims, ascetics, and priests, emphasize that the transmigration of the soul takes thirty-three years and occurs in four stages.

At an annual Gassan Summit conference during my fieldwork in 2015, a local historian lectured with authority on this topic. He explained that in the first stage, the soul is "unstable and dangerous" and must be memorialized frequently. Memorialization ceremonies are thus held at 7, 27, 37, 47, 57, 67, and 77 days after death, typically in the home. In stage two, the soul stabilizes. Memorialization rites then occur at 100 days and one, three, seven, and thirteen years after death. In stage three, memorialization is performed at twenty-five and thirty-three years after death, at which point stage four commences and the ancestral soul becomes a kami for Shintō-oriented practitioners or achieves posthumous Buddhahood for Buddhists. Most pilgrims undertake both Shintō and Buddhist rites depending on the context. There is no exclusive boundary between souls becoming strictly kami or strictly Buddhas.

In the transmigration ontology of Gassan, lower-altitude mountains, referred to as *hayama*, host spirits before they take to Gassan for the final ascent to the afterlife, which is in the Land of Bliss (*gokuraku*).[9] One such mountain in the area is called Mount Mitsumori (Three Forests).[10] Memorialization ceremonies are still performed on the three summits of this small mountain annually by Sōtō Zen monks. Each of its three peaks represent temporally and hierarchically graded zones of posthumous ascension for the souls of the ancestral dead. I attended ancestral *kuyō* (memorialization rites) on Mount Mitsumori in August 2015, just after Obon, the Festival of the Dead. I was surprised to find that it was only 394 feet high. Yet the memorialization ceremonies were elaborate and run by Sōtō Zen monks.

If an ancestral soul is cared for with proper memorialization rites, it is believed to ascend to the peak of Gassan, where it either is enshrined at the summit or rises into the sky. Different rituals indicate a different domain for ancestral souls. It is not agreed upon whether souls reside in the summit shrine, which is overseen by Shintō priests, or in the starry depths above. By name alone, the deathscape of Gassan has a strong association with the moon and the vibrant, star-studded cosmos in which the moon and the mountain as seen from below are embedded. The moon rises over the mountain, and if the sky is clear, the Milky Way can be seen arcing over it as well. The cosmic associations of Gassan signify death through transcendence, since the verticality and altitude of the mountain are the meeting point between heaven and earth. As the highest point in the Shōnai plains, the summit is the bidirectional pathway for the transmigration and annual return of ancestral souls. Poets, artists, and photographers often draw Gassan and the moon together in their creations and emphasize this aesthetic. Recall Bashō's haiku:

the peaks of clouds
have crumbled into fragments
Mount of the Moon

In pre-Meiji times, the ten stations of Gassan represented the Ten Worlds of Buddhist cosmology with the tenth, the summit, being Buddhahood. Yet the word "Buddha" in Japanese (*hotoke*) is also used to refer to a corpse: "She became a Buddha [*hotoke*]" is synonymous with saying "She died." "I see a Buddha" is synonymous with saying "I see a corpse."[11] Ancestors (*senzo*) are also referred to as "Buddhas" (*hotoke*). The association between Buddhahood, death, and ancestors is reflected in the association between Buddhism, funerals, and death anniversaries, but also in the haunted ontology of spirit mountains as spatialized mandalas that ascend to Buddhist enlightenment. In one reading, the cosmos, which is beyond the ten stages, represents the spatialized transcendence of *samsara* (the earthly realm of suffering) and the final resting place for posthumous Buddhas.

Gassan, like Mount Haguro and other spirit mountains in Japan, is historically envisioned as a Buddhist mandala.[12] Buddhists still hold this view, as do many pilgrims.[13] Before a paved road leading all the way up to the eighth station of Gassan was built in the late 1950s, the ten stations of Gassan served pilgrims as sites of practical necessity. They were places to rest, eat, drink tea, take shelter, and acquire supplies, but they also correspond to the Ten Worlds doctrine in Buddhist thought.[14] Like Mount Haguro and the ten steps of Dewa Sanzan Shrine, the physical ascent up the mountain is a symbolic ascent toward Buddhahood through the Ten Worlds. These days, most visitors ascend four-fifths of Gassan by automobile, then hike a three-mile trail to the summit, encountering just the eighth and ninth stations before reaching the summit.[15] Only serious and physically capable ascetics, pilgrims, and hikers do it entirely by foot.

A clear day viewed from the parking lot reveals a remarkable mountain vista of green rice fields, the Japan Sea, and the peak of Mount Chōkai, an active volcano, floating on oceanic haze to the north. A cobblestone stairway leads to an inclined wooden boardwalk that cuts into a lush meadow and then diverges into a labyrinth of paths. Bright-colored flowers and small ponds are strewn about in the deep grassy meadow. Hikers, wearing the latest gear, are often seen kneeling reverently before the flowers, aiming their camera lenses into the yellow blooms of "daylight lilies" (*nikkōkisuge*) and other colorful flora spotting the meadow.

The first time I climbed Gassan was the day after I climbed Mount Haguro with Itō-san in July 2012. Much of what he had to say about the cultural orography of Gassan during that initial ascent was repeated by others. As a Buddhist ascetic, he reveals his bias when reading the palimpsestic landscape, but his individual observations accurately reflect general interpretations.

Entering the meadow after our winding drive up to the eighth station, Itō-san said, "Gassan is a mountain of death. It is the realm of Amida Buddha," the overseer of the afterlife. The ecologically unique meadow we were walking through is found on other spirit mountains in Japan and is referred to as Midagahara, or the Meadow of Amida. After the Meiji period, when Shintō became the dominant religious order in Dewa Sanzan, it was reinterpreted as Mitagahara, or the Meadow of the Rice Deity. The ponds strewn about these alpine meadows are technically referred to as *chitō*. They are found on the damp slopes of extinct or active volcanic mountains. In Gassan and other spirit mountains such as Mount Tateyama in Toyama Prefecture or Mount Haku in Ishikawa Prefecture, these ponds are referred to as Hungry Ghost Fields (*gakita*). Since the mountain is the realm of the dead, the ponds are imagined as the rice fields of hungry ghosts (*gaki*) who, Itō-san explained, "cultivated these dead ponds in their starvation." There are approximately 3,000 chitō scattered across the slopes of Gassan.

The trail to the summit, with its awe-inspiring vistas and flower-spotted fields, is also, like Mount Haguro, a soundscape for the distant echoes of hora gai. Itō-san joined the scattered chorus as we ascended with his own powerful conch calls. There were a few stone cairns along the way, draped with the deteriorating *shime* (stoles worn like necklaces) of ascetics and pilgrims. Itō-san mentioned that "pilgrims stack stones for gaki." The attachment gaki have to the world has prevented them from crossing over so pilgrims make artificial mountains to assist their stunted ascent to the afterlife.

At the ninth station is a large chitō pond with a shrine before it. "It's called *busshōike*," Itō-san explained, the Buddha-Life Pond. "It is the last pond before the summit," he said. After Itō-san performed a Shintō bow and clap as well as a recitation of the Heart Sutra with the *shakujō* and hand *mudras*, he explained that the pond is where the souls of the dead, who climb Gassan thirty-three years after their death, "take their last drink" before ascending to the summit and, in one interpretation, launching off into heaven above or, in another, becoming a Buddha. "This last drink is called *shinimizu*. It's the same word for when water is dripped onto the lips of a dying person or the lips of a corpse during their wake." Before the persecution of Buddhism in the

1870s, there was a large statue of Amida in the busshōike pond, he said, "but it was removed when Nishikawa-san abolished Buddhism in Dewa Sanzan."

The ninth-station lodge, a few feet away from the busshōike, accepts overnight guests and provides meals and drinks to visitors. The lodge also sells unique Gassan merchandise produced by the Japanese mountaineering company Mont Bell. Shirts, coffee mugs, and rain gear are available, all designed with the ideogram of the moon, the *ga* (月) of Gassan. The operators of the ninth-station lodge are not priests but a family that lives on the mountain every summer. The ingredients of their cuisine are picked fresh from the meadows and forests of Gassan, and they carry up backpacks full of supplies daily. The foyer of the ninth station is, on many stormy days, a refuge from the wind and rain.

Just below the summit, Itō-san and I met an eighty-year-old woman, dressed all in white, with her heavily backpacked son. She was absolutely elated, breaking down in tears, when we met her. I could not understand why at first. Then her son explained that they were from Fukushima Prefecture. They had been forced to leave their home after the evacuation order, owing to the nuclear meltdown of the Fukushima Daiichi plant. Calming down, she explained to us that she had climbed Gassan one last time "to offer *kuyō*," a memorialization ritual, "for the ones who disappeared in the tsunami." Overjoyed, she announced, "I feel so purified now!" At the bottom of the mountain, we would see her once more. Before her final step off the trail, she turned, teary-eyed, and said, "*Arigatō!*" (Thank you!) and made a deep bow in the direction of the summit shrine.

The fact that pilgrims, such as the mother and son we met, ascend to the summit to memorialize the ancestral dead and disaster victims is indicative of Gassan's status as a spirit mountain, an elevated domain between worlds. It is a deathscape that is also a place of "cultural therapeutic" value, where pilgrims can be "purified" through "a sanctioned release of [the] negative affect[s]" of disaster.[16] Nowhere is the shared space and time between the living and the dead more apparent in Dewa Sanzan than on the summit of Gassan at eventide every August 13.

A Beacon for the Dead

Obon is held August 13–15 in Japan every year. This holiday, the highlight of the summer, is marked by family reunions and gravesite visitations. Families who make a special effort to visit the graves of their ancestors during Obon typically clean the grave of fallen leaves, offer fresh flowers, incense, perhaps also a meal and a beer or some rice wine, and a respectful bow, maybe a sutra recitation as well. They may even converse with their deceased family member whose cremated remains lie beneath an inscribed tombstone.[17] The peak moment of Obon is large fireworks displays throughout the country, called *hanabi*, or fire flowers.

Obon is markedly different in the heights of Gassan. Every August 13, groups from around Tōhoku hike up its rocky path and gather on its narrow, oval summit to summon the souls of their ancestors before a massive bonfire. Throughout the day, storm or shine, pilgrims clad in white, symbolizing both death and purity, along with yamabushi, Shintō priests, film crews, photographers, and hikers wearing multicolored, brand-name rain gear, trek to the plateaued peak. In overcast conditions, the climb is dreamy and damp. The coastal winds from the Sea of Japan loft rain clouds at the green meadow slopes, and visibility amounts to a cocoon with a tight radius. When it rains, the downpour always seems to strike through strong, sideways winds. On a clear day, the vista reaches deep into the surrounding mountainscape. The ocean can be seen beaming blue beyond the Shōnai rice plains. Forty miles to the north, is the peak of Mount Chōkai, a snow-crowned volcano.

At eventide, when the hues of the sunset begin to fade but a red glow remains on the horizon, the unmistakable hora gai pierces the cool mountain air with its high pitch melody and echoes throughout the natural amphitheater of the Dewa Sanzan range below. Most people, who by that time have gathered in the summit lodge (*yamagoya*) to visit and prepare their bedding for the night, scramble into their jackets and boots, which are often soaked from rain and hanging over a blazing kerosene heater in a small, low-ceiling room. With headlamps and a white Shintō shime stole around their necks, pilgrims walk a few minutes around to the backside of the summit shrine to the apex of the 6,509-foot-high mountain. Approximately fifty people crowd together, some poised on the edge of steep slopes. Pilgrims stand before a large square platform with a bamboo pole erected in each corner and a *shimenawa* rope connecting them into the shape of a square with *shide*, sacred white paper folded into zigzag designs, hanging around it. The platform is the umbilicus of the mountain, the axis mundi, a central portal between "this world" of the living, *kono yo*, and the "otherworld" of the dead, *ano yo*. Stacks upon stacks of vertically laid, wooden funerary tablets (*sotoba*) inscribed with the posthumous names of the ancestors are on it. Similar sotoba stacks are also located at the ninth and eighth stations and were once located at every station all the way down the mountain, leading the souls of the ancestors to the altars (*butsudan*) in the homes of their descendants.

A vertically laid stack of funerary tablets, Eighth Station, Gassan.
Photograph by Shayne Dahl.

At the beginning of the ceremony, while facing the mound of sotoba, Shintō priests, in their robes, call out, over a drumbeat, with a guttural "*Oh–!*" Two yamabushi with large fire-lit torches soon arrive. On cue with the Shintō priests' *norito* incantations, the torches are rammed into either side of the vertical stack of funerary tablets. Multiple Shintō-oriented yamabushi simultaneously blast their hora gai. This includes Hoshino-san, who was present at this ceremony every year I attended. The fire grows quickly by the stoking of coastal winds. It engulfs the sotoba. The names of the ancestors inscribed upon them flash ablaze, then crumble in the flames. The inferno is fierce, and everyone standing before it glows amber from firelight. During the ceremony, there are some norito incantations only the Shintō priests know, but there are also many that all pilgrims know, particularly the Three Word Prayer and the Three Mountain Prayer: "*Ayani ayani kuzushiku tōto tsuki no miyama no kami no mimae wo orogami matsuri*" (With utmost reverence, I worship before the divine presence of the kami of Gassan).

As the fire dies down and after all the Shintō priests have left, a yamabushi leads remaining pilgrims in a few recitations of the Heart Sutra, reasserting the Buddhist dimension of the rite and the legacy of Shintō-Buddhist syncretism in Dewa Sanzan. Behind the glowing embers, a stone monument becomes visible. It is inscribed in Japanese and English, though the translation is not direct. In English, it is called the Tohoku Earthquake Memorial Sutra Mound: 10,000 Shakyo for Japan. In Japanese, *Higashi nihon daishinsai kuyō fukkō kyōhi* (Great East Japan Earthquake Memorial, Recovery, Sutra Monument).

While norito prayers are directed to the various kami of Dewa Sanzan, individual intentions are dedicated to the souls of ancestors whose posthumous names are inscribed on the flaming sotoba. I have seen many pilgrims shed tears on the summit midchant while peering into the blaze of ancestral names. This ceremony is referred to as a *mukaebi*, or Returning Fire. It is at once a Buddhist memorialization of ancestral souls that helps them advance toward posthumous enlightenment (*kuyō*), a Shintō pacification of restless spirits (*chinkon*), and an ancestral summoning, a beacon for the dead to come home for the annual holiday.

It is ironic that Shintō priests, not Buddhist monks, lead this ceremony for the souls of the dead. Typically, Buddhist monks labor in the service of funerary rites in Japan. This is another consequence of the kami-Buddha separation policies of the Meiji period, which replaced and reinterpreted Buddhist rituals in the guise of Shintō (Sekimori 2005a). This is also the case for the Returning Fire ceremony on the summit of Gassan. Shintō priests inherited the rite from Nishikawa's reforms in the early Meiji period.

After norito and the recitation of the Heart Sutra, representatives from different pilgrim confraternities are called on by Shintō priests. They may represent their group, but they may also be an entry-level employee sent on behalf of their company to pay the company's respects. Many companies in the vicinity of Tsuruoka, including the "Yamabushi hot spring" of Tōge, have talismans from the Gassan summit shrine retrieved by a proxy pilgrim who attends the ceremony. Each pilgrim makes their way to the front of the group to offer a small branch of a sacred *sakaki* (*Cleyera japonica*) bush before the embers of a diminishing blaze. They bow twice, clap twice, and bow once in appropriate Shintō fashion.

Members of the pilgrims' group in the crowd synchronize their bows and claps. Once the Shintō priests have completed their ceremonies before the fire, they then climb down and around to the Gassan shrine. At this point, a sendatsu from a shukubō (pilgrim's lodge) in Tōge steps forward, representing all laypeople. He offers a sakaki branch and leads *gongyō* that joins Shintō

Disaster memorial on the summit of Gassan. Photograph by Shayne Dahl.

norito and Buddhist sutra. After the final prayer, everyone climbs down and around the rock-built wall of Gassan shrine and enters the inner sanctuary. Sake is served to each attendee. After drinking it, yamabushi and pilgrims tilt their heads skyward, curl their hands to the side of their mouths, and bellow out, *"Oiii! Oiii!"* (Hey! Over here! Over here!), beckoning souls down from the cosmos to gather for Obon. As mentioned, there are competing claims about where the souls reside. The local historian at the Gassan conference said, "They reside in the summit shrine." However, pilgrims calling skyward to ancestral souls suggests that pilgrims believe they live in the cosmos and descend on the summit when they see the firelight of their enflamed names.

Stories from the Summit

After summoning ancestors on the apex of the mountain, pilgrims return to the summit lodge while priests go to the shrine quarters. Waiting for pilgrims in the summit lodge on woodcut tables in a rustic dining hall is a gourmet alpine-inspired meal, prepared with fresh vegetables gathered on the mountain, and a fair amount of beer and sake. It is a night spent on the summit with people who gather once a year, every year, as an ephemeral spiritual community. Pilgrims generally keep track of how many times they have attended the Returning Fire ceremony, along with how many times they have climbed Gassan and other mountains. They even keep track of how many times they have climbed it from the base of the mountain as opposed to from the eighth station or from the rear entrance as opposed to from the well-trodden path from the front. It is a notable mark of social capital that I have seen among pilgrims. I once met an eighty-two-year-old man who, before telling me his name or where he was from, introduced himself by declaring, proudly, that this was his fortieth ascent of Gassan. Another, younger man, said, in response that although it was "only" his tenth ascent of Gassan, he had summited Mount Fuji 500 times.

The first time I attended the Returning Fire ceremony was in 2013. The sky was crystal clear and the wind was calm. The stars appeared intimately close. I met a middle-aged urban yamabushi-sendatsu from Tokyo who was guiding a group through the mountains for Obon. He led his group outside around midnight and found some flat boulders on the slope near the shrine, which is perched on the peak. There he led a meditation, encouraging his group to contemplate not only their relationship with the cosmos but their feelings of gratitude toward the ancestors. The cosmos and the afterlife are, at least on this night, an indistinguishable domain.[18]

I was also invited to go stargazing with a local politician named Kusajima-san, who had been attending this ceremony for the past twenty years. He is from Tsuruoka but was working in Tokyo as an organic vegetable salesman in the early 1990s. In 1995, after the Great Hanshin Earthquake near Kobe, he decided to organize some volunteers to help with the recovery. At first, he requested three days off work. But once he arrived, he and his volunteers fed some survivors of the earthquake a big *nabe* (hot pot) stew. "They cried because it was the first hot meal they had eaten since the earthquake, five days before," he told me. From that moment, which was pivotal in his life, Kusajima-san resigned from his job in Tokyo and worked for an NGO in Kobe for three years after the quake. He then returned home to Tsuruoka and successfully campaigned for a seat in the city council, where he met Hoshino-san and became a yamabushi. He worked there for about a decade and then successfully ran for a seat in the prefectural government of Yamagata. At the Returning Fire memorialization rite, he represented not only himself—as a person with long-term commitment to the posthumous repose of the souls of the disaster dead—but also the support of the prefectural government for Dewa Sanzan. In June 2025, Kusajima-san informed me of a proposal he put forth to get Dewa Sanzan recognized as a UNESCO World Heritage site.

Every year of my attendance, I also met with the Matsuyama family from Sendai. They had been coming to the summit of Gassan every August 13 for two decades before 3/11 to memorialize their ancestors. They run a family construction business and come as an extended family, two brothers and their children. Living in Sendai, which was hit hard by the earthquake and tsunami, they lost many friends and some family. Their business headquarters was also heavily damaged. For them, ancestral memorialization is the bedrock of their annual mountain pilgrimage, upon which disaster memorialization was added. It was difficult to speak about the specifics of their experience with the disaster since it often provoked tears, but they have said that although we are all helpless before the power of nature and the kami, memorialization rites on Gassan present "a way forward." Something that is within their power to do.

Their interpretations of the disaster are also noteworthy. Once, deep into a box of wine, the leader of their group, the eldest brother, told me that according to his sendatsu in Tōge (the ascetic master of the pilgrim's inn they stay in year after year), the earthquake and tsunami were "divine punishment" (*tenbatsu*) from the ocean kami (a dragonlike figure called *ryūjin*), who was angered by humanity's abuse of water through the industrial development of dams, the pollution of rivers, and overfishing the ocean. I have heard this view stated by several people in Dewa Sanzan, but it echoes earlier interpretations of the disaster as tenbatsu by a former governor of Tokyo, Ishihara Shintarō, and similar claims made following the Great Kantō Earthquake of 1923.[19]

In 2015, I met a pilgrim confraternity leader on the peak, a middle-aged woman from Hachinohe, Aomori Prefecture. A member of her group introduced her to me as "one who can see the otherworld" (*ano yo ga mieru hito*). She told me that Gassan was a "mysterious mountain" (*fushigina yama*) where one can "see the unseen" (*mienai koto ga mieru*). Expressing a psychic sense of orographic perspectivism herself, she said, "Gassan is a place where one can have many different kinds of experiences" (*Gassan de irona taiken ga dekimasu*).

She had come quite a distance to make offerings (*osonae*) and to "provide a feast" for the hotoke (Buddhas or ancestors) not only of her home altar but also on behalf of the ancestral souls of her extended family, her friends, colleagues at work, and the souls of disaster victims. It was a heavy burden to bear, especially since she, as one who can "see," was overwhelmed with visions of the otherworld. Visions, she said, she would rather not have: "It's too much!" (*mō ii*) she repeated many times. This was her second of three planned pilgrimages to Gassan because she had a long list of posthumous names to memorialize. Many of these ancestral souls had been waiting decades to be memorialized from the summit of Gassan, she said, and everyone back home was relying on her. Like the Matsuyama family from Sendai, she, too, had added the souls of disaster victims to her more orthodox agenda of ancestral memorialization. The difference was that the disaster dead would be invoked as a collective but the ancestral dead would be memorialized individually.

Smith (1974, 20) has noted that historically, the souls of people who died in "great fires, floods, volcanic eruptions, and earthquakes" were classified as gaki, wandering spirits or hungry ghosts. As such, they are to be fed, appeased, and placated by ritual offerings and a Buddhist ceremony, *segaki*, especially during Obon.[20] In Japan, non-memorialized ancestors become *muenbotoke* (relationless Buddhas). As "a sign of abandonment and eternal solitude," Allison (2017, 18) explains, "this is an unenviable state." Unkempt graves in temple cemeteries are the last material traces of muenbotoke. They represent a deceased person with either no living descendants or no descendants willing to care for them by memorializing their soul, nurturing it toward posthumous enlightenment. Non-memorialized souls of the disaster dead risk becoming hungry ghosts, which are known to haunt and possess the living and require exorcisms. The whole Sanriku Coast of Tōhoku became a haunted space in the wake of 3/11. Scholars and journalists reported hauntings, ghost sightings, and cases of spirit possession requiring exorcism and ritual placation.[21] The souls of the disaster dead required care before they could let go of this world. The memorial on Gassan contributes to this effort.

A Mountaintop Memorial

There are several observations to make about the 3/11 disaster memorial on the summit. First, it adds a level of meaning to the summit of Gassan and to the paradoxical Shintō Obon ceremony by incorporating the event of the disaster and the souls of the disaster dead into the established ontology of the peak—namely, that it is a portal between the worlds of the living and the dead. In addition to summoning the ancestors during the Returning Fire ceremony, pilgrims are prompted by the memorial to perform kuyō for the souls of those who died in the tsunami and to pray for the recovery of the stricken region. The temporality of the monument simultaneously reaches to the past event of the disaster, the present posthumous suffering of the souls of the disaster dead, and the future recovery of the inundated coast. The recovery (*fukkō*) aspect of the monument is future oriented. It invites pilgrims, priests, and ascetics to pray post-disaster recovery into being. In its temporal orientation toward the future, the recovery dimension of the memorial is an invocation of post-disaster hope.

The monument on Gassan, I was told, is an active memorialization since interred beneath it are more than 10,000 handwritten transcriptions (*shakyō*) of the Heart Sutra.[22] Apart from visitation to gravesites, memorials, exorcisms, and pilgrimage, post-disaster memorialization can also take the form of shakyō. Significantly, 3,800 of the 13,000 sutra transcriptions beneath the monument were hand copied by non-Japanese. Before the 13,000 were interred on the summit beneath the monument on October 9, 2011, yamabushi from Buddhist and Shintō sides of Shugendō in Dewa Sanzan chanted the Heart Sutra once for each transcription. It was a moment of post-disaster collaboration among mountain ascetic rivals. The constant presence of shakyō enshrined beneath the memorial animates the monument as an active, effective, and year-round memorialization.

The story of how these Heart Sutra transcriptions were gathered in Dewa Sanzan from around the world and interred beneath this stone monument is also quite revealing of post–3/11 religious change in Dewa Sanzan, especially regarding Hoshino-san, since he led the effort to establish the monument in the first place.

The Shōnai region, like everywhere else in Tōhoku, suffered food and energy shortages in the months following the disaster. In an area that counts tourism as a reliable source of income, 3/11 was tough, especially for pilgrim lodges, which are operated by resident sendatsu. Each lodge has a *kasumiba*, or designated area of patronage.[23] Hoshino-san's kasumiba was located along the southern coast of Fukushima Prefecture, one of the areas hardest hit by the tsunami and most affected by nuclear radiation. Many of his patrons were displaced and some died. In his own words:

> My shukubō's area [*kasumiba*] was the worst hit. It includes Minami Sōma, Namie, Futaba, and Ōkuma. These towns were in the headlines in the wake of the disaster. They are all in the designated area of Daishōbō. Shortly after 3/11, my patrons needed to evacuate their homes because of the nuclear disaster. At that time, I received phone calls from some patrons living there: "Hoshino-san, may we stay with you?" I accepted four families from March 15 to the beginning of April. Twenty people stayed here. Of course, I wanted to go visit the disaster zone as soon as possible, but I had to host evacuees, so I couldn't leave my house. Every year in the winter, I travel to visit my patrons, right?

Well, in January 2011, I had just traveled to visit my patrons along the coast. I was *just* walking all through that area forty days before. When I returned in April, I saw that *nothing* along the coastline had survived the tsunami. I was stunned . . . speechless. *Absolutely nothing* was left standing! All the homes I had visited were destroyed. I had no idea where my patrons had gone. I hoped they had evacuated. I did meet some people who were still in the region. They said that because so many people died, they were unable to have proper memorial services. That's when I asked myself: "What can I, as a yamabushi, do to help?" That's when I first thought of performing a mass memorial service for the deceased as well as special prayers for the recovery and revival of the inundated coast.

Hoshino-san later told me of the challenges he and his family faced when hosting multiple families in light of the food and fuel shortages after the disaster. Before the disaster, Daishōbō had been a relatively low-key pilgrim's lodge with a stable, reliable flow of patronage. After 3/11, it faced new difficulties. However, Hoshino-san told me that once he fulfilled his responsibility to host his evacuated patrons, his priority became memorialization:

> A woman I know from Tokyo had the idea for a memorial on the summit of Gassan. Through Facebook, we sought 10,000 handwritten transcripts of the Heart Sutra, but we ended up getting around 13,000. The media helped us advertise and we received 3,800 from overseas! We decided to do the memorialization that same year, so we agreed on the last day that Gassan shrine was open, October 9. Since Dewa Sanzan is a *shinbutsu shūgō* [kami-Buddha] mountain, it seemed that the most appropriate place to begin our memorialization was Kōganedo temple. So, we requested the participation of Buddhist ascetics. Shimazu-san, the daisendatsu, accepted our request. Our chanting of each Heart Sutra transcript began there. Then, on the summit of Mount Haguro. After that, Daishōbō. Luckily, the weather was good on October 9. We went up Gassan in the morning, carrying everything to the top except for the monument, which came by helicopter. On the summit, we interred it.

Before the campaign, Hoshino-san was not a social media user. The first posting on his Facebook page is a photo of the enshrining of the disaster memorial monument. Hoshino-san then became increasingly proficient at social media and managed to gain quite a following for his three-day shugyō. The existential crisis that 3/11 provoked in people led to extraordinary demand for shugyō. While some of his critics say he started the shugyō as a financial pivot considering the sudden loss of his kasumiba to the tsunami, Hoshino-san says the popularity of his three-day program is more a reflection of a rise in demand for shugyō as opposed to his own efforts at self-promotion for personal financial gain.

A key ritual during his three-day shugyō is a memorialization for the souls of the disaster victims on the summit of Gassan. Rain or shine and usually facing the strong coastal winds from the Sea of Japan, he leads yamabushi to the 3/11 monument, tells them the standard interpretation of the summit of Gassan, that it is a portal between worlds, and then leads an invigorated recitation of the Heart Sutra before the memorial. Outside of shugyō, he regularly hosts pilgrims from around Japan and guides them to the summit of Gassan for a more intimate memorialization ritual dedicated to the disaster dead.

Conclusion

In this chapter, I have emphasized the relation between the cultural orography of Gassan and its historically entrenched death symbolism. The bidirectional transmigration of souls on the summit, their traveling to and from the afterlife through the portal of the peak, collapses the past and the present in moments of ritual communitas, most especially at eventide on August 13, the first day of the Festival of the Dead. For pilgrims and ascetics, the summit of Gassan is a site of orographic and spiritual transcendence, where natural beauty, ephemeral communities, and ancestor veneration coalesce beneath cosmic vistas for a single evening in the year.

Through the example of the disaster memorial, an effort led by Hoshino-san, we see that mountain ontology, the general doctrine of soul travel that yamabushi and pilgrims take to be true, is flexible and responsive to major events. Mountain pilgrimage on Gassan is not only a form of ancestor veneration and memorialization but a moral response to disaster. It presents a flicker of hope on the summit of a spirit mountain that acknowledges both the ancestral past and the past event of the disaster but also points ahead to future recovery. Hoshino-san, who leads yamabushi and pilgrims to the memorial, always emphasizes prayers for the future recovery of Tōhoku. The peak, though a place of the past in its orientation toward the ancestors, is also a place for the future, where pilgrims and yamabushi who may not have practical means to support the recovery can offer a prayer for the disaster dead while imagining Tōhoku anew.

Spirit mountains in Japan are pathways to the afterlife for the dead but also the living, who seek an intimate connection with their ancestors and wish to maintain bonds beyond the grave while they assist loved ones in their pursuit of posthumous Buddhahood. Natural disasters are cataclysmic events that disrupt the normal passage of time and can throw a nation into a period of prolonged distress and mourning. By adding special rites for the souls of disaster victims to traditional ancestor memorialization rituals on the summit of Gassan, yamabushi have provided a cultural therapeutic for pilgrims in post-disaster Tōhoku while also reorienting the temporality of the summit—transforming it into a place of hope for future recovery.

7 The Buddha Mummies of Mount Yudono
Cosmic Bodies of the Future Past

∙∙∙

I never got a chance to visit Mount Yudono with Itō-san as my guide during my first tour through Dewa Sanzan in July 2012. We explored Mount Haguro and Gassan together but not Mount Yudono. His plan was to drive to the eighth station of Gassan on the second day, climb up to the summit shrine and back down to the eighth station, then drive to Mount Yudono. We simply ran out of time. I was too slow on the trail going up Gassan. I had too many questions. But I couldn't let it go. He had said Mount Yudono was "a mountain of many secrets." What did he mean? Curious, I went to Mount Yudono the next day on my own.

From Tsuruoka Station, I took a ninety-minute bus ride that went around Mount Haguro, Gassan, and Mount Yudono Shrine (featuring the hot spring mound) to a small mountainside hamlet called Ōami. I had read there were some mummies in the temples there. Sounded interesting. After the bus dropped me off at a stop in Ōami, signs pointed the way to the two main temples, Dainichibō and Chūren-ji.[1] An uphill walk leads to a fork in the road. Signs point to either temple. Turn left for Chūren-ji, right for Dainichibō. Without a firm plan, I turned right for Dainichibō. I approached the temple through its Niōmon. Hanging from it were abnormally large straw sandals, honoring pilgrims who journey far.

I walked down a narrow path, then washed my hands and rinsed my mouth in the *temizuya* water basin stations in front of the temple. As I ascended the stairs to the temple, I was greeted by an attendant monk, an old, frail man with a big smile, in a dialect I could barely understand. He accepted my 500-yen entry fee at the door and then led me through a discrete hallway beside the main hall featuring Buddhist statues to a room near the back of the temple. I soon found myself kneeling before the robed remains of a mummified ascetic.[2]

Skeletal in form, with a thin, leathery layer of skin stretched tightly over the skull and hands, he was dressed in the colorful orange silk robes of a temple abbot as if alive. He was inside an elevated, glass-encased reliquary and

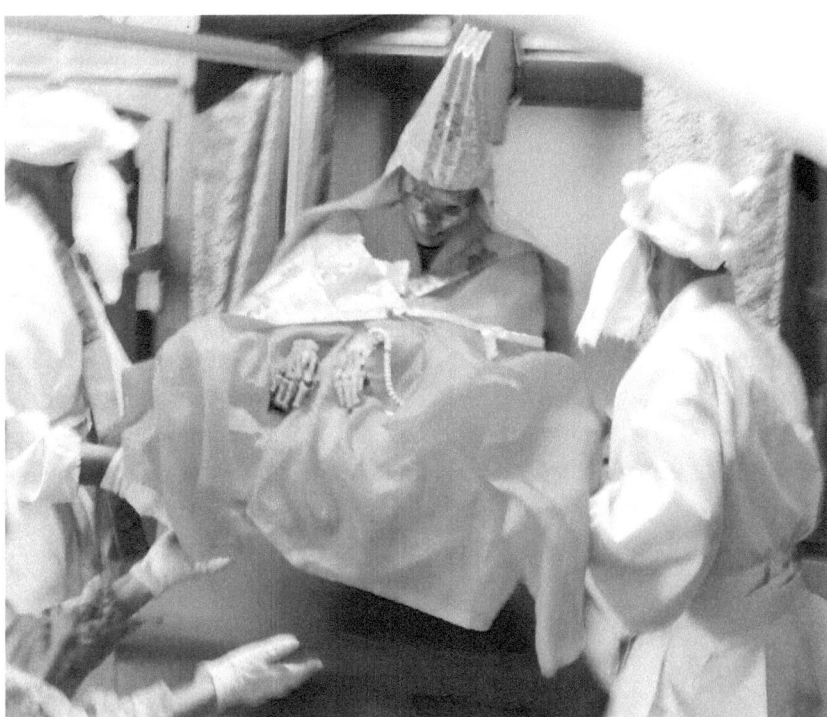

Monks remove a sokushinbutsu from a preservation case, Dainichibō Temple, Mount Yudono. Photograph by Shayne Dahl.

appeared to be seated in a half-lotus position, as though meditating. Before the reliquary, itself adorned with golden curtains, were golden ornaments, a large wooden box for pilgrims to make monetary offerings, stacked rows of gifts and letters, a singing bowl, and dozens of white cloth amulets (*omamori*). In all my travels in Japan and abroad, I had never seen anything like this.

I later learned that this mummified ascetic and others like him are called sokushinbutsu, "one who has attained Buddhahood in this very body." I prefer to translate this more simply as "embodied Buddhas." In the religious studies literature, they have been called "living Buddhas," "self-mummified Buddhas," and "flesh-body icons." They are the curated remains of a special class of ascetic in the history of Mount Yudono called *issei gyōnin*, "lifetime ascetic." According to Andrea Castiglioni (2024, 129–30), the leading expert on religious history in Mount Yudono, issei gyōnin were ascetics from the mid-sixteenth century. They operated outside of mountain entry rites such as Autumn's Peak and were not even ordained as monks. Instead, they engaged in self-seclusion *shugyō*, such as the One Thousand Days Ascetic Training (*sennichi-gyō*). The issei gyōnin "mobilized vast devotional and financial resources" by accruing karmic benefits from the death-defying intensity of their shugyō and transferred the power of those benefits to their patrons. During the One Thousand Days Ascetic Training, "issei gyōnin behaved as a bodily proxy for secular sponsors whose individual vows were fulfilled" through their shugyō.

The most elite of these issei gyōnin received two special treatments of their body upon death (Castiglioni 2024, 132). In the first case, the corpse of the issei gyōnin would be placed in a wooden coffin, then lowered into an underground cell built out of river stones. An earthen mound would be put on top of this underground cell, marked with a memorial stela featuring their name, formal title, temple affiliation, and death date: "The mound itself represented Mt. Yudono and, by extension, a chthonian form of Yudono Gongen [mountain deity] from within which the inhumated corpse of the *issei gyōnin* kept transferring karmic merit . . . to his devotees while remaining buried in his underground cell. Paying their homages to such an ascetic mound . . . worshippers could, at the same time, renew their karmic ties . . . with the eminent *issei gyōnin* they sponsored during life and venerate a miniaturized metamorphic body of Yudono Gongen in the guise of a Gongen mound . . . enshrined within the . . . geography of the village" (132).[3]

The second posthumous treatment of an issei gyōnin involved their remains being excavated from the underground cell after three years. As Castiglioni (2024, 132) writes, "Their corpses were subsequently treated with ad hoc materials such as the extract of *artemisia princeps* [mugwort] . . . and thereby transformed into actual bodies of Buddhas (*sokushinbutsu*). In this case, the desiccated corpse . . . of the *issei gyōnin* was worshipped outside the underground cell, usually with a portable reliquary cabinet . . . and enshrined in a dedicated hall . . . where it was venerated as a flesh-body icon . . . of a buddha." Becoming a sokushinbutsu was a fate reserved for very few owing to the complexity, cost, and risk of failure involved in the years' long procedure. Even so, the corpses of those ascetics who successfully went through these arduous metamorphic procedures have not failed to attract the devotion, curiosity, and scholarly interest of premodern and modern observers alike.

I didn't know any of this while I kneeled before the sokushinbutsu in Dainichibō Temple for the first time. I just remember being thrown into a state of awe at the sight of it. The sokushinbutsu has the physical appearance and spooky feeling of being alive. As Castiglioni (2024, 136) writes, the sokushinbutsu have an "ambiguous agency, which hovers between inert matter and living materiality." They "permanently oscillate between the status of objectified things and living trans-humanized subjects" (127).

This chapter explores how the sokushinbutsu are interpreted by and influence the lives of their attendant monks and temple patrons. Revered as "living Buddhas" by some and treated as historical artifacts by others, sokushinbutsu exist in a truly liminal space that collapses distinctions between life and death and the past, present, and future. Through oral histories, dreams and other paranormal incidents, the sokushinbutsu reveal the enduring power of the past they come from to shape the present they inhabit with their "ambiguous agency," offering protection and meaning to those who seek guidance from them while capturing the attention of pilgrims, tourists, and scholars alike. Drawing on personal anecdotes, ethnographic accounts, and historical insights, I argue that the sokushinbutsu are prisms of historical consciousness for contemporary beholders that inspire visions in their caregivers, cause political divisions between living monks, and generate capital through inventive means in the tourist industry while also unifying devote communities through distinct religious services. In all cases, the sokushinbutsu expand our understanding of agency, memory, and the boundaries of life itself by inserting their mysterious past into a confused present, sparking historical speculation and serious existential reflection.

The Mount of Mount Yudono

Kneeling before the impressive sight of the sokushinbutsu, the elder monk elaborated from a clearly rehearsed script on the historical significance of the temple and its sokushinbutsu.[4] I interrupted him, asking if I could record him. He gave permission, so I scrambled in my backpack to retrieve my recorder. "Let me tell you the story from the very beginning," he began:

> 1,200 years ago, Kōbō Daishi went to China to study Esoteric [Shingon] Buddhism. When he came back to Japan, he came *first* to Mount Yudono in Yamagata Prefecture. . . . The *last* place he would practice was Mount Kōya in Wakayama Prefecture. Kōbō Daishi founded Buddhism in Mount Yudono when he visited the boulder that is shaped like a woman squatting as she gives birth [*gohōzen*], the one with ferrous water pulsating outward. . . . That is why Mount Yudono is not really a mountain. You cannot find it on a topographical map. Mount Yudono is the boulder [*gohōzen*] that expresses hot water. It is not a woman with arms or legs or a head, but she has the organ that gives birth. She is the

boulder that gives birth to all human beings, everyone. She is Dainichi Nyorai [the Cosmic Buddha] incarnate in this world.

As the monk clarifies here, Mount Yudono is not a "mountain" (*yama*) as conventionally understood. It is not a distinctive mountain or dormant volcano with a summit. It is not even a foothill. Orographically, it is located on a spur of Gassan. The "mount" of Mount Yudono refers specifically to the gohōzen, the large ocher mound with a pulsating hot spring on top. The one that Shintō priests now refer to as the Great Boulder (*ōiwa*) and that Sakamoto Daizaburo (2012), placing his hands on the wet surface, compared to a vagina. In an interview with a different monk at Dainichibō a year later, I was told to look in the center of the gohōzen. "There," he said, "you will see a discrete slit that most people fail to see. That is the labia."

Castiglioni (2015, 25) writes that the gohōzen is, in Esoteric Buddhist doctrine, a "gigantic stone-vagina" (*join*). There are two apexes of the mound with open craters. In the past, when Mount Yudono was predominantly a Buddhist domain, "the bigger one on the left side represented the maṇḍala of the Womb Realm and the smaller one on the right was the maṇḍala of the Diamond Realm. Therefore, the entire body of the *gohōzen* was visualized as the maṇḍala of the Two Realms . . . and correspond to . . . the Buddhist notion of non-duality" (27). The gohōzen is "the site where Dainichi Nyorai [the Cosmic Buddha] naturally gushes" (27). It is "perennially coated by a thin layer of hot water" and "was worshipped as a lithomorphic manifestation of Yudono Gongen . . . the principal god of the mountain" (Castiglioni 2024, 129). The water, which is yellow and high in iron content, feeds into the Dabonji River, which leads to the two waterfalls of Mount Yudono described in chapter 2, where yamabushi undertake takigyō (waterfall practice). The area where all these sites are located is called the Valley of Immortals (Senninzawa), and it is where the issei gyōnin practiced their severe shugyō.

Mummified Monks in Esoteric Buddhism

The senior monk at Dainichibō continued his narrative as I gazed at the macabre features of the sokushinbutsu in its elevated, glass-encased reliquary: "In Mount Kōya [in 835 CE], Kōbō Daishi undertook nyūjō [entering a state of suspended animation] and became a Buddha in this very body [sokushinbutsu]. For 1,200 years, Kōbō Daishi has remained in eternal meditation. To this day, he is meditating. He entered his mausoleum while alive and he is still alive! Because he is not dead, monks still feed him. . . . Emulating Kōbō Daishi, this issei gyōnin, who is named Shinnyōkai, said, 'I wish to become a Buddha!' and willfully undertook nyūjō while alive. He entered his tomb and, like Kōbō Daishi, became a sokushinbutsu."

The source of motivation for this specialized deathbed practice is often attributed to a specific Buddhist prophecy that has resonated throughout Asia for millennia. The issei gyōnin are said to have committed themselves to self-mummification because they were convinced that an age of moral and societal degeneration began after the death of the historical Buddha, roughly 2,500 years ago. The prophecy goes that Buddha's teachings will gradually disappear from the collective memory of the world. This will give rise to "a period of catastrophic social turbulence."[5] The global amnesia of Buddha's teachings will ultimately be cured by Maitreya, the Future Buddha (Miroku in Japanese), who will revive the original teachings and usher in a new era of Buddhist awakening. This is slated to occur more than five billion years from the death of the historical Buddha.[6]

Kūkai or, as he is posthumously known, Kōbō Daishi is the eighth patriarch and founder of Shingon Buddhism in Japan. As legend has it, he was the first monk to have successfully practiced self-mummification.[7] After his physical death in Mount Kōya, Wakayama Prefecture, Kōbō Daishi was placed in a mausoleum. His followers claimed that his hair continued to grow and that his skin was warm to the touch.[8] This aligns with the belief that he was not dead but meditating, waiting for the Future Buddha so that he could assist in the salvation of humankind. We see this belief inferred in the narrative that the monk at Dainichibō Temple shared with me as well. The individual motivations of the issei gyōnin of Mount Yudono are often presented to visitors as having been inspired by Kōbō Daishi's saintly example. Following Kōbō Daishi's path, the issei gyōnin sought to preserve their bodies beyond death by entering a state of suspended animation (nyūjō) achieved through rigorous mountain austerities, intentional starvation, and self-entombment, so they could serve the Future Buddha.

The key method by which issei gyōnin of Mount Yudono are said in oral histories to have mummified their bodies involved a rigorous multiyear diet consisting of only tree bark and forest nuts (*mokujiki*) while undertaking prolonged mountain austerities.[9] At the end of their ordeal and after a final forty-two-day fast of only salt and water, the issei gyōnin are said to have drunk lacquer (*urushi*) and entered a stone chamber many feet below the surface. As their followers stacked river stones atop the chamber, they inserted a bamboo pole to connect the chamber with the surface to supply the issei gyōnin with air. Inside this tight space, the issei gyōnin are said to have chanted Buddhist sutras until their last breath. When they needed water, they would ring a hand bell. Once the bell could no longer be heard from the surface, attendant monks removed the bamboo pole and sealed the tomb for three years. After this period, the tomb was reopened, and if the body had not putrefied, the issei gyōnin's practice was deemed successful. He was presumed to have become a Buddha, a sokushinbutsu.[10]

In this pantheistic and panpsychist form of Esoteric Buddhism, "becoming a Buddha" means realizing nondual unification with Dainichi Nyorai, the Great Sun Buddha, who is the source and substance of the universe.[11] One way I have made sense of this over the years is by imagining the cosmos as Dainichi Nyorai's dream. In this analogy, the world is generated by Dainichi Nyorai's dreaming consciousness. As are sentient beings within it. Awakening to Buddhahood, then, is something like a lucid dream, becoming aware that one is dreaming while dreaming. By realizing that the dream world and one's dream self are generated by the same fundamental consciousness, one realizes the nondual nature of the dream state. In other words, the separation between world and self is understood as an illusion.[12] From an Esoteric Buddhist perspective, the nature of waking reality is no different. Human consciousness is a lens through which Dainichi Nyorai—the cosmos itself—experiences and perceives its own ultimate reality. Becoming lucid in waking life to the nondual nature of reality is awakening to Buddhahood.

As Fabio Rambelli (2013, xvii) explains: "Esoteric Buddhism considers the Buddha Mahāvairocana [Dainichi Nyorai, in Japanese] coextensive and identical with the entire universe. . . . Everything that takes place in the universe, either on a macrocosmic or a microcosmic (individual) level, is something done by, and part of, him." Dainichi Nyorai is not a "spiritual entity permeating the universe but envisioned instead as co-substantial with the universe itself." The implication is that everything that occurs is not only a part of its cosmic becoming but is an expression "of its ongoing cosmic sermon" (xviii). This applies also to the hora gai, which represents *Aum*, the cosmically diffuse drone of Buddhist awakening, and its spreading of the dharma, the teachings of Buddha, throughout the world. Life itself may be understood as a fractal emanation of cosmic becoming, the unfolding articulation of Buddha nature.

Having crafted incorruptible bodies through extreme shugyō, the sokushinbutsu are also said by attendant monks to have entered a deep meditation, nyūjō, as they await the Future Buddha.[13] Nyūjō is described by early researchers of the sokushinbutsu as "a state . . . wherein one attains absolute emotional stability and tranquility, complete attenuation of all bodily and intellectual functions."[14] While awaiting the arrival of the Future Buddha, the sokushinbutsu continue serving their temple and its patrons for the interim. They answer prayers, heal the sick, and communicate with patrons through altered states of consciousness. Considering the five-billion-year timescale of the prophecy, the sokushinbutsu are just a few centuries into their nyūjō. It is still early days.

Castiglioni (2024, 43) argues that, contrary to popular oral histories, the issei gyōnin did not self-mummify, were not motivated to follow the example of Kūkai, and did not arbitrarily seek to enter suspended animation: "The majority of *issei gyōnin* conceived ascetic practices as necessary procedures for preparing the body-mind . . . in view of [spirit] possession (*kamigakari*) focused on Yudono Gongen; delivering of oracular messages . . . and, more than anything else, for fulfilling the private vows . . . of those lay patrons who sponsored their religious activities during life. In other words, there was a difference between the internal conceptualizations of asceticism among the *issei gyōnin* and the way in which external social actors understood and narrated their religious activities."

Nevertheless, for contemporary devotees, sokushinbutsu are true immortals who pray incessantly for the welfare of humankind.[15] Every six years (twice in the twelve-year zodiac cycle), the robes of the sokushinbutsu of Dainichibō are completely removed and their frail frame is fitted into new robes.[16] Why six years? Mount Yudono was founded in the year of the ox. Visualizing the Chinese zodiac in a sphere, the reclothing ceremony follows every year of the ox and every year of the sheep, falling on a meridian (*shigosen*) axis of the twelve-year Chinese zodiac. The ox and the sheep are each other's antipodes, reflecting the equinoctial polarity of the zodiac calendar cycle.

According to Castiglioni (2015, 273), "The reclothing ceremony allowed the *sokushinbutsu* to produce other relics, which can be defined as 'contact relics.' The . . . garment[s] worn by the *sokushinbutsu* were believed to have absorbed the ascetic power embedded in the mummified body of the eminent *issei gyōnin* for twelve years and were preserved by the followers as protective amulets [*omamori*]." These *omamori* talisman are sold at the temples to this day. They are very popular.

The Politics of Sokushinbutsu

Beyond their religious significance and relevance to Buddhist prophecies, the sokushinbutsu of Mount Yudono figure prominently in contemporary temple politics in the form of competing claims by temple abbots about their historical authenticity. There is enduring concern with how the sokushinbutsu are represented in historical, popular, and academic discourse. This is especially clear when it comes to their classification as a "sokushinbutsu" or a "mummy" (*miira*). In an interview with a monk at Dainichibō during my primary fieldwork, this distinction was made very clear: "Shinnyōkai [the sokushinbutsu of Dainichibō] is not a mummy! He is *very* different! A mummy is dead. A sokushinbutsu is not dead. Maybe you have seen on TV how mummies are made as in ancient Egypt? They are dead bodies. The embalmer took out the organs from a hole in the side of the belly and pulled the brain matter out from the nostrils. To preserve the body, chemicals are used. *That* is a mummy!"

Speaking more explicitly about the difference between a sokushinbutsu and a mummy, the monk of Dainichibō criticized the authenticity of all other sokushinbutsu in Japan with exception of Kōbō Daishi:

> People who have seen a mummy say, "That mummy was shiny and black. I couldn't see well because it was so black. Is it a real sokushinbutsu or is yours here at Dainichibō real?" A sokushinbutsu should not be black and shiny! There are twenty-five so-called sokushinbutsu in Japan and nine in Yamagata. In Shōnai there are six. However, in Japan there is *only one* that is a true sokushinbutsu in the likeness of Kōbō Daishi and we are now kneeling before him. Just like Kōbō Daishi, Shinnyōkai did not decay after he entered eternal meditation. His organs, everything, are still perfectly intact.

As the monk at Dainichibō indicated, Dewa Sanzan has the highest concentration of sokushinbutsu in Japan.[17] There are six temples with mummified ascetics in the region today, but there are stories of more monks that remain interred, most likely crushed under the weight of a collapsed tomb and forgotten in time. Others burned to ashes in temple fires.

Acknowledgment of the authenticity of Shinnyōkai, the sokushinbutsu of Dainichibō, is of utmost importance to the attendant monks there. They openly criticize claims to authenticity made by monks at nearby temples whose sokushinbutsu have visibly "blackened, shiny faces":

> I will tell you why these mummies at other temples are black. First, the brain was pulled out through the nostrils and the organs were removed from an incision in the side of the belly. They needed to dry the corpse, so they hung the body in a small hut. To handle the smell,

they had to burn a lot of mugwort incense. That is why those so-called sokushinbutsu are blackened. Decades ago, the body [of Tetsumonkai at Chūren-ji] was so dilapidated that researchers from Niigata Medical School took it and did some restorative work with chemical varnish. That is why it is shiny. Many so-called sokushinbutsu like this are around. People think because ours is different from others it is not real, but this is the *only* real sokushinbutsu in Japan apart from Kōbō Daishi! Shinnyōkai did the real shugyō. The others did not. Mummies are treated by others. A true sokushinbutsu is self-fashioned.

The academic discovery of sokushinbutsu only occurred in 1954, when two Japanese researchers found locals of Niigata and Yamagata Prefectures worshipping them.[18] The remains of these long-deceased issei gyōnin, the researchers noted, were gradually eroding because patrons were extracting pieces of the bodies to consume as medicinal tea. This prompted researchers to rush in, conduct a series of medical tests, and commence historical research regarding the meaning of this practice. They also did restorative work.[19] The fact that restorative work was even required signals to the monks of Dainichibo that the sokushinbutsu were not successful in their self-mummification because their bodies were not incorruptible.

The monks at Dainichibō have key points they refer to when justifying their claims of authenticity regarding Shinnyōkai. Apart from the appearance of Shinnyōkai's skin (which is not blackened and is not shiny) is the half-lotus position of his body and his hands. He said: "Shinnyōkai has his head hung and his hands are palm-down, hanging over his lap, right? Clearly, in his final moments he was performing *gasshō* [palms steepled together in prayer]. When his power left [when he died, physically], his head fell forward and his hands, directly from gasshō, fell to his lap. This is what the natural position of one whose bodily functions ended in the middle of meditation looks like." As Zoe Crossland (2009, 76) writes: "The dead body . . . in its indexical referentiality is endowed with force and potential to act." For the monks of Dainichibō, the body of Shinnyōkai indexes its historical authenticity through bodily position as well as the skin coloration (that is, the lack of black charring and varnish).

More than once, the monks at Dainichibō have spoken with disdain about the international attention that the mummified ascetic at nearby Chūren-ji Temple has received (in particular, in *The Michelin Green Guide*) relative to Shinnyōkai. Once, a temple monk at Dainichibō compared the difference between Shinnyōkai and that of all other "so-called sokushinbutsu" to the difference between "a real airplane" and "a paper airplane." Recognition of the historical authenticity of Shinnyōkai is paramount to the monks at Dainichibō.

The head monk at Chūren-ji Temple is less interested in the historical authenticity of the sokushinbutsu at his temple, named Tetsumonkai, than the monks at Dainichibō. He was not interested in being interviewed on this subject in much depth. The only comments I heard from him on this topic were something to the effect of: "Other monks may say various things about Tetsumonkai—for example, questioning his authenticity as a sokushinbutsu—but I would not encourage you to put much stock in it. What is important is not what may or may not have happened during the mummification process but how each sokushinbutsu lived their lives for their communities and how their intentions in life have far surpassed their physical death. What is important is that they continue to positively influence people's lives in the present."

Supernatural Powers and Telepathic Messages

At some point, I realized that no amount of descriptive writing could capture the impressive spectacle of the sokushinbutsu and their associated rituals, so I teamed up with a local director, Watanabe Satoshi, in the summer of 2015, and we collaborated over the next couple of years to make a short documentary, *The Buddha Mummies of North Japan* (Watanabe 2017). We were able to film the reclothing ceremony and interview monks at Dainichibō and other temples as well as patrons of Chūren-ji, who indicated a clear devotion to Tetsumonkai, the sokushinbutsu of Chūren-ji (who has a blackened and shiny face).

An older man whom we interviewed and who is featured in our film, told us that he had lung cancer. Not knowing much about sokushinbutsu history or Esoteric Buddhism, he came to Chūren-ji and prayed with his family before Tetsumonkai many times. When his lung cancer went into remission, he and his family attributed the recovery to Tetsumonkai's healing power and have been devoted ever since. One local and famous chef I met during primary fieldwork confided in me that the success of his restaurant, which sees visitors from all over the country and around the world, is owing to the supernatural assistance of Tetsumonkai, to whom he prays regularly. Many people come to Tetsumonkai with their concerns and believe that in his state of eternal meditation, he can offer supernatural intervention to the faithful.

Kaikōji, a temple in Sakata City, just north of Tsuruoka, has two sokushinbutsu. The wife of the temple abbot there confirmed for me that the historical

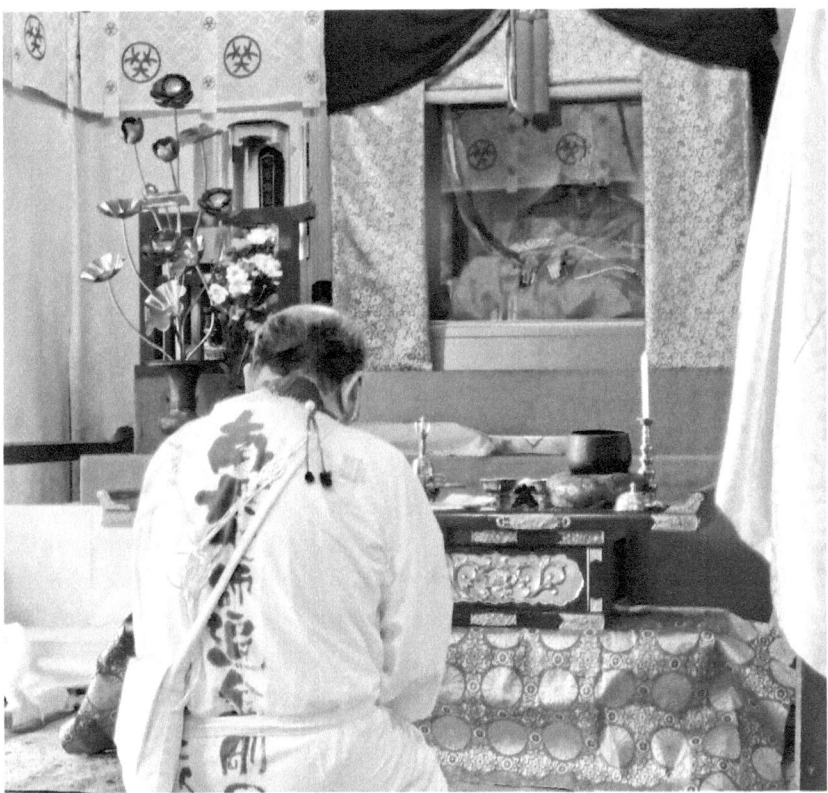

A pilgrim prays to the sokushinbutsu, Dainichibō Temple, Mount Yudono. Photograph by Shayne Dahl.

authenticity of the mummification process has little bearing on the significance of the sokushinbutsu for many contemporary people. In my interview with her, she indicated that some visitors come to sit and "stare into their empty eye sockets" for prolonged periods, contemplating mortality. A culturally unique form of memento mori. Facing the sokushinbutsu is also a face-to-face encounter with a "living Buddha," an enlightened being of the past who can manifest the prayers of the living in the present.

The abbot's wife claimed to receive telepathic "messages" from the sokushinbutsu at her temple. These messages relate directly to her private concerns but also have contained insights that pertain to others who may be experiencing difficulties in their lives and have come to the temple seeking guidance. She said:

> I always listen to the sokushinbutsu to understand what they want to say. People might think I am strange, but I will tell you this: I strongly

feel I have heard the sokushinbutsu. For example, when I got ill, I asked the sokushinbutsu of our temple in all seriousness: "Why did I get this sickness? Everyone comes here to pray for good health and happiness, but why am I, who live here and care for you, ill?" Soon after, I received an answer: "You are ill so that you can realize the true value of happiness, good health, and easy living. Only after struggle and suffering will you realize what is most important." While I was hospitalized with this illness, I really wanted to wash the kids' dishes. Truthfully, while I was sick, that was my greatest desire. After I could not do the dishes, I realized how much I love doing the dishes and other daily household tasks that I used to think were troublesome. When I heard the sokushinbutsu's voice, or not a "voice" but as a thought or a feeling, I understood his teaching: suffering is not a bad thing. It prompts realizations. Shugyō is such a process. Some people choose shugyō in the mountains, others have shugyō come upon them unknowingly in the form of illness or tragedy. I received this teaching from the sokushinbutsu and others like it not through words but through a psychic reception. It was not in Japanese. I translate the telepathic messages into Japanese. I accumulate them within, and when a patron or pilgrim comes and has some concern, I will pull a teaching out from the drawer, so to speak.

Her story draws interesting parallels with Tanya Luhrmann's (2004, 2012) account of American Evangelicals who claim to "hear" God through trained attention on subjective experiences. During prayer, for instance. Luhrmann calls this process "metakinesis." Like the abbot's wife who hears the sokushinbutsu without hearing an audible voice, Luhrmann's interlocutors describe "hearing" God but not audibly: "I felt like God just spoke to my heart. I don't know how else to put it" (2012, 68–69). Yet where the abbot's wife received telepathic messages from the sokushinbutsu that she had to translate into Japanese, Luhrmann's interlocutor did receive a linguistic communication: "It wasn't really a voice, she said, more 'kind of remembering the words on a page'" (69). While both perform metakinesis, attending to subjective experiences interpreted as supernatural communication, the major difference is that the American Evangelical God is disembodied and invisible whereas the sokushinbutsu is embodied and visibly present. As Luhrmann (xi) writes, "It ought to be difficult to believe in God. God is invisible. You cannot shake God's hand, look God in the eye, or hear what God says with your ears. God gives none of the ordinary signs of existence." To the contrary, the sokushinbutsu is visible, you can connect with them in religious services, you can look into their empty eye sockets, and you can, if you have the sensitivity of the abbot's wife, "hear" them. The sokushinbutsu give many signs of existence. The only leap of faith required is in whether they remain sentient in their mummified state. Many believe they do.

Prisms of the Past

For the monks of Dainichibō, the life and status of the sokushinbutsu derives not as much from the extrasensorial perception of them in the present as from the proper execution of their deathbed shugyō in the past. They contest the historical authenticity of other sokushinbutsu based on key points of evidence (such as the blackened face, the shiny skin, and the position of the hands) and insinuate that other sokushinbutsu are inauthentic. They are "just mummified corpses dressed up as sokushinbutsu."

In contrast, the monk of Chūren-ji sees the sokushinbutsu, no matter how the mummification process unfolded, as meaningful in the lives of contemporary patrons. This observation is, in my experience, true. The sokushinbutsu are liminal figures, biologically dead and socially alive, object and person. They are of the past, in the present, and connected to a prophesized future. Their inert bodies become mobile in the hands of temple monks during reclothing ceremonies and in the consciousness of patrons who received messages from them in waking visions or dreams.

Castiglioni contests the legend of self-mummification altogether. He asserts instead that the community of worshippers in Mount Yudono produced every sokushinbutsu. After their beloved issei gyōnin died, the community made it look as though the issei gyōnin mummified themselves. This is because issei gyōnin were adored spiritual leaders who procured karmic merit on behalf of their devotees.[20] Castiglioni (2015, xxxix) suggests that the legend of automummification persisted within the devotional communities that assisted in the mummification process owing to a "psychological removal of the pivotal role they played in mummifying the ascetic's corpse." The rituals of devotion surrounding the sokushinbutsu have no doubt solidified this "psychological removal" across generations.

In recent years, the sokushinbutsu have been featured in popular culture through comics, domestic and international travel tourism promotions, and even a two-part documentary drama on Japan's national broadcaster, NHK.[21] During my visit to Tsuruoka in 2016, I saw a "sokushinbutsu temple passport" available at one temple that visitors can get stamped and that directs visitors to other sokushinbutsu temples in the area. One monk overseeing a temple with a sokushinbutsu that I spoke with expressed concern with the increased presence of tourists in the wake of such coverage. He asked, pointedly: "Is that why they committed their lives to self-mummification? To become a tourist attraction?!"[22]

Public fascination with sokushinbutsu is nothing new, though. It goes back to the 1960s, shortly after their academic discovery. Tetsumonkai was delivered to downtown Tokyo and put on public display in the Seibu department store of Ikebukuro as a part of the *Exhibition on the Mummies of Japan*. This was coordinated with an NHK television special called *Visiting the Mummies' Village*, which reported high ratings. This public relations effort was an aspect of a broader effort by scholars and their financers to generate popular interest in the sokushinbutsu. In exchange for permitting the team of scholars to make a public exhibit featuring Tetsumonkai, monks of Chūren-ji received free restoration services on his body to enhance preservation. This is why Tetsumonkai's face is "shiny" (Castiglioni 2024, 146).

Despite disagreements between contemporary monks about what constitutes a sokushinbutsu, the centuries-old bodies of these mummified ascetics endure in the present. As I have argued in the case of mountains, sokushinbutsu located in temples within mountains warp modern space-time, even in the middle of a department store in downtown Tokyo, stimulating historical consciousness. Sokushinbutsu are not just "living Buddhas." They are also living history. Bodies of history. They are prisms through which history is remembered and interpreted. They immortalize not just a legend of issei gyōnin but key historical events and periods of the past, the speculative circumstances in which they committed their lives to shugyō.

According to the monks of Dainichibō and the historical record, Shinnyōkai, the sokushinbutsu of Dainichibō, entered his own tomb in 1786, at the age of ninety-six. This fact alone reveals that he did not pursue "self-mummification" for the sake of a solely ontological ideal. In 1782, four years before he is alleged to have entered his own tomb, the Tenmei Famine, "one of the worst and longest food crises of the Tokugawa Period," struck.[23] As Ann Jannetta (1992, 428) explains: "In 1782, poor harvests were reported in northern Honshū, Shikoku, and Kyushu, and, in 1783, there were freezing rain and severe floods in northern Honshū during the growing season. In the same year, Mount Asama erupted, covering a large part of the Kantō Plain—a major food-producing region which surrounded the shogun's administrative capital at Edo—with volcanic ash. In 1784, thirty domains in northern Honshū reported no harvest, and other areas reported declines in agricultural production of 40 percent. . . . The census of 1792 . . . [reveals] a loss of 1,119,159 people."

The Tenmei Famine, as with other major famines during the early modern period, from the late sixteenth to mid-nineteenth century, were "as much unnatural disasters as they were natural ones."[24] The chaotic climate in Japan was exacerbated by the eruption of Mount Asama, but it was also caused by the Little Ice Age that volcanic eruptions in Iceland triggered. As Brett Walker (2015, 132–33) writes, "The Edo *bakufu* [shogun administration] might have successfully isolated Japan from global political currents by evicting missionaries, but it could not isolate Japan from global environmental or climatological ones."

It was in this context that Shinnyōkai commenced a diet of forest nuts and tree bark. It was this context in which he, a ninety-six-year-old monk, became not just a Buddha in the eyes of his devotees but one less mouth to feed. "He was buried alive," the monk from Dainichibō explains, "knowing he had to pray for our collective salvation. So many others died of starvation at that time or lost their eyesight from malnutrition. Shinnyōkai felt he had to do something to save them, so he wanted to keep praying on their behalf, even beyond death."

While the historical consciousness of the Tenmei Famine that Shinnyōkai evokes for monks today aligns with the historical record, other sokushinbutsu with no historical records can inspire the same historical reflection. The sokushinbutsu in Zōkōin Temple, Shirataka, in southern Yamagata Prefecture, is one such case. Watanabe-san and I interviewed the attendant monk for *The Buddha Mummies of North Japan* film, but it was my earlier interview with him that revealed the relation contemporary monks make between sokushinbutsu and the Tenmei Famine regardless of historical accuracy. The sokushinbutsu of Zōkōin is named Kōmyōkai. His name is known, but there are no remaining historical records. The records were burned in a temple fire decades ago. Kōmyōkai was exhumed in 1978 by the attendant monk's father. Kōmyōkai's body had been crushed, so his skeletal remains were reassembled and put on display in a glass-encased reliquary.

During my first meeting with the monk of Zōkōin, he explained that although there are no historical records of Kōmyōkai, we can infer from the elaborate tomb in which he was interred and the valuable items found with him that he was highly respected. Speculating, the monk suggested that it is likely he committed himself to pray on behalf of humankind during a time of great societal crisis since that is a pattern among other sokushinbutsu. With tears welling up in his eyes, he imagined what it must have been like:

Kōmyōkai, sokushinbutsu of Zōkōin Temple, Shirataka, Yamagata Prefecture. Photograph by Shayne Dahl

Perhaps it was during one of the famines in the past that Kōmyōkai decided to become a Buddha? Life was very hard in Tōhoku in the past. It got so bad. I have heard stories of mothers killing infants by smashing their heads in a rice pounder just so they would be able to afford to feed older children. Could you imagine raising a child amid such a crisis? In this painful time, the ascetic who would become sokushinbutsu, such as Kōmyōkai, would have thought deeply about what they could do, despite their limited power, to alleviate the suffering. Refusing to eat, becoming one less mouth to feed, is one option. Praying eternally for humans in suffering is another.

As much as the monk of Zōkōin imagined the context in which Kōmyōkai interred himself (if, indeed, he did inter himself), the monk is the first to admit that he does not know because there are no existing records. Even still,

Kōmyōkai is greatly respected. As the monk explained to us in his filmed interview: "The fact that sokushinbutsu like Kōmyōkai left their remains behind suggests to me that their shugyō is incomplete. I believe that even after their mummification, their heartfelt desire to undergo such extreme shugyō on behalf of future generations . . . is something that they are continuing even now as an eternal shugyō. . . . That's something I think about every time I pay my respects to Kōmyōkai."

Conclusion

The sokushinbutsu reveals that mummified bodies, like mountains, affect modern space-time through the historical consciousness they inspire, even in the absence of historical records. The body of Kōmyōkai and the bodies of Shinnyōkai and other sokushinbutsu are prisms of the past—bodies of history to be read through "clues and signs."[25] Claims are made of the legitimacy of sokushinbutsu and whether they are "alive," in a state of eternal meditation, but all sokushinbutsu are agentive in the present, influencing the lives of the living, acting, communicating, and making actual differences in the modern world. They are believed to be capable of treating cancer. A sokushinbutsu may be different than a mummy, but both are prisms to the past, bodies of history that speak without words.

The sokushinbutsu influence monks in the present to imagine the past, but they also influence the consciousness of the living in interesting ways, as we see with the example of the abbot's wife who claims to receive telepathic communications from them. I have met and interviewed other temple patrons who have asserted that the sokushinbutsu appear to them in dreams and telepathically communicate important advice about life to them. I thought this was an obscure aspect of the sokushinbutsu until I had my own dream of Shinnyōkai.

It was just before the production of *The Buddha Mummies of North Japan*. I remember thinking through the ethics of filming the reclothing ceremony. Was it inappropriate to film Shinnyōkai's naked remains when he is worshipped as a living Buddha? In my dream, I was kneeling. Shinnyōkai was beside me. Suddenly, he put his hand on my knee as if to say it was OK to proceed with the film. It seemed to me after waking from this dream that the sokushinbutsu, who are dressed and treated as though they are alive, have a peculiar psychological-spiritual effect on the consciousness of the people who engage with them. Perhaps the sokushinbutsu appear to us as scarecrows do to birds—lifeless but embodied, present, and psychologically effective. Although they are physically inanimate, they become animate in the imaginations of devotees and caretakers through visions of history and in mysterious dreams. The sokushinbutsu clearly exhibit a form of "postmortem agency."[26]

One story shared with me by a monk at Dainichibō was about the tsunami. A patron of the temple had previously bought an *omamori*, a protective cloth amulet that contains a piece of the sokushinbutsu's robe, cut from the redressing ceremony. He hung it from his rearview mirror in his car. On March 11, 2011, he had been driving near the Sanriku Coast when he realized that a tsunami was fast approaching his location but he was stuck in traffic. Just then, the omamori started swinging in a northwestern direction. He felt in that moment that it was a sign from Shinnyōkai telling him where to go. He then drove off-road in that direction and found a path between buildings that led him to safety. Months later, he came to Dainichibō and made a special offering of sake to express his gratitude. Stories like these abound. There is still much research to be done on the enduring influence of the sokushinbutsu.

Epilogue
The Mountain Vista

∙ ∙

In the first pages of this ethnography, I compared memories of fieldwork to a dream. Having arrived at the final chapter, I cannot help but compare the experience of writing this ethnography to a circuitous pilgrimage through the mountains of that dream, up their steep paths and over their luminous summits, in their waterfalls, through their mandalas. Having traversed the mountains of Dewa Sanzan physically many times during fieldwork and now, through a yearslong waking dream, what conclusions can be drawn? What does the mountain vista, a panoramic view of all preceding chapters, reveal?

Each chapter presents distinct episodes of Dewa Sanzan and its representations, offering a fragmented glimpse into the cultural orography and temporality of the mountains for modern tourists, ascetics, and pilgrims. This approach, which has enabled me to convey a range of distinct perspectives of Dewa Sanzan, demonstrates one of the first claims I made about mountains: they are not merely geological formations. A mountain is not just a mountain. In the case of Dewa Sanzan, mountains are living placeworlds populated by people practicing millennium-long religious traditions, which are an integral part of the mountainous landscape. Sacred mountains in Japan absolutely collapse the nature-culture divide.

Where Bernard Debarbieux and Gilles Rudaz (2015) argue for "orogenesis," the social construction of the "mountain" as a concept, I suggest further that specific mountains and mountain ranges are constituted by orographic perspectivism, which I define as the entanglement of multiple orographies by which humans interpret, relate, and react to mountains. Like water taking the shape of its container, mountains manifest differently in the eyes, experiences, and, as this ethnography has shown, rituals and religious lineages of their beholders. Mountains transform over time and across generations in the popular imagination of a given society but are also subject to diverse views between individuals and groups of the same generation, even within the same small community. In the same moment that people engage mountains, mountains affect people, "dialoging" with them through the soles of their feet and the pores of their skin and through the interpretive frameworks of their culture and individual disposition. They inspire awe and wonder, grief and fear, and emotional reflections on gender and sexuality. Mountains are constituted by diverse and often conflicting interpretations that are shaped by the complex interplay of culture, personal experience, religion, and imagination.

The tourist experience described in chapter 1 is very different from the *shugyō* of Hoshino-san's three-day program described in chapters 2 and 3. Shintō-oriented shugyō is markedly different than the shugyō of Autumn's Peak for Buddhist ascetics described in chapter 5. Even within Hoshino-san's shugyō or within the Buddhist version of Autumn's Peak, ascetics have very different experiences of the mountains. Pilgrims of Gassan encountered in chapter 6 have their own motivations and interpretive frameworks for pilgrimage, as do the patrons of the sokushinbutsu temples described in chapter 7. As the spirit medium I met on the summit of Gassan said, "Dewa Sanzan is a place of many experiences" (*irona taiken ga dekimasu*).

Despite the manifold interpretations of orographic perspectivism, it is possible to discern a common thread tying the episodes of Dewa Sanzan I have presented together. The second takeaway from this ethnography is that from an urban Japanese perspective, mountains are and have long been viewed as places of spatiotemporal alterity. They stand in topographical and ontological contrast to capitalist modernity and the world of the living. In this capacity, mountains can be theorized as a geographically fixed *espace autre* (other space), heterotopias animated by competing modes of historical consciousness. Sacred mountains are places where social constructions of time bend, twist, fold, and swirl.

Although this phrasing suggests a conceptual divide between "society" and "mountains," echoing the structuralist divide between "nature" and "culture" (see Descola 2005), it is apparent in the way urban and rural Japanese approach and think about mountains, even if they labor to overcome that divide through shugyō. Despite the push by figures such as Hoshino-san to resurrect the premodern notion of *jinen* (human-nature unity) to emphasize the nondualism beneath the nature-culture schism, it remains intact conceptually, even among contemporary ascetics, and is a productive space where other structural divides, such as modernity and tradition, are being negotiated in the ethics of participation, as discussed in chapter 5.

The irony of the mountain-as-otherworld trope is that it is this nostalgic, idealized view of mountains that has made them into places of intense social activity in modern times. In the same way that the "modernist nostalgia" Ivy

(1995, 10) speaks of "must preserve . . . the sense of absence that motivates its desires," urban Japanese preserve a sense of untrammeled nature in mountains, which motivates their desire to ascend and be immersed within them. As an "other space," mountains enable Japanese people to symbolically break away from the mounting psychological pressures of capitalist modernity and the peculiar "neuroses" it can cause.[1]

Mountains can also be thought of as "key symbols" in Japan that contain a host of "root metaphors," symbols that operate "to sort out experience, to place it in cultural categories, and to help us think about how it all hangs together" (Ortner 1973, 1341). In Japan, mountains are elevated placeworlds where rivers double as thresholds to the otherworld, where gateways double as symbolic vaginas, where summits are portals to the ancestral domain, where caves are wombs and stone pillars are phalluses. Mountains have strong associations with death, the ancestors, and "the otherworld" while engendering uterine symbolism. The ritual process of Shugendō fuses birth, death, and rebirth in the womb of the mountain. Mountains are places where souls of the dead go after they die and where ascetics go to die and be reborn. This ethnography reveals that sacred mountains in Japan are, as they have long been, fertile grounds for the regeneration of self and society.

A word that stands out to me as I reflect on the grand journey of writing this ethnography is something Itō-san said (see chapter 3): "Within nature, there is a birthing power [*umidasu chikara*]." This umidasu chikara is the essence of Shugendō as I have experienced it in Dewa Sanzan. Pillar-shaped boulders and walking staffs held in the left hand are phalluses while anomalous hot spring mounds, lakes, caves, and hora gai held in the right hand are vaginas. The mountains are wombs. The temples are wombs within the womb of the mountain. Ascetics are embryonic fetuses that gestate within them through shugyō and are reborn from them upon its completion. Shugendō is profound in its symbolic ritualization of reproductive biology and for harnessing that symbolism in a highly complex ritual framework to inspire an existential awakening about the varied dimensions of the human condition as well as the fundamental nonduality of consciousness and cosmos. At the core of Shugendō is a deep recognition of the umidasu chikara, the birthing power of nature from which all life emerges.

In this ethnography, I have treated mountains in Japan as vectors of time that not only reach into the past, present, and future but draw together multiple pasts, multiple presents, and possible futures. Although mountain time can be as varied as the subjects who experience and interpret it, there are observable patterns of temporal engagement. In the sense that mountains and Shugendō make present old, anachronistic ways of life for contemporary people, they are also places of moral alterity, places to imagine a more fulfilling life, one that defies cultural norms. By providing critical distance from urban centers, mountains can inspire moral critiques of society and foster new forms of counterculture. Ascetics such as Sakamoto and others interviewed have developed critiques of contemporary Japanese society through the critical distance that shugyō provides. In the case of pilgrimage, mountains can offer a unique form of cultural therapy as well, a way to renew ancestral bonds on sacred peaks while also serving as a moral response to disaster through caring for the posthumous repose of the tsunami dead.

Since the introduction of Buddhism to Japan, mountains have been a place for existential reflection.[2] In 788, the Tendai Buddhist monk Saichō established a monastery on the summit of Mount Hiei. In 816, Kūkai, the founder of Shingon Buddhism in Japan, established his monastery on the plateaued summit of Mount Kōya. Since at least twelve hundred years ago, the mountains of Dewa Sanzan have been used for similar pursuits, as have sacred mountains from every part of the Japanese archipelago. In Asia, mountains are and have long been places set apart from society, places that seekers go to contemplate the meaning of life and practice rebirth.

From the widest possible frame, I have approached this ethnography as a contribution to the anthropology of mountains and time through a specific case study of Shugendō in Japan. Anthropological positions I have developed about mountains such as orographic perspectivism and cultural orography and methods I have pursued in them such as alpine ethnography by working in Dewa Sanzan are applicable to any mountain in or beyond Japan. The case study of Dewa Sanzan illuminates our understanding of the nature-culture dynamic in Japanese capitalist modernity, but it also points to a greater cross-cultural relation between human beings and mountains, a bond that can be explored in a multitude of ways in every inhabited continent and that will certainly yield new disciplinary insights. The anthropology of mountains figures into the social imagination, history, religion, and the creation of new knowledge through the critical distance high altitude provides. In a similar way that ethnography makes the strange familiar through participant observation in a different culture, entering the alternate space-time of mountains creates critical distance from society. This is why mountains attract philosophers, ascetics, and pilgrims alike.

Disciplines such as geography, history, and religious studies have made strides in the study of mountains, but anthropology, despite its attentiveness to place-making and historicity, the delicate sociopolitical dynamics holding communities together, social links between the local, regional, and the global, has only until recently began thinking beyond the human, considering the contexts of research as objects of research themselves. Mountains are ripe for ethnographic discovery and anthropological theory. Throughout a good part of the world, the symbols of a society's highest values are found on the summits of its highest mountains. Much anthropology remains to be done on the slopes and summits of the mountains of the world and much remains to be explored in Dewa Sanzan. This book is just a sampler plate. It's not a definitive account. It's more like an invitation. Many mysteries remain in Dewa Sanzan. There is a lot that I don't yet understand. Shimazu-san, the daisendatsu of Buddhist-oriented Shugendō, certainly left me with that impression during our final interview.

I remember it clearly. The date is December 9, 2015. I enter Shozen-in Temple as I have many times before. First, I kneel before the golden-hued Buddhist statues. I light an incense stick and place it in the incense burner. Then, I steeple my hands in *gasshō* and bow forward to the Buddhas. I stand up and walk to a room to my right side where there is a sit-down table. I kneel across a table from Shimazu-san on the tatami mat floor. It's cold, so I'm relieved when he serves me a steaming cup of green tea. I take a few sips. It warms up my core. We have a wide-ranging interview. I'm checking off my list of questions to consolidate my understanding of everything I have experienced over the past three years of Autumn's Peak. Near the end of the interview, I ask him one last question: "Many scholars have come to study Shugendō. You've seen them come and go. Is there a common aspect of it that, in your opinion, they tend not to understand?"

To focus my energy on comprehending his difficult Japanese, I peer into my cup of green tea on the table, which is now empty. Silence. I assume he is contemplating a response, so I wait in anticipation. Staring into the teacup, at fragments of leaves in a small pool at the bottom, I feel my heart rate increase with the awkwardness of the prolonged silence. After what feels like a full minute or more, I look up, timidly. A jolt of adrenaline surges through me when our eyes meet. A stone cracks open. He is smiling.

Notes

Prologue

1. This scene is also depicted in Minao Kitamura's film *The Autumn Peak of Haguro Shugendo* (2009).

Introduction

1. The reference to Dewa Province in the place-name of Dewa Sanzan, the Three Mountains of Dewa, signals the premodern era of feudal territories in Japan (Hopson 2017, 33).

2. Tōhoku comprises Aomori, Akita, Iwate, Yamagata, Miyagi, and Fukushima Prefectures. The region received global attention in the wake of the earthquake, tsunami, and nuclear disasters that struck off the Sanriku Coast on March 11, 2011.

3. See Allision (2013).

4. Tsing (2005, 174) writes, "Landscape is both social (created within human projects) and natural (outside of human control; populated by non-human species)." It is also temporal, "made by a history of movement and connection" (182).

5. As Bender (2002, 103) observes, "Landscape is time materializing." See also Ingold (2010).

6. Palmié and Stewart (2016, 233) define "historicity" as "cultural paradigms modulating historical experience and practice."

7. Lambek (2018, 14) suggests that "historicity . . . is simultaneously and intrinsically ethically informed and inflected, concerned with how to live and with living as it matters. It is a matter both of finding the world we think we want and of understanding what we owe ourselves, our contemporaries, or predecessors, and our successors as we proceed."

8. Capitalist modernity can be generally characterized through its institutional forms, such as "clock time, industrial work discipline, and nation-state archival practices," and the "linear, homogenous, abstract time" that such forms operate within to pursue production (Bear 2016, 488). In precarious times, capitalist modernity can also appear as a time when "futures have lost their utopian qualities" because of the "emergence of radically unpredictable evacuated near futures" (Bear 2014, 489; see also Guyer 2007).

9. Death from overwork (*karōshi*) (North and Morioka 2016), solitary death in old age (*muenshi*) (Tsuji 2018, 27), and extreme agoraphobia among youth who have locked themselves in their rooms indefinitely (*hikikomori*) (Saito 2013) account for just a few of the effects of this social alienation. In post-bubble, post-disaster Japan,

capitalist modernity is referred to as "relationless society" (*muenshakai*), "a country where the stitching of connectedness between people is fraying at the seams" and where "being alone—literally, psychically, socially—is the new human condition for Japan/ese in the 21st century" (Allison 2012, 346; see also Allison 2015, 131–32).

10. Hope, as Miyazaki (2004, 138) writes, is "an aesthetic of emergence."

11. The Gregorian calendar was introduced to Japan in 1873 (Nishimoto 1997).

12. Gell's (1992) approach to time marks a clear departure from Leach, Geertz, and Munn, each of whom attend closely to social constructions of time and their influence on the experience of life and the structure of society (see also Durkheim 2008; Evans-Pritchard 1990; and Lévi-Strauss 1966). In the conclusion of his sweeping critique of "time-anthropology," Gell (1992, 315) writes, "There is no fairyland where people experience time in a way that is markedly unlike the way in which we do ourselves, where there is no past, present, and future, where time stands still, or chases its own tail, or swings back and forth like a pendulum. All these possibilities have been seriously touted in the literature on the anthropology of time . . . but they are all travesties, engendered in the process of scholarly reflection." My ethnography is more aligned with Munn, Leach, Geertz, and Lambek.

13. *Oros* means "mountain" in ancient Greek. "Orogenesis" was coined in 1840 by Swiss geologist Amanz Gressly (Debarbieux and Rudaz 2015, 1).

14. To draw in a classic line from Geertz's (1973, 5) definition of culture.

15. Alexander von Humboldt (1769–1859) and other Enlightenment geographers first articulated and universalized a scientific notion of "the mountain." Humboldt (1997) is best known for *Kosmos*, a five-volume treatise that converged geography, astronomy, and biology and other disparate disciplines into a unified "cosmography." Having "inspired Charles Darwin to board the *Beagle* and Franz Boas to do fieldwork among the Inuit," the legacy of *Kosmos* is undeniable in anthropology, though not often acknowledged (Morita 2017, 231; Walls 2009, 210–50).

16. As Debarbieux and Rudaz (2015) discuss, the French word *montagnard* was once used as a derogatory term for rural people living near mountains; it was later repurposed by alpinists and nationalistic discourses.

17. See Bolin (2009).

18. See Rhoades and Thompson (1975).

19. See Orlove (2002).

20. Himalayan anthropology has been the most influential in this regard. Since the early twentieth century, when British expeditioners first sought to climb Mount Everest, the Himalayas have captured the orientalist imagination of the West. The best-known British expedition of Mount Everest in the first half of the twentieth century was in 1924, when George Mallory and Sandy Irvine disappeared during their attempt for the summit (Davis 2011). Mountaineers have debated whether they summited before dying for the better part of a century. Tenzing Norgay (1955), a Sherpa mountaineer, and Sir Edmund Hillary (1955) of New Zealand were the first to reach the peak of Everest, and their success has inspired hundreds of mountaineering expeditions up Everest and a vast and growing corpus of mountaineering literature specific to Everest, including failed attempts (Denman 1954), tragedies (Krakauer 1997), and historic successes (Allison and Carlin 1993). This long-standing attention

to the Himalayas through mountaineering worked in tandem to sustain the demand for Himalayan anthropology. A major contribution to Himalayan anthropology, and to the anthropology of mountains specifically, is Sherry Ortner's *Life and Death on Mt. Everest* (1999). Going far beyond a cultural ecology model of mountains, Ortner's account balances Sherpa and Western mountaineer perspectives of and approaches to mountains, specifically to Mount Everest, referred to in Sherpa and Tibetan as Chomolungma, "Goddess Mother of the Earth." Having scoured through hundreds of mountaineering books and memoirs, Ortner characterizes Western mountaineers as romantics seeking transcendent, countermodern experiences at the risk of death in high altitude but who could never have reached the summit without the assistance of the Sherpas who live in the Khumbu Valley below. The Sherpas have figured into the orientalist imaginary of the adventure-seeking Western mountaineer as countermodern mountain people, childlike helpers. For a more recent ethnography of the Himalayas, see Jonathan Miles-Watson's *Christianity and Belonging in Shimla, North India: Sacred Entanglements of a Himalayan Landscape* (2021).

Julie Cruikshank's *Do Glaciers Listen? Local Knowledge, Colonial Encounters, and Social Imagination* (2005) presents another pivotal text in the anthropology of mountains. In it, Cruikshank recounts a colonial mountain politics in the Mount Saint Elias range, which lies on the political border of Alaska, British Columbia, and the Yukon. Where Ortner observed contemporary interactions between Sherpa and Western mountaineers on the mountain, Cruikshank considers "entangled narratives" of mountains through colonial writings and indigenous oral history. She observes that in the oral histories of the Tlingit and Athabascan peoples, "glaciers take action and respond to their surroundings. They are sensitive to smells and they listen. They make moral judgements and they punish infractions" (1). Glaciers are "both animate (endowed with life) and [are] animating (giving life to) landscapes they inhabit" (1). To early colonists who sought to map and overtake the northwest, indigenous paradigms were "casually dismissed as 'superstition'" (20). Cruikshank (259) suggests that even environmentalists who seek to move beyond colonial bureaucratic structures deploy a neocolonial model of environmental protection that unintentionally "appropriates and reformulates" indigenous knowledge under the guise of "co-management" and "sustainable development."

The idea of mountains as a sociopolitical domain between indigenous and Western-colonial ontology is also apparent in South America. In a comprehensive summary of ethnohistorical and archaeological accounts in the Andes, Swenson and Warner (2015) observe many threads of "mountain theology" at play in pre-Columbian societies, where human sacrifices made on summits were a ritually mediated technique for claiming territory and consolidating empires. For centuries, they write, "mountains as living deities, ancestral *apus* [gods], and progenitors of human communities, have played a central role in Andean religious life and political relations" (23). Elevated ceremonial complexes (*huaca*), which are found throughout the Andean archaeological record, functioned as "mimetic mountains" in their capacity to increase the efficacy of ritual. Other ethnographic accounts in the Andes such as Frank Salomon's *At the Mountain's Altar: Anthropology of Religion in an Andean Community* (2018) and Marisol de la Cadena's *Earth Beings: Ecologies of Practice across Andean Worlds*

(2015) demonstrate that traces of such "mountain theology" are alive and finding new footholds in contemporary Andean society and politics. Ausangate (20,945 ft.), a sacred mountain used for pilgrimage in the Vilcanota range of the Peruvian Andes, emerges in *Earth Beings* at the center of a struggle between indigenous-environmental protection and resource extraction by a mining company. In the end, "The mountain won, the mining corporation lost; but to earn the victory, the earth-being was made invisible, its presence withdrawn by the alliance that defended it" (275). Drawing parallels with Cruikshank's account, Ausangate had to be rendered significant and worthy of protection, not for its value to indigenous peoples as an "earth-being," but for its ecological value, which is determined in nonindigenous, environmental discourse. Andean mountain theology takes new, secularized forms to necessitate the protection of indigenous territory and knowledge.

21. Orographic perspectivism is distinct from the perspectivism of Viveiros de Castro (1998, 2004), which has strongly influenced anthropological discourse in the past thirty years. "Perspectival anthropology," in Viveiros de Castro's usage, is an indigenous epistemic critique of anthropology, an attempt to invert the one-nature, multiple-cultures disposition of anthropology and conduct analyses instead through the logic of Amerindian perspectivism, a one-culture, multiple-natures disposition. By dropping the "Amerindian" qualification while still retaining a distinctly "Amerindian" logic to "perspectival anthropology," Viveiros de Castro strives to generalize beyond the "Amerindian" case and make a theoretical provocation in the discipline, reorienting or inverting the way we do anthropology. By launching "perspective anthropology" from a specifically indigenous framework, Viveiros de Castro has fortified a specific model of perspectivism in anthropology, yet the term itself has a much more general meaning than Viveiros de Castro's radical modification implies.

The orographic perspectivism I intend is not an application of Viveiros de Castro's (2004) "perspectival anthropology," nor does it entail "Amerindian perspectivism," a cosmological disposition specific to the Americas in which "humanity is . . . the reflexive condition of a subject to itself, while animality is the condition of the body regarded from an external point of view" (Vanzolini and Cesarino 2014).

22. Referring to Tsing's (2005) ideas on "friction."

23. The furusato and its iconic mountain are emblematic of modernity's wager—the sacrifice of emplaced identity and community in one's ancestral village for the prospect of greater opportunity, prosperity, and an overall better lifestyle in the city. Robertson (1997, 103) explains, "Although *furusato* literally means 'old village,' the word is used most often in an affective capacity to signify not a particular place, that is an actual old village, but rather the generalized nature of such a place and the nostalgic feelings aroused by its mention." The image of furusato is linguistically temporal: *furu(i)* "signifies pastness, historicity, age, quaintness, and the patina of familiarity and naturalness that culture artifacts and human relationships acquire with age, use, and interaction" (104). See also Robertson (1988) and Creighton (1997).

24. As Reader and Tanabe (1998, 158) write: "The name Daikoku . . . is a direct translation of Mahākalā" who is in some Buddhist sutras described as "a manifestation of Mahāvairocana who can subdue demons." He is also described as "a great bodhisattva of good fortune who shares his wealth with the poor, and it is for this

characteristic that he is known as one of the Seven Gods. Well-fed and smiling, Daikoku carries a sack of good fortune over one shoulder; in his other hand he holds a small mallet for hammering out wealth (*uchide no kozuchi*)."

25. See Ivy (1995, 29–65).

26. Caleb Carter (2025, 407) also writes, "Since its modern introduction to Japan, mountaineering has been construed as a secular sport severed from mountain worship."

27. If we were to deconstruct the term "hybrid" we would see that each "half" implied in the term is an assemblage of perspectives that vary greatly between groups and individuals. My use of the term "hybrid" represents the conjoining of two general dispositions toward mountains that are varied within but that mostly adhere to common assumptions about mountains—that is, whether mountains are sacred abodes of the kami that religious specialists must approach through ritual mediation or whether they are material landscapes for the subjective pleasure of secular mountaineers. *One Hundred Mountains of Japan* represents a synthesis of these dispositions, weaving as Fukada does, between religious and secular perspectives of mountains.

28. See Hood (2015, 11–13).

29. See Goodman (2005).

30. Other notable reizan in Japan where Shugendō and other forms of asceticism are practiced include Mount Hiko in Fukuoka Prefecture (Grapard 2016), Mount Ōmine in Nara Prefecture (DeWitt 2015; McGuire 2013), Mount Fuji in Shizuoka Prefecture (Earhart 1989, 2011; Sawada 2022), Mount Ontake, which straddles Gifu and Nagano Prefectures (Blacker 1999, 279–97), Mount Togakushi in Nagano Prefecture (C. Carter 2022), Mount Iwaki (Fujiwara 2021, 151–71; Schattschneider 2003), and Mount Osore in Aomori Prefecture (Ivy 1995, 141–91).

31. See Price (2015).

32. Canadian anthropologist Peter Gose (2018, 488) discusses the meta-personhood of mountains in Andean culture.

33. See Foucault (1984, 1). As Munn (1992, 94) also writes: "Although Western theory frequently treats space as time's antithetical 'Other,' time's Other turns out somewhat embarrassingly to be its Other Self."

34. The collapsing of space and time is not new in anthropology. Bakhtin (1981, 84) has drawn Einstein's formulation of space-time into literary theory to develop the notion of "chronotopes," which has been adopted by anthropologists for a range of analytic purposes. Palmié and Stewart (2016, 218) write: "In contrast to the naively Newtonian nature of Western temporal common sense, Bakhtin's concept analogically recurs to a post-Einsteinian relativity from which a plurality of senses of space and time become not only thinkable but also potentially psychologically and socially inhabitable." Where Foucault's "heterotopias" differ from Bakhtin's chronotopes is in their emphasis on the otherness of certain spaces and how this otherness distorts social space and time, twisting and dividing it into a multitude of other-than-nows and other-than-heres that can be used to gain critical distance from the here and now.

35. See Ian Reader's book *Religion and Tourism in Japan* (2023) for recent examples.

36. According to Hobsbawm (1983, 1), "'Invented tradition' is taken to mean a set of practices, normally governed by overtly or tacitly accepted rules and of a ritual or

symbolic nature, which seek to inculcate certain values and norms of behaviour by repetition, which automatically implies continuity with the past."

37. See Walker (2015, 159–78).

38. See Josephson (2012). This theocracy was unraveled with the "Humanity Declaration" of Emperor Hirohito when he declared that he was, in fact, human and not a kami descended from Amaterasu, the Sun goddess (Ohnuki-Tierney 1991, 206).

39. See Walker (2015, 261–82).

40. See Hopson (2017, 15–16).

41. See Creighton (1997).

42. The "refined high culture" of Nō theater, tea ceremonies, and so on are examples that Ivy (11) draws on to emphasize not only the fetish of authentic tradition in modern Japan but also how certain fetishes are selected for international export as marketable icons of national-cultural identity.

43. See Hopson (2017) and Traphagan and Thompson (2006).

44. See Lindholm (2008).

45. See Hopson (2017, 14–16).

46. Recent works in the study of Shugendō and mountain religion in Japan include: Amada (2019), C. Carter (2022, 2024, 2025), Castiglioni (2015), Castiglioni, Rambelli, and Roth (2020), DeWitt (2015), Earhart (2011), Faure, Moerman, and Sekimori (2009a), Fujita (2005), Hirasawa (2013), Lobetti (2014), Grapard (2016), McGuire (2013), Miyake (2005, 2001), Sawada (2022), Schattschneider (2003), Shimazu (2005), and Suzuki (2015). See Sekimori (2009b) and Suzuki (2020) for more detailed state of the field overviews.

47. Castiglioni, Roth, and Rambelli (2020, 1) write: "On the one hand, [Shugendō] places the natural environment at the core of its practices, with ritualized "mountain entries" . . . as its most defining feature. On the other hand, Shugendō focuses on the acquisition of special powers . . . aimed at both attaining spiritual advancement and ensuring a livelihood through healing and exorcisms, as well as more standard religious services."

48. See also Lobetti (2014), Miyake (2000, 2001, 2005), and Sekimori (2016).

49. Castiglioni, Roth, and Rambelli (2020, 3) write that although Shugendō was "a shadow of its former self" when it began its postwar revival in 1946, "it remains a living tradition to this day . . . currently gaining new momentum, thanks to growing interest, both in Japan and internationally, for eco-spiritual concerns."

50. Caleb Carter (2022, 4) describes the "ideological rigidity" that has characterized "romanticized" images of Shugendō's past, giving early studies of Shugendō a "guise of ahistorical constancy." Acknowledging the importance of contemporary Shugendō, he writes, "Minute attention to ritual preservation or reenactment can stifle contemporary adaptations, closing the door to evolving interests and new participants. Although some practitioners may prioritize continuity with the past, others have been drawn to Shugendō through rising trends in spirituality (*supirichuariti*), mental wellness, and a desire to connect with the rigors and beauty of the mountains."

51. Suzuki (2020, 58–59) writes: "The imaginative power of hybridity," the fusion of tradition and modernity, "is at the root of Japanese culture" and is what generates the most potential for the continuity of Shugendō.

52. See Dahl (2023).

53. See Hori (1962) and Castiglioni (2019, 2024) for influential essays on the mummified ascetics of Mount Yudono.

Chapter 1

1. See Allison (2013), Gill, Steger, and Slater (2015a), Kingston (2012), and Samuels (2013) for accounts of the disasters that struck Tōhoku on March 11, 2011, beginning with a magnitude 9.0 earthquake. An estimated 18,600 people died across Fukushima, Miyagi, and Iwate Prefectures (Gill, Steger, and Slater 2015b, 6).

2. Ascetic training programs are now revived and updated. As Reader (2024, 185–86) writes, "One of the websites Lonely Planet cites talks of how for centuries ascetics have walked in the Dewa Sanzan mountains seeking enlightenment and adds that 'for the first time, you can too' by engaging in what it states are 'authentic ascetic mountain practices' via a variety of courses that have been 'curated specially for an international audience for the first time ever.'"

3. *Kami* loosely translates as "god" or "gods" in English but could also be described as natural or ancestral spirits.

4. As Stausberg (2011, 8) notes: "Tourism, far from being the *other* of religion, is a major arena, context and medium for religion in the contemporary global world."

5. See Horie (2017) and Ivy (1995, 128).

6. Using power as the measure of analysis, Grapard's approach is characteristically Foucauldian. It is an approach Ortner (2016, 50) has described as "a virtually totalizing theory of a world in which power is in every crevice of life, and in which there is no outside to power." Power is present and active in Dewa Sanzan; however, my concern with the power of Dewa Sanzan in this chapter is not in the sense of historical power relations. Here, I am interested in the power of the mountain in terms of the multiple temporalities and modes of historical consciousness that set the space of the mountains apart from their modern surroundings.

7. As Geertz (1973, 10) famously wrote, "Ethnography is thick description."

8. As Lambek (1995, 246) writes, "Time is not fully consecutive; the past is not finished and done with, receding ever further into the distance, but (in grammatical terms) imperfect." Nietzsche ([1874] 1998, 88) also writes that by virtue of memory and a collective sense of past happenings, human existence is basically an imperfect tense.

9. Vignau (2013) has shown how the alphorn has attained global influence while retaining its symbolic value as an icon of Swiss nationalism. She even documents how the alphorn has flourished in Japan and how yamabushi attended and participated in an alphorn event with their conches, finding universal value in their mutual cultural practice of using mountains as amphitheaters with their horns.

10. The *oku* of Bashō's writings has been translated as both "interior" and "deep north." While *oku* literally means "interior," it is also an old geographic reference to northeastern Japan.

11. Alternatively translated as *The Narrow Road to the Deep North*.

12. I draw on a translation by Donald Keene (Matsuo Bashō 1996, 104, 108, 112) here but have made a minor revision on the third line of the second stanza. In Japanese,

the line is *tsuki no yama*. Keene translates it as "Moonlit Mountain," but this is an alternative reference to Gassan (Moon Mountain) that positions the possessive particle (*no*) between moon and mountain. One could translate it as "moonlit mountain," "the moon's mountain," or, as I have, "mount of the moon." In the original Japanese, Bashō's haiku for Dewa Sanzan read as follows. Mount Haguro: 涼しさや、ほの三か月の、羽黒山。**Gassan:** 雲の峰、幾つ崩れて、月の山。**Mount Yudono:** 語られぬ、湯殿にぬらす、袂かな。

13. See Shirane (1998).
14. Yuasa (1967, 37).
15. Ueda (1970, 52).
16. See Qui (2005), S. Carter (2000), and Heyd (2003).
17. Shirane (1998, 212).
18. See Shirane (1998, 182). Here I am using "poetic places" as a gloss for *utamakura* or *haikaimakura*. Literally, the translation is "song pillow" or "haiku pillow," places where poems sleep.
19. *Atarashimi*.
20. Yuasa (1967, 37).
21. See Keene (1997, 11) and Shirane (1998, 227).
22. In tandem with what has been said of ethnography (Geertz 1973, 15). See Shirane (1998, 225).
23. Shirane (1998, 36).
24. See Schattschneider (2003, 28). Mountains throughout Japan have inspired poetry and, for poetry enthusiasts, likely inspired other forms of literary pilgrimage. Mount Iwaki in Aomori Prefecture to the north is a case in point. It also has a rich tradition of poetry and mountain asceticism (see Fujiwara 2021, 151–71).
25. Yamadera, a mountain with a series of Buddhist temples on it, is the most well-known site to which *haiku* pilgrims go in Yamagata Prefecture.
26. See Thompson and Traphagan (2006) and Hopson (2017).
27. The former *niō* of Mount Haguro's gate are now in Koganedō, one of the few remaining Buddhist temples in Tōge.
28. Translating *jigoku* as "hell" is problematic, since hell implies Christian theology; however, this is Itō-san's translation. Scholars also often translate *jigoku* as hell. See Hirasawa (2013).
29. See Bushelle (2018) and Deal and Ruppert (2015, 69–86).
30. See Grapard (1982, 2016) and Miyake (2005).
31. See Earhart (1970, 30).
32. See Castiglioni and Roth (2020, 2).
33. See Hirasawa (2013, 82) for Tateyama in Toyama Prefecture. See Ivy (1995, 141–91), Miyazaki and Williams (2001), and Reader (2024, 20–23, 236) for Mount Osore in Aomori Prefecture.
34. *Avalokiteśvara* in Sanskrit.
35. As Rodrigues (2006, 199) explains: Viṣṇu "holds a discus (*cakra*), a club (*gada*), a conch (*śaṅkha*), and a lotus flower (*padma*)."
36. *Mahāvairocana* in Sanskrit. See also Heisig, Kasulis, and Maraldo (2011, 1251).
37. This was in Mount Hiko in Kyushu.

38. At the hora gai workshop, participants were given a technical manual that described how to play a range of melodies that are specific to Buddhist-oriented Shugendō in Mount Haguro. Different melodies are closely connected with different stages in the ritual procession of annual mountain entry rites. Reflecting the influence of Onmyōdō (Way of Ying Yang), the hora gai pitch notation in the technical manual is signified by the five elements of Chinese metaphysics: wood, fire, earth, metal, and water.

39. Amada (2019) has argued that traditional Shugendō is in decline in Japan but the consumption of Shugendō through heritage tourism is increasing. From an anthropological perspective, I would avoid such value judgments as they are rooted in presumptions about authenticity and tend to diminish the increasingly global complexity of contemporary Shugendō. Just because Shugendō now exists in an era of capitalist modernity and is adapting to its new circumstances doesn't mean that it, as an old religion with new movement, is in decline. Rather, it is undergoing a global transformation.

40. *Ano yo* refers to the "otherworld," a concept that refers to the dimension of ghosts, spirits, sprites, and ancestors.

41. As Keesing (2012, 407) has observed, "The symbolic systems of a community are structured . . . in layers—from outer, transparent, meanings down to inner ones, access to which requires increasing degrees of esoteric knowledge / poetic imagination / philosophical insight."

42. As Keesing (2012, 407) explains: "The existence of such a coherent symbolic structure requires only that enough members of the community have access to the deeper symbolic layers of the culture to perpetuate these structures."

43. See Kawano (2005, 1).

44. Caleb Carter (2018) also discusses the crossover between tourism and power spots in modern-day Shintō shrines but indicates an ambivalence on the clerical side. There is hesitant embrace of the power spot designation by priests because it draws visitors yet also deemphasizes the traditional religious order.

45. See my article "Sutra as Speech Act: Shugendō Rivalries and the Heart Sutra in Northeastern Japan" (Dahl 2023).

46. See Tanahashi (2014) and Dahl (2023).

47. See Saunders (1985, 179).

48. Before the importation of the Gregorian calendar in 1873, the Chinese zodiac calendar was the standard measurement of time in Japan (Nishimoto 1997; Steger and Steineck 2017); however, the zodiac calendar is still used to regulate the ritual cycle in many contexts throughout Japan.

49. Architectural floodlighting, referred to as *raito appu* ("light ups") in Japanese, has become a popular way to illuminate historical buildings and cityscapes throughout Japan. In Mount Haguro, it is used to illuminate the stone stairway, Grandfather Cedar, and five-storied pagoda.

50. The year 2014 was also Heisei 26 in the imperial calendar (that is, the twenty-sixth year of Emperor Akihito's reign). Ironically, at the same time as the Meiji government adopted the Gregorian calendar from the West, the imperial calendar, which counts years in relation to an emperor's reign, was used both to reorient time and to align history with nativist temporal order.

51. North, east, south, and west have one Buddhist deity each, while northwest, northeast, southwest, and southeast each contain two Buddhist deities each, for a total of twelve deities in eight directions. This also connects with the twelve-animal Chinese zodiac.

52. Seishi Bosatsu is *Mahāsthāmaprāpta* in Sanskrit.

53. See Benjamin (1969, 263).

54. In Japanese: 継子坂.

55. See Stausberg (2011, x).

56. Dewa Sanzan has, specifically and vicariously through the regional narratives of Tōhoku, also been subject to a "denial of coevalness" (Fabian 1983) in the national cultural imagination. Fabian's notion of "the denial of coevalness" was originally used in *Time and the Other* to critique twentieth-century anthropologists who pushed the subjects of their research into "primitive" temporalities to make "modern" sense of their lifeways. Fabian described this analytic method, in which ethnographers deny the coevalness of their interlocutors, as "allochronism." The regional exoticism of Tōhoku in Central Japan, which spans more than a millennium, engenders a "denial of coevalness" in its persistent reluctance to emphasize the contemporaneity of Tōhoku and its people, places, and customs.

Chapter 2

1. *Engawa* constitute an outer veranda to traditional homes and are often used as a liminal social space between inside (*uchi*) and outside (*soto*). Visitors who wish to meet only briefly with a person at their home will sometimes enter no further than the engawa to avoid burdening the person from hosting.

2. *Uchi* and *soto* are distinguished in other aspects of Japanese society, relationality, and language. See Bachnik and Quinn (1994).

3. Daytime napping (*inemuri*) is common and tolerated in Japan. It is a "subtle method of showing commitment to work" because it signals exhaustion and a loss in nocturnal sleep time (Steger 2003). I do not think this reading of inemuri is suitable for Hoshino-san, though. Over time, I would come to read his inemuri as a performative combination of disinterestedness and contemplation that signals his authority in relation to other speakers. A person of lower status would certainly not nap or appear to nap before Hoshino-san.

4. Gift exchange is an essential aspect of Japanese sociality (Rupp 2003). Among yamabushi, gifts are usually left in the altar (*kamidana*) as they are accepted on behalf of one's tutelary kami and ancestors and opened later.

5. Ruth Benedict (1946, 223) has argued that shame works as a potent sanction in Japan and furthermore that Japan is a "shame society" when compared with American "guilt society." Although some scholars have argued against this characterization, Creighton (1990) has asserted that Benedict merely intended to identify the relative emphasis that Japanese society places on shame as an aspect of socialization and childrearing.

6. Since I met him, Hoshino-san (2017, 2018) has published two books that reflect his views.

7. Roseman and Badone (2004, 2) have observed that "rigid dichotomies between pilgrimage and tourism, or pilgrims and tourists, no longer seem tenable in the shifting world of postmodern travel." Decades earlier, the Turners (1978, 20) likewise observed that "a tourist is half a pilgrim if a pilgrim is half a tourist."

8. Here, I am mobilizing Bourdieu's (1985) notion of "social capital" to the context of Hoshino-san's community of yamabushi. Bourdieu (1988) has also qualified social capital to particular contexts to show how inequalities emerge (for instance, in his discussion of "academic capital" in *Homo Academicus*).

9. Within Esoteric Buddhist Shugendō, the idealized horizon of selfhood is infinity, the indistinguishable union between self and cosmos, which is imagined in the form of the Great Sun Buddha, Dainichi Nyorai (Rambelli 2013).

10. Ortner (1999, 38–39) observed a similar pattern among mountaineers in the Himalayas: "For these men, modernity is the problem, and mountaineering is the solution. Where modernity is vulgar and materialistic, mountaineering is sublime and transcendental. Where the modern is noisy and distracting, mountaineering is peaceful and conducive to reflection. Where the modern is soft and boring, mountaineering is difficult, challenging and thrilling. The 'there' of Everest contrasts with the 'here' of the modern." Here, she refers to George Mallory's famous line. When asked why anyone would want to or should climb Mount Everest, he answered: "Because it is there!"

11. Van Gennep (1960, 15).

12. See Mauss (1973).

13. See also Reader (1993).

14. See Hardacre (2017, 117).

15. See Dahl (2023) for an account of how the Heart Sutra figures into the history and politics of contemporary Dewa Sanzan. Shultz (2021) draws attention to some of the ways in which the Heart Sutra is being reimagined in Japanese popular culture today.

16. In Japanese: 諸々の罪穢れ祓い禊ぎて清々し.

17. In Japanese: 遠つ神笑み給へ綾威の御霊を幸へ給へ.

18. In Japanese: 天つ日嗣の栄えまさむこと天地の共無窮なるべし.

19. In Japanese: あやに　あやに　くすしく　尊と　月のみ山の　神の御前を拝みまつる.

20. In *The Awakened Ones*, Obeyesekere (2012, 48–49) suggests that "solitude seekers cultivate the space of silence that permits It-thoughts to emerge in consciousness." In his paradigm, "It-thinking" is contrasted with "I-thinking." I-thinking is intentional, conscious, and willfully directed because it is the consciousness of "discursive thought." It-thinking, by contrast, is "passive cerebration" (41), a mode of consciousness that emerges from silence in which "truths" may appear. Interpreted through this lens, the silence of shugyō can be understood as a means to generate "It-thinking," though it is followed by a return to "I-thinking" when yamabushi reflect on their experience afterward.

21. The famed "marathon monks" of Mount Hiei, who practice the most extreme forms of shugyō, likewise report heightened sensitivity to their immediate environment. Some claim to hear the sound of ash falling from an incense stick (see Covell 2004).

22. See also Satsuka (2015, 180).

23. See Mauss (1973).

24. See Sharf (2015). Although the inclusion of zazen, like the chanting of the Heart Sutra, is a Buddhist component of Hoshino-san's shugyō (and he presents it as such, describing his practice as "combinatory" of Buddhist and Shintō elements), Buddhist-oriented Shugendō has no such zazen practice in Dewa Sanzan. Seated meditation is not common practice among most Buddhist monks in Japan. Hoshino-san's inclusion of zazen is more reflective of popular Zen Buddhism and the global mindfulness movement than it is of Japanese Buddhism or Shugendō in or beyond Dewa Sanzan today (see Wilson 2014). He has adjusted the purpose of it, though, teaching that the purpose of zazen is to attend closely to and become present with nature.

25. In Japanese: "修行というと、つらいことの連続のように想像していましたが、実際はそうではありませんでした。昼間、山で見た飾り気のない自然の美しさ、ほんの二切れのタクワンのおいしさ……。日常生活ではなかなか気が付かなかったものです" (Sakamoto 2012, 39).

26. In Japanese: "表へ出ると星がきれいでした。夜でも明るい都会では、見ることのできない夜空です。星座を探している人もいました。怖いくらいの星の数です。天の川も浮かんでいます。星が目のようで、いっせいにこっちを見ているように感じました。江戸時代の頃までは、星を見ることを恐ろしいと感じる人たちもいたという話を思い出しました。僕にもその気持ちがわかったような気がしました" (Sakamoto 2012, 44).

27. In Japanese: "手向から少し離れた森の中を歩いていました。昨晩と同じように「死」の世界を感じます。しかし、昼間、月山で感じた「死」とは種類が違うようです。月山はとても透き通ってクリアな世界でした。月山は、においもシンプルでしたが、羽黒の森の中は、どこか獣じみた、粘り気のあるにおいです。歩くたび少し重みがあるような空気が身体にまとわり付いてくるような感じがします。それは不愉快であったり、恐ろしかったりはしません。ずっと身近にあったはずのもののようです。眠りにつくときに、目を瞑るとあらわれるような暗闇でした。月山や羽黒の闇の違いを感じて、死者の霊が低山に止まり、やがて高い山に登って神になると考えた古代の人々の感覚が、現代人の自分の中にも、同じように流れているように思えました" (Sakamoto 2012, 63–64).

28. In Japanese: "森の先は見晴らしの良い丘でした。あたり一面畑です。眼下には鶴岡の街の夜景が広がっています。僕は街の灯りを眺めました。あそこは家族団欒しているのかな、友達と騒いでいるのかな、恋人とイチャイチャしているのかな……。たった二日間ですが、そんな日常生活から離れていました。無秩序の世界である自然の中では、かえってシンプルな自分が見えてくるようです。山にいると、普段気にしていることが、どうでもいいことのように思てきます。自分も無くなって、普遍的な人間というものが、見えてくるような気もしてきます" (Sakamoto 2012, 64–65).

29. In Japanese: "できるだけ煙を吸い込まないように、鼻で大きな呼吸をして、回数を減らしました。突然、鼻の奥で、いままで感じたことのない刺激を感じました。やばい！これをまともに吸い込んだら大変なことになるぞ！そう直感し、煙を避けようと、身を低くしました。薬味が焼けるパチパチという音ごとに、煙が濃くなり、前が見えなくなっていきました。涙がポロポロとこぼれ落ちてきて、大量の鼻水も流れています。呼吸は……大丈夫です。すると、背後から勤行が聞こえ

てきました。「もろもろのー、つみけがれー、はらいみそぎて、すがーしー...」諸々の罪穢れが、僕の目や鼻から液体になって流れ出ているようでした。煙の中でなんとかやっていけそうだと感じはじめた僕は、みんなと一緒に勤行をしようと口を開きました。それが間違いでした。「もろもろのー、つみーけが...れ...ごほごほごほっ!!!」一度煙の中で咳き込んでしまうと、もう息をすることができません。ああ、自分はこのままだと気絶するな。息が詰まる音が道場に響きました。生命力をかきたてるのではなく、魂が離れて飛んでいってしまいそうです。でも、行の途中で部屋を出ていくのも、せっかく羽黒までやってきて山伏の修行をしているのに、投げ出してしまうよう嫌でした。いろいろな感情がわき起こってきましたが、苦しくて、何がなんだかわからなくなりました" (Sakamoto 2012, 42–44).

30. Cash to the kami and the priests who mediate them in exchange for the fulfillment of prayer has long been custom in Japan (Reader and Tanabe 1998).

31. In Japanese: "湯殿山への道はとても険しく、ほとんど人がいません。足場の悪い崖を鉄ハシゴを頼りに下りて行く場所もあります。後に、古くから出羽三山を信仰している千葉の講の方に聞いたのですが、そういったところを先祖が歩いた道と考えて、同じ道を進み、先祖との一体感を思うのだそうです。霊魂のふるさとである月山で先祖の霊と出会い、先祖の辿った道を歩いて里へもどり、その命のサイクルを次代へと紡いでいったのです。長い年月の中で、どれだけの人が、この道を踏んできたのでしょうか。自分が歩く一歩一歩も、もしかしたら、どこかの誰かから受け継ぎ、受け継がれていく歩みなのかもしれません" (Sakamoto 2012, 54).

32. Schattschneider's (2003, 210) interlocutors, female ascetics in Mount Iwaki in Aomori Prefecture, also describe *amae* (maternal dependence) in relation to the mountain.

33. In Esoteric Buddhism, it is referred to as *gohōzen* (Castiglioni 2015, 25–30). See chapter 7.

34. See Porath (2024, 18).

35. I have fused two translations of this haiku together, Keene's (Bashō 1996, 112) and Yuasa's (Bashō 1968) to best express the context and affective impact of Bashō's account of Mount Yudono. In Japanese: "語られぬ、湯殿にぬらす、袂かな."

36. See Scheid and Teeuwen (2008), Castiglioni and Rambelli (2020), and C. Carter (2022).

37. In Japanese: "岩を登るために、手をついた瞬間です。僕の身体に衝撃が走りました。生々しい弾力が伝わってきたのです。「岩が生きている」人間の身体のようでもありました。僕はその感触に心当たりがありました。それは女性器に触れた感触と同じだったのです。湧き出る温泉が、暖かい愛液のようにヌルヌルと僕の指の間を通り抜けていきました。岩は人間と同じだ。人間は岩と同じだ。そう思うと、僕は自然の中に吸い込まれていくように感じました。その感覚は不思議に懐かしいものでした。子供の頃にみた夢の感覚でした" (Sakamoto 2012, 55–58).

38. Schattschneider (2003, 155) describes a similar practice in Mount Iwaki at a boulder called *ubaishi*.

39. See Sato (2005) for an extensive discussion of takigyō in meaning and practice.

40. See Matthews (1996).

41. In Japanese: *basaitō* (場採灯).

42. In Japanese: "無事に修行を終えた僕たちは、三日間の汚れと疲れを落とすために、手向近くにある温泉に向かいます。待望のこの瞬間、みんなもう大人なの

に、目を見開きキラキラ光らせて、夏休みの小学生のような顔をしていました。何しろ生まれ変わったばかりです" (Sakamoto 2012, 68).

43. Schattschneider's (2003) account of female ascetics doing shugyō in Mount Iwaki is an excellent ethnographic case study, as are Lobetti's (2014) broad survey approach in his book *Ascetic Practices in Japanese Religions* and Caleb Carter's historical account, *A Path into the Mountains: Shugendō and Mount Togakushi* (2022).

44. See Yamabushido (2024).

Chapter 3

1. See Schnell (1997) for more about the significance of *sake* in Japanese religion and culture.

2. In Japanese: "お酒が進んでくると、酒が二升入る真っ赤な大杯が登場します。僕たちは、なみなみそそがれた酒を、みんなで回し飲みするのです。僕もずいぶん飲みました。「おい、ヨカチンやれ！」星野さんから声がかかりました。ヨカチンとは、地方によっていろいろなバリエーションがあるお座敷芸です。大聖坊のヨカチンは羽黒近くの学校に伝わっていたのもだそうです。一升瓶を男根にみたてて、かけ声に合わせてくねくねと踊る、エロスあふれるダンスです" (Sakamoto 2012, 69–70).

3. In a section of his second book, Sakamoto (2013, 141–45) discusses the deep relation between *matsuri* (festivals) and sexuality. He provides examples from early ethnological studies that describe food and reproduction as expressions of "cosmic rhythm." He describes one kind of premodern festival called a *konone* (木の根) matsuri in which attendees were permitted to have sex with people other than their spouse in the nearby forest, using the root of a tree as a pillow. The kami were imagined descending into the bodies of men in a form of spirit possession. The deification of the men consecrated and made socially permissible extramarital sex during the konone matsuri. Sakamoto uses this example to suggest that sexuality, as the driving force of human procreation, is a fundamental element to matsuri culture that has been diluted over time but the vestiges of that sexual culture can be observed in the sexual symbolism of Shugendō rituals and sacred mountain landscapes today.

4. In Japanese: "山に入ると起こした問題が消える。"

5. In Japanese: "僕がはじめて山伏の世界に足を踏み入れたとき、一番驚いたことが自分の身体のことでした。パソコンに向かって仕事をして、ほとんど身体を動かさず都会暮らしで鈍っていた身体が、山を歩き断食をすることで、ほんの些細な変化に気がつくようになったのです。それはお腹がペコペコの時に食べたオニギリやタクワンのおいしさに気がついたとか、そんなに格好いい話ではないのですが、自分自身にとっては大きな発見でした。「山伏になって何が変わった？」と聞かれることがありますが、僕は何かが変わったのではなく、もともと自分の身体の中にあった物を再び見つけ出すことができたように感じました。それはアウトドアや登山をやるだけでも良いんじゃないの？と言われることもありますが、現在のアウトドアスポーツが近代的な西洋文化を背景に持っているのに対して、山伏の世界は日本列島に人が暮らし始めた頃から培われた文化を根底に持っているものなので、より自分にとっては関心が惹かれるものでした。孤独の中を生きていかなくてはならない人間ですが、自分自身の身体に目を向けてみた時、食や性など、そこには自然、

宇宙のリズムと呼応している生々しい自然が息づいていることを見つけ出すことができるはずです。当たり前のことなのかもしれませんが、このことに気づいた時、僕はけっこう感動しました" (Sakamoto 2013, 149–50).

6. "The more you do shugyō, the livelier and more energized your spirit becomes" (修行するほど魂はイキイキと活性化する) (Hoshino 2018, 28).

7. In Hardacre's (2017, 49) description: "The heavenly deities commanded Izanagi and Izanami to make the land solid. The pair then stood on the Heavenly Floating Bridge, lowered a jeweled spear into the brine beneath them, and stirred. The drops that fell from the spear's tip coagulated and formed an island called Onogoro. The pair then descended from the bridge to the island, where they set to work to 'give birth to the land,' by engaging in sexual intercourse."

8. As discussed of Hoshino-san's first book in the section titled "母なる山、母体の海、野生は魂(Mountain as mother, ocean as mother's body, wildness as spirit)" (2017, 97).

9. See Sekimori (2018) for a more nuanced discussion of the role of the ocean in Shugendō religious history.

10. Schattschneider (2003, 210) has drawn on Freud to discuss the "fantasy of infinite *amae*, of complete maternal dependence" apparent in female mountain asceticism in Mount Iwaki in Aomori Prefecture.

11. See Hardacre (2017, 21).

12. For a more historically accurate account, see Nishimoto (1997).

13. In Japanese: "旧暦の時代は太陰太陽暦だった。月の回りの太陰暦で日にちを数え、太陽のめぐりの太陽暦で季節の変化を加える。旧暦時代は一年のサイクルと季節感がピッタリ合っていたんだろう。それに、近世までは、女の人たちの野生が保たれていたと思うね。女性の体は月とつながってルカラ。女の人の野生が強いのは、やっぱり月のものの関係でしょう。ところが、明治五年に太陽暦になった。それで月との関係性が切れちゃった。それから一四〇年以上たってる。今女の人たちに、魂強いんだねっていうと、「ウソー！」っていわれる。野性が強いなんて感覚は、ほとんどわからなくなっている。近世まではしっかり保たれていたんだよ。近代化した明治から、暮らしも習慣も変わってきた。近世、江戸では、女の人はみんな腰巻きだ。今のような生理用品もない時代、女性は経血をコントロールすることができたそうだ。そうした力は、今はなくなってしまったんだね。本来女性の持つ野性とか魂とかは、途絶えてしまったんだ。もったいない。昔、腰巻きだったころ。その頃は旧暦で、季節感、慣習、全てうまくいっていた。野性も保たれていた。それがみんな壊れちゃった。ところが、たとえ三日間でも、山に入って自然の中で修行していると、薄れていた野性が呼び起こされ、体が勝手に目覚めてくる。それがあのいきいき感だ。魂だ。あれが女性本来の美しさだよ。女の人が、化粧っ気なしで、いきいきして、中からあふれ出してくる美しさ。それに気づいたんだよ、俺" (Hoshino 2017, 100).

14. See the cover page of Hoshino (2017).

15. In Japanese: 星野さんは山のような人である。山はなにも話さないけれどももし口あったら星野さんみたいに話すんだと思う．

16. Trouillot (1991; 2003, 7–28).

17. A few times, while introducing me to new disciples, Hoshino-san praised me for being a scholar of Shugendō who not only undertakes *shugyō*, but who does so

repeatedly over the course of years while residing in the Shōnai community, gaining experiential grasp of the knowledge I seek. He expressed hope for an anthropology of Shugendō owing to the participant-observation research method.

18. Obeyesekere (2012, 45–62) similarly argues that exercises conducive to "It-thinking" such as walking for long durations in a mountainous landscape leads to "aphoristic thinking," the spontaneous emergence of linguistically expressible insight.

19. In Japanese: "修行は昔の人のような魂にするため" (Hoshino 2017, 68–69).

20. Schattschneider (2003) writes about shugyō and labor.

21. See Klien (2020) and Traphagan (2021) for more about this emerging trend of "cosmopolitan rurality."

22. The overarching structure of Autumn's Peak is confinement practice (*komori-gyō*). Yamabushi are secluded from the rest of society for seven days, during which they undertake rituals that correspond with the Ten Worlds cosmology with emphasis on the six realms of *samsara*.

23. Although Itō-san's perspective is unique, rice has, as Ohnuki-Tierney (1993, 10) observes, long been used as a metaphor for the self in Japan: "As a metaphor of self, rice paddies are our ancestral land, our ancestral village, are our region and ultimately our land, Japan. They also represent our pristine past before modernity and foreign influences contaminated it. Rice paddies then embody Japanese space and time, that is Japanese land and history."

24. Comaroff and Comaroff (1992, 70) note that religious rites often entail a "dis-membering and re-membering" of participants: "Attempts to remake habit tend to treat the body as a 'memory' in which are lodged, in mnemonic form, the organizing principles of an embracing context. Scrambling this code—that is, erasing the messages carried in banal physical practice—is a prerequisite for retraining the memory, either to deschool the deviant or to shape new subjects as the bearer of new worlds."

25. In Japanese: "一生懸命お祈りすれば成仏できるとか、経済的に豊かに慣れるとか、願い事が叶うといった話は全く信じていません。山伏は厳しい山岳で修行することによって験力というある種の超能力を得ることを目的としている側面もあります。そういったことにも全然興味がありません。そんな僕ですが山に入るとイキイキして身体が軽くなってきますし、自然の豊かさや厳しさを目にした時には、身体の奥底から感動という言葉であらわしたくない強い感情がわき起こってきます。自然は不思議です。そして自然との関わりの中で「自分はどうしてここに存在しているのだろう？」という自らの存在根拠を解き明かそうとします。そんな自然と人との関わりの原型を原始的な自然崇拝信仰の末裔である山伏の文化が今でも持ち伝えているのではないかと考え、自然とはなんだろう？という疑問や生きることに対するヒントを山伏をおこなうことでみつけることができるのではないかと僕は思いました。それが信仰心が薄いかもしれない僕が山伏でいる理由となっています" (Sakamoto 2013, 36–37).

26. In Japanese: "僕がこの世界に入ったのは、偶然ではないような。古代人に手招きされていたみたいです" (Sakamoto 2012, 85).

27. In Japanese: "気になるのは魂のせい。だから気になることをどんどんする" (Hoshino 2018, 92). My translation may appear embellished, but there are unspoken nuances in this sentence. Even his use of terms such as *ki* and *tamashii* add dimension that requires extra detail in translation.

28. Schattschneider (2003, 101, 152, 227) also observed vaginal and reproductive imagery on Mount Iwaki.

29. See C. Carter (2022, 172–76), Bouchy (2009), and Sekimori (2009a) for related accounts of contemporary Shugendō.

Chapter 4

1. Sekimori (2005a) presents the clearest account of this event in Dewa Sanzan's history.

2. Nietzsche ([1887] 1989) argued that much of the Old Testament, with its prophecies of Armageddon and impending punishment and judgment represents the ressentiment of slave morality cloaked in eschatology as a vividly imagined spiritual revenge.

3. Fassin (2013) discusses ressentiment through a case study in post-Apartheid South Africa.

4. See Hardacre (2017, 23–28). In the Kofun period (300–700 CE), the political organization of the Japanese archipelago was known as Wa. It was constituted by clans and chieftainships. Buddhism's introduction to Wa was a consequence of people fleeing escalating wars among the three kingdoms of premodern Korea: Koguryū, Sila, and Paekche. The kingdom of Wa allied with the kingdom of Paekche. It was from this alliance that Buddhism entered premodern Japan in the 550s. As Hardacre (2017, 24) writes, "The tide of emigrants produced a division within Japan between clans and chieftainships whose spiritual authority rested upon continental (including Buddhist) rites, and nativist groups whose leadership rested on the performance of rites for the Kami." Buddhism's eventual acceptance by the court "created a rivalry between the champions of the Kami and Buddhism's advocates."

5. Prominent nativists who opposed the Soga clan's intent to integrate Buddhism into premodern Japan were the Nakatomi and Mononobe clans (Hardacre 2017, 28).

6. The syncretic fusion of Shintō and Buddhism culminated in the medieval period as "esotericization" of Shintō (Hardacre 2017, 147–76; see also Andreeva 2017). A theological paradigm developed at this time was called *honji suijaku*, "original foundation, manifest traces" (see Teeuwen and Rambelli 2003). This paradigm modeled indigenous *kami* (gods) as local manifestations of Buddhist deities. The honji suijaku paradigm subordinates the kami to superior Buddhist deities.

7. A notable example is Nobunaga's sixteenth-century crackdown on the rebellious *ikkō ikki* Jōdō Shinshū groups who drew on Buddhism to develop their political ideology and organize resistance as well as his crackdown on Tendai Buddhism as practiced in Mount Hici (McMullin 1984). Although it could be argued that Nobunaga did not oppose Buddhism based on a sense of ressentiment owing to its foreign origins, this example shows persistent political resistance to Buddhist groups in Japan since its introduction.

8. See Grapard (1984).

9. "Historicity" is defined by Palmié and Stewart (2016, 233) as "cultural paradigms modulating historical experience and practice" from which people form relations with past times. Including academic historiography as a privileged mode of "historicity" democratizes all claims of the past as historical narratives that possess orientations

toward present-day values. As Lambek (2018, 11) writes, historicity appears like a "moving horizon" that is constantly "expanding or retracting in response to social and political circumstances; changing as we move towards or away from them or as they begin to merge with those of new conversation partners."

10. In her original Japanese: 羽黒山はいまなお神道系仏教系に分離しており、明治時代に生じた両者間の溝は未だに深い。出羽三山神社の神職たちは、神道系の大学で教育を受け、明治神宮などの組織で修行をしており、彼らは神道と仏教の間をつなぐことに対しては全く関心を持っていない。仏教系の山伏は、自らを修験道の伝統の真の継承者と任じ、神社方の秋の峰をあまり問題にしていない。手向に宿坊を構える旧修験たちは、両者の間で微妙な立場に立たされている。神社には属してはいても、彼らは自分たちが羽黒修験の重荷を負っていることを自覚している。しかし、根本的な部分で、羽黒修験道の断ち切られた糸が再び一本に紡がれることはほとんどあり得ないだろう。

11. Like Shō-chan on the Inaho train is described in chapter 1.

12. Reader (2024) cites the article version of this chapter (Dahl 2023) to argue that religion has become increasingly fused with tourism in contemporary Japan.

13. This further complicates the role of the museum in the community of ascetics in Mount Haguro. Despite its selective emphasis on Shintō representations of history, it is not an entirely one-sided platform for the shrine. Given the Ideha Cultural Museum's ties with the shrine, which funds half of its operations, I interpret the Buddhist lecture series as a reconciliatory effort organized by curators.

14. Buddhist monks managed to negotiate for the preservation of the niō, the guardian statues at the former Niōmon, and they now stand in Kōganedo Temple in Tōge.

15. For Adam Smith ([1759] 1976), resentment entailed an "unsocial passion" resulting from a perceived injustice that makes a person "contemptible."

16. See Befu (2001).

17. See Reader (2005, 2024) and Reader and Shultz (2021).

18. In her original Japanese: "一見したところ、仏式の秋の峰と神道系の秋の峰にそう大きな違いはない。しかし、神道の勤行は、かつての三山祝言や開山和讃などを神道的に改変下だけのもので、荒澤寺が継承している勤行と神社方の拝式は全く異なり、さらに仏教の要素を排除した結果、神社方の秋の峰では本来の象徴表現や劇的構成の多くは失われてしまっている ... 三山神社は観光客を惹きつけるために修験道を利用しているだけだと避難する声もある。神社、荒澤寺双方が行う紫燈護摩を比べてみると、神社方の紫燈護摩は、見た目のおもしろさや一般受けをねらう方向へ変化したのに対し、荒澤寺の儀礼は本来の神秘性と非公開性を保っている" (Sekimori 2005b, 125).

19. See Clements (2019).

Chapter 5

1. This scene is depicted in Kitamura's (2009) film, *The Autumn Peak of Haguro Shugendo*.

2. See Earhart (1970, 26).

3. Also Shōresai, Winter's Peak, and many other seasonal festivals.

4. Michael Lambek (personal communication, July 14, 2019).

5. Autumn's Peak has been the subject of scholarly interest for eighty years, and there is not enough space here to summarize the full extent of such work. Past approaches, most of which have been conducted by scholars of religion, have identified the ritual structure and reproductive symbolism inherent throughout the rite (Blacker 2000b; Earhart 1965, 1970; Sekimori 2016).

6. Blacker ([1975] 1999, 218–22) emphasizes three other aspects of the "embryo symbolism" of Autumn's Peak: (1) the *oi*, a portable altar representing a womb, which ascetics carry with them through the mountains; (2) a specially adorned *ayaigasa* hat, representing a placenta, which covers the *oi* and is worn by the daisendatsu; and (3) the *bonten*, a long pole with decorative *shide* streamers bulging on top that represents a phallus.

7. See Coleman (2022) for theoretical discussions of laterality in pilgrimage and ritual.

8. I draw on Earhart (1970, 26–27) and Sekimori's (2016, 527–34) list here to supplement my field notes but add missing elements.

9. This symbolism is derived from esoteric Buddhism (Earhart 2006; Hardacre 2006).

10. After showing me his collection of hora gai, this Buddhist ascetic also showed me a collection of brass trumpets and French horns as well as an alphorn. His experiences as a yamabushi had turned him into a horn enthusiast.

11. In Japanese: "装束を着けると、自分が現代人ではなくずっと古い時代の山伏の一員になったような感じがして、気が引き締まります" (Sakamoto 2012, 29).

12. Horton (2007, 3) observes that "Japanese worshippers have treated and continue to treat Buddhist statues as living beings with whom they engage in reciprocal relationships."

13. Sekimori (2005b) describes historical changes to Autumn's Peak in depth.

14. Earhart (1970, 118–19).

15. Earhart (1970, 119).

16. In Japanese: "昔話の中にいるようです" (Sakamoto 2012, 5).

17. For a more detailed account of the aural culture of Buddhist Shugendō, see Ōuchi (2009).

18. See Ōuchi (2021) and Dahl (2023).

19. See Parry (2014).

20. See Thomas (2019).

21. See Earhart (1970, 111) and Clements (2019, 2022).

22. See Fotiou (2016).

23. See Stein (2023) for a detailed account of Reiki, a form of energy channeling and healing.

24. I have never met Koshikidake-san in person, attended any of his shugyō events, or interviewed him or his followers for this study. I have corresponded via e-mail once or twice. My knowledge of Koshikidake-san and his sect derives from Sekimori's (2009a) research, the Internet activity of his sect, including on social media, and the nuanced opinions of members of Shozen-in Temple who are cautious and guarded about making public statements. Nevertheless, from this multisource approach, a portrait of tension does emerge.

25. It's possible that this ritual is a revitalized form of a centuries-old ritual that was lost during the Meiji period.

26. Michael Lambek (personal communication, July 14, 2019).

Chapter 6

1. *Jizō* are Buddhist figures associated with children in the afterlife. The jizō statues at the eighth station of Gassan were salvaged following the post-Meiji persecution of Buddhism.

2. Another famous reizan in Tōhoku is Osorezan ("Mount Fear") in the Shimokita peninsula of Aomori Prefecture (see Miyazaki and Williams 2001). Located in the heart of the northernmost peninsula of the Japanese mainland, Osorezan has, since the Tokugawa period at least, been thought of as the last stop spirits of the deceased make on their journey to the afterlife. It is a site of strong geothermal activity where even the ground hisses and gurgles. It bears many associations with Buddhist hell (*jigoku*). To this day, *itako*, blind spirit mediums, gather there at the annual festival in late July and help paying patrons to converse with their ancestors, whose spirits are believed to possess the itako for the duration of a séance (Perrone 2018).

3. Ian Reader (personal communication, March 30, 2017) also emphasized this translation.

4. As Munn (2013, 360) writes: "Places . . . should be understood as significant, meaningful forms in process rather than as static givens, since their existence is ongoingly subject to the varied ways they enter into human practices—into people's actions, expectations, pasts, and sense of their pasts."

5. See Allison (2012) and Gagne (2021).

6. Janice Boddy's (1988) notion of "cultural therapeutics," which situates religious experience and practice as remedial to sociopolitical and historically particular forms of distress and illness, applies as well. Cultural therapeutics, she writes, are "effective in the repatterning of idiosyncratic conflicts and defenses in culturally appropriate ways and furnishing a corrective emotional experience [to an ailment], the sanctioned release of negative affect" (21).

7. See Hori (1968).

8. See Maddrell and Sidaway (2010, 4).

9. In Japanese: 極楽. See Castiglioni (2015, 8).

10. Referred to in Hori (1968, 170) and R. Smith (1974, 64–65) as *mori no yama*, Forest Mountain.

11. This is the language that disaster relief workers used to identified bodies in the wake of the tsunami (Wilhelm and Delaney 2015, 103).

12. See Hirasawa (2013) and Schattschneider (2003).

13. Mandalas, which are represented in art and orography throughout Japan, are "condensations of the totality of the cosmos . . . fractal reproductions . . . in which the totality is identical to its parts or fragments" (Rambelli 2007, 65). In the Heian period (794–1185), many Japanese mountains were subjected to "systematic mandalization" by Esoteric Buddhists, who were endorsed by the state, "as a way to establish a type of cultural hegemony among the intellectual elites" (Rambelli 2013, 30).

14. See Earhart (1970, 49).

15. The road construction of the paved road began in 1957, when Gassan received national park (*kokuritsu kōen*) and nature sanctuary (*shizen hogoku*) status.

16. See Boddy (1988, 21).

17. This is a description of standard practice, but mortuary rituals are changing in Japan. See Rowe (2011), Boret (2014), Tsuji (2018), and Gould (2023).

18. The nationwide fireworks of the Festival of the Dead (*hanabi*, or "fire flowers," in Japanese), which draw massive crowds, also reflect the equation of the afterlife with the cosmos in Japan since they appear as flower offerings to sky-dwelling ancestral souls.

19. For the example of the disasters of March 11, 2011, being interpreted as *tenbatsu* (divine punishment) (see McLaughlin 2013, 295–96). For examples from the Kantō earthquake of 1923, see Schencking (2008).

20. After Mount Asama erupted in 1788, temples throughout Japan performed the *segaki*. It was widely feared that the wandering spirits would wreak havoc on the living (R. Smith 1974, 20).

21. See Horie (2016), Takahashi (2016), and Parry (2014).

22. See Lowe (2017) for a detailed history of "ritualized writing" practices in Japanese Buddhism.

23. On *kasumiba*, see Earhart (1970, 60–65).

Chapter 7

1. Honmyōji is the third temple in the Ōami area with a mummified monk, but it is less accessible by tourist transportation.

2. See Hori (1962).

3. Drawing striking parallels with the case of the sokushinbutsu are the deathbed practices of the Aghori ascetics in India described by Parry (1982, 96). Through ascetic practices they enter a state referred to as *samādhi*, which is very similar in description to *nyūjō*. Parry (86–87) describes samādhi as "a timeless state of non-duality in which there is neither birth nor death nor any experience of differentiation." Achieving samādhi, the Aghori ascetic then "enters into a perpetual cataleptic condition of suspended animation of deep meditation." Their bodies are fitted "in a box" that is buried in the holy city of Benares, and "a small shrine containing the phallic emblem of Siva is erected over the site of the grave, the emblem transmitting to the worshipper the power emanating from the ascetic's subterranean meditation." By undertaking this practice, "the ascetic unequivocally escapes the normal circumstances of death," making the body "immune to putrescence and decay." In this way, "the body of the model ascetic is perfectly and perpetually preserved in its tomb," with the possibility of reanimation "by the fervent prayers of the devotee." It is a "death that conquers death" (97).

4. This translation omits several historical details he provided about the significance of the temple (that is, which famous feudal lords visited, what the role of the temple was in the Edo period in relation to other major temple complexes, and so on). Instead, the edited account I present focuses specifically on comments made about Mount Yudono and the sokushinbutsu.

5. See Hansen (2008, 56).
6. *Maitreya* is the Sanskrit name for the Future Buddha. It is *Miroku* in Japanese. See Sponberg and Hardacre (1988).
7. See Hakeda (1972, 60) and Abe (1999, 398).
8. See Reader (2005, 43).
9. See Blacker (1999, 64–81).
10. See Rambelli (2013, 125–27). Whereas a mummified ascetic is referred to as a *sokushinbutsu* (Embodied Buddha), the Esoteric Buddhist principle referred to is *sokushinjōbutsu* (Becoming a Buddha in This Very Body).
11. Panpsychism is a philosophical position that models human consciousness as aspectual and fractal to a cosmic consciousness (Skrebina 2017; Bruntrup 2016). See Heisig, Kasulis, and Maraldo (2011, 1251) for a more detailed description of Dainichi Nyorai in Japanese Buddhist philosophy.
12. See Young (1999) for more detail regarding dreams in the Buddhist tradition.
13. See Lobetti (2007).
14. See Group for Research of Japanese Mummies (1993, 5).
15. Lobetti (2014, 130–36) has theorized that the alleged self-mummification of the sokushinbutsu represents the "progression" and "perfection" of the body within an ascetic value system, a process he calls *corpus ascendus*. This theory of ontological progression applies, he argues, to the annual advancement of status in Autumn's Peak, but is most apparent in the sokushinbutsu who attained the ascetic ideal.
16. According to Castiglioni (2024, 148), the reclothing ceremony is called *okoromogae*.
17. See Togawa (1974).
18. See Group for Research of Japanese Mummies (1993, 5).
19. Castiglioni (2024) provides a detailed account of how these initial studies took place.
20. See Sakurai et al. (1998, 325).
21. See Tomi (2006).
22. This ethnographic encounter was originally published in my article "Buddhist Mummy or Living Buddha? The Politics of Immortality in Japanese Buddhism" (Dahl 2020) and discussed in Reader (2024).
23. See Ehlers (2014, 55).
24. Such as the Kannei Famine (1642–43), the Kyōhō Famine (1732), and the Tenpō Famine (1833–37). See Walker (2015, 132).
25. See Crossland (2009, 76).
26. Castiglioni (2024, 151).

Epilogue

1. To refer back to Freud's ([1930] 1961) comments in *Civilization and Its Discontents*.
2. See Bushelle (2018).

Works Cited

Abé, Ryūichi. 1999. *Weaving the Mantra: Kūkai and the Construction of Esoteric Buddhist Discourse.* New York: Columbia University Press.
Allison, Anne. 2012. "Ordinary Refugees: Social Precarity and Soul in 21st Century Japan." *Anthropological Quarterly* 85 (2): 345–70.
Allison, Anne. 2013. *Precarious Japan.* Durham, NC: Duke University Press.
Allison, Anne. 2015. "Discounted Life: Social Time in Relationless Japan." *Boundary 2* 42 (3): 129–41.
Allison, Anne. 2017. "Greeting the Dead: Managing Solitary Existence in Japan." *Social Text* 35 (1): 17–35.
Allison, Stacy, and Peter Carlin. 1993. *Beyond the Limits: A Woman's Triumph on Everest.* Boston: Little, Brown.
Amada, Akinori. 2019. 現代修験道の宗教社会学：山岳宗教の聖地「吉野・熊野」の観光化と文化資源化 [Contemporary Shugendō in the sociology of religion: Mountain religion, tourism, and cultural resources]. Tokyo: Iwata shoin.
Andreeva, Anna. 2017. *Assembling Shinto: Buddhist Approaches to Kami Worship in Medieval Japan.* Cambridge, MA: Harvard University Press.
Bachnik, Jane M., and Charles J. Quinn. 1994. *Situated Meaning: Inside and Outside in Japanese Self, Society, and Language.* Princeton, NJ: Princeton University Press.
Badone, Ellen. 2004. "Crossing Boundaries: Exploring the Borderlands of Ethnography." In *Intersecting Journeys: The Anthropology of Pilgrimage and Tourism*, edited by Ellen Badone and Sharon R. Roseman, 180–89. Champaign: University of Illinois Press.
Bakhtin, M. M. 1981. *The Dialogic Imagination: Four Essays.* Edited by Michael Holquist. Translated by Caryl Emerson and Michael Holquist. Austin: University of Texas Press.
Baldwin, Frank, and Anne Allison, eds. 2015. *Japan: The Precarious Future.* New York: New York University Press.
Basso, Keith H. 1996. *Wisdom Sits in Places: Landscape and Language among the Western Apache.* University of New Mexico Press.
Bear, Laura. 2014. "Doubt, Conflict, Mediation: The Anthropology of Modern Time." *Journal of the Royal Anthropological Institute* 20 (S1): 3–30.
Bear, Laura. 2016. "Time as Technique." *Annual Review of Anthropology* 45: 487–502.
Befu, Harumi. 2001. *Hegemony of Homogeneity: An Anthropological Analysis of "Nihonjinron."* Tokyo: Trans Pacific Press.
Bender, Barbara. 2002. "Time and Landscape." *Current Anthropology* 43 (S4): S103–S113.

Benedict, Ruth. 1946. *The Chrysanthemum and the Sword: Patterns of Japanese Culture*. Boston: Houghton Mifflin.

Blacker, Carmen. (1975) 1999. *The Catalpa Bow: A Study of Shamanistic Practices in Japan*. New York: Routledge.

Blacker, Carmen. 2000a. *Collected Writings of Carmen Blacker*. Tokyo: Japan Library and Edition Synapse.

Blacker, Carmen. 2000b. "Initiation in the Shugendō: The Passage through the Ten States." In *Collected Writings of Carmen Blacker*, 186–200. Tokyo: Japan Library and Edition Synapse.

Bloch, Maurice, and Jonathan Parry, eds. 1982. *Death and the Regeneration of Life*. Cambridge: Cambridge University Press.

Boddy, Janice. 1988. "Spirits and Selves in Northern Sudan: The Cultural Therapeutics of Possession and Trance." *American Ethnologist* 15 (1): 4–27.

Bolin, Inge. 2009. "The Glaciers of the Andes Are Melting: Indigenous and Anthropological Knowledge Merge in Restoring Water Sources." In *Anthropology and Climate Change: From Encounters to Actions*, edited by Susan A. and Mark Nuttall Crate, 228–39. New York: Routledge.

Boret, Sebastien Penmellen. 2014. *Japanese Tree Burial: Ecology, Kinship, and the Culture of Death*. New York: Routledge.

Bouchy, Anne. 2009. "Transformation, Rupture, and Continuity: Issues and Options in Contemporary Shugendō." In *Shugendō: The History and Culture of a Japanese Religion*, edited by Bernard Faure, D. Max Moerman, and Gaynor Sekimori, 17–45. Paris: École française d'Extrême-Orient.

Bourdieu, Pierre. 1985. "The Forms of Captial." In *Handbook for Theory and Research for the Sociology of Education*, edited by J. G. Richardson, 241–58. New York: Greenwood.

Bourdieu, Pierre. 1988. *Homo Academicus*. Translated by Pieter Collier. Stanford, CA: Stanford University Press.

Bruntrup, Godehard, and Ludwig Jaskolla, eds. 2016. *Panpsychism: Contemporary Perspectives*. Oxford: Oxford University Press.

Bushelle, Ethan. 2018. "Mountain Buddhism and the Emergence of a Buddhist Cosmic Imaginary in Ancient Japan." *Japanese Journal of Religious Studies* 45 (1): 1–36.

Carter, Caleb. 2018. "Power Spots and the Charged Landscape of Shinto." *Japanese Journal of Religious Studies* 45 (1): 145–73.

Carter, Caleb Swift. 2022. *A Path into the Mountains: Shugendō and Mount Togakushi*. Honolulu: University of Hawai'i Press.

Carter, Caleb Swift. 2024. "Mountains as Loci of Attraction, Fear, and Spiritual Utility." In *The New Nanzan Guide to Japanese Religions*, edited by Matthew D. McMullen and Joylon Baraka Thomas, 213–28. Honolulu: University of Hawai'i Press.

Carter, Caleb Swift. 2025. "The Metamorphic Spirit: Mountaineering, Secularity, and Spirituality at the Turn of Japan's Twentieth Century." *Religion* 55 (1): 393–410.

Carter, Steven D. 2000. "Bashō and the Mastery of Poetic Space in *Oku No Hosomichi*." *Journal of the American Oriental Society* 120 (2): 190–98.

Castiglioni, Andrea. 2015. "Ascesis and Devotion: The Mount Yudono Cult in Early Modern Japan." PhD diss., Columbia University.
Castiglioni, Andrea. 2019. "Devotion in Flesh and Bone: The Mummified Corpses of Mount Yudono Ascetics in Edo-Period Japan." *Asian Ethnology* 78 (1): 25–51.
Castiglioni, Andrea, Carina Roth, and Fabio Rambelli. 2020. "Introduction: Shugendō and Its Metamophoses." In *Defining Shugendō: Critical Studies on Japanese Mountain Religion*, edited by Andrea Castiglioni, Fabio Rambelli, and Carina Roth, 33–62. London: Bloomsbury Academic.
Castiglioni, Andrea, Fabio Rambelli, and Carina Roth, eds. 2020. *Defining Shugendō: Critical Studies on Japanese Mountain Religion*. London: Bloomsbury Academic.
Clements, Frank. 2019. "The Fall Peak, Professional Culture, and Document Production in Early Modern Haguro Shugendo." *Japanese Journal of Religious Studies* 46 (2): 219–45.
Clements, Frank. 2022. "Refining a Shugenja Elite: Household, Status, and Privilege in the Early Nineteenth-Century Reorganization of Haguro Shugendō." *Journal of Religion in Japan* 11 (3): 236–67.
Coleman, Simon. 2022a. "Laterality: A Sideways Look at Ritual." *Journal of the Royal Anthropological Institute* 29 (4): 727–44.
Coleman, Simon. 2022b. *Powers of Pilgrimage: Religion in a World of Movement*. New York: New York University Press.
Covell, Stephen G. 2004. "Learning to Persevere: The Popular Teachings of Tendai Ascetics." *Japanese Journal of Religious Studies* 31 (2): 255–87.
Creighton, M. R. 1990. "Revisiting Shame and Guilt Cultures: A Forty-Year Pilgrimage." *Ethos* 18 (3): 279–307.
Creighton, Millie. 1997. "Consuming Rural Japan: The Marketing of Tradition and Nostalgia in the Japanese Travel Industry." *Ethnology* 36 (3): 239–54.
Crossland, Zoe. 2009. "Of Clues and Signs: The Dead Body and Its Evidential Traces." *American Anthropologist* 111 (1): 69–80.
Cruikshank, Julie. 2005. *Do Glaciers Listen? Local Knowledge, Colonial Encounters, and Social Imagination*. Vancouver: University of British Columbia Press.
Dahl, Shayne A. P. 2020. "Buddhist Mummy or 'Living Buddha'? The Politics of Immortality in Japanese Buddhism." *Anthropological Forum* 30 (3): 292–312.
Dahl, Shayne A. P. 2023. "Sutra as Speech Act: Shugendō Rivalries and the Heart Sutra in Northeastern Japan." *Pacific World Journal* 4 (4): 5–24.
Davis, Wade. 2011. *Into the Silence: The Great War, Mallory, and the Conquest of Everest*. Toronto: Vintage Canada.
Deal, William E., and Brian Ruppert. 2015. *A Cultural History of Japanese Buddhism*. Hoboken, NJ: Wiley Blackwell.
Debarbieux, Bernard, and Gilles Rudaz. 2015. *The Mountain: A Political History from the Enlightenment to the Present*. Chicago: University of Chicago Press.
de la Cadena, Marisol. 2015. *Earth Beings: Ecologies of Practice across Andean Worlds*. Durham, NC: Duke University Press.
Denman, Earl. 1954. *Alone to Everest*. New York: Coward-McCann.
Descola, Philippe. 2005. *Beyond Nature and Culture*. Chicago: University of Chicago Press.

DeWitt, Lindsey Elizabeth. 2015. "A Mountain Set Apart: Female Exclusion, Buddhism, and Tradition at Modern Ōminesan, Japan." *Asian Languages and Cultures*. Los Angeles: University of California Los Angeles.

Durkheim, Emile. 2008. *Elementary Forms of Religious Life*. Oxford: Oxford University Press.

Earhart, Byron H. 2006. "Shugendō, the Traditons of En No Gyōja, and Mikkyō Influence." In *Tantric Buddhism in East Asia*, edited by Richard K. Payne, 191–206. Somerville, MA: Wisdom Publications.

Earhart, H. Byron. 1965. "Four Ritual Periods of Haguro Shugendō in Northeastern Japan." *History of Religions* 5 (1): 93–113.

Earhart, H. Byron. 1970. *A Religious Study of the Mount Haguro Sect of Shugendō: An Example of Japanese Mountain Religion*. Tokyo: Sophia University.

Earhart, H. Byron. 1989. "Mount Fuji and Shugendo." *Japanese Journal of Religious Studies* 16 (2/3): 205–26.

Earhart, H. Byron. 2011. *Mount Fuji: Icon of Japan*. Columbia: University of South Carolina Press.

Edmondo, Perrone, dir. 2018. *Itako: Visions*. Italy.

Ehlers, Maren. 2014. "Benevolence, Charity, and Duty: Urban Relief and Domain Society during the Tenmei Famine." *Monumenta Nipponica* 69 (1): 55–101.

Eliade, Mircea. (1964) 2004. *Shamanism: Archaic Techniques of Ecstasy*. Translated by Willard R. Trask. Princeton, NJ: Princeton University Press.

Evans-Pritchard, Edward E. 1990. *The Nuer: A Description of the Modes of Livelihood and Political Institutions of a Nilotic People*. Oxford: Oxford University Press.

Fabian, Johannes. 1983. *Time and the Other: How Anthropology Makes Its Object*. New York: Columbia University Press.

Fassin, Didier. 2013. "On Resentment and Ressentiment: The Politics and Ethics of Moral Emotions." *Current Anthropology* 54 (3): 249–67.

Faure, Bernard, D. Max Moerman, and Gaynor Sekimori, eds. 2009. *Shugendō: The History and Culture of a Japanese Religion / L'histoire et la culture d'une religion japonaise*. Paris: École française d'Extrême-Orient.

Fotiou, Evgenia. 2016. "The Globalization of Ayahuasca Shamanism and the Erasure of Indigenous Shamanism." *Anthropology of Consciousness* 27 (2): 151–79.

Foucault, Michel. 1984. "Des espace autres—Of Other Spaces: Utopias and Heterotopias." *Architecture, Mouvement, Continuité*, no. 5: 1–9.

Freud, Sigmund. (1930) 1961. *Civilization and Its Discontents*. Translated by James Strachey. New York: W. W. Norton.

Fujita, Shouichi. 2005. 熊野、修験の道を往く [Kumano: Walking the path of Shugendō]. Kyoto: Tankosha.

Fujiwara, Gideon. 2021. *From Country to Nation: Ethnographic Studies, Kokugaku, and Spirits in Nineteenth-Century Japan*. Ithaca, NY: Cornell University Press.

Fukada, Kyūya. (1964) 2015. *One Hundred Mountains of Japan*. Translated by Martin Hood. Honolulu: University of Hawai'i Press.

Gagne, Nana Okura. 2021. *Reworking Men: Changing Men at Work and Play under Neoliberalism*. Ithaca, NY: Cornell University Press.

Geertz, Clifford. 1973. *The Interpretation of Cultures*. New York: Basic Books.

Gell, Alfred. 1992. *The Anthropology of Time: Cultural Constructions of Temporal Maps and Images*. Oxford: Berg.
Gennep, Arnold van. 1960. *The Rites of Passage*. London: Routledge and Kegan Paul.
Gill, Tom, Brigitte Steger, and David H. Slater, eds. 2015a. *Japan Copes with Calamity*. Oxford: Peter Lang.
Gill, Tom, Brigitte Steger, and David H. Slater. 2015b. "The 3.11 Disasters." In *Japan Copes with Calamity*, 3–23. Oxford: Peter Lang.
Goodman, Roger. 2005. "Making Majority Culture." In *A Companion to the Anthropology of Japan*, 59–72. Malden, MA: Wiley-Blackwell.
Gose, Peter. 2018. "The Semi-Social Mountain: Metapersonhood and Political Ontology in the Andes." *HAU: Journal of Ethnographic Theory* 8 (3): 488–505.
Gould, Hannah. 2023. *When Death Falls Apart: Making and Unmaking the Necromaterial Traditions of Contemporary Japan*. Chicago: University of Chicago Press.
Grapard, Allan G. 1982. "Flying Mountains and Walkers of Emptiness: Toward a Definition of Sacred Space in Japanese Religions." *History of Religions* 21 (3): 195–221.
Grapard, Allan G. 1984. "Japan's Ignored Cultural Revolution: The Separation of Shinto and Buddhist Divinities in Meiji ('Shimbutsu Bunri') and a Case Study: Tōnomine." *History of Religions* 23 (3): 240–65.
Grapard, Allan G. 1994. "Geosophia, Geognosis, and Geopiety: Orders of Significance in Japanese Representations of Space." In *Now Here: Space, Time, and Modernity*, edited by Roger Friedland and Deirdre Boden, 372–401. Berkeley: University of California Press.
Grapard, Allan G. 2016. *Mountain Mandalas: Shugendō in Kyushu*. London: Bloomsbury.
Group for Research of Japanese Mummies. 1993. *Research of Japanese Mummies*. Tokyo: Heibonsha.
Guyer, Jane I. 2007. "Prophecy and the Near Future: Thoughts on Macroeconomic, Evangelical, and Punctuated Time." *American Ethnologist* 34 (3): 409–21.
Hakeda, Yoshito S. 1972. *Kūkai: Major Works*. New York: Columbia University Press.
Hansen, Anne Ruth. 2008. "Gaps in the World: Harm and Violence in Khmer Buddhist Narrative." In *At the Edge of the Forest: Essays on Cambodia, History, and Narrative in Honor of David Chandler*, edited by Anne Ruth Hansen and Judy Ledgerwood, 47–70. Ithaca, NY: Cornell University Press.
Hardacre, Helen. 2006. "The Cave and the Womb World." In *Tantric Buddhism in East Asia*, edited by Richard K. Payne, 207–26. Boston: Wisdom Publications.
Hardacre, Helen. 2017. *Shinto: A History*. Oxford: Oxford University Press.
Heisig, James W., Thomas P. Kasulis, and John C. Maraldo. 2011. *Japanese Philosophy: A Sourcebook*. Honolulu: University of Hawai'i Press.
Heyd, Thomas. 2003. "Bashō and the Aesthetics of Wandering: Recuperating Space, Recognizing Place, and Following the Ways of the Universe." *Philosophy East and West* 53 (3): 291–307.
Hillary, Edmund. 1955. *High Adventure: The True Story of the First Ascent of Everest*. Oxford: Oxford University Press.

Hirasawa, Caroline. 2013. *Hell-Bent for Heaven in Tateyama Mandara: Painting and Religious Practice at a Japanese Mountain.* Leiden: Brill.

Hobsbawm, Eric. 1983. "Introduction." In *The Invention of Tradition*, edited by Eric Hobsbawm and Terence Ranger, 1–14. Cambridge: Cambridge University Press.

Hood, Martin. 2015. "Introduction." In *One Hundred Mountains of Japan*, by Kyūya Fukada. 1–42. Honolulu: University of Hawa'i Press.

Hopson, Nathan. 2017. *Ennobling Japan's Savage Northeast: Tōhoku as Japanese Postwar Thought, 1945–2011.* Cambridge, MA: Harvard University Press.

Hori, Ichiro. 1962. "Self-Mummified Buddhas in Japan: An Aspect of the Shugendō ('Mountain Asceticism') Sect." *History of Religions* 1 (2): 222–42.

Hori, Ichiro. 1968. *Folk Religion in Japan: Continuity and Change.* Chicago: University of Chicago Press.

Horie, Norichika. 2016. "Continuing Bonds in the Tōhoku Disaster Area." *Journal of Religion in Japan* 5 (2–3): 199–226.

Horie, Norichika. 2017. "The Making of Power Spots: From New Age Spirituality to Shinto Spirituality." In *Eastspirit: Transnational Spirituality and Religious Circulation in East and West*, edited by Jørn Borup, 192–217. Leiden: Brill.

Horton, Sarah J. 2007. *Living Buddhist Statues in Early Medieval and Modern Japan.* London: Palgrave Macmillan.

Hoshino, Fumihiro. 2017. 感じるままに生きなさい: 山伏の流儀 [Live by feeling: A Yamabushi method]. Tokyo: Sakurasha.

Hoshino, Fumihiro. 2018. 答えは自分の感じた中にある: 清々しく生きるための山伏のヒント [The answer lies in your own intuitive feelings: Tips from Yamabushi for living refreshingly]. Tokyo: Ie no Hikari Kyoukai.

Humboldt, Alexander von. 1997. *Cosmos: A Sketch of the Physical Description of the Universe.* Vol. 1. Translated by E. C. Otté. Baltimore: John Hopkins University Press.

Ingold, Tim. 2010. "The Temporality of the Landscape." *World Archaeology* 25 (2): 152–74.

International Shugendo Association. 2019. "Homepage." www.shugeninternational.org.

Ivy, Marilyn. 1995. *Discourses of the Vanishing: Modernity, Phantasm, Japan.* Chicago: University of Chicago Press.

Jannetta, Ann Bowman. 1992. "Famine Mortality in Nineteenth-Century Japan: The Evidence from a Temple Death Register." *Population Studies* 46 (3): 427–43.

Josephson, Jason Ananda. 2012. *The Invention of Religion in Japan.* Chicago: University of Chicago Press.

Kasulis, Thomas P. 2004. *Shinto: The Way Home.* Honolulu: University of Hawa'i Press.

Kawabata, Yasunari. (1948) 1996. *Snow Country.* Translated by Edward G. Seidensticker. New York: Vintage Books.

Kawano, Satsuki. 2005. *Ritual Practice in Modern Japan: Ordering Place, People, and Action.* Honolulu: University of Hawai'i Press.

Keene, Donald. 1997. "Preface." In *The Narrow Road to Oku*, by Matsuo Bashō, 5–15. Tokyo: Kodansha International.

Keesing, Roger M. 2012. "On Not Understanding Symbols: Toward an Anthropology of Incomprehension." *HAU: Journal of Ethnographic Theory* 2 (2): 406–30.

Kingston, Jeff. 2012. *Natural Disaster and Nuclear Crisis in Japan: Response and Recovery after Japan's 3/11.* New York: Routledge.

Kitamura, Minao, dir. 2009. *The Autumn Peak of Haguro Shugendo.* DVD, 115 mins. Japan: Visual Folklore Inc. Japan.

Klien, Susanne. 2020. *Urban Migrants in Rural Japan: Between Agency and Anomie in a Post-Growth Society.* New York: SUNY Press.

Krakauer, Jon. 1997. *Into Thin Air: A Personal Account of the Mt. Everest Disaster.* New York: Villard Books.

Laidlaw, James. 2002. "For an Anthropology of Ethics and Freedom." *Journal of the Royal Anthropological Institute* 8 (2): 311–32.

Lambek, Michael. 1995. "The Past Imperfect: Remembering as Moral Practice." In *Tense Past: Cultural Essays in Trauma and Memory,* edited by Paul Antze and Michael Lambek, 235–54. New York: Routledge.

Lambek, Michael. 1997. "Knowledge and Practice in Mayotte: An Overview." *Cultural Dynamics* 9 (2): 131–48.

Lambek, Michael. 2002. *The Weight of the Past: Living with History.* New York: Palgrave Macmillan.

Lambek, Michael. 2018. *Island in the Stream: An Ethnographic History of Mayotte.* Toronto: University of Toronto Press.

Leach, E. R. 1961. "Two Essays Concerning the Symbolic Representation of Time." In *Rethinking Anthropology,* 124–36. London: Althlone.

Lévi-Strauss, Claude. 1966. *The Savage Mind.* London: Weidenfeld and Nicolson.

Lindholm, Charles. 2008. *Culture and Authenticity.* Malden, MA: Wiley-Blackwell.

Lobetti, Tullio Federico. 2007. "Eternal Bodies: The Miira, the Self-Mummified Ascetics of Japan." In *Back to the Future of the Body,* edited by Dominic Janes, 190–215. Newcastle, UK: Cambridge Scholars.

Lobetti, Tullio Federico. 2014. *Ascetic Practices in Japanese Religion.* New York: Routledge.

Lowe, Bryan D. 2017. *Ritualized Writing: Buddhist Practice and Scriptural Cultures in Ancient Japan.* Honolulu: University of Hawai'i Press.

Luhrmann, T. M. 2012. *When God Talks Back: Understanding the American Evangelical Relationship with God.* New York: Vintage Books.

Luhrmann, Tanya M. 2004. "Metakinesis: How God Becomes Intimate in Contemporary U.S. Christianity." *American Anthropologist* 106 (3): 518–28.

Maddrell, Avril, and James D. Sidaway. 2010. "Introduction: Bringing a Spatial Lens to Death, Dying, Mourning and Remembrance." In *Deathscapes: Places for Death, Dying, Mourning and Remembrance,* edited by Avril Maddrell and James D. Sidaway. Surrey, UK: Ashgate.

Marx, Karl. (1844) 1978. "Economic and Philosophic Manuscripts of 1844." In *The Marx-Engels Reader,* 2nd ed., edited by Robert C. Tucker, 66–125. New York: W. W. Norton.

Matsuo, Bashō. (1694) 1966. *"The Narrow Road to the Deep North" and Other Travel Sketches.* Translated by Nobuyuki Yuasa. Harmondsworth, UK: Penguin.

Matsuo, Bashō. 1996. *The Narrow Road to Oku.* Translated by Donald Keene. Tokyo: Kodansha International.

Matthews, Gordon. 1996. *What Makes Life Worth Living? How Japanese and Americans Make Sense of Their Worlds.* Berkeley: University of California Press.

Mauss, Marcel. 1973. "Techniques of the Body." *Economy and Society* 2 (1): 70–88.

McGuire, Mark Patrick. 2013. "From the City to the Mountain and Back Again: Situating Contemporary Shugendo in Japanese Social and Religious Life." PhD diss., Concordia University.

McLaughlin, Levi. 2013. "What Have Religious Groups Done after 3.11? Part 1: A Brief Survey of Religious Mobilization after the Great East Japan Earthquake Disasters." *Religion Compass* 7 (8): 294–308.

McMullin, Neil. 1984. *Buddhism and the State in Sixteenth-Century Japan.* Princeton, NJ: Princeton University Press.

Miles-Watson, Jonathan. 2021. *Christianity and Belonging in Shimla, North India: Sacred Entanglements of a Himalayan Landscape.* London: Bloomsbury Academic.

Miyake, Hitoshi. 2000. 羽黒修験: その歴史と峰入り [The history and mountain entry practices of Shugendō in Mt. Haguro]. Tokyo: Iwata shoin.

Miyake, Hitoshi. 2001. *Shugendō: Essays on the Structure of Japanese Folk Religion.* Edited by H. Byron Earhart. Ann Arbor: Center for Japanese Studies, University of Michigan.

Miyake, Hitoshi. 2005. *The Mandala of the Mountain: Shugendō and Folk Religion.* Edited by Gaynor Sekimori. Tokyo: Keio University Press.

Miyazaki, Fumiko, and Duncan Williams. 2001. "The Intersection of the Local and the Translocal at a Sacred Site: The Case of Osorezan in Tokugawa Japan." *Japanese Journal of Religious Studies* 28 (3–4): 399–440.

Miyazaki, Hirokazu. 2004. *The Method of Hope: Anthropology, Philosophy, and Fijian Knowledge.* Stanford, CA: Stanford University Press.

Morita, Atsuro. 2017. "In between the Cosmos and 'Thousand-Cubed Great Thousands Worlds': Composition of Uncommon Worlds by Alexander von Humboldt and King Mongcut." *Anthropologica* 59 (2): 228–38.

Munn, Nancy D. 1992. "The Cultural Anthropology of Time: A Critical Essay." *Annual Review of Anthropology* 21: 93–123.

Nelson, John K. 2000. *Enduring Identities: The Guise of Shinto in Contemporary Japan.* Honolulu: University of Hawai'i Press.

Nietzsche, Friedrich. (1901) 1968. *The Will to Power.* Edited by Walter Kaufmann. Translated by Walter Kaufmann and R. J. Hollingdale. New York: Vintage Books.

Nietzsche, Friedrich. (1887) 1989. *On the Genealogy of Morals and Ecce Homo.* Edited by Walter Kaufmann. Translated by Walter Kaufmann and R. J. Hollingdale. New York: Vintage Books.

Nietzsche, Friedrich. 1995. *Unfashionable Observations.* Translated by Richard T. Gray. Sanford, CA: Stanford University Press.

Nishimoto, Ikuko. 1997. "The 'Civilization' of Time: Japan and the Adoption of the Western Time System." *Time and Society* 6 (2–3): 237–59.

Norgay, Tenzing. 1955. *Tiger of the Snows: The Autobiography of Tenzing of Everest.* Edited by James Ramsey Ullman. London: George G. Harrap.

North, Scott, and Rika Morioka. 2016. "Hope Found in Lives Lost: Karoshi and the Pursuit of Worker Rights in Japan." *Contemporary Japan* 28 (1): 59–80.

Obeyesekere, Gananath. 2012. *The Awakened Ones: Phenomenology of Visionary Experience*. New York: Columbia University Press.

Ohnuki-Tierney, Emiko. 1991. "The Emperor of Japan as Deity (Kami)." *Ethnology* 30 (3): 199–215.

Ohnuki-Tierney, Emiko. 1993. *Rice as Self: Japanese Identities through Time*. Princeton, NJ: Princeton University Press.

Orlove, Benjamin. 2002. *Lines in the Water: Nature and Culture at Lake Titicaca*. Berkeley: University of California Press.

Orlove, Benjamin S., and David Guillet. 1985. "Theoretical and Methodological Considerations on the Study of Mountain Peoples: Reflections on the Idea of Subsistence Type and the Role of History in Human Ecology." *Mountain Research and Development* 5: 3–18.

Ortner, Sherry B. 1973. "On Key Symbols." *American Anthropologist* 75, no. 5: 1338–46.

Ortner, Sherry B. 1999. *Life and Death on Mt. Everest: Sherpas and Himalayan Mountaineering*. Princeton, NJ: Princeton University Press.

Ortner, Sherry B. 2016. "Dark Anthropology and Its Others: Theory since the Eighties." *HAU: Journal of Ethnographic Theory* 6, no. 1: 47–73.

Ōuchi, Fumi. 2009. "The Lotus Repentance Liturgy of Shugendō: Identification from Vocal Arts." In *Shugendō: The History and Culture of a Japanese Religion*, edited by Bernard Faure, D. Max Moerman, and Gaynor Sekimori, 169–94. Paris: École française d'Extrême-Orient.

Ōuchi, Fumi. 2021. "Sound." In *The Bloomsbury Handbook of Japanese Religions*, edited by Erica Baffelli, Fabio Rambelli, and Andrea Castiglioni, 209–15. London: Bloomsbury.

Palmié, Stephan, and Charles Stewart. 2016. "Introduction: For an Anthropology of History." *HAU: Journal of Ethnographic Theory* 6 (1): 207–36.

Parkes, Lorna. 2023. "Finding Balance on a Nature Pilgrimage with Japan's Yamabushi Mountain Priests." *National Geographic*, October 6. www.nationalgeographic.com/travel/article/nature-pilgrimage-japan-yamabushi-priests.

Parry, Jonathan. 1982. "Sacrificial Death and the Necropagous Ascetic." In *Death and the Regeneration of Life*, edited by Maurice Bloch and Jonathan Parry, 74–110. Cambridge: Cambridge University Press.

Parry, Richard Lloyd. 2014. "Ghosts of the Tsunami." *London Review of Books*, February 6, 2014, 13–17.

Price, Martin F. 2015. *Mountains: A Very Short Introduction*. Oxford: Oxford University Press.

Qiu, Peipei. 2005. *Bashō and the Dao: The Zhuangzi and the Transformation of Haikai*. Honolulu: University of Hawai'i Press.

Rambelli, Fabio. 2007. *Buddhist Materiality: A Cultural History of Objects in Japanese Buddhism*. Stanford, CA: Stanford University Press.

Rambelli, Fabio. 2013. *A Buddhist Theory of Semiotics: Signs, Ontology, and Salvation in Japanese Esoteric Buddhism*. New York: Bloomsbury.

Rappaport, Roy. 1992. "Ritual, Time, and Eternity." *Zygon* 27 (1): 5–30.

Reader, Ian. 1991. *Religion in Contemporary Japan*. Honolulu: University of Hawai'i Press.

Reader, Ian. 1993. "Dead to the World: Pilgrims in Shikoku." In *Pilgrimage in Popular Culture*, edited by Ian Reader and Tony Walker, 107–36. London: MacMillan.

Reader, Ian. 2005. *Making Pilgrimages: Meaning and Practice in Shikoku*. Honolulu: University of Hawai'i Press.

Reader, Ian. 2024. *Religion and Tourism in Japan: Intersections, Images, Policies and Problems*. London: Bloomsbury Academic.

Reader, Ian, and John Shultz. 2021. *Pilgrims until We Die: Unending Pilgrimage in Shikoku*. Oxford: Oxford University Press.

Reader, Ian, and George J. Tanabe Jr. 1998. *Practically Religious: Worldly Benefits and the Common Religion of Japan*. Honolulu: University of Hawai'i Press.

Rhoades, Robert E., and Stephen Thompson. 1975. "Adaptive Strategies in Alpine Environments: Beyond Ecological Particularism." *American Ethnologist* 2 (3): 535–51.

Riessland, Andreas. 2000. "Mountain of Problems: Ethnography among Mount Haguro's Feuding Yamabushi." In *Globalization and Social Change in Contemporary Japan*, edited by Harumi Befu, J. S. Eades, and Tom Gill, 180–202. Melbourne: Trans Pacific Press.

Robertson, Jennifer. 1988. "*Furusato* Japan: The Culture and Politics of Nostalgia." *International Journal of Politics, Culture, and Society* 1: 494–518.

Robertson, Jennifer. 1997. "Empire of Nostalgia." *Theory, Culture and Society* 14, no. 4: 97–122.

Rodrigues, Hillary. 2006. *Introducing Hinduism*. New York: Routledge.

Rousseau, Jean-Jacques. (1755) 2009. *Discourse on the Origin of Inequality*. Translated by Franklin Philip. Oxford: Oxford University Press.

Rowe, Mark Michael. 2011. *Bonds of the Dead: Temples, Burial, and the Transformation of Contemporary Japanese Buddhism*. Chicago: University of Chicago Press.

Rowthorn, Chris, Ray Bartlett, Andrew Bender, Matthew Firestone, Wendy Yanagihara, Michael Clark, and Tim Hornyak. 2007. *Lonely Planet Japan*. 10th ed. Carlton, Victoria, Australia: Lonely Planet Publications.

Ruffell, Ben, dir. 2012. *Uketamau*. Short film, 8 min., 31 sec. Green Valley. Available at www.youtube.com/watch?v=3lQoheSuoEE&ab_channel=BenRuffell.

Rupp, Katherine. 2003. *Gift-Giving in Japan: Cash, Connections, Cosmologies*. Stanford, CA: Stanford University Press.

Saito, Tamaki. 2013. *Hikikomori: Adolescence without End*. Minneapolis: University of Minnesota Press.

Sakamoto, Daizaburo. 2012. 山伏と僕 [Yamabushi and I]. Tokyo: Little More.

Sakamoto, Daizaburo. 2013. 山伏ノート：自然と人をつなぐ知恵を武器に～ [Yamabushi notebook: Connecting nature and people with wisdom as a weapon]. Tokyo: Gijutsu hyōronsha.

Sakurai, Kiyohiko, Tamotsu Ogata, Iwataro Morimoto, Peng Long-Xiang, and Wu Zhong-Bi. 1998. "Mummies from Japan and China." In *Mummies, Disease, and Ancient Cultures*, edited by Aidan Cockburn, Eve Cockburn, and Theodore A. Reyman, 308–35. Cambridge: Cambridge University Press.

Salomon, Frank. 2018. *At the Mountain's Altar: Anthropology of Religion in an Andean Community*. New York: Routledge.

Samuels, Richard J. 2013. *3.11: Disaster and Change in Japan*. Ithaca, NY: Cornell University Press.

Sato, Michiko. 2005. 滝行 大自然の中、新しい自分と出会う [Waterfall meditation: Meeting your new self in the midst of nature]. Tokyo: Kosumosu raiburari.

Satsuka, Shiho. 2015. *Nature in Translation: Japanese Tourism Encounters the Canadian Rockies*. Durham, NC: Duke University Press.

Saunders, E. Dale. 1985. *Mudrā: A Study of Symbolic Gestures in Japanese Buddhist Sculpture*. Princeton, NJ: Princeton University Press.

Sawada, Janine Anderson. 2022. *Faith in Mount Fuji: The Rise of Independent Religion in Early Modern Japan*. Honolulu: University of Hawai'i Press.

Schattschneider, Ellen. 2003. *Immortal Wishes: Labor and Transcendence on a Japanese Sacred Mountain*. Durham, NC: Duke University Press.

Scheid, Bernhard, and Mark Teeuwen, eds. 2008. *The Culture of Secrecy in Japanese Religion*. New York: Routledge.

Schencking, J. Charles. 2008. "The Great Kanto Earthquake and the Culture of Catastrophe and Reconstruction in 1920's Japan." *Journal of Japanese Studies* 34 (2): 295–331.

Schnell, Scott. 1997. "Sanctity and Sanction in Communal Ritual: A Reconsideration of Shintō Festival Processions." *Ethnology* 36 (1): 1–12.

Schnell, Scott. 2007. "Are Mountain Gods Vindictive? Competing Images of the Japanese Alpine Landscape." *Journal of the Royal Anthropological Institute* 13 (4): 863–80.

Sekimori, Gaynor. 2005a. "Paper Fowl and Wooden Fish: The Separation of Kami and Buddha Worship in Haguro Shugendō, 1869–1875." *Japanese Journal of Religious Studies* 32 (2): 197–234.

Sekimori, Gaynor. 2005b. 秋の峰の歴史を歩む [A walk though the history of autumn's peak]." In 千年の修験道 羽黒山伏の世界 [A millennium of Shugendō: The world of the Haguro Yamabushi], 88–127. Tokyo: Shinjuku shobo.

Sekimori, Gaynor. 2009a. "Defining Shugendō Past and Present: The 'Restoration' of Shugendō at Nikkō and Koshikidake." In *Shugendō: The History and Culture of a Japanese Religion*, edited by Bernard Faure, D. Max Moerman, and Gaynor Sekimori, 47–71. Paris: École française d'Extrême-Orient.

Sekimori, Gaynor. 2009b. "Shugendo: Japanese Mountain Religion—State of the Field and Bibliographic Review." *Religion Compass* 3 (1): 31–57.

Sekimori, Gaynor. 2016. "Foetal Buddhism: From Theory to Practice—Embryological Symbolism in the Autumn Peak Ritual of Haguro Shugendo." In *Transforming the Void: Embryological Discourse and Reproductive Imagery in East*

Asian Religions, edited by Anna Andreeva and Dominic Steavu, 552–58. Leiden: Brill.

Sekimori, Gaynor. 2018. "Shugendo and the Sea." In *The Sea and the Sacred in Japan: Aspects of Maritime Religion in Japan*, edited by Fabio Rambelli, 101–18. London: Bloomsbury.

Sharf, Robert H. 2015. "Is Mindfulness Buddhist? (And Why It Matters)." *Transcultural Psychiatry* 52 (4): 470–84.

Shiga, Shigetaka. (1894) 1995. 日本風景論 [Theory of Japanese landscape]. Edited by Kondo Nobuyuki. Tokyo: Iwanami shoten.

Shimazu, Kókai, and Minao Kitamura. 2005. 千年の修験：羽黒山伏の世界 [1,000 years of asceticism: The world of the Mt. Haguro Yamabushi]. Tokyo: Shinjuku shobo.

Shirane, Haruo. 1998. *Traces of Dreams: Landscape, Cultural Memory and the Poetry of Bashō*. Stanford, CA: Stanford University Press.

Shultz, John. 2021. "'Heart Sutra Pop': Religious Textual Democratization by a Sexy Vocal Android." *Journal of Religion and Popular Culture* 33 (1): 29–47.

Skrebina, David. 2017. *Panpsychism in the West*. Cambridge, MA: MIT Press.

Smith, Adam. (1759) 1976. *The Theory of Moral Sentiments*. Edited by D. D. Raphael and A. L. Macfie. Oxford: Clarendon Press of Oxford University Press.

Smith, Robert J. 1974. *Ancestor Worship in Contemporary Japan*. Stanford, CA: Stanford University Press.

Sponberg, Alan, and Helen Hardacre. 1988. *Maitreya, the Future Buddha*. Cambridge: Cambridge University Press.

Stausberg, Michael. 2011. *Religion and Tourism: Crossroads, Destinations and Encounters*. New York: Routledge.

Steger, Brigitte. 2003. "Getting Away with Sleep: Social and Cultural Aspects of Dozing in Parliament." *Social Science Japan Journal* 6 (2): 181–97.

Steger, Brigitte, and Raji C. Steineck. 2017. "Introduction from the Guest Editors to the Special Issue 'Time in Historic Japan.'" *Kronoscope* 17: 7–15.

Stein, Justin B. 2023. *Alternate Currents: Reiki's Circulation in the Twentieth-Century Northwest Pacific*. Honolulu: University of Hawai'i Press.

Suzuki, Masataka. 2015. 『山岳信仰―日本文化の根底を探る』中央公論新社 [Mountain worship: Exploring the basis of Japanese culture]. Tokyo: Chuokoraon-shinsha.

Suzuki, Masataka. 2020. "A Critical History of the Study of Shugendō and Mountain Beliefs in Japan." In *Defining Shugendō: Critical Studies on Japanese Mountain Religion*, edited by Andrea Castiglioni, Fabio Rambelli, and Carina Roth, 33–59. London: Bloomsbury Academic.

Swenson, Edward, and John Warner. 2015. "Landscapes of Mimesis and Convergence in the Southern Jequetepeque Valley, Peru." *Cambridge Archaeological Journal* 26 (1): 23–51.

Takahashi, Hara. 2016. "The Ghosts of Tsunami Dead and Kokoro no kea in Japan's Religious Landscape." *Journal of Religion in Japan* 5 (2–3): 176–98.

Tanahashi, Kazuaki. 2014. *The Heart Sutra: A Comprehensive Guide to the Classic of Mahayana Buddhism*. Boston: Shambhala.

Teeuwen, Mark, and Fabio Rambelli, eds. 2003. *Buddhas and Kami in Japan: Honji Suijaku as a Combinatory Paradigm*. New York: Routledge.

Thomas, Jolyon Baraka. 2019. *Faking Liberties: Religious Freedom in American-Occupied Japan*. Chicago: University of Chicago Press.

Togawa, Anshō. 1974. 出羽三山のミイラ仏 [The Buddha mummies of Dewa Sanzan]. Tokyo: Chūō shoin.

Tomi, Shinzō. 2006. *Testumonkai Shōnin: Even If Love Fades*. Vol. 2. Tokyo: Magazine Five.

Traphagan, John W. 2021. *Cosmopolitan Rurality, Depopulation, and Entrepreneurial Ecosystems in 21st Century Japan*. New York: Cambria.

Traphagan, John W., and Christopher S. Thompson, eds. 2006. *Wearing Cultural Styles in Japan: Concepts of Tradition and Modernity in Practice*. New York: State University of New York Press.

Trouillot, Michel-Rolph. 1991. "Anthropology and the Savage Slot." In *Recapturing Anthropology: Working in the Present*, edited by Richard G. Fox, 17–44. Santa Fe, NM: School of American Research Press.

Trouillot, Michel-Rolph. 2003. *Global Transformations: Anthropology and the Modern World*. New York: Palgrave Macmillan.

Tsing, Anna Lowenhaupt. 2005. *Friction: An Ethnography of Global Connection*. Princeton, NJ: Princeton University Press.

Tsuji, Yohko. 2018. "Evolving Mortuary Rituals in Contemporary Japan." In *A Companion to the Anthropology of Death*, edited by Antonius C. G. M. Robben, 17–30. Hoboken, NJ: John Wiley and Sons.

Turner, Victor, and Edith L. B. Turner. 1978. *Image and Pilgrimage in Christian Culture: Anthropological Perspectives*. New York: Columbia University Press.

Turner, Victor. 2008. *The Ritual Process: Structure and Anti-Structure*. New Brunswick and London: Aldine Transaction.

Ueda, Makoto. 1970. *Matsuo Bashō*. New York: Twayne.

Vanzolini, Marina, and Pedro Cesarino. 2014. "Perspectivism." *Oxford Bibliographies*. Last modified August 26. www.oxfordbibliographies.com/display/document/obo-9780199766567/obo-9780199766567-0083.xml.

Veteto, James R. 2009. "From Mountain Anthropology to Montology? An Overview of the Anthropological Approach to Mountain Studies." In *Horizons in Earth Science Research*. Vol. 1, edited by Benjamin Veress and Jozsi Szigethy, 1–17. Hauppauge, NY: Nova Science.

Vignau, Charlotte. 2013. *Modernity, Complex Societies, and the Alphorn*. Lanham, MD: Lexington Books.

Viveiros de Castro, Eduardo. 1998. "Cosmological Deixis and Amerindian Perspectivism." *Journal of the Royal Anthropological Institute* 4 (3): 469–88.

Viveiros de Castro, Eduardo. 2004. "Perspectival Anthropology and the Method of Controlled Equivocation." *Tipití: Journal of the Society for the Anthropology of Lowland South America* 2 (1): 3–22.

Walker, Brett L. 2015. *A Concise History of Japan*. Cambridge: Cambridge University Press.

Walls, Laura Dassow. 2009. *The Passage to Cosmos: Alexander von Humboldt and the Shaping of America*. Chicago: University of Chicago Press.

Watanabe, Satoshi, dir. 2017. *The Buddha Mummies of North Japan*. DVD, 20 mins. Watertown, MA: Documentary Educational Resources.

Wilhelm, Johannes, and Alyne Delaney. 2015. "No Homes, No Boats, No Rafts: Miyagi Coastal People in the Aftermath of Disaster." In *Japan Copes with Calamity*, 2nd ed., edited by Tom Gill, Brigitte Steger, and David H. Slater, 99–124. Oxford: Peter Lang.

Wilson, Jeff. 2014. *Mindful America: The Mutual Transformation of Buddhist Meditation and American Culture*. Oxford: University of Oxford Press.

Yuasa, Nobuyuki. 1966. Introduction to *The Narrow Road to the Deep North and Other Travel Sketches*, by Matsuo Bashō. Translated and edited by Nobuyuki Yuasa, 9–49. Harmondsworth, UK: Penguin.

Zhuāngzǐ. 2024. *The Complete Writings*. Translated by Chris Fraser. Oxford: University of Oxford Press.

Index

Page numbers in italics refer to illustrations.

alpine affects, 71; and ancestral communion, 97, 98; and break from capitalist modernity, 27; and contact with birthing power (*umidasu chikara*), 105; and inner silence, 69, 70, 215n20, 215n21; and sensory stimulation, 65; and temporal alterity of body, 98, 106

alpine ethnography, 10, 20, 33, 202–3

ancestral connection, 22, 34, 97; and authentic identity, 22; and balance with modern life, 7, 9; and conch trumpet (*hora gai*), 47; and cosmic deathscape of Mount Gassan, 164, 165, 166, 168; and Gassan pilgrimage, 162, *162*, 163, 179; and Matsuo Bashō, 38; and Obon festival, 168, 169, 170, *170*, 171, 172, *172*; on path between Gassan and Yudono mountains, 76, 77; and pilgrimage, 202; and Sakamoto Daizaburo, 73; and temporality of Dewa Sanzan, 32; and 3/11 aftermath and memorial, 28, 178; and womb of mountain, 105, 201

ascetic guides (*sendatsu*): and ancestral memorialization, 171, 173; and Autumn's Peak, 124; and Esoteric Buddhist cosmos, 144; and pilgrim lodges, 176; 3/11 interpreted by, 174; Shintō-oriented, 87; trust in, 25. *See also* Hoshino Fumihiro; Shimazu Kokai

ascetics, 24; and ancestor veneration on Mount Gassan, 163, 178; and ancestral powers, 19; aspiring, 26; and birth symbolism, 25, 27, 201; and break from capitalist modernity, 8, 9, 27, 202; and Exorcism River, 49; and Heart Sutra, 53; and memorial to 3/11 victims, 176; and mountain water, 14; and phronesis, 28; and post-3/11 identity crisis, 7; in pursuit of hopeful future, 8; in search of cyclical temporality, 9, 27; amid Shōnai tourist crowds, 23; and spiritual rejuvenation, 29; stereotypes of, 46, 47; and transmigration of soul, 164. *See also* ascetic guides (*sendatsu*); Autumn's Peak, Buddhist version of; Buddhist-Shintō divide, in Mount Haguro; mummies, Buddha; shugyō, yamabushi testimonies of

Asumi-san (ascetic): and countercultural element of shugyō, 104, 105, 106, 107; interpretation of waterfall practice (*takigyō*) of, 83, 84; and post-3/11 crisis, 83, 101, 102, 146, 147

attire, of ascetics, 44, 45, 67, 115, 129, 138, 139, *139*, 140, 141, 142, 223n6

Autumn's Peak, Buddhist version of: and ascetic phronesis, 133, 134, 138, 147, 159; and ascetics' opposition to innovation, 158, 159; and attire, 138, 139, *139*, 140, 141, 142; and Chinese zodiac and temporal alterity, 143, 144; and concluding rituals, 129, 130, 131, 132; and daisendatsu Shimazu Kokai, 150, 151, 158, 203; and death symbolism, 132, 136, 137, 141, 144; and ethics and capitalist modernity,

Autumn's Peak, Buddhist version of (*continued*)
132, 133, 134, 137, 138, 147, 159, 160; and first bath (*basaitō*), *130*, 131; and global connections of ascetics, 155, 156; and initial rituals, 135, 136; and internet and social media restrictions, 148, 151; and kami, 131, 134, 157; and medieval grammar and lexicon, 145, 146; and moral dilemmas for participants, 147–54, 159; and negotiation of ethics, 155, 156, 157, 158, 159, 160, 200; and New Age ascetics, 153; and nostalgia, 137, 147; and rebirth symbolism, *130*, 131, 132, 134–39, 144; and reproductive symbolism, 223n5; and spatiotemporality, 132, 133, 134, 137, 138, 147, 159, 160; and spirit possession, 146, 147, 158, 224n25; and Tendai Buddhism, 134; and Ten Worlds, 134, 135, 136; and use of word *yamabushi*, 150, 151; and yamabushi in Mexico, 154, 155, 156. *See also* Buddhist-Shintō divide, in Mount Haguro; Kōtakuji Temple

Autumn's Peak, Shintō version of, 111, 132, 161; and Buddhist-oriented Autumn's Peak, 108, 126; and disaster pilgrimage, 161; and Shintō historicity, 113, 114; and yamabushi attire, 115, 141, 142. *See also* Buddhist-Shintō divide, in Mount Haguro

birthing power (*umidasu chikara*), 103, 105, 107, 201

Buddha mummies. *See* mummies, Buddha

Buddhism, 40; arrival in Japan of, 110, 202, 221n4, 221n5; and cosmic deathscape of Gassan, 166; and cosmology of, 54, 134, 135, 140; Esoteric, 46, 53, 54, 140, 184, 185, 186, 190, 223n9; and historical symbolism of mountains, 42, 43; Indian origins of, 45; Meiji persecution of, 142, 144, 147, 167, 168; and numerology, 44; and river symbolism, 48, 49; Shingon, 24, 42, 52, 183, 185, 202; Tendai, 24, 42, 52, 112, 134, 151, 157, 202, 221n7; Zen, 86, 165, 216n24. *See also* Buddhist-Shintō divide, in Mount Haguro; Haguro Shugen Honshū; Heart Sutra; mummies, Buddha; Shimazu Kokai; Shozen-in Temple; Ten Worlds

Buddhist-Shintō divide, in Mount Haguro, 26, 27, 28, 108; and anti-Western historicity of Buddhist ascetics, 121–24; and author's neutrality, 132; and Autumn's Peak tourist infrastructure, 115, 116, 117, 124; and Buddhist ressentiment, 117–21, 128; and Dewa Sanzan public relations campaign, 124; and Heart Sutra, 120; and historicities of shugyō, 111–15, 127, 128, 132, 133, 142; and Meiji period, 52, 108, 109, 110, 111, 112, 114, 127; and Meiji separation orders, 111, 117, 118; and nativist hostility, 109, 110, 111, 221n5, 221n7; and political neutrality of ascetics, 3, 126; and politics of Shugendō scholarship, 124, 125, 126, 127. *See also* Autumn's Peak, Buddhist version of; Autumn's Peak, Shintō version of; Buddhism; Haguro Shugen Honshū; Shugendō, Shintō-oriented

capitalist modernity: and alienation from society, 8, 9, 205n8; and anti-Western resentment of Buddhist ascetics, 124; and ascetic attire, 142; in contrast to mountains, 200, 201; as counterpoint to human agency, 27, 28, 65; and ethics of Buddhist ascetics, 133, 134, 137, 138, 147, 159, 160; and Japan, 21–22, 25, 202, 213n39; and nostalgia, 21, 22; and overstimulated mind, 70; and 3/11, 206n9; and self-estrangement, 65, 107; shugyō-enabled suspension from, 66,

95, 106, 132, 202; and soundscapes, 47; and temporal alterity of shugyō, 86, 100; and trammeled spirits (*tamashii*), 90; and yamabushi experience retreat, 27, 65, 66, 70, 72, 73, 107; vs. zodiac space and time, 144

Chōnan-san: and narrative of Buddhist Shugendō, 117–20, *118*; and politics of Shugendō scholarship, 127

conch trumpet (*hora gai*), 45, 46, 47; and ancestral communion, 47; and Buddhist version of Autumn's Peak, 139, 140, 141, 145, 151, 213n38; and cosmic deathscape of Gassan, 167; and Esoteric Buddhism, 186; and Hoshino Fumihiro, 61, 67; at Ideha Cultural Museum, 34, 35; and marking of time, 145; in Mexico, 155, 156; and Obon festival, 169, 170; and reproductive and sexual symbolism, 139, 140, 141, 201; and tourism, 47, 48, *48*, 49, 116

cultural orography. *See* orography, cultural

Dainichibō temple, Buddha mummies in, 180, 181, *181*; and lifetime ascetic Shinnyōkai, 185, 188, 189, 190, 194, 195, 197; and Mount Yudono reproductive symbolism, 183, 184; and politics of historical authenticity, 188, 189, 190, 193; and supernatural powers, 190, *191*; and Tenmei Famine, 194, 195. *See also* mummies, Buddha

Dainichi Nyorai, 25, 184, 215n9, 226n11; and conch trumpet (*hora gai*), 46; and Fudō Myōō, 140, 158; and historicities of Mount Haguro, 116; and kami and trees, 52; and Mount Yudono, 56, 138; and mummified monks, 186; and temporal alterity of Autumn's Peak, 145

daisendatsu. *See* Shimazu Kokai

Daishōbō, 60, 71, 76, 111; and beast practice (*chikushōgyō*), 75; and final feast (*naorai*), 69, 87; and first bath (*basaitō*), 84; and pepper smoke ritual (*nanban ibushi*), 73; and post-3/11 crisis, 176, 177; and separation from capitalist modernity, 66; and yamabushi attire, 67; and zazen seated meditation, 72. *See also* Hoshino Fumihiro

death symbolism, 7, 25; and attire of ascetics, 141; and Autumn's Peak, 132, 136, 137, 141, 144; and capitalist modernity, 132; and cultural orography, 18, 178; and cyclical returns to mountains, 8, 9; and Gassan pilgrimage, 28, 164–68, 178; and Japanese character ん (Un), 40; and Obon festival, 169; and river crossing, 49; and symbolic womb, 5, 57, 80. *See also* Gassan, pilgrimage on

Dewa Sanzan, 5, 6; and ancestral space-time, 163; and anthropology of mountains, 202, 203; in contrast to cultural modernity, 22, 27, 33, 85, 159; and econostalgia, 105; and gendered landscape, 87, 106; and mountains as living placeworlds, 199; and power spots, 32, 53; regional context of, 22–24; and religion's proximity to tourism, 27, 57, 85; religious politics in, 27, 28, 108, 109, 127, 128; and self-reflection, 159, 202; and Shugendō, 201; significance after 3/11 of, 107, 163; social and temporal dimensions of, 7, 8, 9, 57, 58, 162; and spatiotemporal alterity of mountains, 200

Dewa Sanzan Shrine, 26; Autumn's Peak of, 132, 133, 150; and Buddhist ressentiment, 118, 120, 124; and Chinese Zodiac, 55, 56; and Grandfather Tree, 50; and Great Boulder, 78; and historicities of shugyō, 111, 113, 114; and politics of Shugendō scholarship, 124, 125, 127; and sworn secrecy, 1; ten stairs of, 84, 129, 166; and tourist infrastructure, 117

Index 243

earthquake, Great Hanshin, 21, 173
earthquake, tsunami, and nuclear disaster, 2011. *See* 3/11
Edo period, 73; dramatization of, 21, 23; and embodied Buddhas (*sokushinbutsu*), 225n4; and eruption of Mount Asama, 194, 195; and exoticization of Tōhoku, 40; in Hoshino Fumihiro's historical narrative, 93
embodied Buddhas (*sokushinbutsu*), 180–84, 186, 188, 189, *191*, 192–95, 197, 225n4
Esoteric Buddhism, 46, 53, 54, 140, 184, 185, 186, 190, 223n9
ethics: of research, 2, 197; and Autumn's Peak participants, 28, 140, 150, 151, 152, 155; and capitalist modernity, 132, 133, 134, 137, 138, 147, 159, 160; negotiation of, 155, 156, 157, 158, 159, 160, 200; and 3/11 victims, 164. *See also* Autumn's Peak, Buddhist version of
Exorcism River, 49, 50, 116

filmmaking, 153; *Buddha Mummies of North Japan*, 190, 195, 197; and fame of Hoshino Fumihiro, 98, 105; and Japanese public broadcasting, 17, 98, 193; and Kitamura Minao, 125, 205n1, 222n1; and Koshikidake Shōkai, 157, 158; and mountaineering documentaries, 16; and Obon, 169; and politics of Shugendō scholarship, 124, 125; Shōnai industry of, 23, 24; *Uketamau*, 94
final feast (*naorai*), 69, 87, 88, 90, 96
first bath (*basaitō*), 84, *130*, 131
forests and trees: and birthing power (*umidasu chikara*), 103; and ecosystem and vegetation, 5, 41, 59, 60, 168; and Grandfather Tree, 50, *51*, 52, 53, 71, 213n49; and kami, 52; and paths and walking, 50, 72, 79, 151

Gassan, 5, 6, 10; and ascetic guides' (*sendatsu*) knowledge of symbolism, 50; and Buddhist deities, 138; and heterotopia, 20; and snowfall and water, 14, 15; and Kyūya Fukada's list of spirit mountains (*reizan*), 18; and Matsuo Bashō's haiku, 37, 39, 211n12; and orographic location of Mount Yudono, 5, 76, 184; temporality of, 179; and yamabushi testimonies of shugyō, 94; and zodiac, 15, 56. *See also* Gassan, pilgrimage on; yamabushi experience retreat
Gassan, pilgrimage on, 28, 200; and ancestral memorialization, 168–72, *170*, *172*; and Heart Sutra, 176, 177, 178; and Hoshino-san, 170, 173, 176, 177, 178, 180; and Itō-san's observations of deathscape, 167, 168; and kami, 164, 165, 170, 171, 174; and lodges (*shukubō*), 5, 40, 60; and memorialization of disaster dead, 173, 174, 175; and Naitō-san (spirit medium), 161, 162, 164; and orography, 163, 164, 167, 178; and post-3/11 temporality, 163, 164, 168, 175; and Shintō incantations (*norito*), 170, 171, 172; and spirit mountains (*reizan*), 162; and sutras, 172, 176; and ten stations, 161, 166, 167, 168, 169, 173, 224n1, 225n15; and transmigration of soul, 5, 162, *162*, 164, 165, 167, 178; and 3/11 memorial, 28, 175–78. *See also* Daishōbō; Hoshino Fumihiro; pilgrims
Gate of Dual Deities. *See* Zuishinmon
gendered landscape and imagery, 19, 27, *80*, 90, 91, 92; and genitalia, 56, 78, 79, 87, 106, 141, 184, 201, 221n28, 223n6, 225n3; and Ohama lake, 79; and placenta, 135; and uterine symbolism, 43, 78, 201; and waterfall practice (*takigyō*), 83, 91, 94. *See also* conch trumpet (*hora gai*); womb of mountain, symbolic
globalization, 16; and adaptability of Shugendō, 25, 26, 213n39; and alphorn, 211n9; and contrast with

premodern cyclical time, 56; and friction between Buddhist morality and capitalist modernity, 138, 159, 160; and history of Western encroachment, 123, 195; and integrity of Shugendō, 28; and interpretation of locales and mountains, 15, 18; and Native American spirituality, 154, 155, 156; and religion's proximity to tourism, 211n4, 213n39; and zazen seated meditation, 216n24

gongyō. *See* Haguro Shugen liturgy (*gongyō*)

Grandfather Tree, 50, *51*, 52, 53, 71, 213n49

Great Boulder, 77, 78, 81, 184

Haguro, Mount, 1, 2, 4, 5, 6, 13, 69; and confinement practice (*komorigyō*), 102; and cultural orography, 13, 14, 20; god body (*gōshintai*) of, 84; and Haguro Shugen liturgy (*gongyō*), 72, 74, 89, 145, 146; and Heart Sutra after 3/11, 177; as hub for ascetics and pilgrims, 24; and Matsuo Bashō's haiku, 212n12; and multiple temporalities, 20; and muscular guardian statues (*niō*), 212n27; and pepper smoke (*nanban ibushi*), 74, 75; shrine on, 26; spring water from, 14; and stairway of rebirth, 43, *44*, 45, 52, 56, 57, 115, 116, 131; and torii, 60. *See also* Autumn's Peak, Buddhist version of; Autumn's Peak, Shintō version of; Buddhist-Shintō divide, in Mount Haguro; Dewa Sanzan Shrine; Haguro, Mount, guided tour of; womb of mountain, symbolic

Haguro, Mount, guided tour of: and attire, 44, 45; and Buddhist-Shintō rift, 40, 41, 42; and Chinese zodiac, 55, 56, 213n49; and conch trumpet (*hora gai*), 45, 46, 47, 48, 49, 213n38; and Exorcism River, 49–50; and five-storied pagoda, 53, 54; and Grandfather Tree, 50, *51*, 52, 53, 213n49; and guidebooks, 30, 31; and Heart Sutra, 53; and hell imagery, 42, 45; and journey to Tōge, 31; and kami, 31, 40, 41, 49, 50, 52, 54, 56; and Matsuo Bashō's haiku on stone, 35–40, *36*, 58; and multiple temporalities of Dewa Sanzan, 27, 40, 57; and nostalgia, 44, 46, 49; and power spots, 45, 54, 57; and regional narratives of Tohoku, 36, 37, 38, 39, 40; and rituals and temporality, 46, 47, 53, 55, 57; and river symbolism, 49, 50; and sutras, 49, 50, 53; and tea shop, 54, 55; and torii, 31, 32, 55; and tourism, 45, 53, 54, 55, 57; and Zuishinmon, 40, 41, *41*, 49, 56, 57. *See also* conch trumpet (*hora gai*); Haguro, Mount; Ideha Cultural Museum; Itō-san (yamabushi guide)

Haguroha Koshugendō. *See* Shugendō, Shintō-oriented

Haguro Shugen Honshū, 109, 121; attire of, 129, 138; and Buddhist ressentiment, 117, 119; and criticism of Dewa Sanzan public relations campaign, 124; and ethics of yamabushi, 150, 151; and Hell Realm (*jigokudō*), 134; and historicities of shugyō, 114; low profile of, 126; opposition to yamabushi experience retreats of, 132; and origins lore, 26; and politics of Shugendō scholarship, 124, 125, 126, 127; post–World War II revitalization of, 142, 147; and resistance to capitalist modernity, 133. *See also* Autumn's Peak, Buddhist version of; Shozen-in Temple

Haguro Shugen liturgy (*gongyō*), 68, 87; and ancestral memorialization, 172; in Daishōbō, 84; on Gassan summit, 72, 76, 71; at Great Boulder, 78; and Hell Realm (*jigokudō*), 146; and Kōtakuji Temple, 120; at Ohama lake, 79; during nocturnal journey, 72;

Index 245

Haguro Shugen liturgy (*continued*) during pepper smoke ritual (*nanban ibushi*), 74; and politics of Shugendō scholarship, 125; and temporal disorientation, 145; and waterfall practice (*takigyō*), 81, 83; and yamabushi testimonies of shugyō, 89, 91, 120

Heart Sutra, 53, 68, 120, 121, 145, 146, 176, 177, 178, 215n15. *See also* Haguro Shugen liturgy (*gongyō*)

hell, imagery and symbolism of, 42, 43, 45, 134, 146

historical consciousness: and anthropology of mountains, 11; Buddhist, 137, 138, 142, 143; and embodied Buddhas (*sokushinbutsu*), 183, 194, 195, 197; evoked by mountains in Japan, 7, 20, 200; evoked by rituals, 9; of Japanese modernity, 21; and modern peoples' attraction to Dewa Sanzan, 33, 57, 162, 211n6. *See also* Buddhist-Shintō divide, in Mount Haguro

Hoshino Fumihiro, 59–63, 85; and anthropology of Shugendō, 90, 219n17; and counterculture of shugyō, 103, 104, 105; and flexible Shugendō, 86, 90, 94, 96; and fusion of Shugendō and tourism, 62, 63, 66, 85, 86; on gendered landscape, 91; and historical narrative of Buddhist-Shintō divide, 112–15; on human-nature unity (*jinen*), 71, 200; on necessity of shugyō in modern times, 95, 96, 97, 219n6; nostalgic and spiritual framework of, 98; fame of, 94; reflections on role of sendatsu of, 89, 90; and Shintō version of Autumn's Peak, 111, 112; and 3/11 aftermath, 176, 177, 178; and uketamau of, 71, 83, 95, 96, 97; on yamabushi's wildness within, 94, 95, 106. *See also* Daishōbō; yamabushi experience retreat

Huichol people of Mexico, 154, 155, 156

hungry ghost practice (*gakigyō*), 42, 72, 75, 87

Ideha Cultural Museum, 30, 34, 35, 62, 105, 111, 98, 99, 115, 116, 117, 222n13

Itō-san (yamabushi guide): on birthing power (*umidasu chikara*) of Shugendō, 201; on Chinese zodiac, 55, 56; and conch trumpet (*hora gai*), 45, 46, 47; and Exorcism River, 49, 50; and final descent from Mount Haguro, 56; and five-storied pagoda, 53; former samurai residence of, 59; and Grandfather Tree, 50; and Heart Sutra, 53; on hell (*jigoku*), 42, 43; and Hoshino Fumihiro, 59, 60; and Ideha Cultural Museum, 34, 35; and interview with Japanese public broadcasting, 99, 102, 103, 104; on labor of shugyō, 99; on Matsuo Bashō's haiku, 35; and Mount Gassan pilgrimage, 167, 168; and personal transformation through shugyō, 104; and religion-tourism dynamic of Dewa Sanzan, 57; and stairway of rebirth, 43, 44, *44*; and tea shop, 54, 55; and winter's generative power, 102, 103; and Zuishinmon, 40, 41

Ivy, Marilyn, 17, 18, 21, 22, 48, 49, 200–201, 210n42

Japan: capitalist modernity in, 20–22; cultural orography in, 13–20. *See also* Buddhism; Edo period; globalization; Meiji period; Shugendō; Shugendō, Shintō-oriented; tourism; 3/11; *and individual place names*

kami, 9, 56; and Buddhist-oriented Autumn's Peak, 131, 134, 157; and Buddhist-Shintō conflict, 112, 121, 122, 123, 221n4, 221n6; and cultural orography, 13, 15, 16, 17; and Emperor Hirohito, 210n38; and Great Boulder, 78; and konone matsuri festival, 218n3; of Mount Gassan, 73, 164, 165, 170, 171, 174; and Mount Haguro, 31, 40, 41, 49, 50, 52, 54, 56; sacred

246 Index

abodes of, 52, 209n27; in translation, 211n3; and yamabushi experience retreat, 67, 68, 73, 74, 78, 81, 83, 84, 217n30

Kōtakuji Temple, 120, 124, 125, 126, 129, 142, 143, 144, 148, 152

Matsuo Bashō, haiku of, 36–40, *36*, 78, 165, 166

meditation, seated (zazen), 71, 72, 75, 216n24

Meiji period, 21; and Buddhist place names, 116; and competing Buddhist and Shintō historicities, 127; and Gregorian solar calendar, 93; and Meiji Restoration, 36, 52, 54, 108; and separation orders, 111, 117, 118; and Shintōization of Shugendō, 109, 110, 111, 112, 114, 119, 122

memorial to 3/11 victims, 28, 163, 171, *172*, 174–78

mountains, 29; and deathscape, 164; and disengagement with capitalist modernity, 8, 9, 200; and ethnographic discovery, 29, 203; and Japanese language, 19, 20; and modes of historical consciousness, 7; and moral alterity, 201–2; as spatiotemporal vortex, 9, 20. *See also individual mountain names*

mountains, anthropology of, 10–13, 20, 27, 33, 200, 202–3, 207. *See also* orographic perspectivism; orography, cultural

mummies, Buddha, 5, 143, *191*, 211n53; and academic discovery of embodied Buddhas (*sokushinbutsu*), 189, 194; agency of, 198; and *Buddha Mummies of North Japan*, 190, 197; Andrea Castiglioni on, 181, 182, 184, 187, 193; of Chūren-ji temple, 180, 189, 190, 193, 194; in Esoteric Buddhism, 184–87; historical consciousness inspired by, 194–97, 198; and metakinesis, 192, 193; and nomenclature of mummified ascetics, 181, 182; and politics of historical authenticity, 28, 29, 187–90; in popular culture, 193; and power of embodied Buddhas (*sokushinbutsu*), 183; and self-mummification in oral history, 183, 184, 185, 225n4; and supernatural powers, 190, 191, 192, 193, 197, 198; and Tetsumonkai temple, 189, 190, 194; and 3/11, 198; and tourism, 29, 183, 193, 194; of Zōkōin temple, 195, 196, *196*, 197. *See also* Dainichibō temple, Buddha mummies in

Naitō-san (*reinōsha*), 161, 162, 164

Narrow Road to the Interior, 36, 37, 38, 39, 40

Nomura-san (*ascetic*), 154, 155, 156

nostalgia: and Buddhist-oriented Autumn's Peak, 137, 147; and Buddhist ressentiment, 118, 119; and capitalist modernity, 21, 22, 137, 147; and conch trumpet (*hora gai*), 46, 47; and cultural orography, 13, 14, 16, 18, 33, 162, 164, 200–201, 208n23; and Dewa Sanzan as power spot, 32; evoked by yamabushi attire, 44; and Hoshino Fumihiro's shugyō framework, 98; and Japanese film industry, 23, 24; for Japanese identity, 89; and tourism, 48, 49, 58, 105

Obon (Festival of the Dead), 161, 163, 168–73, *170*, 175

Oki-san (*yamabushi*), 80, 81, 83, 108, 126, 127

orographic perspectivism, 12, 13, 15, 16, 18, 103, 107, 199, 200, 202, 208n21. *See also* orography, cultural

orography, cultural, 12, 45, 167, 199–200; and alpine affects, 71; and alpine ethnography, 10, 33, 202–3; and anthropology of mountains, 10, 202; and death symbolism, 18, 19, 164, 178; and ecological significance

Index 247

orography, cultural (*continued*)
of mountains, 14, 15; and European notions of landscape, 16; and Japanese ethnicity and modern literature, 17, 18; and kami, 13, 15, 16, 17; and Kyūya Fukada, 16, 17, 18, 19; and mountain-as-womb motif, 57; and nostalgia, 13, 14, 16, 18, 33, 162, 164, 200–201, 208n23; and rebirth symbolism, 57, 71; and Ellen Schattschneider, 19, 220n20; and Scott Schnell, 16; and spatiotemporality, 20, 162, 163; and Yanagita Kunio, 15, 16, 18

pagoda, five-storied, *51*, 53, 54, 71, 116, 213n49
pepper smoke ritual (*nanban ibushi*), 73, 74, 75, 134, 146
peyote, 154–56
phronesis, 28, 133, 134, 138, 147, 150, 159, 160
pilgrim lodges (*shukubō*), 5, 35, 40, 60, 111, 114, 171, 174, 176
pilgrims, 24; and Buddhist-Shintō rift, 120, 129; and conch trumpet (*hora gai*), 46; and embodied Buddhas (*sokushinbutsu*) 180, 181, 183, *191*, 192; and esoteric hand gestures (*mudras*), 53, 54; and Great Boulder, 78, 79; in guidebooks, 30; and Heart Sutra, 53; and hungry ghost realm practice, 146; and leisure travel to Shōnai after 3/11, 23; literary, 212n24, 212n25; and lodges (*shukubō*), 5, 35, 40, 60, 111; at main shrine of Mount Yudono, 77; and Matsuo Bashō, 39, 40, 212n25; and means of travel, 119, 120, 137; in Mexico, 155; and place-based observance rituals (*omairi*), 53, 54, 55; and politics of Shugendō scholarship, 124; and rebirth and self-transformation in mountains, 43, 55, 202; and religion's proximity to tourism, 215n7; and Shikoku, 123, 153; and spatiotemporality of path between Gassan and Yudono mountains, 76, 77; and wide-brimmed hat (*ayaigasa*), 141; at Zuishinmon, 40, 41. *See also* Gassan, pilgrimage on

place-based observance rituals (*omairi*), 53, 54, 55, 71, 79, 119, 120, 197
power spot, 32, 45, 53, 54, 57, 213n44

rebirth symbolism, 1, 19; and birthing power (*umidasu chikara*), 103, 105, 107, 201; and countermodern temporality, 8, 9, 27; and first bath (basaitō), 84, *130*, 131; and Great Boulder, 78; Hoshino-san on, 91; and Ohama lake, 79; and mountains in Asia, 202; and stairway of rebirth, 43, *44*, 45, 52, 56, 57, 115, 116, 131; after 3/11, 164; waterfall practice (*takigyō*), 91. *See also* Autumn's Peak, Buddhist version of; Haguro, Mount; womb of mountain, symbolic
ressentiment, 27, 109, 110, 11, 117–21, 124, 128, 221n2, 221n7
rituals, 52, 53; and bond between yamabushi, 85, 90; and counter-modern space and time, 9, 46, 56, 65, 66, 86, 133, 213n48; and domains for ancestral souls, 165; as expression of resilience of Buddhist Shugendō, 119; global context of, 26; and hierarchy of ascetics, 149, 150; and historical consciousness, 9, 57; and Eric Hobsbawm, 209n36; and Koshikidake Shōkai, 157, 158; of mourning and memorializing, 163, 164, 168, 175, 178, 179, 225n17, 225n22; and present and future of Shugendō, 210n5; and proximity of religion to tourism, 63, 85, 86; and Shugendō in Mexico, 154; and Tendai Buddhism, 134; and veneration of mountains, 15. *See also* Autumn's Peak, Buddhist version of; conch trumpet (*hora gai*); death symbolism; Dewa Sanzan Shrine; Gassan,

pilgrimage on; Haguro, Mount; Haguro Shugen liturgy (*gongyō*); Heart Sutra; Kōtakuji Temple; pilgrims; rebirth symbolism; Shugendō; Ten Worlds; yamabushi experience retreat

river symbolism, 48, 49, 50

Sakamoto Daizaburo (ascetic), 129; on ascetics' attire, 142; and countercultural element of shugyō, 104, 105, 106, 202; on final feast (*naorai*), 87; on nightwalking, 73; on path between Gassan and Yudono mountains, 76, 77; on pepper smoke ritual (*nanban ibushi*), 74; and sexual descriptions of landscape and ritual, 78, 184, 218n3; and temporal alterity of Autumn's Peak, 145; and waterfall practice (*takigyō*), 83; and *Yamabushi and I*, 72; and *Yamabushi Notebook*, 89; and Yamabushi Onsen hot spring, 85, 90

Sato-san (senior yamabushi), 100, 101, 103, 104, 106, 107

Sea of Japan, 5, 13, 14, 22, 31, 39, 47, 76, 169

Shimazu Kokai: academic approach to Shugendō of, 117; on attire of ascetics, 139, 140, 223n6; and Buddhist-Shintō rift, 129; and completion of Autumn's Peak, 131; on ethics of Autumn's Peak participants, 150, 151, 152; on ethics of research, 2, 3, 4; and Hoshino Fumihiro, 114; and Koryū Shugen Honshū's online activities, 158; and mysteries of Dewa Sanzan, 203; and spirit possession, 146, 147; on Ten Worlds, 134, 135; and *Thousand Years of the Haguro Yamabushi*, 125; and zodiac during Autumn's Peak, 144

Shintō. *See* Shugendō, Shintō-oriented

Shintō incantations (*norito*), 76, 84; and Three Mountain Prayer, 68, 74, 77, 170; and Three Word Prayer, 68, 74, 75, 77, 170; and Obon festival, 170, 171, 172; and waterfall practice (*takigyō*), 81, 83

Shōnai, 22, 23; and embodied Buddhas (*sokushinbutsu*), 188; and film industry, 23, 24; and international exchange and tourism, 2, 23, 32, 47, 66, 161, 176; plains of, 54, 71, 161, 165, 169; and regionalism, 102, 117, 132; and textile tradition, 99; after 3/11, 23, 176

Shozen-in Temple, 4, 203; and author's interview with *daisendatsu*, 2, 3; and Buddhist-oriented Autumn's Peak, 131, 138, 142, 143, 155, 158; and Buddhist ressentiment, 117; and historicities of shugyō, 112, 114; and Koshikidake Shōkai, 223n24; and politics of Shugendō scholarship, 127

Shugendō: and anthropology of mountains, 202, 203; and counterculture of shugyō, 98, 100, 101, 107; and equilibrium between tradition and modernity, 66, 156, 158, 159, 160; and essence in birthing power (*umidasu chikara*), 201; ethnographic context of, 24–26; as flexible religion, 24, 25, 26, 63, 86, 90, 94, 96; fusion with tourism of, 48, 62, 85; and influence of Esoteric Buddhism, 40, 46, 53; institutional, 62, 94; and Koshikidake Shōkai, 156, 157, 158, 223n24; and Mexico, 154, 155, 156; and morphology and translation, 24, 43, 63, 64; and reproductive symbolism, 87, 88, 201, 218n3; and shamanism, 25, 110, 136; and syncretism, 24, 96, 108, 109, 110, 115, 128, 134. *See also* Autumn's Peak, Buddhist version of; Buddhist-Shintō divide, in Mount Haguro; shugyō, yamabushi testimonies of; tourism, encounters with religion of; yamabushi experience retreat

Shugendō, Shintō-oriented, 24, 221n6; and ascetics' attire, 141, 142; and

Index 249

Shugendō, Shintō-oriented (*continued*) conch trumpet (*hora gai*), 45, 46; and disaster pilgrimage, 161, *162*, 165, 167, 169, 170, 171; and historicity, 113, 115, 116, 132, 137, 222n13; and religion's proximity to tourism, 213n44; and syncretism of Shugendō, 24, 96, 115; and use of word *yamabushi*, 150. *See also* Autumn's Peak, Shintō version of; Buddhist-Shintō divide, in Mount Haguro; Dewa Sanzan Shrine; Hoshino Fumihiro; Shintō incantations (*norito*)

shugyō, 25, 26, 46; around the world, 154, 158; as central to Shugendō, 105, 124, 150, 152; counterculture of, 99, 100, 101, 102, 103, 104, 105, 106; definition and translation of, 63, 64, 85; and demand after 3/11, 177, 178; and embodied Buddhas (*sokushinbutsu*), 181, 182, 184, 186, 189, 192, 193, 194, 197; historicities of, 111–15; and laterality, 86; multiple forms of, 85, 200, 218n43; and ritual process, 65, 66. *See also* Autumn's Peak, Buddhist version of; Hoshino Fumihiro; shugyō, yamabushi testimonies of; yamabushi experience retreat

shugyō, yamabushi testimonies of: and birthing power (*umidasu chikara*), 105; and emergence of childhood memories, 88; and final feast (*naorai*), 69, 87, 88, 90, 96; and gender and sexual references to landscape, 90, 91; and gendered sense of time, 92, 93, 94; and generative power of winter, 102, 103; and heightened sensory perception, 88, 89; and nostalgia for national identity, 89; and refuge from capitalist modernity, 107; on social media, 90; and sensitivity to spirits (*tamashii*), 83, 90, 92, 93, 98, 105, 106. *See also* yamabushi experience retreat

silence, code of, 1, 78, 69, 70, 71, 76, 77, 79, 88, 95

social media, 69, 90, 148, 151, 153, 154, 155, 157, 158, 177

spirit mountains (*reizan*), 18, 19, 28, 162, 209n30, 224n2

spirit possession (*kamigakari*), 146, 147, 158, 224n25

spirits (*tamashii*), 83, 90, 92, 93, 98, 105, 106

stairway of rebirth, 43, *44*, 45, 52, 56, 57, 115, 116, 131

supernatural powers, 25, 64, 104, 190, 191, 192

syncretism, Buddhist-Shintō, 108, 109, 112, 119, 134, 171, 221n6

telepathy, 28, 190–92, 197

ten stations of Gassan, 161, 166, 167, 168, 169, 173, 224n1, 225n15

Ten Worlds, 42, 134, 129, 152; and confinement practice (*komorigyō*), 220n22; and Dewa Sanzan Shrine, 55, 120; and Hoshino Fumihiro's shugyō retreats, 75; and Koshikidake Shōkai, 157, 158; and Kōtakuji Temple, 129; and rebirth symbolism, 136, 144; and six realms, 136, 140; and structure of Autumn's Peak ritual, 143; and temporality of Autumn's Peak, 137; and ten stations of Gassan, 166; and Yamabushi Onsen hot spring, 85

3/11, 205n2, 211n1; and Asumi-san (ascetic), 83, 84, 101, 102, 146, 147; author's recollection of, 30; as divine punishment, 174, 225n19; and haunted spaces, 175; and Hoshino Fumihiro, 176, 177, 178; and identification of bodies, 224n11; and Kusajima-san (local politician), 173; and Matsuyama family, 174; and meaning and temporality of Mount Gassan, 28, 163, 164, 168, 175; and memorialization, 28, 163, *172*, 175, 176, 177, 178, 202; and optimism about future, 28,

163, 164; and pessimism and existential crisis in Japan, 7, 9, 21, 163, 177, 178, 179, 205n9; and radiation exposure, 97; and reorientation of priorities, 107; and Shōnai, 23, 176. *See also* Gassan, pilgrimage on

Three Mountain Prayer, 68, 74, 77, 170. *See also* Haguro Shugen liturgy (*gongyō*)

Three Word Prayer, 68, 74, 75, 77, 170. *See also* Haguro Shugen liturgy (*gongyō*)

Tōge, 4, 30, 34; and Buddhist ressentiment in Mount Haguro, 118; and journey to Mount Haguro, 31; and Koganedō temple, 212n27, 222n14; pilgrim lodges in, 5, 60, 114, 171, 174; political dynamics in, 117, 118, 119, 127; and Shozen-in Temple, 2, 131, 142; and tourist infrastructure, 32; and Yamabushi Onsen hot spring, 85, 171

Tōhoku, 5, 14; as contrast to modern capitalist Japan, 22, 57, 63; and ethnographic context, 22, 23, 24; and Hoshino Fumihiro's fame, 94; and Matsuo Bashō, 36, 37, 38, 39, 40; and monk of Zōkōin, 196; and Obon festival, 169, 171; regional narratives of, 27, 36, 37, 38, 39, 40, 214n56; and 3/11, 7, 30, 175, 176, 178, 179, 205n2, 211n1; and spirit mountains (*reizan*), 162, 224n2; yamabushi from, 47

torii, 31, *31*, 32, 33, 55, 60, 77, 84, 144

tourism: anti-Western resentment of Buddhist ascetics, 123, 124; and Exorcism River, 50; and five-storied pagoda, 53; and guidebooks, 30, 31, 62; and Kyūya Fukada, 18; and marketing, 23, 32, 41, 44, 115, 116, 117, 123, 193; and Matsuo Bashō, 39; and 1960s boom, 60; and nostalgia, 48, 49, 58, 105; and railways, 47, 48; and Shōchan, 47, 48, 49; and Shōnai, 2, 23, 32, 47, 66, 161, 176; and stairway of rebirth, 43; and Way of the Yamabushi enterprise, 86; and Yanagita Kunio, 16; at Zuishinmon, 49. *See also* tourism, encounters with religion of

tourism, encounters with religion of, 27, 58, 62, 66, 85, 222n12; and Autumn's Peak, 130, 137, 147, 149; and Buddha mummies, 29, 183, 193, 194; and commoditization of tradition, 21; and conch trumpet (*hora gai*), 46, 47, 48, *48*, 49, 116; and Dewa Sanzan Shrine, 117, 124, 126, 129; and globalization, 211n4, 213n39; and Hoshino Fumihiro's shugyō, 62, 63, 66, 85, 86; and Mount Haguro, 44, 54, 55, 57; and pilgrims, 215n7; and reimagining of past, 33; and rituals, 52, 53, 63, 85, 86; and Shintō-oriented Shugendō, 115, 116, 117, 213n44; and torii, 32. *See also* tourism

Tsuruoka City, 2, 6, 24, *48*, 87, 96, 116, 117, 127

uketamau, 1, 68, 71, 83, 95, 96, 97, 130

waterfall practice (*takigyō*), 64, 81–84, *82*, 91, 94, 96, 97, 217n39

womb of mountain, symbolic, 78, *80*, 131, 164, 223n6; and ascetics' rebirth experience, 25, 27, 65, 66, 67, 85, 105, 106; and bodily empowerment of female yamabushi, 91, 106; and Buddhist-oriented Autumn's Peak, 28, 135, 136, 141, 143, 144, 147, 152, 159; and connection to past, 106; and Diamond and Womb Realms, 79, 139, 140, 184; and Great Boulder, 78; Hoshino Fumihiro on, 91, 105; and male yamabushi, 91, 106; and Shugendō's fusion of death, birth, and rebirth, 5, 201; and stairway of rebirth, 43, *44*, 45; and Taste-of-the-Suffering-of-Birth Hill (*mamago saka*), 57; and Womb Mandala, 4; in yamabushi testimonies of shugyō, 91, 94, 102

Index 251

Womb Realm, 79, 139, 140, 184
World War II, 21, 37, 122, 123

yamabushi experience retreat: and alpine affects, 27, 65, 69, 70, 71, 72; and ancestral connection, 73, 76, 77; and capitalist modernity, 27, 65, 66, 70, 72, 73; and changing of garments, 66, 67, *67*; and code of silence, 69, 70, 71, 76, 77, 79, 88, 95; and dynamic and flexible Shugendō, 63; and fusion of tourism and religion, 27, 62, 66, 85, 86; and gendered aspect of mountains, 27, 71, 78, 79, *80*, 105, 106; and gender of yamabushi, 69, 79; and Great Boulder, 77, 78, 81; and Heart Sutra, 68, 74; and hungry ghost practice (*gakigyō*), 72, 75; and kami, 67, 68, 73, 74, 78, 81, 83, 84; and laterality between Buddhism and Shintō, 86; and Mount Gassan, 61, 62, 75, 76, 77; and Mount Haguro, 60, 69, 72, 78; and Mount Haguro and Sakamoto Daizaburo, 73, 74, 75; and Mount Yudono main shrine, 77, 78, 79; and memorialization of 3/11 victims, 178; and nightwalking, 72, 73; and nocturnal journey, 72, 73; and ocean submersion, 91, *92*; and pepper smoke ritual (*nanban ibushi*), 73, 74, 75; and rituals and temporality, 63, 65, 66; and secrecy regarding Great Boulder, 78; and Shintō incantations (*norito*), 68, 69, 76, 77, 81, 83; and shugyō in translation, 63, 64; and spatiotemporality of path between Gassan and Yudono mountains, 76, 77; and stages of shugyō ritual process, 65, 66; and Three Mountain Prayer, 68; and yamabushi's return to Daishōbō, 84; and waterfall practice (*takigyō*), 81, *82*, 83, 84; and womb of boulders, *80*; and Yamabushi Onsen, 85, 87; and *zazen* (seated meditation), 71, 72, 75, 216n24. *See also* Haguro Shugen liturgy (*gongyō*); Hoshino Fumihiro; Ideha Cultural Museum; shugyō, yamabushi testimonies of

Yamagata Prefecture, 5, 6, 13, 36; and embodied Buddhas (*sokushinbutsu*), 183, 189, 195, *196*; and ethnographic context, 22, 26; and Hoshino Fumihiro, 62, 90; and Koryū Shugen Honshū, 157; and Matsuo Bashō, 39; Nomura-san (*ascetic*), 154; ordained monks in, 151; and Shōnai regionalism, 117; and tourism, 47, 66; and Yamadera mountain, 212n25

Yudono, Mount, 5, 6, 13, 20; and Buddhist deity Dainichi Nyorai, 138; and Chinese Zodiac, 56, 76, 187; and Great Boulder, 78; and Great Waterfalls, 81, 94; and kami, 73; main shrine of, 77, 79; and Matsuo Bashō's haiku, 37, 39, 78, 212n12, 217n35; and sexual descriptions of landscape, 78, 90, 91, 184; and spatiotemporality of Dewa Sanzan, 76; as spur of Mount Gassan, 5, 76, 184; and Three Mountain Prayer, 68; and yamabushi experience retreat, 61, 76, 77, 78, 79, 81, 84, 89. *See also* mummies, Buddha

zodiac, 15, 55, 56, 76, 143, 144, 187, 213n49
Zuishinmon, 40, 41, *41*, 49, 56, 57; under pre-Meiji Buddhist name Niōmon, 40, 118, 119

www.ingramcontent.com/pod-product-compliance
Lightning Source LLC
Chambersburg PA
CBHW020328240426
43665CB00044B/886